中華古籍保護計劃

ZHONG HUA GU JI BAO HU JI HUA CHENG GUO

·成 果·

海外中華古籍書志書目叢刊

加拿大多倫多大學
慕氏藏書目（外一種）

1

加拿大多倫多大學　編
東　亞　圖　書　館
喬　曉　勤　主編

國家圖書館出版社

圖書在版編目(CIP)數據

加拿大多倫多大學慕氏藏書目:外一種／加拿大多倫多大學東亞圖書館編,喬曉勤主編.—北京:國家圖書館出版社,2022.9

(海外中華古籍書志書目叢刊)

ISBN 978－7－5013－6041－3

Ⅰ.①加… Ⅱ.①加… ②喬… Ⅲ.①古籍—善本—圖書館目録—加拿大 Ⅳ.①Z838

中國版本圖書館 CIP 數據核字(2017)第 013196 號

書　　名　加拿大多倫多大學慕氏藏書目(外一種)(全五冊)
著　　者　加拿大多倫多大學東亞圖書館　編　喬曉勤　主編
責任編輯　張愛芳　代　坤
助理編輯　王若舟
封面設計　程言工作室

出版發行　國家圖書館出版社(北京市西城區文津街 7 號　100034)
　　　　　(原書目文獻出版社　北京圖書館出版社)
　　　　　010－66114536　63802249　nlcpress@nlc.cn(郵購)
網　　址　http://www.nlcpress.com
印　　裝　北京華藝齋古籍印務有限公司
版次印次　2022 年 9 月第 1 版　2022 年 9 月第 1 次印刷

開　　本　787×1092(毫米)　1/16
印　　張　202
書　　號　ISBN 978－7－5013－6041－3
定　　價　2600.00 圓

多倫多大學圖書館總館（The Robarts Library）外景

多倫多大學鄭裕彤東亞圖書館古籍閱覽室

廿一史彈詞註 卷之一

成都楊　慎用修編著　　富平楊　浚松林重刻

漢陽張三異禹木增定

　　　　男仲璜別麓註　孫坦含坤章

　　　伯琮鶴淵訂　　　坦麟盡臣

　　叔斑鵠巖泰　　　坦驄青御

　　　　　　　　　坦熊男祥仝校

第一段　總說　西江月

天上烏飛兔走人間古往今來沉吟屈指數英才、多少

是非成敗　富貴歌樓舞榭凄凉廢塚荒臺萬般回首

化塵埃只有青山不改　詩曰

廿一史彈詞註十卷　（明）楊慎編著　（清）張三異增訂
（清）張仲璜註　清康熙四十九年佚名刻　清雍正五年佚名
重刻

高祖皇帝

帝姓李氏諱淵字叔德其先隴西成紀人後徙長安祖虎

佐周有功爲柱國追封唐公帝生襲封隋大業十二年十

二月爲太原留守明年五月舉義兵十一月入長安尊立

恭帝自爲大丞相進爵爲王義寧二年戊寅五月受禪建

元武德在位九年八月傳位太子年七十一諡曰大武皇

帝廟號高祖追尊神堯大聖大光孝皇帝

授老人等官教

欽定全唐文 （清）董誥編 清內府刻本

増廣註釋音辯唐柳先生集卷之一

南城先生童宗說註釋

新安先生張敦頤音辯

雲間先生潘緯音義

唐雅

獻平淮夷雅表

案毛詩注云淮夷在淮浦師夷行也吳元濟
在淮蔡故故曰淮夷宗元擬江漢之詩而作也

臣宗元言臣員聚竄伏違尚書幾奏十有四年
官掌尚書幾
聖恩寬宥命守邊壤十年
陛下坤云禮部郎
冊也詩序周室
中興又特賜洛本有方
剛

聖文武皇帝陛下天造神斷克清大憝之德
柳州刺史懷印曳綬有社有人臣宗元誠感誠荷頓首頓首伏惟
冊也
吳楚聚
中唯仲切
忠州
越東

唐聖文武皇帝陛下天造神斷克清大憝之德
剌史懷印曳綬有社有人臣宗元誠感誠荷頓首頓首伏惟

濟金鼓一動萬方畢臣太平之功中興之
中興推校千古無所與讓因伏自忖度
為 方剛

増廣註釋音辯唐柳先生集、柳宗元年譜四十九卷 （唐）柳宗元撰 （宋）文安禮撰 （宋）童宗說註釋 （宋）張敦頤音辯 （宋）潘緯音義 宋刻本

周易上經

周代名也。易。書名也。其卦本伏羲所畫有交易

變易之義。故謂之易。其辭則文王周公所繫故繫之

周以其簡袠重大。故分爲上下兩篇。經則伏羲之畫

文王周公之辭也并孔子所作之傳十篇。凡十二篇。

中間頗爲諸儒所亂近世晁氏始正其失而未能盡

合古文。呂氏又更定著爲經二卷傳十卷。乃復孔氏

之舊云。或問伏羲始畫八卦。其六十四者文王重之

邪。抑伏羲已自畫了。那看先天圖。則有八卦

便有六十四卦。是伏羲之時已有六畫矣。如何朱子

曰同禮三易。經卦皆八。其別皆六十有四。便見不是

周易傳義大全二十九卷 （明）胡廣輯　明内府刻本

誠意格 凡八目

審幾　立志　謀慮　感應
儆戒　敬天　敬祖考　畏民

臣若水序曰誠意何以言格物也程順曰

格者至也物者理也至其理乃格物也至

也者知行並進之功也於意焉而至之也

至其意之理也是故審幾也立志也謀慮

也感應也儆戒也敬天也敬祖考也畏民

也皆意之事也人主讀是編焉感通吾意

之理念念而知於斯存存而行於斯以有

聖學格物通一百卷　（明）湛若水撰　明嘉靖十二年陳陞

刻本

總　目

古籍回歸故里　功德澤被千秋（代序）

"史在他邦，文歸海外"，這是鄭振鐸先生面對中華古籍流失海外時的慨歎。流傳海外的珍貴典籍，無論是文化交流、贈送、交換、販售，還是被掠奪、偷運，抑或是遭非法交易、走私等，都因其具備極高的文物價值和文獻價值，而爲海外所看重。因此，其中多珍善版本，甚而還有不少是孤本秘笈。據估算，海外中文古籍收藏數量超過 300 萬册件，北美、歐洲、亞洲等許多大型圖書館、博物館和私人機構、寺廟等都收藏有中文古籍。甲骨、竹木簡、敦煌西域遺書、宋元明清善本、拓本輿圖和中國少數民族古籍等，在海外都有珍稀孤罕的藏品。

中華文化綿延五千年，是全世界唯一没有中斷的古老文明，其重要載體就是留存於世的浩瀚典籍。存藏於海外的典籍，同樣是中華燦爛輝煌文化的重要見證，是釐清中華文明發展脉絡不可或缺的組成部分。要促成中華民族最重要的智慧成果歸於完璧、傳承中華文化優秀成果，就必須高度重視海外古籍回歸工作。

新中國成立以來，黨中央、國務院始終高度重視海外中華古籍的回歸與保護工作。1981 年中共中央在《關於整理我國古籍的指示》中，明確指出"通過各種辦法爭取弄回來，或者複製回來，同時要有系統地翻印一批珍本、善本"。2007 年，國務院辦公廳頒佈《關於進一步加强古籍保護工作的意見》，指出要"加强與國際文化組織和海外圖書館、博物館的合作，對海外收藏的中華古籍進行登記、建檔"。同年，"中華古籍保護計劃"正式啓動，中國國家圖書館加掛"國家古籍保護中心"牌子，負責牽頭與海外藏書機構合作，制訂計劃，有步驟地開展海外古籍調查工作，摸清各國藏書情況,建立《國家珍貴古籍名録》(海外卷)。2011 年文化部頒佈《關於進一步加强古籍保護工作的通知》,指出“要繼續積極開展國際合作,調查中華古籍在世界各地的存藏情況,促進海外中華古籍以數字化方式回歸”。

按照黨中央、國務院的要求,半個世紀以來,海外中華古籍的回歸工作一直在不斷推進,并取得了一系列的重要成果。1955 年和 1965 年,在周恩來總理親切關懷和支持下,中國國家圖書館兩度從香港購藏陳清華舊藏珍籍;2004 年,又實現了第三批陳清華海外遺珍的回歸。2010 年,在國際學者和學術機構的幫助下,中國國家圖書館在館網上建立了海外中文古籍專題網站,發佈了“哈佛燕京圖書館藏中文善本特藏資源庫”。2013 年,北京大學中國古文獻研究中心團隊所承擔的《日本宮内廳書陵部所藏宋元本漢籍叢刊》由上海古籍出版社出版;2013 年 5 月、2014 年 7 月,中國國家圖書館出版社分別影印出版了《哈佛燕京圖書館藏〈永樂大典〉》《普林斯頓大學東亞圖書館藏〈永樂大典〉》;2014 年日本大倉汲古館藏書整體入藏北京大學圖書館。這些不同形式的海外古籍回歸,均有利於學術研究,促進了中外文化交流。但總體説來,這些僅係海外古籍中的極少部分,絕大多數仍沉眠於海外藏書機構或藏家手中,國人無緣得見。

在海外中華古籍實物回歸、數字化回歸、影印出版等幾種方式中,採取以影印出版的方式永久保存承載華夏文明的中華古籍特藏,是古籍再生性保護的重要手段,是繼絶存真、保存典籍的有效方式,也是傳本揚學、惠及士林的最佳方式,它不僅有利於珍本文獻原件的保存和保護,更有利於文獻的利用和學術研究,而且也有效地解決了古籍保護與利用之間的矛盾。與實物回歸相比較,影印出版的方式更爲快捷,規模也更大。

爲進一步做好海外中華古籍的回歸工作,2014 年國家古籍保護中心(中國國家圖書館)彙集相關領域專家、國外出版機構、出版工作者等多方力量，在已有工作的基礎上，整合資源、有序推進，策劃啓動了“海外中華古籍書志書目叢刊”“海外中華古籍珍本叢刊”兩大海外中華古籍回歸項目。“海外中華古籍書志書目叢刊”編纂出版海外圖書館、博物館、書店等單位或個人所藏中華古籍新編書目、歷史目錄、專題書目、研究書志書目、藏書志、圖錄等；“海外中華古籍珍本叢刊”則以影印的方式，按專題或收藏機構系統整理出版海外圖書館或個人存藏的善本文獻、書籍檔案，對具有典型性、文物性、資料性和藝術性的古籍則採用仿真影印的形式出版；希望通過“海外中華古籍書志書目叢刊”“海外中華古籍珍本叢刊”的持續出版，促進海外古籍的影印回歸。

　　“海外中華古籍書志書目叢刊”“海外中華古籍珍本叢刊”編纂出版項目作爲“中華古籍保護計劃”的一部分，它的實施對保存保護中華傳統典籍、推進海外散藏文獻爲學界利用、促進學術研究深入開展均具有重要意義，也必將極大促進中外文化交流的實質性拓展。

　　是爲序。

國家古籍保護中心（中國國家圖書館）

2015 年 3 月

序

　　八年前,加拿大多倫多大學東亞圖書館館長喬曉勤博士和他的同事趙清治博士依據館藏慕氏藏書精華編纂出版了《加拿大多倫多大學東亞圖書館藏中文古籍善本提要》(廣西師範大學出版社,2009 年)。如今,喬曉勤博士百尺竿頭更進一步,將館藏義理壽(Irvin Van Gillis,1875—1948)編 *The University of Toronto Chinese Library*(《多倫多大學中文圖書館目録》)原稿整理出版,完整地揭示慕氏藏書與懷履光(Bishop William Charles White,1873—1960)藏書八十多年前西移加拿大時的全貌,爲中加文獻交流史、加拿大中國學研究和中國目録學史增添了新的篇章和新的光彩。

　　國際漢學研究大致可以分爲東亞漢學、歐洲漢學和美國漢學三大地域,三者自成體系,各具特色,各有千秋。東亞漢學,以日本爲主,起源於中國文化學術的傳播與影響,源遠流長,與中國的傳統漢學大致亦步亦趨,頗爲相似。歐洲漢學,以俄、法、英、荷、瑞、德爲主,肇始於十八世紀歐洲各國對遠東中國的探索,以注重研究中國傳統文化學術的漢學(Sinology)最爲顯著。北美漢學,以美國爲主,發端於二十世紀初中國學術與藏書的流入,二戰以後纔開始普遍興起,以注重研究現代中國的中國研究(China Studies)最爲顯著,且後來居上,在諸多方面扮演着國際漢學的引領作用。

　　雖然北美的中國學研究肇始於中國學術與藏書的流入,且無不以建立中國藏書爲基石,但是,美、加的情形又略有不同。一般説來,美國的中國學研究藏書大多是在少量捐贈藏書的基礎上逐步建立起來的,而加拿大的中國學研究藏書則基本上是在批量購置個人專藏的基礎上逐漸建立起來的,其中三次中國藏書的流入對加拿大的中國學研究和東亞圖書館具有里程碑意義:

一、葛思德藏書。葛思德藏書原爲美國人葛思德(Guion Moore Gest,1864—1948)早年來華時收集的中國藏書,共約七萬五千册。1926年,葛思德將個人藏書從中國移藏加拿大蒙特利爾市麥吉爾大學賴德派斯圖書館(McGrill University Redpath Library),設立了北美第一個東亞圖書館——葛思德中國研究圖書館(The Gest Chinese Research Library)。1937年,葛思德將藏於麥吉爾大學的葛思德藏書悉數售予美國普林斯頓大學(Princeton University),於是,普林斯頓大學據此建立了葛思德東方圖書館(The Gest Oriental Library)。

二、慕氏藏書。慕氏藏書原爲山東蓬萊人慕學勳(1880—1929)的個人收藏,共約四萬餘册。慕學勳去世後,加拿大中華聖公會河南教區主教懷履光於1933年將慕氏藏書約四萬餘册悉數收購,并於1935年將慕氏藏書與懷履光個人另外收購的約一萬册圖書共計約五萬册圖書一起運至加拿大多倫多,藏於當時隸屬加拿大多倫多大學的皇家安大略博物館(The Royal Ontario Museum),建立了安大略省第一個中文圖書館——慕學勳教授中文圖書館。後來,慕氏藏書被一分爲二,一部分留作皇家安大略博物館的 H. H. Mu 遠東圖書館(H. H. Mu Far Eastern Library)藏書,另一部分則歸於多倫多大學。1961年,多倫多大學以慕氏藏書爲基礎建立東亞圖書館(The East Asian Library),并逐漸將其發展成爲加拿大乃至北美的中國學研究重鎮。

三、蒲坂藏書。蒲坂藏書原爲中國澳門姚鈞石的蒲坂書樓藏書,共約四萬五千册。蒲坂藏書大部分爲廣州著名藏書家徐信符南州書樓的舊藏,1959 年被加拿大卑詩大學（University of British Columbia）收購,并從中國澳門運至加拿大温哥華,由此加拿大卑詩大學建立了亞洲圖書館（The Asian Library）,并迅速發展成爲加拿大乃至北美的中國學研究重鎮。

葛思德藏書、慕氏藏書和蒲坂藏書西移加拿大時均有目録。

葛思德藏書的目録爲義理壽與白炳騏合編《葛思德東方藏書庫書目》（Title index to the catalogue of the Gest Oriental Library）,原稿二十册,藏於普林斯頓大學東亞圖書館,1941 年曾在北京印行,一函四册。

慕氏藏書的目録則有兩種:一種是慕學勳自編自刊的《蓬萊慕氏藏書目》,2005 年商務印書館出版的《中國著名藏書家書目匯刊·近代卷》第 31 册有收録。另一種是義理壽編 The University of Toronto Chinese Library（《多倫多大學中文圖書館目録》）,其中包括慕氏藏書和懷履光藏書,稿本藏於加拿大多倫多大學東亞圖書館。

蒲坂藏書則有嚴文郁編《蒲坂書樓藏書目録》稿本五册,應藏在加拿大卑詩大學亞洲圖書館,但未見刊本。

這些藏書目録在藏書運抵加拿大成爲各大學東亞圖書館館藏書後逐漸失去了其原有的作用與意義,很快被各東亞圖書館的館藏目録所取代。二十世紀七十年代以後,電腦目録（MARC）流行,各東亞圖書館的館藏目録相繼轉爲機讀目録,并匯入各聯機聯合目録,如今均可在網上檢索利用。然而,從文獻交流史、文獻學、版本學和書志學的角度來看,現代電腦目録偏重於檢索利用的功能,喪失了辨章學術、考鏡源流的傳統目録學功用。正因爲如此,半個多世紀以來,大凡有能力的北美東亞圖書館都會編纂各自的中文古籍目録或者書志。在這方面,美國的東亞圖書館起步較早,且以哈佛大學哈佛燕京圖書館最爲顯著,而加拿大的東亞圖書館相對滯後。如今,喬曉勤博士將義理壽編 The University of

Toronto Chinese Library（《多倫多大學中文圖書館目錄》）原稿和慕學勳編《蓬萊慕氏藏書目》彙集成《多倫多大學慕氏藏書目》整理出版,迎頭趕上,令人贊賞。

慕學勳編《蓬萊慕氏藏書目》分書名、著(註)者、版本、卷(册)數、函數、備考(出版年、紙張等)、編列號數七欄,以表格形式排印,其中尤以備考項中有關紙張的著錄最見功底,最有特色,屬於傳統的中式目錄。

義理壽編 *The University of Toronto Chinese Library*(《多倫多大學中文圖書館目錄》)與慕學勳編《蓬萊慕氏藏書目》殊异,有索書號(Accession No.)、索引號(Index No.)、(英中對照)題名(Title)、(英中對照)分類(Classification)、主題(Subject)、參考(References)、(英中對照)著者(Author)、版本(Edition)、索引(Index)、裝幀(Bound in)、註釋(Remarks)共十一個著錄項目,屬於典型的西式目錄。

義理壽的目錄與慕學勳的目錄的最大區別在於義理壽的目錄是供大眾使用的現代圖書館目錄,而慕學勳的目錄則是供個人使用的傳統私藏目錄。在二十世紀三十年代,我國的圖書館目錄尚無統一規制,而歐美東亞圖書館的中文目錄尚處在探索之際,作爲公用的圖書館目錄,義理壽的目錄就顯得特別有價值和意義。

義理壽目錄的款目起首著錄索書號(Accession No.)和索引號(Index No.),這是現代西方圖書館目錄的典型特徵。這種索書號和索引號應該是義理壽的獨創,誠如喬曉勤博士在《編者的話》中所言"懷履光也不太明白義理壽分類系統中不同的數位序列的含義",昔人尚且難以明白其究竟,今人就更加難以知道其所以,恐怕祇有義理壽本人瞭然於心。

爲什麼會出現如此情形? 其實此情并不難理解。義理壽是一位美國軍人,在中國北京擔任美國駐華大使館海軍武官多年,在 1919 年從美國海軍退役之前,可以説是地地道道的美國海軍情報人員。長期的對華情報工作,使義理壽養成了對中國文化的興趣和對中國古籍的愛好,這種興趣與愛好又使得他在 1919 年退役以後仍然樂於繼續在中國生活,并娶中國人爲妻,直到客死异鄉。因爲對中國文化的興趣和對中國古籍的愛好,義理壽相繼促成了葛思德藏書和慕氏藏書西移加拿大,并親自爲這兩宗藏書編纂目録。大約在編纂這兩個藏書的目録期間,義理壽還編纂過《〈四庫全書〉書名索引》《〈天禄琳琅書目〉索引》《〈皕宋樓藏書志〉索引》《千字文索引》等。筆者未看過這些索引,不知其索引法爲何,但是,可以猜想其索引方法可能與 *The University of Toronto Chinese Library*(《多倫多大學中文圖書館目録》)英文目録大致相仿。也就是説,義理壽自創了一套"義理壽索引法",并不斷自用。這種做法在二十世紀三十年代中國索引運動興起時十分普遍。二十世紀初,卡片目録傳入中國以後,漢字排檢始終是一個難題,於是索引法和漢字排檢法的創造發明層出不窮,差不多有近百種。所有的索引法和漢字排檢法發明者無不認爲自己的方法最爲精良,但是能夠實際應用的并不多,即使能夠實際應用的基本上也都是在自己的職權範圍之内,例如,做館長的可以在自己主管的圖書館目録中應用,做學者的可以在自己編的目録索引中使用,例如義理壽自編的目録。還有一種情形是,所有的索引法和漢字排檢法發明者都希望自己的方法可以推廣應用,例如洪業(煨蓮)對自己發明的中國字庋擷法頗爲得意,更著《引得説》予以闡發,希望得以推廣,但是他人并未得見。最後,洪業也祇不過是在自己主持的哈佛燕京學社引得編纂處所編引得中使用而已。唯獨商務印書館王雲五先生從電報編碼中得到啓示發明的四角號碼法,因爲具有簡單明瞭、易記易識的特點,纔得以比較普遍地使用。

　　姚名達在《中國目録學史》中言:"我國古代目録學之最大特色爲重分類而輕編目,有解題而無引得。"從這一點上説,義理壽的目録僅憑索書號(Accession No.)和索引號(Index No.)就要比慕學勳的目録更加現代和先進。更爲重要的是,義理壽編纂葛思德藏書目録和慕氏藏書目録實質上是在爲東亞圖書館的中文古籍編目做十分有益的探索,這種探索在某種程度上與哈佛燕京圖書館館長裘開明博士的探索具有同樣重要的歷史意義和學術價值。

在 *The University of Toronto Chinese Library*(《多倫多大學中文圖書館目録》)的著録項目中,義理壽在題名(Title)、分類(Classification)和著者(Author)三個項目的著録中采用了英中對照的著録方式,這是很了不起的創意,與後來東亞圖書館普遍使用的純威妥瑪拼音題名和著者的著録方式相比,更具有可用性和實用性。特別是分類(Classification)項的著録采用了英文字母加阿拉伯數字的分類號與漢字類名的方式,例如:"C-263 譜録—器物",這種雙語著録方式可謂中西結合、古今一體,對於任何一種語言的使用者都有明確的分類指向。

義理壽目録的主題(Subject)、參考(References)、版本(Edition)、索引(Index)、裝幀(Bound in)、註釋(Remarks)等著録項目在今天看來并不規範,例如主題(Subject)沒有使用主題詞,而是陳述句,參考(References)、索引(Index)也是用陳述句説明所著録圖書的目録頁數和附録數量等,沒有英美描述目録(Descriptive Bibliography)或者分析目録(Analytical Bibliography)那種用符號和縮寫字著録的簡明,但是其版本(Edition)項則著録了出版年、版本、紙張等項目,既保持了與慕學勳目録的一致性,也凸顯了義理壽對版本的重視。

總而言之,義理壽編 *The University of Toronto Chinese Library*(《多倫多大學中文圖書館目録》)著録了慕氏藏書和懷履光藏書,真實地記録了慕氏藏書西移加拿大時的原貌,是十分珍貴的中加文獻交流史史料和加拿大中國研究史史料;而喬曉勤編《加拿大多倫多大學慕氏藏書目》

將義理壽編 *The University of Toronto Chinese Library*（《多倫多大學中文圖書館目錄》）和慕學勳編《蓬萊慕氏藏書目》熔於一爐，中西合璧，相映成趣，相輔相成，相得益彰，可圈可點，可喜可賀。

　　是爲序。

程煥文

2017 年 7 月 5 日

於中山大學康樂園竹帛齋

　　【程煥文：中山大學信息管理學院教授，圖書館館長，校長助理，國際圖書館協會聯合會（IFLA）管理委員會委員，中國圖書館學會副理事長。】

I. V. GILLIS: CATALOGER OF THE MU AND GEST COLLECTIONS

Irvin Van Gorder Gillis (Yi Lishou 義理壽,1875-1948), the individual responsible for the cataloging of the Mu Collection at the University of Toronto Library, is a complex man whose multifaceted life is far from having been exhaustively described. The recent book *A plain sailorman in China*[1] describes his life until the end of WWI, a life which either directly or occasionally indirectly revolved around the US Navy (governmental and private interests were intrinsically linked in the US approach to China in the first decades of the twentieth century). After 1919 however, we have a much more restricted view of him. The letters and reports from Gillis kept with the East Asian Library and the Gest Collection Archives at Princeton University[2], which form the basis of my previous research on Gillis (which was excerpted in the same book), only show one singular activity of his, albeit a very important one: his collecting of Chinese books for what was to become the Gest Library, located first at McGill University, and since

---

[1] Bruce Swanson *et al.*, *A plain sailorman in China: The Life and Times of Cdr. I. V. Gillis, USN*, 1875-1948, Annapolis, Md.: Naval Institute Press, 2012.

[2] Series 26: East Asian Library Records; 1916-1988; Princeton University Library Records. For this article, mostly boxes 412 and 415 were used.

1936 at Princeton University[1]. This trove of material has not yet been exploited fully; much more cross-referencing of its various strands are required before a researcher who would know the complicated workflow would know when a book was bought, from whom, for how much; but that is in principle attainable.

Yet, all that detailed information only tells us about one fact of Gillis' life. There is much else we do not know. We barely know that he was married and had adopted children from scraps of sentences and the memory of a niece. We do not know that part of his life, not even the names of his children; on the other hand, his Chinese wife seems to have no interest in his book-collecting activities. We certainly do not know how Gillis lived in China, or where his income came from. He was on retainer for Gest; but he could not have survived on that income only, and was often complaining he was not paid for his efforts; yet he seems to have been reasonably well off, had many servants, and could invest in book purchases for other libraries with his own money. Certainly, from a too-short unpublished memoir written by his mason friend Thomas Sze, we can conclude that his book-collecting was central to him; but I would not be at all surprised if he were simultaneously also on retainer for many other companies, naval, general defense or

---

[1] See my "The East Asian Library and the Gest Collection at Princeton University", in: Peter X. Zhou, ed., *Collecting Asia: East Asian Libraries in North America, 1868-2008* (Ann Arbor: Association for Asian Studies, 2010), pp. 120-135; translated, with corrections, as "Pu lin si dun da xue Dong ya tu shu guan yu Ge si de wen ku 普林斯頓大學東亞圖書館與葛思德文庫", in: Peter X. Zhou, ed., *Dong xue xi jian: Bei Mei zhu ming Dong ya tu shu guan* 1868-2008 東學西漸:北美著名東亞圖書館 1868-2008 (Beijing: Gao deng jiao yu chu ban she 高等教育出版社, 2012 年), pp. 119-132.

otherwise, during the same period. As the documented first part of his life showed, one of Gillis' strengths was building up networks with people from many areas of life, business men, missionaries, scholars, diplomats, to gather information others could use. Before 1919, part of this was done as an intelligence "officer", but no strict divisions applied at that time among foreigners: it was the kind of consultancy any business and occasionally governmental offices would require. It hardly can have been all or largely government-related: Gillis remained in Peking, when the center of government life had moved to Nanking. Socially he was vice-president of the American Chamber of Commerce, president of the Peking Club, and particularly active in the Masons; a concentrated focused effort to search for remnants of this life in other people's memoirs may prove fruitful; at Princeton, Gillis' relationship with John MacMurray only came to light when the papers of the latter were analyzed. Some of his contacts occasionally surface even in that small snapshot of his life as preserved in the East Asian Library Archives at Princeton, such as the art historian John Ferguson, or Paul Pelliot, who was French military attaché when Gillis was the US naval attaché; others will have to be diligently searched for. In Gillis' letters, these acquaintances are always commented upon in a rather critical, acerbic way: it is that attitude above all (as well as his very prickly demeanor whenever he was asked to account for expenses) which tells us that Gillis remained the same person in his pre- and post-1919 lives after all; "Gillis is just being Gillis" seemed to have been the attitude of his friends whenever he seemed to criticize yet another individual.

One of those people who surface in the EAL letters between Gillis and the Gest Library curator, Nancy Lee Swann (Sun Nianli 孫念禮, 1881-

1966), was indeed Bishop William C. White. On April 4, 1933 Gillis wrote to Swann, who then was still in Montreal:

I shall be "carrying coals to Newcastle" probably when I tell you that the University of Toronto has established a Chinese department, and that in connection therewith Bishop W. C. White has recently bought the H. H. Mu collection of some forty thousand (40000) volumes. This was the collection I inspected about two years or more ago and "turned down" on account of our having a large proportion of the works. He has asked my advice and general assistance, and this I have cheerfully given him, being a firm believer in co-operation in such matters of common interest. I am told that $ 30000 local currency was paid for this collection, so it was not a bad "buy" it seems to me[1].

A month later, on May 21, more information was forthcoming. Gillis had shown Bishop White his classification system, i. e., his reworking of the subject organization based upon the *Si ku quan shu* 四庫全書, and White wished to use the same system with some changes:

The Bishop suggested one or two minor changes, and I am of the opinion that although not of very great importance, nevertheless they are worth considering. You know that both he himself and the Toronto University are greatly interested in Chinese archaeology so he considers it desirable to make a few sub divisions to the main classes covering this and related subjects and matter. Standard Chinese catalogues

---

[1] Series 26: East Asian Library Records, Box 412. All following letters from Gillis to Swann come from this box.

4

differentiate naturally, but do not place the works in separate classes. For example, our class C-263 would have sub divisions for (1) *bronzes and brasses*; (2) *monuments, petroglyphs, tombs, etc.* ; (3) *arms and armour*; (4) *numismatics*; (5) *paper, ink, etc.* ; (6) *ceramics in general*; (7) *textile and embroideries*; (8) *jade*; *ivory*; *etc.* [1] Then he proposes two additions to the general religious classes—(1) *ancestral worship and* (2) *folk-lore.* Of the necessity of the last two I am somewhat doubtful.

This correspondence is all to be put against a background of intense interest Swann, Gillis, and their library directors had about how the master catalogue would look like, how the cards (horizontal or vertical; the first kind called by Gillis "à la Toronto"), by which number (subject, accession) they should be filed, how index entries (for the Chinese) would refer to them, what place transliteration should play, which colors to use—for the characters, for lines on the card, or for the whole card; as usual Gillis would be quite opinionated on all this. "WHAT IS THE MISSION OF A CATALOGUE AND OF AN INDEX?" was the title, in capitals and underlined, of a four-page letter of July 10, 1932 and it would remain a hotly debated topic in the decade to come. Another worry both libraries had in common, was about the difficulty in the mid-30s of shipping Chinese books to North America, because of the opposition of the Kuomintang's Cultural Society. Still,

---

[1] Italics as in the original. Gillis' letters normally use two types of fonts (the second one usually comprising italics, but occasionally small caps), have drop-ins, headings, etc. Gillis always had a great interest in typewriters, and the layout of his letters would even not be simple to be replicated in current word processing programs. Chinese characters in his letters were probably written by his assistants.

Gillis called his relationship with the Toronto University Library "purely personal and voluntary, and due to my friendship with Bishop White." [1]

On January 11, 1938 Gillis reported that in the previous November Toronto had received the Mu collection, and had started to unpack the items—four years after its purchase. They "have beaten you to it," as he wrote Swann, referring to boxes still unpacked in Princeton, knowing full well that he was not telling her anything new, since he rightly supposed Swann and Bishop White themselves were also in correspondence with each other.

Indeed, they were [2]. And with cause: on October 23, 1937 a few weeks before the official opening of the Mu Chinese Library on November 5, 1937-the formal invitation to Swann is extent—a frantically handwritten letter (all others were typed) was sent from Bishop White to Swann: in Toronto they had been opening up the cases, and setting out the books, but found they only had Gillis' catalog notes for the first 1000 items, not yet for the following 1500-and, moreover, White did not completely understand the various number schemes. Did Dr. Swann have the full list of the Mu items by any chance, or any other information on the schemes? Nancy Lee Swann answered on October 28, with an explanation of the classification number versus the accession number, how duplicate books had to be dealt with using cross-references, but also the possibility on filing index cards by title or au-

---

[1] November 15, 1933.

[2] A letter of August 23, 1934 from White to Swann mentioned that they had met many years before in Kaifeng; in this letter White set up a meeting with Swann in Montreal for the general Synod of their Church, and hoped he would there meet Gest himself for the first time, "since I have heard Capt. Gillis speak so much of him." All letters quoted here between White and Swann are from Series 26: East Asian Library Records, Box 415.

thor indexes, referring White to Gillis' *Title index to the Ssŭk'uch'üanshu.*

These interconnections between Gest and Toronto did not go completely one-way. Gillis' final, red-silk bound descriptive catalog notes for the Gest collection (revisions of earlier shipment and packing notes), had largely the same series of headings as those he made for the Toronto items; but Toronto had all the data compactly on one sheet, while the Gest data were on two sheets—therefore Swann asked for some blank Toronto copies in order to use them at Gest as well (she received those sheets, but they don't seem to have been used).

The catalog notes made by Gillis reference many traditional Chinese catalogs, and Gillis knew quite well that he was probably the westerner most familiar with the Chinese systems; he once let Swann know, in his usual acerbic way, that John Ferguson may know a lot of other things, but that he, Gillis, was the authority on classifications [1]. His final index work for the Gest collection [2], probably finished just before his house-arrest in 1941 and copies of which were gathered after his release in 1945 (they were sent to Princeton in installments, and the chronology is not fully clear), lists 239 traditional Chinese catalogs, thirty of which the Gest index referred to in detail: that is, an entry for a book present in the Gest Library would be listed in this work according to its index number (composed of the radical number of the first character of the title, plus the number of the non-radical

---

[1]　July 23, 1933; in Box 412.

[2]　Gillis and Bai Bingqi 白炳騏, *Geside dong fang cangshuku shumu* 葛思德東方藏書庫書目,［Beiping : n. p.］, 1941.

7

strokes [1] of the first four characters), would also refer to the page and entry numbers on that page where the same book was listed in those thirty catalogs.

In addition to those catalogs which he had analyzed into a set of 40000 cards [2], Gillis occasionally wrote to other specialists. Thus, in a copy of a still difficult-to-understand Ming edition of a *Wen gong xian sheng zi zhi tong jian gang mu* 文公先生資治通鑑綱目 （TB22/1427Q）, we have a photostat copy of his correspondence with Yuan Tongli 袁同禮（1895-1965）of the National Library of Beiping on this copy; while elsewhere we can see interest of Jiang Fucong 蔣復璁（1898-1990）of the National Central Library at Nanking for Gillis' cataloging scheme [3]. Wang Zhongmin 王重民（1903-1975）, when he came at several points in time in 1946 to assess the Gest collection (and write a catalog draft of its rarer items), had high praise for Gest descriptive capabilities ("almost without mistakes"), although he occasionally missed to point out the importance of a certain edition [4]. And indeed, with hindsight we can also say that sometimes it is Gillis', and not Wang Zhongmin's assessment which proved to be correct, most notably in the case of one of the Gest library's rarest items, the *Qisha Da zang jing* 磧砂大藏經. Gillis has left a catalog where each of its almost 6000 volumes has been categorized as a Song original print, a Yuan original print, a later

---

［1］ A list of frequently used non-radical components and their stroke counts was also given—with, typically Gillis, many instances pointed out where the Kangxi dictionary had been inconsistent in its counts.

［2］ Hu Shi, "The Gest Oriental Library at Princeton University", *Princeton University Library Chronicle* 15:3（Spring 1954）, pp. 113-141, here p. 116, from a letter from Gillis to Swann, April 17, 1941.

［3］ Box 415: a letter of May 23, 1938 from Jiang to Swann.

［4］ See Hu Shi, op. *cit.*, p. 116.

Ming reprint, or a handwritten still later version (now thought to be early Qing). For some still unknown reason, Wang Zhongmin decided that the collection was "a ca. 1850 recut." (Most books in 1946 were packed up, and difficult to access. Did Wang Zhongmin perhaps only happened to have seen one of the very few later printed copies printed? His mistake is otherwise difficult to explain). Hu Shi would soon re-correct Wang's assessment, comparing the Gest copy in detail to the recent 1935 republication of the work, and readopting the assessments of Gillis, volume by volume, making only 6 changes. Hu Shi is very clear about the accuracy of Gillis, and the mistake of Wang Zhongmin, although some later researchers wrongly assume that Gillis had made the mistakes, and Hu Shi the corrections, rephrasing the episode as the Chinese specialist correcting the Westerner's ignorance[1]. The data in the Gest Library are very clear, as Hu Shi already clarified. Similar volume-by-volume assessments are extant in the Gest Library for the various sets of the *Wu ying dian ju zhen ban shu* 武英殿聚珍版書 Gillis had painstakingly collected, and for the *Gu jin tu shu ji cheng* 古今圖書集成: for each single volume of the latter Gillis cites page, line and number of those characters which prove that that volume was one of the small run of the palace edition, and not one of the much more numerous provincial reprints.

Gillis was a knowledgeable, intelligent bibliophile indeed.

Director, East Asian Library, Princeton University   *Martin J. Heijdra*

In February, 2017

---

[1] One has to refer to the original article, Hu, *op. cit.*, pp. 130-134.

義理壽:慕氏藏書與
葛思德文庫的編目者

　　作爲多倫多大學圖書館慕氏藏書編目工作的負責人,義理壽是一位複雜的人物;以往描述遠未窮盡他多面的人生。最近出版的《一個在中國的普通水手》①一書集中講述了他在第一次世界大戰結束前的生活;這段生活直接或偶爾間接地圍繞着他在美國海軍中的服役而展開(在二十世紀初,政府與私人利益共同關聯於美國的對華政策與在華活動)。至於其在 1919 年後的活动,我們則所知有限。我根據普林斯頓大學葛思德東亞圖書館現保存一批義理壽的信件與報告②進行研究,并在本書中有所摘録。這批資料僅僅反映了他在華所從事的對中文書籍收集的一項活動。但毋庸置疑,此項活動具有極爲重要的意義,因爲這批藏書最終構成了最初葛思德圖書館藏書的主體(這批資料最初藏於麥吉爾大學,并於 1936 年遷往普林斯頓大學)。③ 然而,這批出於義理壽之手的

---

　　① Bruce Swanson et al. , A Plain Sailorman in China: The Life and Times of Cdr. I. V. Gillis, USN, 1875-1948, Annapolis, Md. : Naval Institute Press, 2012.

　　② Series 26: East Asian Library Records: 1916-1988, Princeton University Library Records. 本文主要使用了其中 Box 412 和 415 中的資料。

　　③ 見拙著 "The East Asian Library and the Gest Collection at Princeton University", 收入 Peter X. Zhou, ed. , Collecting Asia: East Asian Libraries in North America, 1868-2008 (Ann Arbor: Association for Asian Studies, 2010), 頁 120-135;修訂版中文翻譯見何義壯(Martin J. Heijdra), "普林斯頓大學東亞圖書館與葛思德文庫", 收入周欣平主編,《東學西漸:北美著名東亞圖書館,1868—2008》(北京:高等教育出版社,2012 年),頁 119-132。

材料還遠未得到充分的利用。在一位對書籍收藏的複雜工作流程有所瞭解的研究人員眼中，通過各個環節的交叉比對，更多關於購書時間、對象與相關花費的具體細節可以從這些資料中挖掘出來。而這在理論上是完全可以實現的。

即便如此，通過所有詳細信息，我們也祇知道義理壽生活的一個方面，對其生命中的其他方面仍所知甚少。從其文字中的一些零散段落以及他姪女的回憶，我們纔知道他曾結婚并收養了幾個孩子。除此之外，關於其婚姻、家庭生活的記錄則付之闕如。我們甚至都不知道他孩子的名字，祇瞭解到他的中國籍妻子似乎對其藏書活動興味索然。我們也并不知道他是如何在中國謀生以及他的收入來源，祇知道他受雇於葛思德，但僅靠此項工作帶來的收入很難維持其生活，而且他還經常抱怨自己的努力沒有換來應得的回報。儘管如此，他似乎還算富裕，有幾個仆人，而且可以用自己的錢爲其他圖書館投資購書。從他的共濟會成員好友施肇祥(Thomas Sze)所寫的一本未發表的簡短回憶錄中，我們可以肯定的是，圖書收集是義理壽最核心的工作；但同時，他又可能也受雇於其他公司或軍事機構。正如關於其前半生的相關記錄所顯示的那樣，義理壽擅長與各行各業人士(商人、傳教士、學者、外交官)聯繫，并進而從中收集可用的信息。在 1919 年之前，這部分工作顯示其履行着情報"官員"的職責，但當時在華外國人之間并沒有相關嚴格的職業劃分：他所提供的是任何企業和政府部門偶尔都需要的那種咨詢服務。這項工作也很難說是完全與政府相關，因爲當中國的中央政府遷往南京去後，他依然留在北平活動。在社交方面，義理壽是美國商會的副會長，北京俱樂部的主席，并且在共濟會中特別活躍。在其他人的回憶錄中集中精力尋找關於這種生活的殘篇斷簡可能是有效的：在普林斯頓，直到分析完後者的手稿，義理壽與馬慕瑞(John MacMurray)的關係纔浮出水面。至於在上文提及的保存於普林斯頓東亞圖書館檔案庫的那批僅僅反映其生命一小段剪影的資料中,其他一些聯絡人亦會偶爾顯現出來,比如說藝術史學者福開森(John Ferguson)或者是漢學家伯希和(Paul Pelliot)。後者在擔任法國駐華武官之時,義理壽亦在美國駐華海軍武官任上。至於其他人,還有待更徹底地研究。在義理壽的信中,這些提及到的熟人總是被他以一種相當批判、尖刻的方式所評論,而正是這種態度(以及每當被要求說明開支時表現出來的鋒芒畢露的舉止)告訴我們,無論是1919之前還是之後,他并未有所變化。每當發現他似乎找到了一個新的對象來大加撻伐之時,他的朋友們祇是覺得他"本性難移"而已。

在義理壽與葛思德圖書館館員孫念禮(Nancy Lee Swann, 1881 – 1966)之間的一系列通信中,所涉人物當然有懷履光主教(Bishop William C. White)。1933年4月4日,他給當時在蒙特利爾的孫念禮寫有一封信:

> 也許我是多此一舉,但還是想告訴你多倫多大學新近成立了一個中文系,并且通過懷履光主教買下了總量達40000卷之巨的慕氏藏書。兩年前我已檢閱過這批藏書,并以大量標題重復爲由"拒絕"了對其的采購。懷氏曾向我尋求相關的建議與協助,作爲在此類關乎共同利益的事務中展開合作的支持者,我亦樂意之至。聽說購買這批藏書總共花費了30000銀元,在我看來,這筆"買賣"不算糟糕。①

在寫於一個多月後的5月21日的信件中,披露出來更多信息。義理壽向懷履光主教展示了他基於四庫全書四部分類法所改造出的書目

---

① Series 26: East Asian Library Records, Box 412. 以下所有義理壽與孫氏之間的書信都來自此。

分類系統,而懷履光亦希望在運用同一系統時做些許修改:

　　　　主教提出了一兩處的細微修改建議,在我看來,它們雖然不太重要,但依然值得考慮。你知道,他本人和多倫多大學都對中國考古學非常感興趣,因此他認爲最好在書目的主類之下設置幾個分部來涵蓋相關主題與事項。標準的中文書目自然有不同類別,但祇有一種考古相關的作品類別。比方説,在我們的 C－263 類中有如下細分:(1)青銅與銅器;(2)碑刻、岩畫、墓葬等;(3)武器與甲冑;(4)古錢幣;(5)紙,墨等;(6)一般陶瓷;(7)紡織品與刺繡;(8)玉器、象牙等。① 然後主教他還建議在一般宗教類下添加兩個額外分部,即(1)祭祖和(2)民俗。對於此二者的必要性,我有些懷疑。

　　以上討論須置於此一背景之下,即孫氏、義理壽以及他們背後的圖書館館長們對於該批藏書的總目應該如何呈現,以何種目錄卡片(橫向或豎向;前者被義理壽稱之爲"多倫多風格")、號碼(主題號,登錄號)歸檔,索引條目(針對中文部分)如何導引至這批卡片,何處應該有中文原文的英文,字母、綫條以至整張卡片應該使用哪種顏色等等表現出濃厚的興趣;像往常一樣,義理壽對這一切都很有自己的看法。在一封寫於 1932 年 7 月 10 日的有着四頁長的信中,他即以"書目與索引的任務是什麼?"(WHAT IS THE MISSION OF A CATALOGUE AND OF AN INDEX)爲標題,用大寫字母和下劃綫寫成;而在之後的十年裏,這依然是一個激烈爭論的話題。此外,兩家圖書館(譯註:即多倫多大學圖書館與葛思德東亞圖書館)還有一個共同的擔憂,即在 1930 年代中期,由於國

---

① 此處英文原文以斜體强調。義理壽在其信件中通常使用兩種字體(其中第二種字體常以斜體方式呈現,偶爾則改爲小體大寫字母),并有各式標註、標題等等。他總對各式打字機表現出極大興趣,而他的信件的布局已很難用現今的文字處理程序來完整再現。至於其信件中的漢字則極大可能由其助手們所寫。

民政府古物保管會的反對,很難將購買到的中文古籍運往北美。儘管如此,義理壽仍稱他與多倫多大學圖書館的關係"純屬個人自願,是基於其與懷履光主教之間的友誼"。[①]

　　在一封於 1938 年 1 月 11 日寫給孫氏的信中,義理壽提及在前一年的 11 月多倫多大學收到了慕氏藏書,并已開始拆封(這已是購書的四年後)。相對於那些還在普林斯頓拆封的古籍,"他們在進度上已經走在了你的前面",他向孫氏寫道。在該信中,義理壽清楚意識到他并未告訴對方什麼新消息,因爲其正確估計到孫氏與懷履光主教之間同樣有聯絡。

　　事實上他們的確如此,[②]且有一定原因。1937 年 10 月 23 日,也就是 11 月 5 日慕氏中文圖書館正式開館的幾周前(給孫氏的官方邀請信依然保存至今),懷履光主教焦急地手寫下一封信(其他的信件都是由打字機打印出來)寄給了孫氏。他提及到在多倫多,拆箱整理書籍的工作一直在進行中,但是他們發現手上祇有義理壽爲前 1000 件藏品所作的編目説明,而之後 1500 件的説明則付之闕如。此外,主教還表示没法完全弄懂義理壽在書目中所使用的編碼。因此他在信中詢問孫博士是否正好有慕氏藏書的完整清單,或是否對那些編碼有所瞭解。孫氏的回信寫於 10 月 28 日,她在信中解釋了分類號與登録號的分别以及如何使用對照參考來處理重復的書籍。此外,她還提及了使用書名或著者索引

---

① 1933 年 11 月 15 日。

② 在一封寫於 8 月 23 日的信中,懷履光向孫氏提及多年前他們曾在開封見過對方;在同一封信中,他還以教會會議爲契機安排了與孫氏在蒙特利爾的會面,并表示希望在那可以第一次見到葛思德本人,"因爲我聽聞義理壽上尉對他評價很高"。此處引用的懷履光與孫氏之間的信件來自於 Series 26:East Asian Library Records,Box 415。

的方式來排檢索引卡片的可能性，并向對方介紹了義理壽所寫的"四庫全書書名索引"。

葛思德與多倫多圖書館之間的聯繫并不是完全單向的。比如説，在義理壽爲葛思德文庫所作的由紅色絲綢裝訂的編目説明的定本中，其一系列標題與他爲慕氏藏書所作的標題幾乎一致。其不同之處在於，在多倫多，所有的信息都被緊湊地置於紙張單面，而在葛思德圖書館則是雙面。因此，孫氏向多倫多方面索取了一些單面空白的副本希望也能在葛思德使用（她收到了這些副本，但似乎并未使用）。

義理壽所制訂的編目説明參考了許多傳統的中文書目，他也相當清楚他可能是對此最爲熟悉的西方人；他曾經以其一貫的尖刻方式讓孫氏知道，儘管福開森可能知道許多其他事物，但他，義理壽，纔是書籍分類方面的權威。[1] 他爲葛思德文庫所作的最後一項索引工作，可能是在他1941年被軟禁前完成[2]，其他幾本書在他1945年獲釋後被收集起來（它們被分批送到普林斯頓，但時間順序并不完全清楚）。其中列出了239個傳統中文書目，而葛思德文庫的索引詳細參考了其中的30個書目。也就是説，一本葛思德圖書館藏書的款目會根據其索引號（由書名中第一個字的部首及前四個字的非部首偏旁筆畫數組成）[3]在該作品中列出，并會提及該頁上同一本書在那30個書目中的頁碼和款目號。

除了那些被他分析拆解爲一套40000張索引卡片的書目外，[4]義理

---

① 1933 年 7 月 23 日，Box 412。

② 義理壽、白炳騏合編，"葛思德東方藏書庫書目"，北平 1941 年。

③ 義理壽還提供了一份列出了常用非部首偏旁及其筆畫數的清單，并且，符合其固有的風格，他還指出了許多《康熙字典》中筆畫數不一致的情况。

④ Hu Shi, "The Gest Oriental Library at Princeton University", Princeton University Library Chronicle 15:3 (Spring 1954)，頁 113-141。其中第 116 頁中的内容來自於 1941 年 4 月 17 日義理壽寫給孫氏的信。

壽偶爾也會寫信給其他專家們。因此，在一件至今仍然難以解讀的明版《文公先生資治通鑑綱目》(TB22／1427Q)中，我們找到了一份他與北平國立圖書館袁同禮(1895—1965)之間通信的影印件；而在其他地方，我們能夠知道位於南京的中央圖書館的蔣復璁(1898—1990)對他的編目法很感興趣。[①] 在 1946 年的某些時間段，王重民(1903—1975)來到葛思德圖書館以評估該館藏品，并爲其中的珍本寫下了一份編目草稿。儘管義理壽偶爾沒有指出某些書籍特定版本的重要性，但王重民對義理壽的描述能力給予了高度評價("幾乎毫無瑕疵")[②]。事實上，依後見之明我們也可以説，有時是義理壽而非王重民的評估被證明是正確的，而其中最顯著的例子就是作爲葛思德圖書館最珍貴藏品之一的《磧砂大藏經》。在其爲此有 6000 卷之巨的叢書所寫的編目中，義理壽爲每卷進行了詳細分類：有些是宋刻原版，有些是元刻原版，有些是明代翻刻，而有些則是更晚期的手寫本(現在認爲它們來自於清初)。與之相對，出於某些不知名的原因，王重民則認定該套藏書祇是"1850 年左右的重刻本"(1946 年大部分葛思德文庫的藏書都被裝箱而難以審閱，也許王重民祇是湊巧看到了該叢書中極少的幾本晚期翻刻的副本？ 如果不是這樣的話，那麼他的錯誤實在難以解釋)。通過將葛思德所藏與 1935 年再版的《大藏經》進行逐卷詳細的比較，胡適很快就糾正了王氏的評估。在此過程中，他重新采用了義理壽的編目説明，并且祇做出了 6 處修改。儘管胡適對義理壽描述的準確性與王重民所犯的錯誤非常清楚，後來的研究者們卻往往認定是義理壽最初犯下了許多錯誤，而胡適所做的工作

---

① Box 415：見於一封 1938 年 5 月 23 日由蔣寫給孫氏的信件。
② 見前引胡適一文，頁 116。

則是糾正前者,從而將原有的情節改寫成了中國專家在克服西洋人的無知。① 但無論如何,留在葛思德的紀録非常清楚,正如胡適所澄清的那樣。此外,與前述類似,現存於葛思德圖書館的還有義理壽爲其費盡心力收集而來的各套《武英殿聚珍版書》以及一套《古今圖書集成》所寫的逐卷説明。對於後者的每一卷,義理壽都徵引其頁數、行數及字數以證明該卷來自於清雍正間少量刊刻的内府版本,而非之後數量更多的地方重印版。

總之,義理壽確實是一位知識淵博、聰慧的藏書家。

何義壯(Martin J. Heijdra),普林斯頓大學東亞圖書館館長

撰於 2017 年 2 月

翁若陽,多倫多大學東亞研究系

譯於 2022 年 8 月

---

① 見前引胡適一文,頁 130-134。

編者的話

　　1935 年，當時隸屬於加拿大多倫多大學的皇家安大略博物館（Royal Ontario Museum）收到了加拿大英國聖公會河南教區主教懷履光（Bishop William Charles White，1873—1960）由中國所購得的私人收藏"慕氏藏書"四千餘種四萬餘册，成爲加拿大最早收藏中文圖書的學術機構之一。這批圖書現分藏於多倫多大學鄭裕彤東亞圖書館和皇家安大略博物館的 H. H. Mu 遠東圖書館（H. H. Mu Far Eastern Library）。"慕氏藏書"的原收藏者爲慕學勳（又名慕元甫，1880—1929），字玄父，山東蓬萊人，曾就讀於天津北洋大學堂，民國元年畢業。畢業後，慕學勳任職於北京德國公使館，共計十七年，其職位是公使館的中文秘書。網羅各類古今圖書是慕氏的愛好，其收藏活動持續的時間長達二十餘年，所收集圖書的範圍以中國古籍爲主，遍及經、史、子、集各部。他曾自編、自刊《蓬萊慕氏藏書目》（收録於《中国著名藏書家書目匯刊·近代卷》第 31 册，北京：商務印書館，2005 年，此次一并印行。參見圖八），并印行方宗誠（1818—1888）的《柏

圖一　慕學勳（左二）與梅蘭芳（左五）等友人在一起

1

堂詩語言行集》,清朱錫珍輯《忍字輯略》(民國十年鉛印本)。

慕學勳去世後,其子慕守一因要與慕學勳好友達古齋主人霍明志遠赴歐洲舉辦中國文物展,從而希望將其父的圖書完整出售。得知此消息後,懷履光認爲這一收藏對於剛剛設立的多倫多大學中國研究科目意義非常,於是到處奔走,籌措購書經費。經過洽談,慕守一最後同意,將其父的所有古籍收藏以一萬零五百加拿大元的價格出售給懷履光。此批中國古籍收藏後被命名爲"慕氏藏書"。慕氏藏書中明版古籍計有二百三十餘種,清乾隆六十年(1795)以前古籍四百二十餘種,歷代鈔、稿本五十餘種。另有《增廣註釋音辯唐柳先生集》《樂書》等被前人分別鑒定爲宋版及元版的圖書,稀見善本約占整個藏書的十分之一。

在懷履光洽購慕氏藏書的過程中,他曾求助於當時多倫多大學校長科迪(Dr. Henry John Cody, 1868—1951),在科迪的幫助下,皇家安大略博物館的長期支持者薩繆爾(Dr. Sigmund Samuel, 1868—1962)與孟德(Sir Robert L. Mond, 1867—1938)很快捐出了六千五百加元,加上當時身在中國的多倫多大學教授弗格森(Professor John C. Ferguson)捐助的四千五百加元,懷履光共籌得捐款一萬一千加元。1933 年,慕

圖二　懷履光像

氏藏書購買成交後，在北京的美國公使館退休的海軍武官義理壽（Irvin Van Gillis，1875—1948）招募了十名中國助手爲慕氏藏書編目。本書即是義理壽所編的稿本《慕氏藏書目》，原書共有三十八冊，其中十七冊於1935年完成，另外二十一冊爲運至多倫多後補編而成。由於當時的國民政府剛剛通過法令，嚴格限制中國古物的出口，其中包括禁止1851年前出版的中國古籍的出口，慕氏藏書無法在1935年初如期裝船赴運加拿大。在弗格森教授等人的斡旋下，由袁同禮、張庾樓、徐鴻寶等組成的"古物保管會"成員，在北京對慕氏藏書進行了鑒定。其結果是抽出了三種明版書，入藏北平圖書館（即今中國國家圖書館的前身），并將數十種廣東地方志及有關地方文化的圖書交給故宮博物院，其他圖書則准予放行。到1935年6月該批圖書運抵多倫多時，圖書的總量爲五萬餘冊。其中包括有懷履光在1933至1935年間又陸續在中國各地購得的一萬餘冊中文圖書，這批後來采購的圖書中包括了山東與河南兩省的舊方志和民國時期出版物。1937年11月，被命名爲"慕學勳教授中文圖書館"（H. H. Mu Chinese Library）的安大略省第一家收藏中文圖書的圖書館在皇家安大略博物館開館（圖三）。

圖三　"慕學勳教授中文圖書館"1937年在皇家安大略博物館開幕時的情景

慕氏藏書除具有與其他中國傳統私人藏書類似的共同特點外，還具有以下的獨有特色：1. 以慕氏所任職位來看，他不可能有當時著名私人藏書家所具有的殷實的經濟實力來搜羅古本、善本圖書，但他獨具慧眼、揚長避短，得身在京城之利，搜羅清代的官刻圖書、鈔本、稿本、宮廷舊檔等。本書所收錄的《福堂寺人小草》《六壬圖像》、清代旗人《成婚檔案》《京察滿司官履歷清册》等均屬這類珍本、善本。其中明劉若愚撰《福堂寺人小草》清鈔本爲二十一卷，比同書的刻本多出一卷，堪稱珍貴。是書爲劉若愚涉魏忠賢案下獄後所述之宮廷事項記略。《六壬圖像》二十四卷，清鈔本，不著撰人名氏，各卷卷首均有工筆重彩方位神煞畫像，畫像後爲占卜項目及結果，該書在海內外并無其他存本可考，應爲孤本（圖四）。2. 慕氏所藏之史部古籍，方志所占比例頗大。其中山東、河南兩省的縣志尤多。這些縣志多爲清乾隆時期所修。部分縣志的紙張、印刷質量皆不佳，字迹漫漶，可能屬於坊刻本或翻刻本。3. 由於慕學勳長期在德國公使館任職，對域外風土文化、西學東漸等頗有興趣，這些方面的圖書也自然是他收藏的重點之一。《西域瑣談》《欽定蒙古源流》《皇明北虜考》《衛藏圖識》等皆述西域、北疆的風物與歷史，《海島算經》《御製耕織全圖》《遠西奇器圖説録最》《新製諸器圖説》《宋明兵制備覽》《礶花做法》則反映出慕氏對算學、農學、西方器用、兵制、民間工藝等的興趣。其中鈔本《礶花做法》不著撰者，内容詳述各類烟花的製作方法、烟花之品種、製作烟花所使用的器具、材料等，甚爲珍奇。《遠西奇器圖説録最》亦爲鈔本，其撰者爲德國耶穌會士鄧玉函，由明王徵譯繪。書中所附多幅工筆白描器物圖十分精美，該鈔本用《大清律例》書葉背面書寫并裝訂成書，在流傳的中國古籍鈔本中頗爲稀見。4. 慕學勳曾搜集了一些其他藏家所藏的善本。例如，《福堂寺人小草》曾爲士禮居所藏，《增廣註釋音辯唐柳先生集》曾爲華陽高氏蒼茫齋所藏，後均爲慕氏弄藏。《廣文苑英華》

這一中土罕見的珍本亦爲慕氏所購得。從藏書印看,慕氏還入藏有朱樫之、孔繼涵、阮元、惠棟、完顔景賢、方功惠、張敦仁、田達村、丁丙、潘祖蔭、周之楨、張師亮等人的舊藏。

圖四 《六壬圖像》書影

關於慕氏藏書的介紹與研究,較詳者有吳曉玲《加拿大多倫多大學東亞圖書館所藏蓬萊慕氏書庫述概》(《文獻》1990 年第 3 期);朱維信、Shuzo Uyenaka《多倫多大學東亞圖書館的收藏》(Pacific Affairs, vol. 46, no. 4);余梁戴光《多倫多大學的東亞收藏》(載於周欣平主編 Collecting Asia, Association for Asian Studies, Inc. 2010;《東學西漸:北美東亞圖書館

1868—2008》,高等教育出版社,2012 年)等已發表的文章。另在《山東藏書家史略》(山東大學出版社,1992 年)、《中國舊書業百年》(科學出版社,2005 年)、《海外漢學資源調查録》(漢學研究資料及服務中心,1982 年)等書中都有對慕氏藏書的簡介。王汝梅的《多倫多東亞圖書館藏〈金瓶梅〉版本考》(《吉林大學學報(社科版)》1994 年第 4 期)對本館藏第一奇書本《金瓶梅》的評介和米列娜在《近代中國的百科辭書》(北京大學出版社,2007 年)中對本館藏黃摩西《普通百科大辭典》的評介均屬對慕氏藏書中特色圖書的專項研究。

上述《蓬萊慕氏藏書目》一書,除有書名、著(註)者、版本、卷(册)數、函數等內容外,尚有備考一欄,記述各書的刊印情況與用紙。筆者與本館中文編目專家趙清治博士曾編纂《加拿大多倫多大學東亞圖書館藏中文古籍善本提要》一書。該書第一版由廣西師範大學出版社於 2009 年出版,增訂版於 2019 年出版。書中收録了慕氏藏書中的善本部分,共著録圖書計七百零一種,書後并附有多倫多大學東亞圖書館所藏慕氏藏書古籍的總目録。

就目前所知的相關材料看,除了慕氏藏書目外,義理壽所編纂的中國古籍目録還包括《葛思德東方藏書庫書目》(*Title index to the catalogue of the Gest Oriental Library*,與白炳騏合編,1941 年北平印本,一函四册)。該目録的原始稿本如慕氏藏書目一樣,采用英文打字和手寫的方式撰寫。普林斯頓大學東亞圖書館現藏有該原始稿本,共計二十册(圖九),并同時撰寫了約四萬張編目卡片(參見 Martin J. Heijdra 何義壯:*Cataloging Chinese rare books at Princeton—a history*,未刊稿)。義理壽還編纂過《〈四庫全書〉書名索引》《〈天禄琳琅書目〉索引》《〈皕宋樓藏書志〉索引》《千字文索引》等。當筆者示以館藏的《慕氏藏書目》給普林斯頓大學東亞圖書館榮休館長馬泰來先生、現任館長何義壯先生時,他們均認定其與《葛思德東方藏書庫書目》的稿本從格式、紙張和包含內容等方面都存在很大的相似性。根據何義壯先生的研究,1933 年義理壽寫給當時葛思德東方圖書館館長孫念禮(Nancy Lee Swann,1881—1966)的信中提到:"多倫多大學有計劃設立中國研究系,這與懷履光主教新近購得多達四萬餘册的中國古籍藏書——'慕氏藏書'有關。我在兩年前曾仔細看過這一藏書,但未購買。原因是我已有其中的大部分圖書了。懷履光希望聽取我專業的意見并對他提供協助,我本人非常樂於相助。我聽説他花了本地貨幣三萬元來購買這批古籍,我覺得這是非常合算的交易。"在此後不久(1933 年 5 月)義理壽與孫念禮的通信中,義理壽提到向懷履光介紹自己按《四庫全書》分類而建立起來的中文古籍分類系統,後者表示新購的"慕氏藏書"也可按此方法分類。義理壽特別指出,懷履光和多倫多大學都對中國考古學研究有濃厚興趣。他認爲可以將自己的分類系統的相關類別加以細化。如 C‒263 可以細分出子目(1)青銅與銅器;(2)碑刻、岩畫、墓葬等;(3)武器與甲胄;(4)古錢幣;(5)紙、墨等;(6)一般陶瓷;(7)紡織品與刺繡;(8)玉器、象牙等。他還計劃在宗教類別内細分出(1)祖先崇拜,(2)民俗學。義理壽將其與多倫多大學的關係界定爲基於與懷履光的個人友誼基礎上的純私人和義務性質(參見何義壯館長爲本書撰寫的英文序言:*I. V. Gillis*:*Cataloger of the Mu and Gest Collections*)。

　　在來到中國、對中華文化産生興趣之前,義理壽是一名軍人。他以在美國海軍服役開始了他的軍旅生涯。1901 年他第一次以安納波利斯號(USS Annapolis)的首席領航員和首席工程師的身份遠赴亞洲。1904 至 1905 年在東京任美國海軍武官的職位。1907 至 1908 年轉往北京任美國駐華大使館海軍武官。1911 至 1914 年義理壽繼續任職於北京及東京的美國大使館,并代表伯利恒鋼鐵公司爭取與中國政府的合作,爲中國政府創建海軍提供鋼鐵與船隻。在短期回國後,1914 年 9 月他作爲格羅頓和康涅迪格州的電船公司代表及伯利恒鋼鐵公司的代表再次來到中國。1917 至 1919 年間，義理壽返回海軍，再任美國駐北京公使館海軍武官。1919 年底義理壽正式從美國海軍退役。

圖五　義理壽像，攝於美國海軍退役後

在華工作期間,義理壽利用他在中國的外交人員和工業代表的身份,結識了一批學者、教育家、人類學家、考古學家、商人和傳教士。由於他超凡的中文閱讀與交流能力,使其成爲美國政府在華收集情報的得力人選。從有關的文獻中我們可以看出義理壽對中國文化的深刻瞭解及他個人的愛好。1914 年義理壽與江蘇吳江實業家施肇曾(1867—1945)在北京相遇,在施肇曾未出版的回憶錄中提到,義理壽在任美國駐北京公使館海軍武官期間,對中國事物有極大的興趣。他不僅學會了中文的日常會話,還掌握了書面用語,而且有很多中國文化界的朋友,其中包括國立北平圖書館館長袁同禮先生。袁先生曾向友人談起,義理壽可以用放大鏡觀察書寫時手指用力的力度,并能根據字體觀察出一份文件是否使用了兩臺或三臺打字機打出來。當他把這些技能運用到古籍版本鑒定方面時,取得了意想不到的成果。他投入大量的時間學習中國歷史文化和風俗,瞭解中國人。義理壽在1920 年左右與比他小十八歲的中國女子趙玉彬結婚。據説趙出身於滿族皇室。義理壽可能也是受到其妻家族的影響,對中國古籍逐漸產生興趣,開始了書商的生涯。他以"趙玉彬"的名義在北京購置了家宅并打算在這古老的都城度過自己的後半生(對此推測,何義壯先生認爲并沒有充足的證據來證明)。在北京生活期間,他參加了諸多團體組織的各種社交活動。施肇曾提到,他經常在全是中國人的聚會中遇到義理壽。美國公使館也經常請義理壽陪同一些到北京訪問的重要客人。自 1919 年從美國海軍正式退役後,義理壽一直留在中國直到其 1948 年在北京逝世。在此期間,他曾經試圖爲幾個美國造船公司在中國開展業務,但由於當時中國政局混亂,他的努力并沒有取得太大成果,相關的美國公司在中國開展業務也困難重重。義理壽在不同的時期也給中國的政府部門做過顧問,其中包括內閣辦公室、海軍部(圖六)、通信部、海巡署等(參見 Tomasko, N. N. 2009, *I. V. Gillis and*

His Biographer, Bruce Swanson, Princeton：The East Asian Library Journal, vol. XIII, No. 2）。

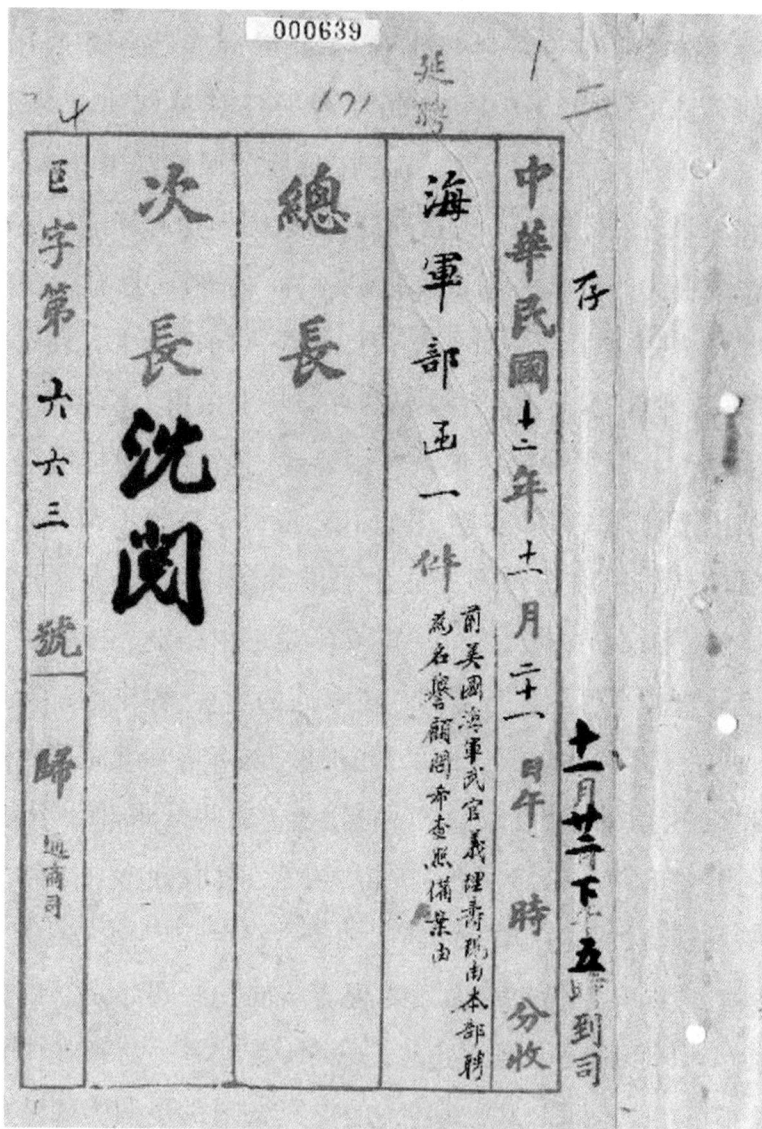

圖六　中華民國海軍部聘請義理壽爲特別顧問的聘書

　　義理壽的中國古籍收藏活動是在他與葛思德相遇後開始的。葛思德（Guion M. Gest，1864—1948）是美國葛氏工程公司（Gest Engineer

Company）的創始人，該公司與建築相關的業務涵蓋北美和亞洲。葛思德長期受青光眼疾病的困擾，在歐美各地嘗試各種辦法醫治，效果一直不佳。在其來華的公務旅行中，葛思德結識了義理壽。義理壽曾建議葛思德嘗試用中醫藥來治療他的眼疾。在試用"馬應龍定州眼藥"後，葛思德的病症得到了很大的緩解。雖然服用中藥未能達到根治其眼疾的效果，但還是取得了不錯的療效，這使葛思德對中醫藥產生了極大的興趣，并把中醫類的圖書作爲其采購中文圖書、建立中文圖書收藏的最初目標。爲購書方便，葛思德還在美國銀行建立起了一個賬户，來支付義理壽收購中文書籍的花費。中醫也許是最初讓葛思德對中文善本收藏感興趣的領域，但一直以來對佛教的興趣也是他收藏中文圖書的主要動因之一。在首批爲葛思德收購的善本書中也包含有除醫學、佛學外的其他類別的書籍，從中我們可以看出在葛思德和義理壽收購善本書的背後，有對中華文化更全面認識的動機。義理壽爲葛斯德在十餘年間共購得中文古籍十餘萬册，其中善本書達一千一百三十六種二萬四千五百册。義理壽曾建議葛思德在資金有限的情況下，把收購的重點放在珍貴明版古籍上，而不必與人競争專求宋代善本。在葛思德收藏的明版書中，如明惠帝建文元年（1399）所刻的佛經和錢謙益明崇禎十六年（1643）所刊印的文集等，均非常珍貴。王重民先生曾指出，義理壽的中國目録學功底非常深厚，他所做的葛思德藏書目録英文註解幾乎没有錯誤。義理壽選書的獨到眼光還反映在他所采購的《武英殿聚珍版重印叢書》上，這套書可能現存祇有五套，而義理壽竟可以收集到其中四套（第五套現藏北京故宫博物院）。義理壽以他一如繼往的對細節的關注和嚴格的自律投入到了善本收藏的工作中。他在自己家裏設立辦公室，并雇用了幾個中國人爲他工作。凡有他認爲有興趣的古書出現在市場上時，他就會請教相關領域的行家和圈中好友，并對照國立北平圖書館（即今中國國家圖書館的前身）的目録來判别它的價值。在這之後繼是對書的購買價格的談判。他對所購入的每本書都要進行細緻的檢查,以確定是否需要重新裝訂或修復強化。由於慕氏藏書中的大多數都有重新製作的函套,函套上署名的題簽在書法風格上也十分的整齊劃一,部分圖書還經過重新裝訂,有理由相信經義理壽之手的這批圖書在赴運加拿大之前在北京也經過了如同葛思德藏書相似的處理過程。

日軍占領北平後,於 1941 年命令義理壽搬到山東。但在出發的那天,義理壽突然病倒在火車站,這使得他能夠繼續留在北平,但也開始了他在英國公使館的長達近四年的被軟禁生活。1946 年 2 月義理壽恢復自由後,在他給葛思德東方圖書館的孫念禮的信中,提到日本軍人收走了他的藏書、書目、記錄和備忘錄等。這些在日軍占領期間丟失的資料,也是義理壽的傳記中關於他在日據時期個人資料缺失的主要原因。晚年的義理壽在試圖找回和整理葛思德圖書館索引目録中度日。在共濟會北京分部(District Grand Lodge of Peking)的名單上記録了義理壽於 1948 年 9 月 1 日在北京去世,享年 73 歲。在美國海軍學院校友雜志上也記録了義理壽於 1948 年 9 月 2 日在北京去世,去世原因及義理壽墓的具體位置都不詳。其精心收藏的圖書和用於古籍版本目録學研究的大量資料也就此流失,非常遺憾。

義理壽的《慕氏藏書目録》以"多倫多大學中文圖書館"(The University of Toronto Chinese Library)的名義編纂,每一條目下有十一項記録,分別是:索書號(Accession No.)、索引號(Index No.)、書名(Title)、分類(Classification)、主題(Subject)、參考(References)、著者(Author)、版本(Edition)、索引(Index)、裝幀(Bound in)、注釋(Remarks)。此書目編纂的時間應為 1933 年至 1935 年之間。書目編纂的體例和義理壽編纂的另一套中國古籍書目《葛思德東方藏書庫書目》有諸多相似之處。《慕氏藏書目録》共分兩種體例:一種是黑色布面現代裝訂,高 33.5 厘米,寬 24 厘米,封面空白,書眉處印有"The University of Toronto Chinese

Library"燙金書名及條目順序號(1—100)(圖七),此類目錄共有十七冊。第一冊在條目開始之前有註釋"首100個條目中三種書的參考索引號:163—ggcz,037—ahhg,167—mhfm 的頁碼是舊目錄中的頁碼,因此,這些頁碼也出現在新目錄中"。一些條目的背後可見水印"Hammermill, Made In USA" 可知此目錄是使用 Hammermill 的紙品。該公司是 1898 年成立於美國賓夕法尼亞州的大型紙製品公司。條目均采用印製好的包含上述十一項內容的標準格式紙,每葉左邊有黑色雙竪欄綫,右下角有長方格。條目的英文部分爲打字機輸入,中文用毛筆

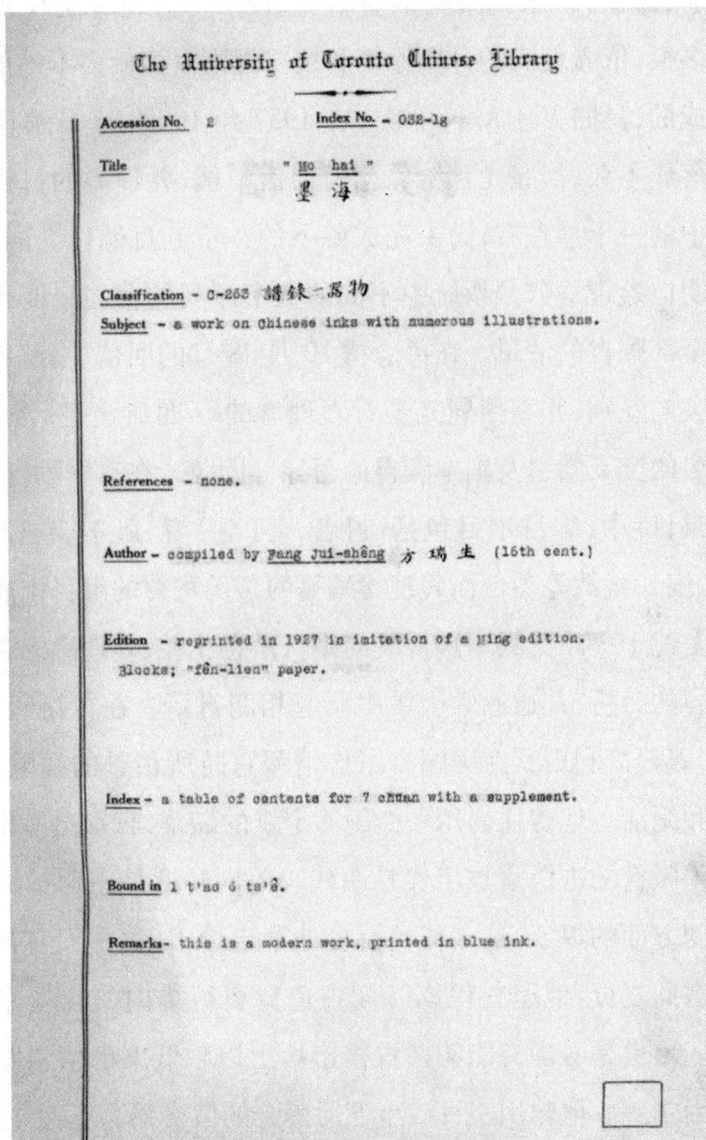

The University of Toronto Chinese Library

Accession No.   2   Index No. - 032-1g

Title   " Mo hai "
                         墨 海

Classification - C-253 譜錄一器物
Subject - a work on Chinese inks with numerous illustrations.

References - none.

Author - compiled by Fang Jui-shêng 方瑞生 (16th cent.)

Edition - reprinted in 1927 in imitation of a Ming edition.
  Blocks; "fên-lien" paper.

Index - a table of contents for 7 chüan with a supplement.

Bound in 1 t'ao 6 ts'ê.

Remarks- this is a modern work, printed in blue ink.

圖七　義理壽所編《慕氏藏書目錄》裝訂書册式條目內文

小楷書寫。中英文均爲黑色。另一種采用三孔活頁夾形式,高 29.5 厘米,寬 24 厘米,是美國 CPPC 公司於 1930—1940 年代生產的"The Superior"品牌的產品。目錄條目均用活頁紙打字而成,條目仍爲十一項。項目采用紅色,條目内容爲黑色,中文爲鋼筆手寫。此類目錄共計有二十一册(圖十)。根據最新的資料看,後一部分目錄是在慕氏藏書運抵多倫多後,依義理壽的分類原則和撰寫規則由多倫多本地的學者逐步撰寫而成的,具體責任人不可考。在 1937 年 10 月 23 日慕氏中文圖書館剛剛落成不久,懷履光寫給孫念禮的信中稱,義理壽的目錄祇包含慕氏藏書中的一千種左右,尚未完成餘下的一千五百餘種。同時,懷履光也不太明白義理壽分類系統中不同的數字序列的含義。他詢問孫念禮是否有全部圖書的清單。在孫念禮 10 月 28 日的回信中,解釋了分類號與索書號的區別,并請懷履光參看義理壽的《〈四庫全書〉書名索引》來瞭解書名的交叉索引及副本圖書的著録等問題。在慕學勳自編的《蓬萊慕氏藏書目》中,編目項目包括:書名,著(註)者、版本、卷(册)數、函數、備考、編列號數等項。而義理壽編纂的慕氏藏書的編目中所包括的内容則爲上述十一項。與中國傳統的編目信息比較,義理壽的書目更加注重對内容的分析,并通過索引號串聯起相關書籍。在古籍版本、年代鑒定方面,義理壽利用其在美國海軍作情報官時所積纍的經驗,有其特有的辦法和絶活。他曾通過用顯微鏡鑒定紙的纖維,識別出一本被其他人認定是宋版書的古籍實際年代爲明代。他同時還是一位指紋鑒定和手寫體辨認方面的專家,這一特長對於他鑒定鈔本、稿本大有裨益。在充當職業書商之後,他還對民國時期古書買賣行業内的各種作假伎倆瞭如指掌。這也是義理壽能夠在古書市場上以較低廉的價格購得善本古籍的原因之一。他曾用三百二十五元美金的價格爲葛思德文庫購得《永樂大典》三册。

	四書合講	龍龕字鑑	五經備旨	五經圖彙	鱗經摘珠	左傳事緯	六藝書綱目	正字字略	六書字通	詩經讀本
著者	清翁復編次		清鄒梧岡纂輯	愚山紹	胡傳明抄本	清馬驌撰	清舒天民述	清王葆友著	清閔寓五輯	宋朱熹集傳
刊本	愛日堂劉本	鼓堂軒刊	大同書局石印	寫堂銅刻		敏德堂刊	東武劉氏校刊	家藏版	家藏版	桂垣書局
冊卷	十二冊	四冊	十二冊	三冊	二冊	十二冊卷	上下二冊	八冊	八冊	四冊 八卷
	二	一	一	一	一	二	一	一	一	二
紙	毛太紙	白毛邊紙	夾油板光緒紙十三年印	夾板進史紙光緒十六年劉	毛邊紙	光緒年劉 竹紙	白綿棉紙温陵黃氏藏書	白綿連紙	毛邊紙	夾板毛邊紙光緒年劉
部	肆	肆	肆	肆	肆	伍	伍	伍	伍	伍

圖八　慕學勳自編《蓬萊慕氏藏書目》內文

15

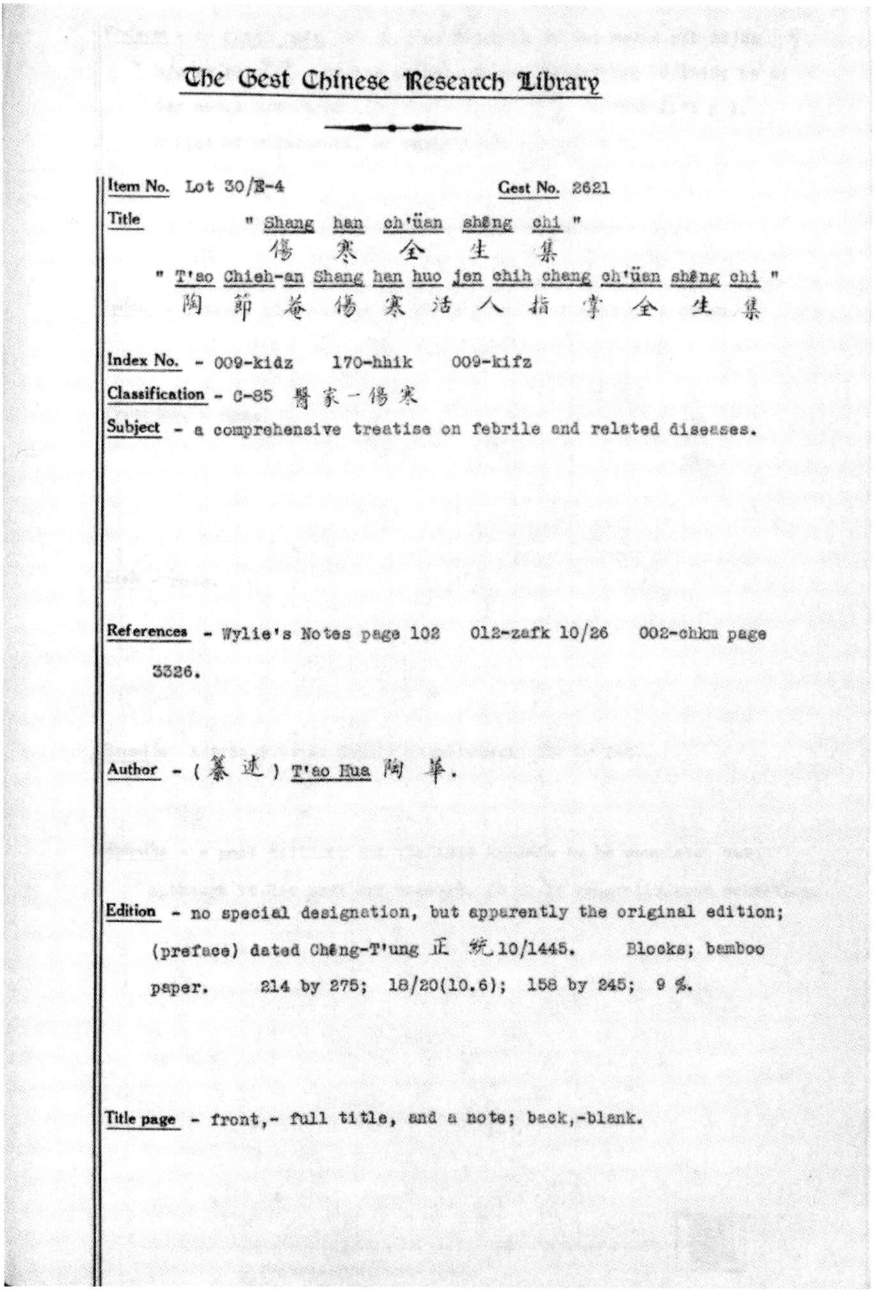

The Gest Chinese Research Library

Item No. Lot 30/B-4　　　　　　　　Gest No. 2621

Title　" Shang han ch'üan shêng chi "
傷　寒　全　生　集
" T'ao Chieh-an Shang han huo jen chih chang ch'üan shêng chi "
陶　節　菴　傷　寒　活　人　指　掌　全　生　集

Index No. - 009-kidz　170-hhik　009-kifz

Classification - C-85 醫家一傷寒

Subject - a comprehensive treatise on febrile and related diseases.

References - Wylie's Notes page 102　012-zafk 10/26　002-chkm page 3326.

Author - (纂述) T'ao Hua 陶華.

Edition - no special designation, but apparently the original edition; (preface) dated Chêng-T'ung 正統 10/1445.　Blocks; bamboo paper.　214 by 275; 18/20(10.6); 158 by 245; 9 %.

Title page - front,- full title, and a note; back,-blank.

圖九　義理壽所編《葛思德藏書目録》内文

義理壽逐步積纍的中文古籍善本目録學的知識受到中國學者的廣泛認同和贊賞，其中包括後來任普林斯頓大學葛思德東亞圖書館館長的胡適以及中國古籍目録學家王重民。在致友人的一封信件中,義理壽提到他編製了一個由梳理上百種不同的中國古代目録組成的包括多達四萬張卡片組成的綜合目録。這個卡片式目録幫助他更好地從事古籍善本的收購、收藏工作。

二十世紀初,當很多漢學家都認爲需要建立一套新的中文注音系統的時候,像義理壽這樣的善本收藏家們却開始設立獨有的中文書籍分類系統。義理壽對裘開明爲哈佛燕京圖書館開發的分類系統并不滿意,認爲它僅是把西方的模式套用在中國文化上。義理壽獨立建立的系統更加傾向於中國傳統的分類系統。他的索引系統曾受到了美國國會圖書館中國圖書部(現亞洲部)首任主任恒慕義博士(Dr. Arthur William Hummel,1884—1975)的贊賞,作爲哈佛燕京學社創始人洪業(William Hung,1893—1980)的友人,恒慕義對此系統的認同似乎在當時更具權威性。按照恒慕義的看法,義理壽的系統是當時唯一重視對單個漢字的索引和對一組漢字索引加以區別的系統。

這套由義理壽創建的索引系統也用在其他一些藏書上,其中包括1941年出版的他與白炳騏合編的《葛思德東方藏書庫書目》,1934年出版的《辦理四庫全書檔案》,和他爲《天禄琳琅書目》和《皕宋樓藏書志》做的索引。德國漢學家衛德明(Hellmut Whihelm,1905—1990)認爲,作爲一個新的索引系統,義理壽的索引系統既不要求讀者記住繁複的數字編碼,也不需要像哈佛燕京索引那樣需要對照筆畫數索引和威妥瑪拼音表來使用。這就使得義理壽的索引系統具有很強的實用性。義理壽索引的數字部分代表着書名的第一個漢字的部首的序號,部首的序號來自《康熙字典》,後面的字母部分代表書名前四個漢字的非部首部分的筆畫數。即 a 代表 1,b 代表 2,以此類推,最後 z 代表 0。例如:《墨海》的編號 032—lg,032 代表"墨"的部首"土","l"是字母表中第 12 個字母,代表非部首部分的"黑"的筆畫數 12,"g"代表"海"中的"每"的筆畫

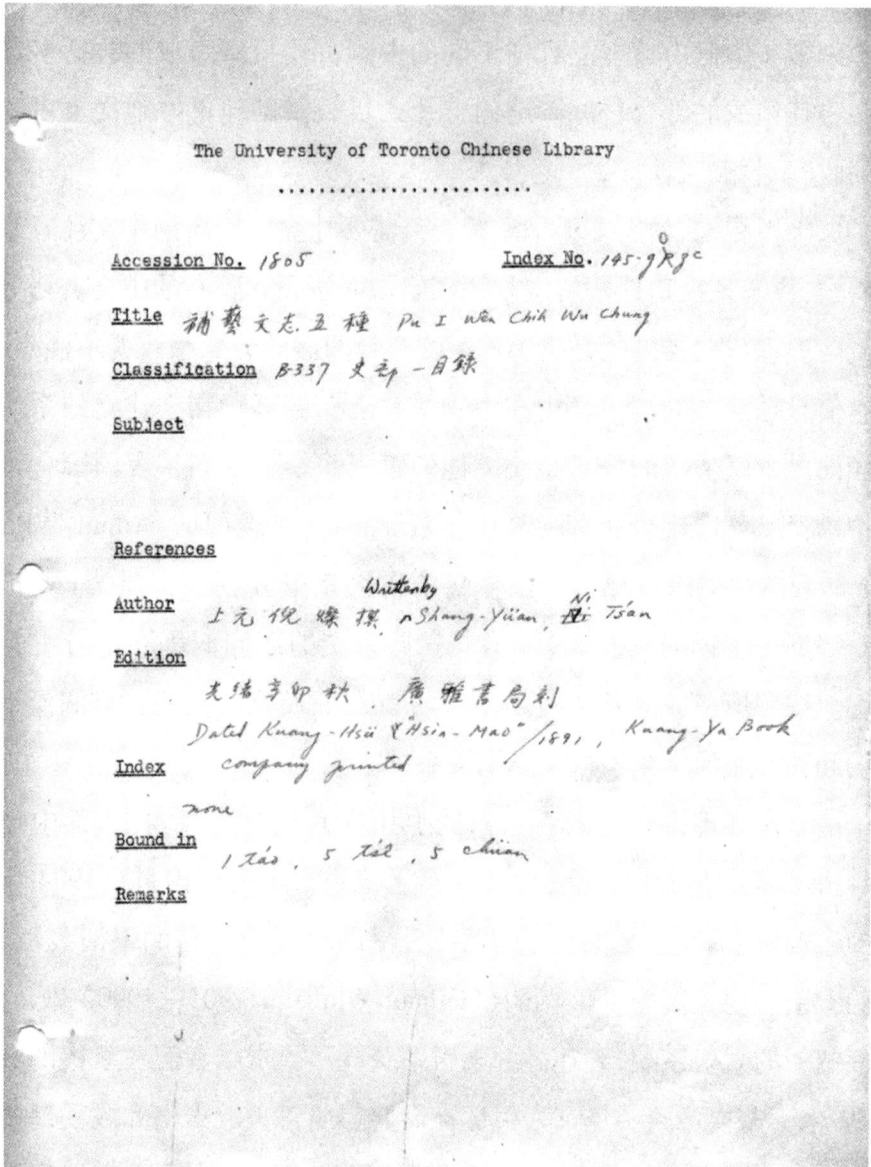

The University of Toronto Chinese Library

....

Accession No. *1805*   Index No. *145·9k8c*

Title   補藝文志五種 *Pu I Wên Chih Wu Chung*

Classification *B337 史部—目錄*

Subject

References

Author   上元倪燦撰 *Written by* *Shang-Yüan, Ni Ts'an*

Edition
           光緒辛卯秋，廣雅書局刻
           Dated Kuang-Hsü & Hsin-Mao 1891, Kuang-Ya Book
Index   *company printed*

           none

Bound in   *1 Tao, 5 Tsê, 5 chüan*

Remarks

圖十　義理壽所編《慕氏藏書目録》活頁式條目內文

數7。《古文淵鑑》一書的索引號是30—bzhn，30 是"口"的部首編號，字母代表非部首部分的筆畫數為2，0，8，14。《補藝文志五種》的編號為145—gozc，145 代表衣補旁，gozc 代表非部首部分的筆畫數為7，15，0，3。

　　今天義理壽所編纂的《慕氏藏書目録》稿本在經過八十餘年的滄桑

之後能夠和讀者見面，可以説是中國古籍善本目録學的一件幸事。傳統上西方學者所進行的古籍版本目録學的研究和探索并没有引起學術界的應有關注和重視。這一被認爲是純粹國學的研究領域似乎不太注意域外人士的参與與貢獻。義理壽《慕氏藏書目録》的出版，給我們提供了一個機會，藉此來深入觀察和分析西方人士所進行的古籍版本目録學的研究。筆者在此也要特別感謝中國國家圖書館出版社的總編輯和責任編輯們的獨具慧眼及辛勤努力，使得這一獨特的中國古籍目録得以影印出版，爲相關的專家、學者提供了不可多得的研究資料。

喬曉勤謹識於多倫多大學東亞圖書館

2017 年 3 月初稿，2022 年 2 月改定

出版説明

　　本書爲影印加拿大多倫多大學東亞圖書館藏慕氏藏書的目録稿本
而成。"慕氏藏書"的原收藏者爲山東蓬萊人慕學勳(1880—1929)。慕
學勳去世後,其子慕守一將圖書出售給加拿大主教懷履光,時在北京的
義理壽爲慕氏藏書編目。每頁書眉處印有"The University of Toronto Chinese Library",内容包括索書號(Accession No.)、索引號(Index No.)、
(英中對照)題名(Title)、(英中對照)分類(Classification)、主題(Subject)、參考(References)、(英中對照)著者(Author)、版本(Edition)、索
引(Index)、裝幀(Bound in)、註釋(Remarks)共十一項。此目主要供大
衆使用,屬典型的西式目録。關於慕氏藏書西移多倫多的過程,詳見本
書文前"序"、"I. V. GILLIS, CATALOGER OF THE MU AND GEST COL-
LECTIONS"與"編者的話"中的介紹。

　　爲便於學術研究,此次將慕學勳自編自刊《蓬萊慕氏藏書目》一并
印行。該目録以表格形式排印,分書名、著者、版本、卷(册)數、函數、附
註(出版年、紙張等)、編號七欄。此目主要供個人使用,屬傳統的中式
目録。

　　此次出版,特編製了總目、册目録與"書名拼音索引"。總目中各册
均標出了所含"慕氏藏書目"索書號(Accession No.),册目録依原稿順
序列出中文書名(包括同一種書的不同版本)與頁碼。對於同一種書有
兩個以上并列書名者,則僅列第一個書名:如第一册第33頁,正文著録
有三個并列書名《列子》《冲虚真經》《冲虚至德真經》,目録僅列第一個

書名《列子》;對於不同種書,則分別列出:如第二册第 601 頁,正文著録有兩種書名《居業録粹語》《讀書録粹語》,目録則將列爲兩條。對於著者姓名,統一采用規範字體,如"峯"改"峰"、"羣"改"群"、"畧"改"略"等。"書名拼音索引"置於全稿最後(第五册正文之後)。

本書爲"海外中華古籍書志書目叢刊"之一種。該系列自 2015 年啓動以來,已先後出版《文求堂書目》(田中慶太郎編,高田時雄、劉玉才整理,2015 年 3 月出版)、《西班牙藏中國古籍書録》(杜文彬編著,2015 年 11 月出版)、《美國埃默里大學神學院圖書館藏中文古籍目録》(美國埃默里大學神學院圖書館編,劉明整理,2016 年 9 月出版)、《普林斯頓大學圖書館藏中文善本書目》(美國普林斯頓大學東亞圖書館編,2017 年 3 月出版)、《美國芝加哥大學圖書館藏中文古籍善本書志·集部》(李文潔著,2019 年 6 月出版)、《美國芝加哥大學圖書館藏中文古籍善本書志·叢部》(李文潔著,2019 年 6 月出版)、《美國芝加哥大學圖書館藏中文古籍善本書志·經部》(張寶三著,2020 年 5 月出版)、《英國國家圖書館藏中文古籍目録》(廖可斌、王惠明、高虹飛、林旭文編著,2021 年 10 月出版)等。希望繼續得到讀者的大力支持。

國家圖書館出版社

二〇二二年二月

第一册目録

NOTE,-The page numbers in the three "reference works",- 163-ggcz; 037-ahhg; 167-mhfm,-appearing in the first 100 items refer to old catalogues; and thereafter the page numbers are those of new editions.

The University of Toronto Chinese Library

Accession No. - 1   **Index No.** - 085-gber

Title -   " <u>Hai nei ch'i kuan</u> "

海 內 奇 觀

Classification - B-222 地理—遊記

Subject - an illustrated description of famous mountains and places in China based upon extensive travel.

References - 012-zafk 8/23.

Author - <u>Yang Êrh-tsêng</u> 楊爾曾·

Edition - apparently original; the "<u>I-pai-t'ang</u>" 夷白堂 ; (preface) dated Wan-Li "chi-yu" 37/1609. Blocks; "bamboo" paper.

Index - a table of contents for 10 chüan.

Bound in 1 t'ao 8 ts'ê; doubly interleaved.

Remarks - this is a complete work and is in very good condition, except the last (8th) ts'ê which is a replacement printed on "mien" paper.

Accession No. 2   Index No. - 032-1g

Title   " Mo hai "
                  墨 海

Classification - C-263 譜錄一器物

Subject - a work on Chinese inks with numerous illustrations.

References - none.

Author - compiled by Fang Jui-shêng 方 瑞 生 (16th cent.)

Edition - reprinted in 1927 in imitation of a Ming edition.
 Blocks; "fên-lien" paper.

Index - a table of contents for 7 chüan with a supplement.

Bound in 1 t'ao 6 ts'ê.

Remarks - this is a modern work, printed in blue ink.

Accession No.   3   Index No. - 001-agkz

Title   " Ch'i ching lou wên chi "
                七　經　樓　文　集

Classification - D-43 別集一文

Subject - an individual collection of prose.

References - 012-zafk   18/14.

Author - Chiang Tzŭ-hsiao　蔣子瀟 .

Edition - no particular notation; (title-page) dated Tao-Kuang
     27/1847. Blocks; "fên" paper.

Index - a detailed table of contents for 6 chüan.

Bound in 1 t'ao 6 ts'ê.

Remarks - this is an ordinary edition without defects.

The University of Toronto Chinese Library

Accession No.   4   Index No. - 058-jefe

Title   " Hui yüan hsiang chu "
                  彙   苑   詳   註

Classification- C-348 類書

Subject - a general encyclopaedia covering miscellaneous subjects.

References - 012-zafk 13/24   031-bgdf   137/39

Author - said to be by <u>Wang Shih-chêng</u> 王世貞 , and revised
  by <u>Tsou Shan-ch'ang</u> 鄒善長·

Edition - a Ming edition; (preface) dated Wan-Li "i-wei" 23/1595.
  Blocks; "bamboo" paper.

Index - a general classified table of contents for 36 chüan.

Bound in 2 t'ao 14 ts'ê.

Remarks- this is a good edition; and the item is in generally
  good condition, except that a number of worm-holes are found
  throught the work.

The University of Toronto Chinese Library

Accession No.   5   **Index No.**   009-zkzn

Title   " <u>Jên shou chin chien</u> "

人 壽 金 鑑

Classification – B-117 傳記一總錄

Subject – a classified collection of notes of a biographical
character.

References – none.

Author – （輯）<u>Ch'êng Tê-ling</u> 程得齡·

Edition – the "<u>Ch'ung wên shu chü</u>"崇文書局 ; dated Kuang-Hsü
"i-hai" 1/1875.   Blocks; "fên" paper.

Index – a table of contents for 22 chüan; arranged according to ages.

Bound in 1 t'ao 6 ts'ê.

Remarks – this is a good edition, and the item is in perfect condition.

The University of Toronto Chinese Library

Accession No.   6   **Index No.** - 128-g11f

Title   " Shêng yü hsiang chieh "
                      聖　諭　像　解

Classification - C-128 儒家

Subject - explanation of the " Sacred Edict ", with numerous
   illustrations of ancient worthies noted for their good reputation
   and virtuous conduct.

References - Wylie's Notes page 87   160-1j

Author - Liang Yen-nien 梁延年

Edition - a reprint by "Wei-ching-t'ang" 味經堂 ; (title-page)
   dated Hsien-Fêng "ping ch'ên" 6/1856.   Blocks; "fên" paper.

Index - separate at the beginning of each of 20 chüan.

Bound in 1 t'ao 10 ts'ê.

Remarks - this is a comparatively new edition, and is in very good
   condition.

Accession No.   7   Index No. - 128-gilf

Title   " Sheng yü hsiang chieh "
                聖　諭　像　解

see C 13

Classification - C-128 儒家

Subject - explanation of the "Sacred Edict" with numerous illustration of ancient worthies noted for their good reputation
and virtuous conduct.

References - Wylie's Notes page 87   160-1j

Author - Liang Yen-nien 梁 延 年 .

Edition - a reprint by "Pao-shan-t'ang" 寶 善 堂 ; (title-page)
dated Kuang-Hsü "ting hai" 13/1887. Blocks; "fen" paper.

Index - separate at the beginning of each of 20 chüan.

Bound in 1 t'ao 10 ts'e.

Remarks - this is a fairly new edition in very good condition.

Accession No.   8   Index No. – 128-gilf

Title   " Sheng yü hsiang chieh "
             聖   諭   像   解

                    ell C 13
Classification – C-128 儒家

Subject – explanation of the "Sacred Edict" with numerous illus-
    trations of ancient worthies noted for their good reputation
    and virtuous conduct.

References – Wylie's Notes page 87   160-1j

Author – Liang Yen-nien 梁延年.

Edition – a reprint by "Wei-ching-t'ang" 味經堂 ; (title-page)
    dated Hsien-Feng "ping ch'en"   6/1856. Blocks; "fen" paper.

Index – separate at the beginning of each of 20 chüan.

Bound in 1 t'ao 10 ts'e.

Remarks – this is a comparatively new edition and is in exceedingly
    good condition.

Accession No.   9   Index No. - 030-bz1j

Title   " Ku wên tz'ŭ lei tsuan "
                          古 文 辭 類 纂 "

Classification - D-63 總集一詩文
Subject - a general collection of prose with some poetic writings.

References - 012-zafk 19/26.

Author - Yao Nai 姚鼐 .

Edition - the "Tu-mên-yin-shu-chü" 都門印書局 ; (preface) dated
  Min-Kuo "i mao" 4/1915.   Blocks; "mao pien" paper.

Index - a general table of contents for 74 chüan covering some
  700 literary selections with compiler's notes at the end.

Bound in 2 t'ao 16 ts'ê.

Remarks - this is a modern work without defects.

Accession No.   10   Index No. -030-bzlj

Title   " Ku wên tz'ǔ lei tsuan "
                 古 文 辭 類 纂

Classification - D-63 總集一詩文

Subject - a general collection of prose with some poetic writings,
   grouped into 13 classifications.

References - 012-zafk 19/26.

Author - Yao Nai 姚 鼐 .

Edition - the "Li-shih-ch'iu-yao-t'ang" 李氏求要堂 ; (title-page)
   dated Kuang-Hsü "hsin ch'ou" 27/1901.   Blocks; "mao t'ai" paper.

Index - a general table of contents for 75 chüan covering some 700
   literary selections with compiler's notes at the end.

Bound in 1 t'ao 12 ts'ê.

Remarks - this is an ordinary work, complete and without defects.
   Some marginal notes were written in the first 2 ts'ê by the
   owner.

—·—

Accession No. 11(a)   **Index No. -** 030-bzlj

Title   " <u>Ku wên tz'ŭ lei tsuan</u> "
古 文 辭 類 纂

Classification - D-63 總集一詩文

Subject - a general collection of prose with some poetic writings
grouped into 13 classifications.

References - 012-zafk   19/26.

Author - <u>Yao Nai</u> 姚 鼐 .

Edition - the "<u>Wên-chang-shu-chü</u>" 文章書局 ; (title-page) dated
Kuang-Hsü "<u>jên ch'ên</u>" 18/1892.   Blocks; "fên" paper.

Index - a general table of contents for 74 chüan covering some 700
literary selections with compiler's notes at the end.

Bound in 1 t'ao 11 ts'ê.

Remarks - this is an ordinary work, complete and without defects.

Accession No.   11 (b)   Index No. - 120-obzl

Title   " Hsü ku wên tz'ǔ lei tsuan "
                         績 古 文 辭 類 纂

Classification - D-63 總集一詩文
Subject - a general collection of prose with some poetic writings
    under 10 classifications, being supplementary to Ku wên tz'ǔ
    lei tsuan 古文辭類纂.

References - none.

Author - (纂集) Wang Hsien-ch'ien 王 先 謙.

Edition - privately published; (title-page) dated Kuang-Hsü
    "jên wu" 8/1882.   Blocks; "fên" paper.

Index - a general table of contents for 34 chüan with compiler's
    notes at the end.

Bound in 1 t'ao 7 ts'ê.

Remarks - an ordinary but good edition; and the item is complete.

The University of Toronto Chinese Library

Accession No.   12 (a)   **Index No.** - 030-bzlj

Title   " Ku wên tz'ú lei tsuan "
             古　文　辭　類　篡

Classification - D-63 總集一詩文

Subject - a general collection of prose with some poetic writings
 grouped under 13 classifications.

References - 012-zafk 19/26

Author - Yao Nai 姚 鼐 ·

Edition - the "Ssŭ-hsien-chiang-shê" 思 賢 講 舍 ; (title-page)
  dated Kuang-Hsü "kuei ssŭ" 19/1893. Blocks; "fên" paper.

Index - a general table of contents for 74 chüan covering some
  700 literary selections.

Bound in 12 ts'ê in 3 t'ao with (b).

Remarks - a modern edition and the item is as if new.

Accession No.   12 (b)   Index No. - 120-obz1

Title   " Hsü ku wên tz'ü lei tsuan "
                續 古 文 辭 類 纂

Classification - D-63 總集一詩文

Subject - a general collection of prose with some poetic writings

grouped under 10 classifications, being supplementary to

Ku wên tz'ü lei tsuan 古文辭類纂(12 a).

References - none.

Author -(纂集) Wang Hsien-ch'ien 王先謙.

Edition -the "Hsü-shou-t'ang" 虛 受 堂 ; (title-page) dated

Kuang-Hsü "jên wu" 8/1882.   Blocks; "fên" paper.

Index - a general table of contents for 34 chüan with compiler's

notes at the end.

Bound in 8 ts'ê in 3 t'ao with (a).

Remarks - a modern edition and the item is as if new.

Accession No.　　13　　　　　Index No. - 120-obzl

Title　　　　　" Hsü ku wên tz'ŭ lei tsuan "

續 古 文 辭 類 纂

Classification - D-63 總集－詩文

Subject - a collection of prose and poetic writings (all not
　included in Ku wên tz'ŭ lei tsuan) in three "pien" and under
　many classifications.

References - none.

Author - (纂敘) Li Shu-ch'ang　黎 庶 昌.
　　　　　(校) Chiang Tzŭ-fan　蔣 子 蕃.

Edition - the "Chin-ling-shu-chü" 金 陵 書 局 ; (title-page)
　dated Kuang-Hsü "kêng yin" 16/1890.　Blocks; "fên" paper.

Index - a detailed table of contents for 28 chüan.

Bound in　1 t'ao　8 ts'ê

Remarks - an ordinary good edition and the item is complete.
　On pages 20 and 21 chüan 5, there are slight defects; worm-
　holes in ts'ê 5.

The University of Toronto Chinese Library

Accession No.   14   Index No. – 021-cgd   187-bcgd

Title   " Pei hai chi "

北　海　集

" Fêng pei hai chi "

馮　北　海　集

Classification – D-33 別集一詩文

Subject – an individual collection of writings, poetry and prose
arranged according to the style of composition.

References – 012-zafk   16/31

Author – Fêng ch'i 馮 琦 .

Edition – a Ming edition; (preface) dated Wan-Li "chi yu"
37/1609.   Blocks; "bamboo" paper.

Index – a general table of contents for 58 chüan with a detailed
table of contents preceeding each chüan.

Bound in 2 t'ao 16 ts'ê.

Remarks – this is a very good Ming edition and the item appears
to be complete; but there are a number of repaired blemishes.

Accession No. 15   **Index No.** – 066-kfc

Title

"Shu tu yen"

數 度 衍

Classification – C-138 天文算法一算書

Subject – "After some iniatory chapters on the source of numbers and music, it gives a treatise on Geometry, drawn up from Ricci's translation of Euclid; next is given the Method of Calculation by the Abacus, after the Suan fa t'ung tsung 算 法 統 宗, a treatise on the abacus published in the Ming dynasty; next are successive chapters on Written Arithmetic, the use of Napier's Rods, and Calculations by the Sector, all which he seems to have learned from the #

References – Wylie's Notes page 121   163-ggcz   8/16

031-bgdf   107/28   031-bgld   11/11   012-zafk   11/5.

Author – (衍) Fang Chung-t'ung 方 中 通 ·

Edition – apparently published by one of the author's descendants; (title-page) dated Kuang-Hsü 4/1878. Blocks; "mao pien" paper.

Index – a general table of contents for 3 首 and 23 chüan; detailed tables at the beginning of each chüan. (chüan 15 is missing)

Bound in 1 t'ao 8 ts'ê.

Remarks – this is an ordinary edition and the item is complete.

#T'ung wên suan chih 同 文 算 指, and the Hsin fa suan shu 新 法 算書; after these the several rules of the Chiu Chang 九 章 are expounded at great length, following the same order in which they are given in the Shu li ching yün 數 理 精 蘊 · (Wylie's Notes page 121)

Accession No. 16   **Index No.** - 018-mcig   173-cigm

Title

" Liu hsüeh hu mei p'u "

劉 雪 湖 梅 譜

" Hsüeh hu mei p'u "

雪 湖 梅 譜

Classification - C-283 譜錄一草木

Subject -an esthetical monograph on the plum-tree (and more especially its blossoms), consisting in the main of poetical references; together with related matter, including sketches of various aspects of its branches and blossoms.

References - 012-zafk   12/9

Author - (編輯) Wang Ssŭ-jên 王 思 任.

Edition - the "Mo-miao-shan-fang" 墨 妙 山 房; (postscripts) dated K'ang-Hsi "hsin yu" 20/1681. Blocks; "fên" paper.

Index - a table of contents for 2 chüan (上 下).

Bound in 1 t'ao 2 ts'ê; doubly interleaved.

Remarks - this is a very good edition, and apparently reprinted from Ming blocks, with a few resultant defects. Pages 31 and 32 of the 2nd. chüan are missing. Liu Hsüeh-hu is Liu Shih-ju 劉 世 儒 and the illustrations are by him.

19

The University of Toronto Chinese Library

Accession No.   17   Index No. - 075-cazz

Title   " Li t'ai po wên chi chi chu "
               李　太　白　文　集　輯　註

Classification - D-33 別集－詩文

Subject - collection of poems and prose of Li Po 李白 ; with
         six appendixes (last 6 chüan).

References - none.

Author - (輯註) Wang Ch'i 王琦 .

Edition - the "Chü-chin-t'ang" 聚錦堂 ; (preface) dated
         "Ch'ien-Lung" 23/1758.   Blocks; "mao-t'ai" paper.

Index - a detailed table of contents for 36 chüan.

Bound in   2 t'ao 16 ts'ê.

Remarks - this is an ordinary edition but a valuable work; and
         the item appears to be complete except the top and bottom
         margins of the pages are somewhat stained.

The University of Toronto Chinese Library

Accession No.   18   Index No. - 032-1z

Title   " Mo tzŭ "

墨 子

Classification - C-308 雜家 一 雜文

Subject - the writings of the philosopher Mo Ti 墨翟 , on moral
and political subjects, as well as certain matters of a
military nature.

References - Wylie's Notes page 157   160-1j   163-ggcz 10/1
031-bgld 13/1   030-iaff 18/13   106-gdkn 55/1
012-zafk 12/13   031-bgdf 117/3.

Author - original work - Mo Ti 墨翟 . See 160-1j Giles B D 1537.
        this work- Pi Yüan 畢沅 .   See 160-1j Wylie's Notes
pp. 78 & 217 Giles B D 1647.

Edition - the " Ling-yen-shan-kuan " 靈巖山館 ; dated
Ch'ien-Lung "chia ch'ên" 49/1784. Blocks; "bamboo" paper.

Index - a table of contents for 15 chüan at end of last ts'ê;
篇 目 考 1 chüan.

Bound in 1 t'ao 6 ts'ê; doubly interleaved.

Remarks - this is a complete work and in good condition.

The University of Toronto Chinese Library

Accession No.   19   Index No.   - 030-gzh

Title   " T'ang wên sui "
                          唐 文 粹

Classification - D-63 總集一詩文

Subject - a comprehensive general miscellaneous collection of
prose and poetry.

References - 160-1j 163-ggcz 16/3 031-bgld 19/9 037-ahhg 3/38
167-mhfm 23/12 030-iaff 38/11 106-gdkn 112/17 012-zafk 19/3
031-bgdf 186/34.

Author - (纂) Yao Hsüan 姚 鉉 .

Edition - the "Chiang-su-shu-chü" 江 蘇 書 局 ; dated Kuang-Hsü
"kuei wei" 9/1883.   Blocks; "fên" paper.

Index - a table of contents for 100 chüan, with separate lists at
beginning of each chüan.

Bound in 2 t'ao 16 ts'ê .

Remarks - this is an ordinary edition and the item is complete
and in good condition.

————•————

Accession No.　20　　　　　Index No. - 040-dzn

Title

" Sung wên chien "
宋　文　鑑

Classification - D-63 總集一詩文

Subject - an extensive collection of prose and poetical compositions
of officials and scholars of the Sung Dynasty period, arranged
under 61 classes; many of the items being of historical
interest and importance.

References - 160-1j　163-ggcz 16/6　031-bgld 19/12　037-ahhg (hsü)
20/1　167-mhfm 23/26　030-iaff 38/14　106-gdkn 113/20
012-zafk 19/3　031-bgdf 187/10.

Author - (編) Lü Tsu-ch'ien 呂 祖 謙.

Edition - the "Chiang-su-shu-chü" 江 蘇 書 局 ; dated Kuang-Hsü
"ping hsü" 12/1886.　Blocks; "fên" paper.

Index - a general table of contents for 150 chüan, arranged under
61 classes of writings, with a detailed list at beginning of
each chüan.

Bound in 2 t'ao　24 ts'ê.

Remarks - an ordinary edition; complete and without defects.

Accession No. 21   Index No. - 167-zzd

Title   " Chin wên ya "
                          金 文 雅

Classification - D-63 總集一詩文

Subject - a miscellaneous collection of prose and poetry by the
emperors and scholars of the Chin Dynasty period.

References - none.

Author - (述) Chuang Hsiu-fang 莊秀方.

Edition - the " Chiang-su-shu-chü " 江蘇書局 ; dated Kuang-Hsü
"hsin mao" 17/1891.   Blocks; "fên" paper.

Index - a general table of contents for 16 chüan and separate
lists for each chüan.

Bound in 1 t'ao 4 ts'ê.

Remarks - an ordinary edition; complete and without defects.

Accession No. 22   Index No. - 010-bzj

Title   " Yuan wên lei "
                    元 文 類

Classification - D-63 總集一詩文

Subject - a general collection of prose and poetry by authors

of the Yuan Dynasty period from its beginning to the

Yen-Yu 延祐 period, grouped under 43 classes.

References - 031-bgdf 188/16-17   012-zafk 19/6

Author - Su T'ien-chio 蘇天爵.

Edition - the "Chiang-su-shu-chu" 江蘇書局 ; dated Kuang-Hsü

"chi-ch'ou" 15/1889.   Blocks; "fên" paper.

Index - a general table of contents for 70 chüan with separate

lists for each chüan.

Bound in 2 t'ao 10 ts'ê.

Remarks - an ordinary edition; complete and without defects.

Accession No.   23   Index No. - 072-dzc

Title   " Ming wên tsai "
                          明　文　在

Classification - D-63 總集一詩文
Subject - a general collection of prose and poetry by officials
    and scholars of the Ming Dynasty period.

References - 012-zafk 17/22   031-bgdf 194/37

Author - (編) Hsüeh Hsi 薛熙 .

Edition - the "Chiang-su-shu-chü" 江蘇書局 ; dated Kuang-Hsü
    "chi-ch'ou" 15/1889.   Blocks; "fên" paper.

Index - a general table of contents for 100 chüan with separate
    lists for each chüan.

Bound in 1 t'ao 10 ts's.

Remarks - an ordinary edition; complete and without defects.

Accession No.   24   Index No. - 030-bhbi   030-bhzi

Title

      " Ku lun yüan chu "
      古 論 元 著
      " Ku lun hsüan chu "
      古 論 玄 著

Classification - D-43   總集一文

Subject - a collection of discourses written by the most famous
ancient authors on literature, politics, history, biography,
etc.

References - 012-zafk   19/11   031-bgdf   193/18.

Author - Fu Chên-shang   傳 振 商 .

Edition - the "Kuo-shih-shu-yüan" 國士書院 ; dated Wan-Li
"jen tzŭ" 40/1612.   Blocks; bamboo paper.

Index - a detailed table of contents for 8 chüan.

Bound in   1 t'ao 8 ts'ê; doubly interleaved.

Remarks - a very good edition; and the item is complete.   Many
pages are stained; defects on the left-hand margins of the pages
repaired.

The University of Toronto Chinese Library

Accession No.   25   Index No. - 024-gdjg

Title   " Nan-Sung tsa shih shih "

南 宋 雜 事 詩

Classification - D-68   總集一詩

Subject - a collection of 700 poems composed by seven authors,
each contributing 100 poems, based upon facts and events
from nearly one thousand works, to arouse interest in the
history of their native district, the location of the capi-
tal of the Southern Sung (Nan-Sung) Dynasty; compiled   (#)

References - 031-bgdf   190/37   012-zafk   19/21

Author - Shěn Chia-ch'ě 沈 嘉 轍 , Wu Ch'uo 吳 焯   and others.

Edition - the "Fu-li-shan-fang" 扶 荔 山 房 ; dated Tao-Kuang
"chi-ch'ou" 9/1829.   Blocks; bamboo paper.

Index - a table of contents for 7 chüan.

Bound in 1 t'ao 8 ts'ě; doubly interleaved with red paper.

Remarks - a good edition, complete, but with very many worm-holes.

    (#)   by the seven authors under rules of compilation into
       7 chüan.

The University of Toronto Chinese Library

Accession No. 26-A   Index No. - 125-zzil   162-11g

Title   " Lao-tzŭ Tao-tê-chên-ching "

老 子 道 德 真 經

" Tao-tê-ching "

道 德 經

Classification - C-751 道家

Subject - the so-called "Canon of Reason and Virtue"; a basic

work of the Taoist gospel.

References - 160-1j Wylie's Notes page 216   012-zafk 14/30

031-bgdf 146/5.   The above are general references and not
to this particular edition.

Author - reputed to be Lao-tzŭ 老子 , but extremely doubtful.

Edition - no notation; no date; but of the Ming period.   Blocks;
"mien" paper.

Index - none; 2 "p'ien" 上 下 .

Bound in 1 ts'ê in 1 t'ao with (b); doubly interleaved with margins.

Remarks - a very good edition; complete, and without defects.

Accession No.   26-B   Index No.   - 140-gzgh   024-gheg

Title   " Chuang-tzŭ Nan-hua-chên-ching "
               莊 子 南 華 真 經
               " Nan-hua-chên-ching"
               南 華 真 經

Classification - C-731 道家

Subject - the Taoist writings in 33 sections, devided into three
    main divisions, (1) Nei p'ien 內 篇 ; (2) Wai p'ien 外 篇 ;
    and (3) Tsa p'ien 雜 篇 ; with marginal commentaries in red.

References - Wylie's Notes page 218   160-1j   012-zafk 14/32
    031-bgdf 146/22.   The above are general references and not
    to this particular edition.

Author - usually credited to Chuang Chou 莊 周 .

Edition - no notation; no date; but of the Ming period.   Blocks;
    "mien" paper.

Index - a table of contents for 4 chüan.

Bound in 10 ts's in 2 t'ao with (a) (c); doubly interleaved with
    margins.

Remarks - a very good edition; complete and without defects.

30

Accession No. 26 (c)   **Index No.** - 018-dzdf 015-dfeg 015-dfzl

Title   " Lieh-tzŭ Ch'ung-hsü-chên-ching "
列 子 冲 虚 真 經
" Ch'ung-hsü-chên-ching "
冲 虚 真 經
" Ch'ung-hsü-chih-tê-chên-ching "
冲 虚 至 德 真 經

Classification - C-731 道家

Subject - a work on metaphysical philosophy; one of the principal
works of the Taoist gospel, with marginal commentaries in red.

References- Wylie's Notes page 217   012-zafk 14/32 031-bgdf 146/18
160-1j. The above are general references and not to this particular edition.

Author - reputed to be Lieh Yü-k'ou 列 禦 寇 , but the actual
existence of such a person is very doubtful indeed. See 160-1j
Giles B D 1251.

Edition - no notation; no date; but of the Ming period. Blocks;
"mien" paper.

Index - a table of contents for 8 chüan.

Bound in 5 ts'ê in 1 t'ao with (b); doubly interleaved with margins.

Remarks- a very good edition; complete and without defects.

31

The University of Toronto Chinese Library

Accession No.   27   **Index No.** - 024-gheg 140-gze

Title

" Nan-hua-chên-ching "

南 華 真 經

" Chuang-tzŭ chu "

莊 子 註

Classification - C-731 道家

Subject - the Taoist writings of Chuang Chou 莊 周 with commentaries and explanations.

References - 031-bgdf 146/21   012-zafk 14/32   Wylie's Notes page 218.

Author - (註) Kuo Hsiang 郭 象 .

Edition - the " Shih-tê-t'ang " 世 德 堂 of the Ming period; no date.   Blocks; "mien" paper.

Index - a general table of contents for 10 chüan.

Bound in   1 t'ao 4 ts'ê.

Remarks - 7 out of the 10 chüan are in good condition. The rest 3 chüan (1,4,10) are as under:-
Chüan 1 badly stained; a portion of page 30 torn and missing.
Chüan 4 hand written with the exception of pages 1,2,3,4, 24,25,26,27.
Chüan 10 being a replacement in bad condition, and with numerous blemishes.
The whole work is, however, complete.

The University of Toronto Chinese Library

Accession No. 28   **Index No.** -018-dz   015-dfeg   015-dfzl

Title

" Lieh-tzŭ "

列 子

" Ch'ung-hsü-chên-ching "

沖 虛 真 經

" Ch'ung-hsü-chih-tê-chên-ching "

沖 虛 至 德 真 經

Classification - C-731 道家

Subject - a work on metaphysical philosophy; one of the principal
works of the Taoist gospel, with commentaries.

References - Wylie's Notes page 217.   012-zafk   14/32   031-bgdf
146/18   160-1j.   The above are general references and not to
this particular edition.

Author - reputed to be Lieh Yü-k'ou 列 禦 寇 , but the actual
existence of such a person is very doubtful indeed.   See 160-1j
Giles B D 1251.   (注) Chang K'an 張 湛 .

Edition - based upon the Sung edition; dated Kuang-Hsü "chia shên"
10/1884.   Blocks; "fên" paper.

Index - none.

Bound in 1 t'ao 2 ts'ê; doubly interleaved.

Remarks - a good edition, and the item is complete and in excellent condition.

Accession No.   29   Index No.   -067-zzhz

Title

"Wên hsin tiao lung"
文 心 雕 龍

Classification - D-93 詩文評

Subject - The earliest "critique on poetry and literature" now
extant, originally in 50 sections, with commentaries and marginal notes in red ink.

References - Wylie's Notes page 244   012-zafk   20/1   031-bgdf
195/1

Author - (撰) Liu Hsieh 劉勰 ; (注) Huang Shu-lin 黄叔琳;
(評) Chi Yün 紀昀 .

Edition - the "Han-mo-yüan" 翰墨園 ; dated Tao-Kuang
13/1833. Blocks; "fên" paper.

Index - a general table of contents for 10 chüan.

Bound in 1 t'ao 4 ts'ê.

Remarks - an ordinary edition; complete and without defects.

The University of Toronto Chinese Library

Accession No. 30   Index No. - 140-fzz

Title   " Ts'ao mu tzŭ "
                    草　木　子

Classification - C-308 雜家一雜文

Subject - " a series of notes embracing nearly every department of
literature, written by Yeh Tzŭ-ch'i during his imprisonment
in 1378." (Wylie's Notes page 168)

References - Wylie's Notes page 168   160-1j   031-bgdf   122/17
012-zafk   12/30.

Author - Yeh Tzŭ-ch'i 葉子奇·

Edition - privately published; (preface) dated T'ung-Chih
"chia hsü" 13/1874.   Blocks; "fên" paper.

Index - a table of contents for 8 chüan.

Bound in 1 t'ao 3 ts'ê; doubly interleaved.

Remarks - an ordinary edition; complete and without defects.

Accession No.   31   **Index No.** - 169-gjfh   120-clid

Title

" Yüeh wei ts'ao t'ang pi chi "

閱 微 草 堂 筆 記

" Chi Hsiao-lan hsien-shêng pi chi "

紀 曉 嵐 先 生 筆 記

Classification - C-368 小 說 家

Subject - five collections of notes and jottings on a variety of
subjects.

References - 012-zafk 14/10

Author - (撰) Kuan i tao jên 觀 弈 道 人 i. e. Chi Yün 紀 昀 .

Edition - " Kuang-chou-ts'ai-chêng-ssŭ " 廣 州 財 政 司 :
(preface) dated Tao-Kuang "i wei" 15/1835.   Blocks;
"fên" paper.

Index - a general table of contents for the 5 collections in
24 chüan.

Bound in 2 t'ao 10 ts'ê.

Remarks - an ordinary edition; and the item is as if new.

36

Accession No. 32   Index No. - 085-hccz

Title   " Ch'ing-tai ming jên shu cha "

清 代 名 人 書 札

Classification - D-73 總集一文

Subject - a collection of autograph letters written by some 40
famous scholars and officials of the Ch'ing Dynasty.

References - none.

Author - (採集) Tzŭ yen shê 資研社.

Edition - the " Chung-hua-yin-shua-chü " 中華印刷局; dated
Min-Kuo 16/1927.   Blocks; "fên" paper.

Index - a list of the authors, with biographical notes arranged
in accordance with the order of their letters.

Bound in 1 t'ao 2 ts'ê; singly interleaved.

Remarks - a new book.

37

Accession No.　33　　　　Index No.　-140-gzdf

Title

　　　" Chuang-tzŭ chi chieh "
　　　莊　子　集　解

Classification　- C-731 道家

Subject　- the Taoist writings by Chuang Chou 莊　周　in 33 sections
with notes and explanations.

References　- 031-bgdf 146/21 012-zafk 14/32 Wylie's Notes
page 218. The above are general references and not to this
particular edition.

Author　- Wang Hsien-ch'ien 王　先　謙.

Edition　- the "Ssŭ-hsien-shu-chü" 思 賢 書局 ; (title-page)
dated Hsüan-T'ung "chi yu" 1/1909. Blocks; "fên" paper.

Index　- none.

Bound in　1 t'ao 3 ts'ê.

Remarks　- an ordinary edition; and the item is new.

The University of Toronto Chinese Library

Accession No. 34   Index No. - 140-gzfe

Title   " Chuang-tzŭ p'ang chu "

莊 子 旁 注

Classification - C-731 道家

Subject - the Taoist writings by Chuang Chou 莊 周 in 33 sections
with explanations and some hand-written marginal notes.

References - 031-bgdf 146/21   012-zafk 14/32   Wylie's Notes
page 218. The above are general references and not to this
particular edition.

Author - (輯注) Wu Ch'êng-chien 吳 承 漸.

Edition - the "Ssŭ-hsün-t'ang" 思 訓 堂 ; (preface) dated
K'ang-Hsi "chi mao" 38/1699. Blocks; bamboo paper.

Index - a table of contents for 5 chüan.

Bound in   1 t'ao 5 ts'ê.

Remarks - a fair edition; and the item appears to be complete.

Accession No.　　35　　　　Index No. - 162-jccd

Title　　　" Hsün chih chai chi "
　　　　　　遜　志　齋　集

Classification - D-33 別集一詩文

Subject - an individual collection of prose and poetry with a

Shih i 拾遺　for 10 chüan.

References - 012-zafk 16/14　163-ggcz　15/5　031-bgdf 170/5

160-1j.　The above are general references and not to this

particular edition.

Author - (撰) Fang Hsiao-ju 方孝儒 .

Edition - the "Hu-wei-shan-chü" 胡味善居 ; (title-page)

dated Min-Kuo "wu ch'ên" 17/1928.　Blocks; "mao t'ai" paper.

Index - a detailed table of contents for 30 chüan with a separate

list for 10 chüan for the Shih i 拾遺 .

Bound in　2 t'ao　18 ts'ê.

Remarks - an ordinary modern edition; and the item is complete.

Accession No. 36 **Index No.** - 149-ofhd

Title " Tu shu t'ang ch'üan chi "

讀　書　堂　全　集

Classification - D-33 別集一詩文

Subject - an individual collection of prose and poetry.

References - 012-zafk 17/12.

Author (撰) Chao Shih-lin 趙 士 麟 .

Edition - the " Chê-chiang-shu-chü " 浙江書局 ; (title-page)
dated Kuang-Hsü "kuei-ssŭ" 19/1893. Blocks; "mao-pien" paper.

Index - a detailed table of contents for 46 chüan.

Bound in 1 t'ao 12 ts'ê.

Remarks - an ordinary edition; complete and without defects.

Accession No. 37   **Index No.** - 077-ngzd 173-gzdz

Title   " Kuei Chên-ch'uan hsien shêng ch'üan chi "

歸　震　川　先　生　全　集

" Chên-ch'uan hsien shêng ch'üan chi "

震　川　先　生　全　集

Classification - D-33 別集一詩文

Subject - an individual collection of prose and poetry with a
pieh chi 別 集 for 10 chüan.

References - 012-zafk 16/29   031-bgdf 172/44.

Author - Kuei Yu-kuang 歸 有 光 . See 160-1j.

Edition - published by one of the author's descendants; (title-page)
dated Kuang-Hsü 1/1875. Blocks; "mao-pien" paper.

Index - a detailed table of contents for 30 chüan and a separate
list for 10 chüan for the pieh chi 別 集 .

Bound in 2 t'ao 12 ts'ê.

Remarks - a fairly good edition; and the item is complete and without
defects.

42

Accession No.   38   **Index No.** - 030-edg

Title
            " <u>Shên</u> <u>yin</u> <u>yü</u> "
            呻   吟   語

Classification - C-13 儒家

Subject - a treatise on mental philosophy and conduct.

References - 160-1j 012-zafk 10/7   031-bgdf 96/26

Author - <u>Lü K'un</u> 呂 坤 .

Edition - the " <u>Hua-lin-shu-wu</u> " 華林書局 ; dated T'ung-Chih
"kêng-wu" 9/1870.   Blocks; "fên" paper.

Index - a table of contents for 6 chüan divided into 2 p'ien (內外).

Bound in 1 t'ao 6 ts'ê.

Remarks - this work is complete and in good condition; but a portion of the last ts'e is slightly stained.

Accession No.　　39　　　　Index No. - 075-izeb　213-zzd

Title

" Yang Wên-ching kung chi "
楊　文　靖　公　集

" Kuei shan chi "
龜　山　集

Classification - D-33 別集一詩文

Subject - an individual collection of prose and poetry with a
nien p'u 年譜 for 2 chüan.

References - 012-zafk　15/19　031-bgdf　156/11　160-1j.

Author - Yang Shih 楊 時 .

Edition - privately published; (preface) dated K'ang-Hsi "ting-ch'ou"
36/1697.　Blocks; bamboo paper.

Index - a detailed table of contents for 40 chüan.

Bound in　1 t'ao 8 ts'ê.

Remarks - a good edition; and the item is complete.　There are a
number of worm-holes and the work is slightly stained at the
top.　However, these defects are not at all serious.

———•———

Accession No.   40   Index No. 140-fghz

Title   " Ju ching t'ang wên chi "
                茹　經　堂　文　集

Classification - D-43 別集一文

Subject - an individual collection of prose under 7 classes.

References - none.

Author - T'ang Wên-chih 唐 文 治 .

Edition - no notation; (preface) dated Min-Kuo "ping-yin"
    15/1926.   Blocks; bamboo paper.

Index - a detailed table of contents for 6 chüan.

Bound in 1 t'ao 8 ts'ê; doubly interleaved.

Remarks - this is a new work.

Accession No.   41   Index No.   - 009-zzao

Title   " Jên   shêng   pi   tu   shu "

人 生 必 讀 書

Classification - C-13 儒家

Subject - a treatise on subjects connected with the moral and ethical training of man.

References - none.

Author - T'ang Piao 唐彪.

Edition - no notation (title-page torn) ; dated Kuang-Hsü "chia-wu" 20/1894. Blocks; "mao-pien" paper.

Index - a detailed table of contents for 12 chüan.

Bound in 1 t'ao 6 ts'ê.

Remarks - an ordinary edition; complete and without defects.

46

Accession No. 42   Index No. - 040-qhhd

Title

" Pao lun t'ang chi "
寶 綸 堂 集

Classification - D-33 別集一詩文

Subject - an individual collection of prose and poetry with a
shih i 拾遺 .

References - 012-zafk 17/5.

Author - Ch'ên Hung-shou 陳 洪 綬 .

Edition - a reprint by the "Tung-shih-ch'ü-ssŭ-t'ang" 董氏取思堂 ;
dated Kuang-Hsü "wu tzŭ" 14/1888. Huo tzŭ pan 活字板.
Blocks; bamboo paper.

Index - none; not divided into chüan.

Bound in 1 t'ao 8 ts'ê; doubly interleaved.

Remarks - an ordinary edition; complete and without defects. The
last ts'ê is slightly stained.

Accession No.   43   Index No. - 075-gjd   040-dzdz

Title

" Mei   hsi   chi "
梅　溪　集

" Sung wang chung wên kung chi "
宋　王　忠　文　公　集

Classification - D-33 別集一詩文

Subject - an individual collection of prose and poetry.

References - 160-1j   012-zafk 15/24   031-bgdf 159/22.

Author - (撰) Wang Shih-p'êng 王　十　朋．

(重編) T'ang Chuan-hsing 唐　傳　銌．

Edition - privately published; dated Kuang-Hsü "ping-tzŭ"
2/1876.   Blocks; "mao-t'ai" paper.

Index - a detailed table of contents for 50 chüan.

Bound in 1 t'ao 12 ts'ê.

Remarks - a fair edition; complete and in good condition.

48

Accession No.　　44　　　　　Index No. - 024-gzd　052-ngzd

Title　　　　　　　　" Nan-shan　chi "
　　　　　　　　　南　山　集
　　　　　　　　" Tai　Nan-shan　chi "
　　　　　　　戴　南　山　集

Classification - D-43 別集一文

Subject - an individual collection of prose with a pu i 補遺 for

　3 chüan.

References - 085-hchm　2/52.

Author - Tai Ho-fu 戴　褐夫．

Edition - no notation; (index) dated Tao-Kuang "hsin-ch'ou"

　21/1841.　Blocks; "mao-pien" paper.

Index - a detailed table of contents for 14 chüan with a separate

　list for 3 chüan (上 中 下) for the pu i 補遺．

Bound in　1 t'ao 10 ts'ê．

Remarks - an ordinary edition; complete and in good condition.

Accession No.   45   Index No. - 212-fekd   040-ekdd

Title

" Kung Ting-an ch'üan chi "

龔　定　盦　全　集

" Ting-an ch'üan chi "

定　盦　全　集

Classification - D-33 別集一詩文

Subject - an individual collection of prose and poetry with
   supplements.

References - none.

Author - (撰) Kung Tzŭ-chên 龔　自　珍．

Edition - the "Ch'êng-tu-kuan-shu-chü" 成都官書局; dated
   Kuang-Hsü "wu-shên" 34/1908.   Blocks; "mao-pien" paper.

Index - a general table of contents for 15 chüan with separate lists
   for the supplements.

Bound in 1 t'ao 6 ts'ê.

Remarks - an ordinary edition; complete and in good condition.

Accession No.   46   Index No. – 212-fekd   040-ekdd

Title   " Kung Ting-an ch'üan chi "
                龔 定 盦 全 集
                " Ting-an ch'üan chi "
                定 盦 全 集

Classification – D-33 別集一詩文

Subject – an individual collection of prose and poetry with
   supplements.

References – none.

Author – (撰) Kung Tzŭ-chên 龔 自 珍 .

Edition – the "Wan-pên-shu-t'ang" 萬 本 書 堂 ; dated Kuang-Hsü
   "ting-yu" 23/1897.   Blocks; "mao-pien" paper.

Index – separate lists for different parts of the work.

Bound in 1 t'ao 5 ts'ê.

Remarks – an ordinary edition; but incomplete,– sections on 雜詩
   and 詞選 missing. The last ts'ê for 4 chüan is a replacement
   from a different copy.

Accession No.   47   Index No. - 073-hzeb   010-bkjj

Title

" Tsêng Wên-ting kung ch'üan chi "
曾 文 定 公 全 集
" Yüan fêng lei kao "
元 豐 類 稿

Classification - D-43 別集一文

Subject - an individual miscellaneous collection of prose.

References - 012-zafk 15/14   031-bgdf 153/17.

Author - Tsêng Kung 曾鞏 . See 160-1j.

Edition - the "Ch'i-yeh-t'ang" 七 業 堂 ; dated K'ang-Hsi
"jên-shên" 31/1692. Blocks; bamboo paper.

Index - a general table of contents for 17 chüan.

Bound in 1 t'ao 12 ts'ê.

Remarks - a fairly good edition, and the item is complete and
without defects.

Accession No.   48   Index No.   -085-1fdz   024-gzd   062-ngzd

Title   " Ch'ien-hsü hsien shêng wên chi "
               潛　虛　先　生　文　集
               " Nan-shan chi "
               南　山　集
               " Tai Nan-shan chi "
               戴　南　山　集

Classification - D-43 別集一文

Subject - an individual collection of prose.

References - 085-hchm 2/52.

Author - Tai Ho-fu 戴　褐　夫.

Edition - no notation; dated Kuang-Hsü "i-yu"(?) 11/1885.

    Blocks; bamboo paper.

Index - a detailed table of contents for 14 chüan.

Bound in 1 t'ao 8 ts'ê.

Remarks - this item is complete and without defects but the edition

    is not very good.

The University of Toronto Chinese Library

Accession No.   49   Index No. - 189-zzlf

Title
                    " Kao-tzŭ i shu "
                    高 子 遺 書

Classification - D-33 別集一詩文
Subject - an individual literary collection,-poetry and prose;
  grouped under 12 classifications together with a nien p'u
  年譜 , a supplement and some marginal notes.

References - 012-zafk 16/32   031-bgdf 172/53   163-ggcz 15/14.

Author - (撰) Kao P'an-lung 高 攀 龍 .

Edition - no notation; dated K'ang-Hsi "kêng-wu" 29/1690.
  Blocks; "fên" paper.

Index - a detailed table of contents for 12 chüan.

Bound in 1 t'ao 8 ts'ê.

Remarks - this edition is a very good one; and, with the exception
  of some slight stains, the item is complete and in excellent
  condition.

Accession No.　　50 (a)　　Index No. - 173-gzao　077-ngza

Title

" Chên-ch'uan　ch'ih　tu "

震　川　尺　牘

" Kuei　Chên-ch'uan　ch'ih　tu "

歸　震　川　尺　牘

Classification - D-43 別集一文

Subject - a collection of extracts from the letters of Kuei Yu-kuang
歸有光.

References - 012-zafk 16/29.

Author - (撰) Kuei Yu-kuang 歸有光.

Edition - privately published; (preface) dated K'ang-Hsi "chi-mao"
38/1699.　Blocks; bamboo paper.

Index - a detailed table of contents for 2 chüan.

Bound in 2 ts'ê in 1 t'ao with (b); doubly interleaved with margins.

Remarks - an exceedingly good edition; and the item appears to be
complete and without defects.

Accession No.　　50 (b)　　　Index No. - 093-dcao　167-hdca

Title　　　　　" Mu-chai ch'ih tu "
　　　　　　　牧　齋　尺　牘
　　　　　　　" Ch'ien Mu-chai ch'ih tu "
　　　　　　　錢　牧　齋　尺　牘

Classification - D-43 別集一文

Subject - a collection of extracts from the letters of Ch'ien Ch'ien-i
錢 謙 益 .

References - none.

Author - (撰) Ch'ien Ch'ien-i 錢 謙 益 .

Edition - uniform with (a).

Index - a detailed table of contents for 3 chüan.

Bound in 3 ts'ê in 1 t'ao with (a); doubly interleaved with margins.

Remarks - an exceedingly good edition; and the item appears to be
complete and in good condition with the exception of a few repaired blemishes.

Accession No.　51 (a)　　　　Index No. -085-ggzd　018-mggz

Title

" Hai-fêng wên chi "
海　峯　文　集
" Liu Hai-fêng wên chi "
劉　海　峯　文　集

Classification - D-43 別集一文

Subject - an individual collection of 231 literary writings grouped into 9 classifications.

References - 012-zafk　17/18.

Author - (撰) Liu Ta-k'uei 劉 大 櫆 .

Edition - no notation; (title-page) dated T'ung-Chih "chia-hsü" 13/1874.　Blocks; "fên" paper.

Index - a detailed table of contents for 10 chüan followed by the editor's notes.

Bound in 4 ts'ê in 1 t'ao with (b).

Remarks - an ordinary edition; complete and without defects.

Accession No.   51 (b)   Index No. - 085-ggfd   018-mggf

Title

" Hai-fêng shih chi "
海 峯 詩 集
" Liu Hai-fêng shih chi "
劉 海 峯 詩 集

Classification - D-38 別集一詩

Subject - an individual miscellaneous collection of poems.

References - 012-zafk 17/18.

Author - (撰) Liu Ta-k'uei 劉 大 櫆 .

Edition - no notation; (title-page) dated T'ung-Chih "chia-hsü"
13/1874.   Blocks; "fên" paper.

Index - a detailed table of contents for 4 chüan.

Bound in 2 ts'ê in 1 t'ao with (a).

Remarks - an ordinary edition; complete and without defects.

58

The University of Toronto Chinese Library

Accession No. 52   **Index No.** - 018-dz   015-dfeg

Title

" Lieh-tzŭ "
列 子

" Ch'ung-hsü-chên-ching "
冲 虛 真 經

Classification - C-731 道家

Subject - a work on metaphysical philosophy; one of the principal works of the Taoist gospel with notes and explanations.

References - Wylie's Notes page 217   160-1j   012-zafk 14/32   031-bgdf 146/18. The above are general references and not to this particular edition.

Author - (注) Chang Chan 張 湛 .

Edition - the "Chê-chiang-shu-chü" 浙 江 書 局 ; (title-page) dated Kuang-Hsü "ping-tzŭ" 2/1876. Blocks; "mao-pien" paper.

Index - a table of contents for 8 chüan.

Bound in 1 t'ao 2 ts'ê .

Remarks - an ordinary edition; complete and in good condition.

Accession No.   53   Index No. - 140-fz

Title   " Hsün-tzŭ "
                     荀 子

Classification - C-13 儒家

Subject -a philosophical work based on the doctrine of "original
    sin"; together with commentary.

References - Wylie's Notes page 82. 160-1j 163-ggcz 7/1
    031-bgld 9/1 167-mhfm 13/1 030-iaff 15/2 106-gdkn 39/1
    12-zafk 10/1 031-bgdf 91/5.

Author - of the original work - Hsün K'uang 荀 况 . See 160-1j
    Giles B.D. 807. （注）Yang Liang 楊 倞 .

Edition - the "An-ya-t'ang" 安 雅 堂 ; dated Ch'ien-Lung
    "ping-wu" 51/1786. Blocks; "fên" paper.

Index - a table of contents for 20 chüan.

Bound in 1 t'ao 8 ts'ê; doubly interleaved.

Remarks - this edition is fairly good, and the item appears to b
    complete; but numerous worm-holes are found throughout this work
    of which chüan 15 and chüan 20 are badly affected. This work is
    also stained.

60

Accession No.　　54　　　Index No. - 030-bge

Title　　　　　　　" Ku　shih　yüan "

　　　　　　　　　古　事　苑

Classification - C-348 類書

Subject - a classified encyclopaedia covering miscellaneous subjects.

References - 031-bgdf 139/10　012-zafk 13/26.

Author - Têng Chih-mo 鄧 志 謨 .

Edition - no notation; (preface) dated Wan-Li "ting-ssŭ" 45/1617.

　　Blocks; bamboo paper.

Index - a table of contents for 24 chüan.

Bound in 1 t'ao 6 ts'ê; singly interleaved.

Remarks - a very good edition; complete and in good condition

　　with the exception of a few slight defects.　The work is also

　　stained.

Accession No.　　55　　Index No. - 074-gjd

Title　　　　" Wang hsi chi "
　　　　　　望　溪　集

Classification - D-43 別集一文

Subject - an individual classified collection of literary compositions many of which are of historical and biographical character.

References - 031-bgdf 173/48　012-zafk 17/19　163-ggcz 15/18 160-1j.

Author - (撰) Fang Pao 方苞 .

Edition - no notation; (preface) dated Ch'ien-Lung "ping-yin" 11/1746.　Blocks; bamboo paper.

Index - a classified list of contents but not divided into chüan.

Bound in　1 t'ao 8 ts'ê; doubly interleaved.

Remarks - a good edition; complete and in good condition with the exception of some slight stains.

Accession No.　　56 (a)　　　Index No. - 009-zm

Title

" Jên　p'u "
人　　譜

Classification - C-13 儒家

Subject - a short brochure on "man",-his nature and conduct.

References - 160-lj　163-ggcz 7/9　031-bgld 9/21　012-zafk 10/7

031-bgdf 93/26.

Author - Liu Tsung-chow 劉 宗 周.

Edition - the "shan-kan-tu-shu" 陝 甘 督 署 ; (title-page)

dated Hsüan-T'ung "chi-yu" 1/1909. Blocks; "fên" paper.

Index - none; complete in 1 chüan.

Bound in 1/2 ts'ê in 1 t'ao with (b)

Remarks - a modern edition; complete and without defects.

Accession No. 56 (b)   Index No. - 009-zmjo

Title   " Jên p'u lei chi "
       入 譜 類 記

Classification - C-13 儒家

Subject - "Life" and human conduct,- being a continuation and
   development of (a); and consisting of classified references
   to the writings of renowned scholars on various phases of the
   subject; together with comments thereon by the author.

References - as under (a)

Author - as under (a)

Edition - as under (a)

Index - none; complete in 2 chüan 上 下 or 6 篇.

Bound in 1 1/2 ts'ê in 1 t'ao with (a).

Remarks - as under (a).

The University of Toronto Chinese Library

Accession No. 57   **Index No.** - 030-dzih

Title   " Lü-tzŭ chieh lu "
            呂 子 節 錄

Classification - C-13 儒家

Subject - selections from the " Shên yin yü " 呻 吟 語, - a
treatise on mental philosophy and " conduct " , with annotations.

References - 031-bgdf 96/26   031-bgld 9/20   012-zafk 10/7
163-ggoz 7/9.

Author - of the original work (著) Lü K'un 呂 坤 . See Giles
B. D. 1448. of this item (評 輯) Ch'ên Hung-mou 陳 宏 謀 .
See 160-1j Giles B. D. 228 Wylie's Notes page 223.

Edition - the "Kan-su-fan-shu" 甘 肅 藩 署 ; (title-page) dated
Hsüan-T'ung "chi-yu" 1/1909. Blocks; "fên" paper.

Index - a table of contents for 4 chüan.

Bound in 1 t'ao 2 ts'ê.

Remarks - a modern edition; complete and without defects.

The University of Toronto Chinese Library

Accession No.   58   Index No. - 061-id

Title   " I lin "
意 林

Classification - C-328 雜家一雜纂

Subject - selections from works by famous philosophers and scholars since the Chou 周 and Ch'in 秦 dynasties.

References - 160-1j   106-gdkn 58/17   031-bgld 13/29   012-zafk 13/3
031-bgdf 123/13.

Author - (編) Ma Tsung 馬 總 .

Edition - the "Wu-ying-tien-chü-chên-pan" 武英殿聚珍版;
(index) dated Ch'ien-Lung "jên-yin" 47/1782.   Blocks; bamboo paper.

Index - a table of contents for 5 chüan.

Bound in 1 t'ao 5 ts'ê; doubly interleaved.

Remarks - this is a very good edition; and the item is complete and in good condition.

66

Accession No.   59   Index No. - 075-czhd

Title   " Tu Kung-pu chi "

杜 工 部 集

Classification - D-38 別集一詩

Subject - a collection of poems by Tu Fu with critical punctuations
and annotations.

References - 012-zafk 15/6   106-gdkn 68/11

Author - (撰) Tu Fu 杜甫 .   See 160-lj   Giles B.D. 2058.

Edition - no notation; no date. Blocks; "fên" paper.

Index - separate lists for each of 20 chüan.

Bound in 2 t'ao 10 ts'ê.

Remarks - a fairly good edition; complete and without defects.
The punctuations are in five colours.

Accession No.   60   Index No. - 075-gjd   040-dzdz

Title   " Mei hsi chi "
                            梅 溪 集

              " Sung Wang Chung-wên kung chi "
                   宋 王 忠 文 公 集

Classification - D-33 別集一詩文

Subject - an individual collection of prose and poetry.

References - 160-1j   012-zafk 15/24   031-bgdf 159/22.

Author - (撰) Wang Shih-p'êng 王 十 朋 .
         (重 編) T'ang Chuan-hsing 唐 傳 鉎 .

Edition - no notation; (preface) dated Yung-Cheng "mou-shên"
         6/1728.   Blocks; "fên" paper.

Index - a detailed table of contents for 50 chüan.

Bound in 1 t'ao 10 ts'ê.

Remarks - this is a good edition; and the item appears to be
         complete, but its condition is affected to some extent by a
         few repaired blemishes (the most serious one on page 21 in
         chüan 24), as well as many stained pages.

Accession No.   61   **Index No.** - 048-bkd

Title   " tso-an chi "

左 盒 集

Classification - D-43 別集一文

Subject - an individual collection of prose.

References - none.

Author - Liu Shih-p'ei 劉 師 培．

Edition - the "Hsiu-kêng-t'ang" 修 綆 堂 ; (title-page) dated Min-Kuo "mou-ch'ên" 17/1928.   Blocks; "mao-pien" paper.

Index - a detailed table of contents for 8 chüan.

Bound in   1 t'ao 6 ts'ê．

Remarks - a new book.

Accession No.　　62　　　　Index No. - 140-qnhl

Title

　　" Lan　hsün　kuan　i　kao "
　　蘭　薫　館　遺　稿

Classification - D-33 別集—詩文

Subject - an individual collection of prose and poetry.

References - none.

Author - (著) T'ao Yü-k'o 陶　玉　珂 .

Edition - the "Shang-hai-chü-chên-fang-sung-yin-shu-chü" 上海聚
珍倣宋印書局 ; (preface) dated Min-Kuo "ting-ssŭ" 6/1917.
Blocks; "fên" paper.

Index - a detailed classified table of contents for 4 chüan.

Bound in 1 t'ao 4 ts'ê; doubly interleaved.

Remarks - this is a new edition; and the item is complete and in
good condition.

Accession No.　　63　　　**Index No.** - 181-gnhl

Title　　　　　" P'in lo an i chi "
　　　　　　　　頻　羅　庵　遺　集

Classification - D-33 別集一詩文

Subject - an individual miscellaneous collection of prose and poetic writings under 7 classifications.

References - 012-zafk 17/32.

Author - (撰) Liang T'ung-shu 梁　同　書 .

Edition - the "Hsiu-kêng-shan-chuang" 修　綆　山　莊 ; (preface) dated Kuang-Hsü "ting-hai" 13/1887.　Blocks; "mao-t'ai" paper.

Index - a general classified table of contents for 16 chüan.

Bound in 1 t'ao 8 ts'ê.

Remarks - a very ordinary edition; but complete and without defects.

Accession No.   64   Index No. - 030-dzih

Title

" Lü-tzŭ chieh lu "
呂　子　節　録

Classification - C-13 儒家

Subject - selections from the "Shên yin yü" 呻 吟 語 ,- a treatise
on mental philosophy and "conduct", with annotations and a
supplement of 2 chüan.

References - 031-bgdf 96/26   031-bgld 9/20   012-zafk 10/7
163-ggoz 7/9.

Author - of the original work (著) Lü K'un 呂 坤 .   See
Giles B.D. 1448. of this item (評 輯) Ch'ên Hung-mou
陳　宏　謀 .

Edition - the "Chiang-hsi-shu-chü" 江 西 書 局 ; (title-page)
dated Kuang-Hsü "ting-hai" 13/1887.   Blocks; "fên" paper.

Index - a table of contents for 4 chüan; none for the supplement.

Bound in 1 t'ao 4 ts'ê.

Remarks - an ordinary edition; the item is complete and in good
condition.

Accession No.   65   Index No. - 001-azzh

Title   " Ch'i shih êrh hou chien "
                 七　十　二　候　牋

Classification - C-223 藝術一書畫

Subject - a collection of sketches to illustrate the 72 five day
  periods of the year.

References - none.

Author - Ch'ien Chi-shêng　錢　吉　生 .

Edition - the "wên-mei-chai" 文　美　齋 ; (preface) dated Kuang-
  Hsü "mou-hsü" 24/1898. Blocks; "fên" paper.

Index - at the beginning of each month.

Bound in 1 t'ao 2 ts'ê; doubly interleaved.

Remarks - an ordinary edition, and without defects.

Accession No.   66   **Index No.** - 030-bbjk

Title

" <u>Ku chin lei chuan sui shih pu</u> "
古　今　類　傳　歲　時　部

Classification - B-157 時令

Subject - a work on chronography which treats in detail first
the year, next the four seasons of the year, the twelve months,
the solar periods, and the days of each month; with historical
notes introduced as examples.

References - 012-zafk 5/32.   031-bgdf 67/7.

Author - (同輯) <u>Tung Ku-shih</u> 董　穀　士 and <u>Tung Ping-wên</u>
董　炳　文 .

Edition - no notation; (preface) dated K'ang-Hsi "jên-shên"
31/1692.   Blocks; bamboo paper.

Index - a table of contents for 4 chüan arranged in the order of the
four seasons.

Bound in 1 t'ao 4 ts'ê.

Remarks - a fair edition in good condition.   The item is complete.

74

The University of Toronto Chinese Library

Accession No.   67   **Index No.** - 149-1boe

Title   " <u>T'an shih chih ch'i</u> "
                    譚　史　志　奇

<u>Classification</u> - C-368 小説家

<u>Subject</u> - a miscellaneous and general collection of historical
    anecdotes and minor incidents dating from the <u>Han</u> 漢 down
    to the <u>Ming</u> 明 Dynasty.

<u>References</u> - none.

<u>Author</u> - <u>Yen Ch'ên</u> 彦 臣 .

<u>Edition</u> - the "<u>Wu-chih-t'ang</u>" 五 知 堂 ; dated "mou-tzŭ" 1888.
    Blocks; "mao-t'ai" paper.

<u>Index</u> - detailed tables of contents at the beginning of chüan
    1-3-5-7; 8 chüan in all.

<u>Bound in</u> 1 t'ao 4 ts'ê.

<u>Remarks</u> - this is a very ordinary edition. The item is complete
    and without defects.

75

Accession No.   68   Index No. - 067-zffg

Title   " Wên chang chih nan "
                    文　章　指　南

Classification - D-73 總集一文

Subject - a general collection of literary compositions written
   by famous ancient scholars; classified into 5 general headings
   with subdivisions for each.

References - 031-bgdf 192/41

Author - (編) Kuei Yu-kuang 歸　有　光 ．
         (蒐 輯) Hsü Hsiao-lien 許　筱　蓮 ．

Edition - the "Wan-chiang-chieh-shu" 皖　江　節　署 ; (title-page)
   dated Kuang-Hsü "ping-tzŭ" 2/1876. Blocks; "fên" paper.

Index - a detailed table of contents for 5 集 , each consisting
   of a few subdivisions; separate lists for each subdivision.

Bound in 1 t'ao 4 ts'ê.

Remarks - an ordinary edition; and the item is complete. The
   last two ts'ê are stained and with repaired defects on the
   top left-hand corner.

76

Accession No.   69   Index No. - 181-izgc

Title

" Yen shih chia hsün "

顏 氏 家 訓

Classification C-308 雜家一雜文

Subject - a collection of twenty essays consisting of precepts of a moral and ethical character.

References - 160-1j 031-bgld 13/5 030-iaff 18/20 106-gdkn 55/9 012-zafk 12/14 031-bgdf 117/22.

Author (撰) Yen Chih-t'ui 顏 之 推.

Edition - a reprint by the "Chang-ching-chi-t'ang" 章 經 濟 堂; dated Kuang-Hsü "kêng-yin" 16/1890. Blocks; "mao-pien" paper.

Index - a general table of contents for 7 chüan; 攷證 1 chüan.

Bound in 1 t'ao 4 ts'ê; doubly interleaved.

Remarks - an ordinary edition; the item is complete and without defects.

———•———

Accession No.　　70　　　　　**Index No.** – 057-hzbd　　057-hzbb

Title

" Chang Wên-chêng chi "

張　文　貞　集

" Chang Wên-chêng kung chi "

張　文　貞　公　集

Classification – D-43 別集一文

Subject – an individual collection of literary compositions,- prose; under 20 classifications.

References – 031-bgdf 173/34　012-zafk 17/15　031-bgld 18/40

Author – (撰) Chang Yü-shu 張 玉 書.

Edition – the "Sung-yin-t'ang 松 蔭 堂; (title-page) dated Ch'ien-Lung 57/1792. Blocks; "fên" paper.

Index – a detailed classified table of contents for 12 chüan.

Bound in – 1 t'ao 6 ts'ê.

Remarks – a fairly good edition; with a few defects and apparently complete.

Accession No.   71   Index No. - 006-gdgc

Title   " Shih wu i ming lu "
                事 物 異 名 録

Classification - C-348 類書

Subject - a work of an encyclopaedia character, consisting of 39
main subjects.

References - 012-zafk 13/28.

Author - (原輯) Li Ch'üan 屬荃 . (增纂) Kuan Huai 關槐 .

Edition - no particular notation; (title-page) dated Ch'ien-Lung
"mou-shên" 53/1788. Blocks; "fên" paper.

Index - a general table of contents for 40 chüan.

Bound in 2 t'ao 12 ts'ê (6.6).

Remarks - a good edition; and apparently complete. Page 14 in chüan
40 is hand-written. No furthur defects are noted.

Accession No.　　72　　　　Index No. - 149-oozf

Title　　　　　" <u>Tu Tu hsin chieh</u> "
　　　　　　　讀 杜 心 解

Classification - D-38 別集－詩

Subject - a collection of some 1500 poems written by the famous poet
<u>Tu Fu</u> 杜甫; classified, rearranged and with annotations and
explanations.

References - 012-zafk 15/6　031-bgdf 147/14.

Author - (講解) <u>P'u Ch'i-lung</u> 浦 起 龍.

Edition - the "<u>Ning-ê-chai</u>" 寧 我 齋; (preface) dated Yung-Chêng
2/1724.　Blocks; bamboo paper.

Index - a general table of contents for 6 chüan; separate detailed
lists for each subdivision of the 6 chüan.

Bound in 1 t'ao 8 ts'ê.

Remarks - a very good edition; and the item is apparently complete
and without defects except some slight stains.

The University of Toronto Chinese Library

Accession No. 73 (a)   **Index No.** - 194-zzz

Title   " Kuei-ku-tzŭ "
鬼 谷 子

Classification - C-308 雜家 — 雜文

Subject - (a) a philosophical miscellany of a semi-political character and tinged with Taoist notions; (b) a commentary on the "Yin fu ching" 陰 符 經 , a Taoist work that "professes to reconcile the decrees of Heaven with the current of mundane affairs". (Wylie)

References - 160-1j 163-ggcz 10/2 031-bgld 13/3 030-iaff 18/15 106-gdkn 53/3 012-zafk 12/13 031-bgdf 117/12.

Author - generally given as Kuei-ku tzŭ , but his actual name is doubtful, but said by some to have been Wang Hsü 王 詡 . (校) Wu Mien-hsüeh 吳 勉 學 .

Edition - no notation; no date; but of the Ming period. Blocks; bamboo paper.

Index - a table of contents for 14 items and a "Wai-p'ien"; complete in 1 chüan.

Bound in 1/2 ts'ê in 1 t'ao with (b); doubly interleaved.

Remarks - a very good edition; complete and in very good condition.

Accession No. 73 (b)   Index No.- 120-df   201-zzbd

Title

" Su shu "

素 書

" Huang Shih-kung su shu "

黃 石 公 素 書

Classification - C-33 兵家

Subject - a short treatise on military matters from the psychological view-point.

References - Wylie's Notes page 90   160-lj   163-ggcz 7/12   031-bgld
9/26   167-mhfm 13/17   106-gdkn 42/2   012-zafk 10/13   031-bgdf
99/10.

Author - （撰）Huang Shih-kung 黃 石 公.   See 160-lj
Giles B.D. 866.   （校）Wu Mien-hsüeh 吳 勉 學 .

Edition - as under (a).

Index - none; in 6 章 .

Bound in 1/2 ts'ê in 1 t'ao with (a); doubly interleaved.

Remarks - as under (a).

The University of Toronto Chinese Library

Accession No.   74 (a)   **Index No.** - 048-bdkb

Title   " <u>Tso Chung-i kung chi</u> "
                    左　忠　毅　公　集

Classification - D-33 别集一詩文

Subject - an individual literary collection,- prose and poetry.

References - 012-zafk 16/28.

Author - (撰) <u>Tso Kuang-tou</u> 左　光　斗 .

Edition - privately published; (postcripta) dated Ch'ien-Lung 4/1739.
 Blocks; "mao-pien" paper.

Index - separate lists of contents for each of 3 chüan.

Bound in 3 ts'ê in 1 t'ao with (b) and (c).

Remarks - a good edition; complete and in good condition.

Accession No.   74 (b)   Index No. - 048-bfhb   048-bfhb

Title   " Tso Shih-yü kung chi "
                左　侍　御　公　集
               " Tso Shih-yü kung tsou i "
                左　侍　御　公　奏　議

Classification - B-72 詔令奏議一奏議

Subject - a collection of memorials, reports etc.

References - none.

Author - Tso Kuang-tou 左　光　斗 .

Edition - as under (a).

Index - a table of contents; not divided into chüan.

Bound in 1 ts'ê in 1 t'ao with (a) and (c).

Remarks - as under (a).

84

Accession No.   74 (c)   Index No. - 048-bdkb

Title

" Tso Chung-i kung nien p'u "
左　忠　毅　公　年　譜

Classification - B-107 傳記一獨録
Subject - the biographical record of Tso Kuang-tou 左　光　斗 .

References - none.

Author - Tso Tsai 左　宰 .

Edition - as under (a).

Index - none; complete in 2 chüan 上　下 .

Bound in 2 ts'ê in 1 t'ao with (a) and (b).

Remarks - as under (a).

The University of Toronto Chinese Library

Accession No.   75   Index No. - 096-zzgb

Title   " Wang Wên-min kung i chi "
                王 文 敏 公 遺 集

Classification - D-33 別集─詩文

Subject - a miscellaneous collection of literary compositions,-
    prose and poetry.

References - none.

Author - (著) Wang I-jung 王懿榮. (編) Liu Ch'êng-kan
    劉 承 幹 .

Edition - the "Ch'iu-shu-chai" 求 恕 齋 ; (title-page) dated
    Hsüan-T'ung "kuei-hai" 1923. Blocks; "mao-pien" paper.

Index - a table of contents for 8 chüan.

Bound in 1 t'ao 2 ts'ê.

Remarks - a modern edition; the item is complete and as new.

Accession No. 76 Index No. - 064-mhh

Title " Tsê chih lu "
擇 執 錄

Classification - C-328 雜家 — 雜纂

Subject - a collection of extracts from the "Classics" and the works of famous philosophers; aiming at the training of man along the lines of morality, ethics etc.; classified into 34 groups.

References - 031-bgdf 133/7.

Author - (編次) Wang Chia-ch'i 王 家 啓.

Edition - no notation; (preface) dated K'ang-Hsi "kuei-ch'ou" 12/1673. Blocks; bamboo paper.

Index - a general table of contents for 12 chüan.

Bound in 1 t'ao 3 ts'ê.

Remarks - this is a fairly good edition; the work is stained, having two or three defects, but appears to be complete.

———•·•———

Accession No. ·   77,   Index No. - 140-hfl

Title   " Ts'ai kên t'an "
                          菜 根 譚

Classification - C-328 雜家－雜纂

Subject - a comprehensive collection of short notes or jottings
    treating of the principles of the affairs of the universe,
    both psychologically and practically; the principles of
    "cause and effect" etc.

References - 012-zafk 13/6.

Author - （撰） Hung Ying-ming 洪 應 明 .

Edition - published by the "Hsiu-yün-ssŭ Temple" 岫 雲 寺 ;
    (preface) dated Ch'ien-Lung 33/1768. Blocks; bamboo paper.

Index - none; complete in 1 chüan.

Bound in 1 t'ao 1 ts'ê; doubly interleaved.

Remarks - a very good edition; complete and with some slight defects.

The University of Toronto Chinese Library

Accession No.   78   **Index No.** - 140-hf1

Title

" <u>Ts'ai kên t'an</u> "
菜 根 譚

Classification - C-328 雜家一雜纂

Subject - a comprehensive collection of short notes or jottings
treating of the principles of the affairs of the universe,
both psychologically and practically; the principles of
"cause and effect" etc.

References - 012-zafk 13/6.

Author - (撰) <u>Hung Ying-ming</u> 洪 應 明 .

Edition - no particular notation; (preface) dated Tao-Kuang 6/1826.
Blocks; "mao-pien" paper.

Index - none; complete in 1 chüan.

Bound in 1 t'ao 2 ts'ê; doubly interleaved.

Remarks - an ordinary edition; complete and in very good edition.

Accession No.   79   Index No. - 085-kjfe

Title   " Han hsi shu fa t'ung chieh "
                    漢　溪　書　法　通　解

Classification - C-223 藝術一書畫

Subject - a treatise on Chinese penmanship (calligraphy) with sketches
illustrating the methods of using the brush and including the
discussions on the subject by ancient famous calligraphists.

References - 012-zafk 11/22   031-bgdf 114/25.

Author - (纂著) Ko Shou-chih 戈　守　智.

Edition - the "Chi-yün-ko" 霽　雲　閣 ; (preface) dated Ch'ien-
Lung "kêng-wu" 15/1750. Blocks; "fên" paper.

Index - a table of contents for 8 chüan.

Bound in 1 t'ao 6 ts'ê; doubly interleaved.

Remarks - a very good edition; the item is stained at the left-
hand margin and on the top, and has a number of repaired defects
in chüan 3.

Accession No.   80   Index No. - 001-dgig

Title

" <u>Shih   shuo   hsin   yü   pu</u> "

世　說　新　語　補

<u>Classification</u> - C-368 小說家

<u>Subject</u> - appendix to a collection of minor incidents from the
<u>Han</u>漢 to the <u>Chin</u>晉 Dynasty inclusive.

<u>References</u> - Wylie's Notes page 189   012-zafk 14/8   031-bgdf 143/31.

<u>Author</u> - <u>Ho Liang-chün</u> 何　良　俊．

<u>Edition</u> - the "<u>Mao-ch'ing-shu-wu</u>" 茂　清　書　屋; dated Ch'ien-Lung
"jên-wu" 27/1762. Blocks; bamboo paper.

<u>Index</u> - a table of contents for 20 chüan.

<u>Bound in</u> 1 t'ao 10 ts'ê.

<u>Remarks</u> - a good edition; apparently complete and in good condition,
with the exception of a bad defect on page 15 chüan 3.

Accession No. 81   Index No. - 085-ggd

Title
" <u>Lang yü chi</u> "
浪 語 集

<u>Classification</u> - D-33 別集－詩文

<u>Subject</u> - an individual comprehensive collection of literary
compositions,- prose and poetry.

<u>References</u> - 012-zafk 15/26 031-bgdf 160/19 031-bgld 16/21.

<u>Author</u> - (撰) <u>Hsüeh Chi-hsüan</u> 薛 季 宣 .

<u>Edition</u> - no notation; no date; but evidently a late <u>Ch'ing</u> 清
edition. Blocks; "mao-pien" paper.

<u>Index</u> - a detailed classified table of contents for 35 chüan.

<u>Bound in</u> 1 t'ao 8 ts'ê.

<u>Remarks</u> - an ordinary edition; in good condition and appears
to be complete.

Accession No.   82   Index No. - 057-hzbd   057-hzbb

Title

" Chang Wên-chêng chi "

張　文　貞　集

" Chang Wên-chêng kung chi "

張　文　貞　公　集

Classification - D-43 別集一文

Subject - an individual collection of literary compositions,- prose; under 20 classifications.

References - 031-bgdf 173/34 012-zafk 17/15 031-bgld 18/40

Author - (撰) Chang Yü-shu 張 玉 書 ．

Edition - no particular notation; (title-page) dated Kuang-Hsü "hsin-ch'ou" 27/1901. Blocks; "mao-pien" paper.

Index - a detailed classified table of contents for 12 chüan; 年 譜 1 chüan.

Bound in 1 t'ao 13 ts'ê.

Remarks - an ordinary modern edition; the item appears to be complete and is very neat.

Accession No.   83   Index No. - 096-zzcb   096-zzcd

Title   " Wang Wên-ch'êng kung wên hsüan "
            王 文 成 公 文 選
            " Wang Wên-ch'êng chi "
            王 文 成 集

Classification - D-33 別集一詩文

Subject - an individual collection of poetry and prose.

References - 012-zafk 16/20   031-bgdf 171/33   031-bgld 18/23

   163-ggcz 15/10. The above are general references and not
   to this particular edition.

Author - （撰）Wang Shou-jên 王 守 仁. （選定）Wang Chi
   王 畿

Edition - the "Hsi-hsiang-kuan" 溪 香 舘 ; (preface) dated

   Ch'ung-Chêng "kuei-yu" 6/1633. Blocks; bamboo paper.

Index - a detailed table of contents for 6 chüan; 年 譜 2 chüan.

Bound in 1 t'ao 8 ts'ê.

Remarks - a good edition; the item appears to be complete and in
   good condition with the exception of some slight defects.
   This work is stained in places.

———◆———

Accession No. 84   **Index No.** - 102-hccg

Title   " <u>Tang tai ming hua ta kuan</u> "
當 代 名 畫 大 觀

Classification - C-223 藝術一書畫

Subject - a work on paintings by 20 modern artists.

References - none.

Author - (主編) <u>Wang Nien-tz'ŭ</u> 王 念 慈.

Edition - lithographed by the "<u>Pi-wu-shan-chuang-of-Shanghai</u>"
上 海 碧 梧 山 莊; dated "Min-Kuo" 12/1923. Blocks;
"fên" paper.

Index - none.

Bound in 1 t'ao 6 ts'ê; doubly interleaved.

Remarks - this is a new book.

Accession No.   85 (a)   <u>Index No.</u> - 009-zm

<u>Title</u>   " Jên p'u "
                              人   譜

<u>Classification</u> - C-13 儒家

<u>Subject</u> - a short brochure on "man",-his nature and conduct.

<u>References</u> - 160-1j 163-ggcz 7/9 031-bgld 9/21 012-zafk 10/7
    031-bgdf 93/26.

<u>Author</u> - <u>Liu Tsung-chou</u> 劉 宗 周 .

<u>Edition</u> - published by "<u>Ting-shih-of-Wu-hsing</u>"吳興 丁 氏 ;
    (title-page) dated T'ung-Chih "mou-ch'ên" 7/1868. Blocks;
    "mao-pien" paper.

<u>Index</u> - none; complete in 1 chüan.

<u>Bound in</u> 1/2 ts'ê in 1 t'ao with (b).

<u>Remarks</u> - an ordinary edition; complete and in good condition.

96

Accession No.   85 (b)   Index No. - 009-zmjc

Title   " Jên p'u lei chi (tsêng ting) "
             人 譜 類 記 增 訂

Classification - C-13 儒家

Subject - "Life" and human conduct,- being a continuation and
development of (a); and consisting of classified references
to the writings of renowned scholars on various phases of the
subject; together with comments thereon by the author.

References - as under (a).

Author - as under (a).

Edition - as under (a).

Index - none; complete in 2 chüan 上 下 or 6 篇 .

Bound in 1 1/2 ts'ê in 1 t'ao with (a).

Remarks - as under (a).

Accession No.　　86　　Index No. - 061-js

Title

"Shên yen"
慎 言

Classification - C-13 儒家

Subject - a collection of miscellaneous philosophical notes; and some
critiques upon the various philosophers after Confucius; main-
taining that heretical teachings arose following the death of
Confucius.

References - 031-bgdf 95/40.

Author - (撰) Wang T'ing-hsiang 王 廷 相.

Edition - no particular notation; (preface) dated Chia-Ching "ting-
hai" 6/1527.　Blocks; bamboo paper.

Index - a table of contents for 13 chüan.

Bound in 1 t'ao 2 ts'ê; doubly interleaved.

Remarks - this is a very good edition; and the item appears to be
complete and in very good condition, but page 2 in chüan 3 is
missing.　It seems that the work was printed from old blocks
in some later year than the one given in the preface.

Accession No. 87   Index No. – 024-ghg

Title " Nan-hua-ching "
南 華 經

Classification – C-731 道家 –

Subject – the Taoist writings in 33 sections, divided into three
main divisions, (1) Nei p'ien 内 篇 ; (2) Wai p'ien 外 篇 ;
and (3) Tsa p'ien 雜 篇 ; punctuated and with commentaries
and marginal notes.

References – Wylie's Notes page 218 160-1j 012-zafk 14/32
031-bgdf 146/22. The above are general references and not to
this particular edition.

Author – usually credited to Chuang Chou 莊 周 . (註 輯)
Kuo Hsiang 郭 象 .

Edition – no notation; no date; but of the Ming period. Blocks;
"fên" paper.

Index – separate lists for the 3 "p'ien" as given under the
"Subject".

Bound in 1 t'ao 8 ts'ê.

Remarks – this is a good edition; and the item appears to be complete. Numerous worm-holes as well as water stains are found
in places in the work. The punctuations are in red; and the
marginal notes in various colours.

The University of Toronto Chinese Library

Accession No. 88   **Index No.** - 162-jzem

Title " Yüan-hsi ch'i ch'i t'u shuo lu tsui "

遠 西 奇 器 圖 說 録 最

Classification - C-238 藝術 － 雜技

Subject - a description of Western machinery and tools of the 17th century; with illustrations and a supplement.

References - none.

Author - (口 授) Têng Yü-han 鄧 玉 函 . (譯 繪) Wang Chêng

王 徵 .

Edition - no notation; a manuscript copy on "fên" paper; (preface) dated T'ien-Ch'i 7/1627.

Index - none.

Bound in 1 t'ao 6 ts'ê; doubly interleaved with leaves from some old books.

Remarks - a good work; apparently complete (pages not numbered), but with some repaired defects in the last ts'ê. This work was evidently copied sometime in Ch'ing Dynasty. However, it is a very interesting work and the illustrations are especially well drawn.

———•———

Accession No.   89   Index No. - 149-ogcg   024-gdgh

Title

" Tu-hua-chai (ch'ung k'o) Nan-Sung Ch'ün hsien hsiao chi "
讀 畫 齋 （重 刻）南 宋 羣 賢 小 集
" Nan-Sung Ch'ün hsien hsiao chi "
南 宋 羣 賢 小 集

Classification - C-338 雜 家 一 叢 書

Subject - a collection of reprints of some 80 works by famous authors of the Southern-Sung period.

References - 029-pffz 290.

Author - （原 輯）Ch'ên Ch'i 陳 起 . （重 刊）Ku Hsiu 顧 修 .

Edition - the "Tu-hua-chai" 讀 畫 齋 ; (preface) dated Chia-Ch'ing "hsin-yu" 6/1801. Blocks; "fên" paper.

Index - a general table of contents for 32 冊 .

Bound in 8 t'ao 40 ts'ê. (5 each).

Remarks - a good edition; apparently complete and in very good condition except the first 5 ts'ê which are stained on the corners.

Accession No.　　90　　　　　Index No. - 162-ech

Title　　　　　　　　" Ti chi lu "
　　　　　　　　　迪　吉　録

Classification - C-328 雜家一雜纂

Subject - a comprehensive collection of essays treating of "retribution" in connection with man's conduct; with historical
incidents introduced as examples.

References - 012-zafk 13/6　031-bgdf 132/30.

Author - （撰）Yen Mao-yu 顏 茂 猷 .

Edition - the "Fu-chou-Hsi-chiang-pieh-shu" 福 州 西 江 別 墅;
(title-page) dated Kuang-Hsü "ping-hsü" 12/1886.　Blocks;
"mao-pien" paper.

Index - a table of contents for 9 chüan.

Bound in 1 t'ao 8 ts'ê.

Remarks - a good modern edition; the item is complete and without
defects.

Accession No.   91   Index No. – 032-1zde

Title   " Mo-tzŭ hsien ku "
                 墨 子 閒 詁

Classification – C-308 雜家 — 雜文

Subject – a commentary on "Mo-tzŭ" 墨 子 ,– "the writings of the
philosopher Mo Ti 墨翟, on moral and political subjects, as
well as certain matters of a military nature"; with supplements.

References – none to this particular work; the general references
are,– Wylie's Notes page 157 160-1; 163-ggoz 10/1 031-bg1d
13/1 030-iaff 18/13 106-gdkn 55/1 012-zafk 12/13 031-bgdf 117/3.

Author – Sun I-jang 孫 詒 讓 .

Edition – no notation; (preface) dated Kuang-Hsü 21/1895. Blocks;
"fên" paper.

Index – a general table of contents for 19 chüan consisting of,–
閒 詁 15 chüan; 目 錄 1 chüan; 附 錄 1 chüan; 後語 2 chüan.

Bound in 1 t'ao 8 ts'ê.

Remarks – a good modern edition; complete and in perfect condition.

——— • ———

Accession No.   92   **Index No.** - 061-idcg

Title

" I lin yao yü "
意 林 要 語

Classification - C-328 雜家 — 雜纂

Subject - selections from works by famous philosophers and scholars
since the Chou 周 and Ch'in 秦 dynasties; similar to the
"I lin" 意 林 , but certain parts therein omitted from the
present work.

References - 030-iaff 19/21. Other general references are,-
160-1j 106-gdkn 58/17 031-bgld 13/29 012-zafk 13/3
031-bgdf 123/13.

Author - (編) Ma Tsung 馬 總 .

Edition - no notation; a manuscript copy on bamboo paper; (preface)
dated Chia-Ching "chi-ch'ou" 8/1529.

Index - a detailed table of contents for 5 chüan.

Bound in 1 t'ao 5 ts'ê; doubly interleaved with margins.

Remarks - a very good work; complete and in excellent condition
with the exception of two well-repaired defects.

Accession No.   93   Index No. - 037-azg   037-abg

Title   " T'ai-hsüan (yüan) ching "
                太　玄　(元)　經

Classification - C-163 術數 一 數學
Subject - a comprehensive treatise on numerical divination based
    upon the "diagrams" with supplements.

References - 160-1j 167-mhfm 15/8 163-ggcz 9/1 031-bgld 11/12
    030-iaff 17/3 106-gdkn 49/1 012-zafk 11/9 031-bgdf 108/2.

Author - (撰) Yang Hsiung 楊雄． (解贊) Fan Wang 范望．

Edition - no particular notation; dated Chia-Ching "chia-shên"
    3/1524. Blocks; "mien" paper.

Index - none; in 10 chüan; 太玄論 5 篇 ; 釋文 1 chüan.

Bound in 1 t'ao 4 ts'ê; doubly interleaved.

Remarks - this is a very good edition; and the item is complete and
    in excellent condition with the exception of some water stains.
    The second ts'ê is a very good manuscript copy on "mien" paper.
    The supplements are as follows;-

        " T'ai-hsüan lun " or " Shuo hsüan "
           太　玄　論   説　玄
        " T'ai-hsüan-ching Shih wên "
           太　玄　經　釋　文

Accession No.　　94　　Index No. - 145-dzeh

Title

" Yüan wên ho chien "
袁　文　合　箋

Classification - D-43 別集一文

Subject - an individual collection of prose.

References - 012-zafk 17/38.

Author - (著) Yüan Mei 袁枚 .　(集箋) Wang Kuang-yeh 王廣業 .

Edition - the "Ch'ing-hsiang-shu" 青箱塾 ; (title-page) dated
Kuang-Hsü "jên-wu" 8/1882.　Blocks; "fên" paper.

Index - a detailed table of contents for 16 chüan.

Bound in 1 t'ao 8 ts'ê.

Remarks - an ordinary edition; complete, but with a number of worm-
holes as well as water stains.　The punctuations and the marginal
notes are in red.

———•———

Accession No.   95   Index No. - 096-zhzh

Title

" <u>Yü t'ang ts'ai t'iao chi</u> "
玉　堂　才　調　集

<u>Classification</u> - D-68 總集一詩

<u>Subject</u> - a general collection of poems by famous poets from the
<u>T'ang</u> 唐 down to the <u>Ming</u> 明 dynasty.

<u>References</u> - 012-zafk 19/18.

<u>Author</u> （編） <u>Yü P'êng-chü</u> 于　朋　舉.

<u>Edition</u> - no notation; (preface) dated K'ang-Hsi "i-mao" 14/1675.
Blocks; bamboo paper.

<u>Index</u> - none; not divided into chüan; some 30 separate lists of
authors throughout the work.

<u>Bound in</u> 1 t'ao 8 ts'ê.

<u>Remarks</u> - a fair edition; appears to be complete (pages not numbered)
and without defects.

Accession No.   96   Index No. - 128-gilc 120-lmgi

Title

" <u>Shêng yü kuang hsün</u> "
聖 諭 廣 訓
" <u>Fan-i Shêng yü kuang hsün</u> "
繕 繹 聖 諭 廣 訓

Classification - C-13 儒家

Subject - an expansion of the so-called "Sacred Edict", being a
collection of short explanatory homilies on the sixteen maxims
contained therein; with original Manchu text.

References - Wylie's Notes page 87 160-1j (聖 諭) 031-bg1d 9/21
012-zafk 10/8 031-bgdf 94/2.

Author - of original - the <u>Emperor K'ang-Hsi</u> 康 熙 . of the expansion - the <u>Emperor Yung-Chêng</u> 雍 正 . of the translation-
not stated.

Edition - a palace edition; (preface) dated Yung-Chêng 2/1724.
Blocks; "k'ai-hua" paper.

Index - none; complete in 1 chüan

Bound in 1 t'ao 4 ts'ê; doubly interleaved.

Remarks - a very good edition; the item is complete and in perfect
condition.

Accession No.   97   **Index No.** - 128-gilc

Title   " <u>Shêng yü kuang hsün chih chieh</u> "
聖 諭 廣 訓 直 解

Classification - C-13 儒家

Subject - an explanation in plain dialect of the "<u>Shêng yü kuang hsün</u>"
聖 諭 廣 訓.- "an expansion of the so-called "Sacred Edict",
being a collection of short explanatory homilies on the sixteen
maxims contained therein." (# 96)

References - O12-zafk 10/8.

Author - of original-the <u>Emperor K'ang-Hsi</u> 康 熙 . of the expansion-
the <u>Emperor Yung-Chêng</u> 雍 正 . of this explanation-not stated.

Edition - officially published; (preface) dated Yung-Chêng 2/1724.
Blocks; "fên" paper.

Index - none; complete in 1 chüan.

Bound in 1 t'ao 2 ts'ê.

Remarks - a good edition; the item is complete and as if new.

Accession No. 98   **Index No.** – 039-zbhz

Title   " <u>Tzŭ shih sui yen</u> "

子 史 粹 言

Classification – C-308 雜家 — 雜文

Subject – a collection of short passages selected (part 1) from works
of famous philosophers; and (part 2) from the official history
of China from the <u>Han</u> 漢 down to the <u>Yüan</u> 元 dynasty.

References – 012-zafk 12/25.

Author – (述) <u>Ting Yen</u> 丁晏.

Edition – the "<u>I-chih-chai</u>" 頤 志 齋; (title-page) dated Tao-Kuang
"ping-wu" 26/1846. Blocks; bamboo paper.

Index – none; in 2 chüan 上下.

Bound in 1 t'ao 2 ts'ê; doubly interleaved with margins.

Remarks – a very good edition; the item is complete and in excellent
condition.

———— • ————

Accession No.   99   **Index No.** - 030-ghbe

Title
" T'ang hsien san mei chi "
唐　賢　三　昧　集

Classification - D-68 總集一詩

Subject - a general collection of poetry, with explanations and marginal notes in red.

References - 012-zafk 19/16   031-bgdf 190/24   031-bgld 19/35.

Author - （撰）Wang Shih-chêng 王　士　禎.

Edition - the "T'ing-yü-chai" 聽　雨　齋 ；(title-page) dated Kuang-Hsü 9/1883. Blocks; "fên" paper.

Index - a general table of contents for 3 chüan 上 中 下.

Bound in 1 t'ao 3 ts'ê.

Remarks - the item is complete and in good condition.

—— · ——

Accession No.   100   **Index No.** - 030-bzkm

Title   " Ku yü t'u p'u "
                        古 玉 圖 譜

Classification - C-265 譜録一珠寶玉器

Subject - a work on ancient jade objects with coloured illustrations.

References - 160-1j 012-zafk 12/1 031-bgdf 116/7 031-bgld 12/13
163-ggcz 9/13.

Author - prepared by a commission headed by Lung Ta-yüan 龍大淵
under imperial orders.

Edition - a reproduction; based upon the Sung edition; no date; but
of the Ch'ing period. Blocks; "fên" paper. *There was no Sung copy JMM*

Index - a table of contents for 32 chüan with separate lists of
objects for each chüan.

Bound in 2 t'ao 10 ts'ê; doubly interleaved.

Remarks - a very good edition; the item is complete and in very good
condition with the exception of some water stains.

The University of Toronto Chinese Library

<u>Accession No.</u>　　101　　　<u>Index No.</u> - 006-gzjh　030-bbgz　069-iibb

<u>Title</u>　　　" <u>Shih wên lei chü</u> "
　　　　　　事 文 類 聚

　　　　　" <u>Ku chin shih wên lei chü</u> "
　　　　　古 今 事 文 類 聚

　　　　" <u>Hsin pien ku chin shih wên lei chü</u> "
　　　　新 編 古 今 事 文 類 聚

<u>Classification</u> - C-348 類書

<u>Subject</u> - a work of an encyclopaedic character; classified according
　　to subjects; and with literary selections,-prose and poetry,-
　　introduced in illustration of the items under discussion.

<u>References</u> - 163-ggcz 10/13　031-bgld 14/9　037-ahhg 9/50　030-iaff
　　20/6　106-gdkn 60/1　012-zafk 13/21　031-bgdf 135/36.

<u>Author</u> - of the main work（前後續別）<u>Chu Mu</u> 祝 穆；of 外集
　　<u>Fu Ta-yung</u> 富 大 用.

<u>Edition</u> - apparently the original Yüan edition; (preface) dated
　　Shun-Yu "ping-wu" 6/1246.　Blocks; bamboo paper.

<u>Index</u> -（前集）a general table of contents arranged in 13 "pu"（部）
　　according to subject matter; a detailed table of contents in 60
　　chüan.　(#)

<u>Bound in</u> 16 t'ao 96 ts'ê; doubly interleaved.　(6.6.6.6.6.6.6.6.6.6.6.
　　6.8.8.4.4)

<u>Remarks</u> - this is indeed a very good edition; the item is complete
　　and in generally good condition with the exception of some re-
　　paired defects.　Two pages are missing as follows:-
　　　　後集 chüan 2 page 8.
　　　　別集目 page 61.

113

(#)　(後集) 13 pu - 50 chüan
　　(續集) 13 pu - 28 chüan
　　(別集) 8 pu - 32 chüan
　　(新集) 14 pu - 36 chüan
　　(外集) 9 pu - 15 chüan

114

The University of Toronto Chinese Library

Accession No.　　102　　　　Index No. – 001-bicg

Title　　　" Shang yü ch'êng yü "
　　　　　　　上　　諭　　成　　語

Classification – A-161 小學 – 字書

Subject – a Chinese-Manchu dictionary of terms and phrases generally
in use in the issuing of imperial edicts and mandates and in other
forms of official documents; arranged according to the radicals.

References – none.

Author – not stated.

Edition – a manuscript copy on "hsüan" paper; no date.

Index – none.

Bound in 1 t'ao 6 ts'ê.

Remarks – a very good and useful work; the item seems to be complete
(pages not numbered) and is in perfect condition.

Accession No.   103   Index No. - 120-fcd

Title   " Chieh chai chi "

絜 齋 集

Classification - D-33 別集 — 詩文

Subject - an individual collection of prose and poetry.

References - 012-zafk 15/25 031-bgdf 160/9 031-bgld 16/19

029-pffz 262.

Author - (撰) Yüan Hsieh 袁 燮 .

Edition - the "Yüan-shih-Chin-hsiu-t'ang" 袁氏進修堂; dated

T'ung-Chih 11/1872. Blocks; "mao-pien" paper.

Index - a general table of contents for 24 chüan; 從祀錄6 chüan.

Bound in 1 t'ao 8 ts'ê.

Remarks - the first ts'ê is a replacement from another copy; much
smaller in size, stained and with a few defects; but is made
uniform in size with the other ts'ê by leaving the inter-leaves
with wide margins. The work is otherwise in good condition.

Accession No.   104   Index No. - 140-hfl

Title   " Ts'ai kên t'an "
                    菜 根 譚

Classification - C-328 雜家 — 雜纂

Subject - a comprehensive collection of short notes or jottings treating of the principles of the affairs of the universe, both
psychologically and practically; the principles of "cause and
effect" etc.

References - 012-zafk 13/6.

Author - (撰) Hung Ying-ming 洪 應 明.

Edition - the "Tzŭ-fu-ssŭ-Temple" 資 福 寺 ; dated Tao-Kuang
13/1833. Blocks; "mao-pien" paper.

Index - none; complete in 1 chüan.

Bound in 1 t'ao 2 ts'ê; doubly interleaved with leaves from some
old books.

Remarks - an ordinary edition; complete and with some defects in
the last 2 pages and in the preface.

Accession No.   105   Index No. - 123-gddk

Title   " Ch'ün fang lieh chuan "
                   羣　芳　列　傳

Classification - C-283 譜録一草木

Subject - a collection of short essays presumed to be the biographical
   records of 50 various kinds of flowers, fruits and other plants
   which are personified, named and with an illustration in each
   case.

References - none.

Author - Ma Ta-k'uei 馬　大　魁.

Edition - the "Ts'an-hsiu-ko" 餐　秀　閣; (title-page) dated Tao-
   Kuang "kuei-wei" 3/1823. Blocks; "fên" paper.

Index - at the beginning of each of 4 chüan.

Bound in 1 t'ao 4 ts'ê; doubly interleaved with margins.

Remarks - a good edition; complete and in perfect condition.

The University of Toronto Chinese Library

—— • ——

Accession No. 106   **Index No.** - 072-dedz   178-hz

Title   " Ch'ang-li hsien-shêng ch'üan chi "

昌　黎　先　生　全　集

" Han wên "

韓　文

Classification - D-33 別集—詩文

Subject - an individual comprehensive collection of prose and poetry.

References - 012-zafk 15/8   167-mhfm 19/23   106-gdkn 67/7.

Author - (撰) Han Yü 韓愈．   (編) Li Han 李漢．

Edition - published in Japan; no date. Blocks; Japanese paper.

Index - a detailed table of contents for 40 chüan for the main work;
外集 10 chüan; 集傳 1 chüan; 遺集 1 chüan.

Bound in 1 t'ao 6 ts'ê.

Remarks- a good edition; the item is complete and in perfect condition.

Accession No.   107   Index No. - 032-khbz   030-bzk1

Title   " Shu k'o ku wên hui hsüan "
                 塾 課 古 文 匯 選
                 " Ku wên hui hsüan "
                 古 文 匯 選

Classification - D-73 總集一文

Subject - a general collection of literary compositions,-prose, by
    ancient famous scholars and officials; many of which are of
    historical interest and importance.

References - none.

Author - (評選) Wên Ch'êng-hui 溫 承 惠.

Edition - the "Pao-yang-tu-shu" 保 陽 督 署; (title-page) dated
    Chia-Ch'ing "kuei-yu" 18/1813. Blocks; "fên" paper.

Index - detailed table of contents for 8 chüan.

Bound in 1 t'ao 8 ts'ê.

Remarks - an ordinary edition; in good condition and apparently
    complete.

Accession No.   108   Index No. - 067-zlne   075-gedz

Title   " Wên   hsüan   tsuan   chu "
             文   選   纂   註
             " Liang   Chao-ming   wên   hsüan "
             梁   昭   明   文   選

Classification - D-63 總集一詩文

Subject - a general collection of literary compositions,- prose
and poetry; with annotations and explanations.

References - 012-zafk 19/1   031-bgdf 191/1

Author - (撰) Chang Fêng-i 張 鳳 翼.

Edition - the "Sun-hsi-Yüan-hao-t'ang" 蓀 溪 顧 好 堂; (preface)
dated K'ang-Hsi 11/1672. Blocks; bamboo paper.

Index - a detailed table of contents for 12 chüan.

Bound in 2 t'ao 12 ts'ê (6.6)

Remarks - a fairly good edition; the item is complete and without
defects.

Accession No.　　109　　　Index No. - 024-ghgh　024-ghgl

Title　　　　　" Nan-hua-ching　chien　chu "
　　　　　　　南　華　經　箋　註
　　　　　　　" Nan-hua　fa　fu "
　　　　　　　南　華　發　覆

Classification - C-731 道家

Subject - a commentary on "Nan-hua-ching",- "the Taoist writings in

33 sections, divided into three main divisions, (1) Nei p'ien

內 篇 ; (2) Wai p'ien 外篇 ; and (3) Tsa p'ien 雜篇 ."

References - Wylie's Notes page 218　160-1j　012-zafk 14/32

031-bgdf 146/22.　The above are general references and not to

this particular edition.

Author - (注) Hsing T'ung 性　通 .

Edition - the "Huai-tê-t'ang" 懷　德　堂 ; (title-page) dated

Ch'ien-Lung "chi-ssŭ" 14/1749.　Blocks; bamboo paper.

Index - none; in 8 chüan.

Bound in 1 t'ao 6 ts'ê.

Remarks - a good ordinary edition; in generally good condition and

apparently complete.

The University of Toronto Chinese Library

Accession No.　110　　Index No. - 145-gicz

Title　　　" Pu-kuo-chai　jih　chi "
補　過　齋　日　記

Classification - C-308 雜家 一 雜文

Subject - miscellaneous notes and expositions, mainly of a philosophical character; and consisting of references to and extracts from works of various renowned philosophers.

References - none.

Author - Yang Tsêng-hsin 楊 增 新·

Edition - no notation; (preface) dated Min-Kuo 10/1921.　Blocks;
"fên" paper.

Index - none; in 19 chüan; 陰 符 經 1 chüan.

Bound in 2 t'ao 20 ts'ê (10 each).

Remarks - a good modern edition; the item is complete and in excellent condition.　The following is a supplement to this work:-
" Yin-fu-ching "
陰 符 經

Accession No.   111   **Index No.** – 145-giez

Title   " Pu-kuo-chai jih chi "
補 過 齋 日 記

Classification – C-308 雜家 一 雜文

Subject – miscellaneous notes and expositions mainly of a philosophical character; and consisting of references to and extracts
from works of various renowned philosophers.

References – none.

Author – Yang Tsêng-hsin 楊 增 新.

Edition – no notation; (preface) dated Min-Kuo 10/1921. Blocks;
"fên" paper.

Index – none; in 19 ch'üan; 陰 符 經 1 ch'üan.

Bound in 2 t'ao 20 ts'ê (10 each)

Remarks – a good modern edition; the item is complete and in excellent condition. The following is a supplement to this work:-
"Yin-fu-ching"
陰 符 經

The University of Toronto Chinese Library

Accession No. 112   **Index No.** - 145-gico

Title   " Pu-kuo-chai tu Lao-tzŭ jih chi "
補 過 齋 讀 老 子 日 記

Classification - C-731 道家

Subject - an explanatory commentary on "Lao-tzŭ Tao-tê-ching",- "the so-called 'Canon of Reason and Virtue'; a basic work of the Taoist gospel."

References - none to this work. The general references to "Tao-tê-ching" are,- Wylie's Notes page 216 012-zafk 14/30 031-bgdf 146/5.

Author - of the original work,- reputed to be Lao-tzŭ 老子, but extremely doubtful; of this work - Yang Tsêng-hsin 楊 增 新.

Edition - no notation; (title-page) dated "ping-yin" 1926. Blocks; "fên" paper.

Index - none; in 6 chüan.

Bound in 1 t'ao 6 ts'ê.

Remarks - a good modern edition; complete and in excellent condition.

The University of Toronto Chinese Library

Accession No.   113   **Index No.** - 145-gico

Title   " Pu-kuo-chai   tu   Yin-fu-ching   jih   chi "

補 過 齋 讀 陰 符 經 日 記

Classification - C-731 道家

Subject - an explanatory commentary on the "Yin-fu-ching" 陰 符 經,- "a Taoist work that professes to reconcile the decrees of Heaven with the current of mundane affairs." (Wylie)

References - none to this work. The general references to "Yin-fu-ching" are,- Wylie's Notes page 216   160-1j   012-zafk 14/30 031-bgld 14/44   031-bgdf 146/1   163-ggcz 11/9.

Author - of original - Huang Ti 黃 帝 ; of this work - Yang Tsêng-hsin 楊 增 新·

Edition - no notation; (title-page) dated "ping-yin" 1926. Blocks; "fên" paper.

Index - none; in 1 chüan or 3 p'ien.

Bound in 1 t'ao 1 ts'ê.

Remarks - a good modern edition; the item is new.

126

Accession No.   114   Index No. – 010-dafz

Title   " Hsien chêng ko yen "
                 先 正 格 言

Classification – G-328 雜家 一 雜纂

Subject – a comprehensive collection of short essays, selected from
  works of famous authors and philosophers; consisting mainly of
  precepts and maxims to be applied by man in various phases of
  his life.

References – none.

Author – compiled by the Pan Hsiang Shu Wu 辮香書屋.

Edition – the "Pan-hsiang-shu-wu" 辮香書屋 ; (title-page) dated
  Tao-Kuang "i-wei" 15/1835. Blocks; bamboo paper.

Index – a general table of contents for 10 chüan.

Bound in 1 t'ao 4 ts'ê.

Remarks – the item is complete, and no defects are noted.

127

Accession No.   115   Index No. - 072-eefh

Title   " Hsing yao chih chang "
                          星 軺 指 掌

Classification - B-257 職官

Subject - a complete treatise on international principles and laws
governing the mutual despatch of diplomatic representatives
between nations; as well as their principal duties and functions;
translated from a certain European work; together with a supplement containing the articles of administration and duties of the
American consuls and consulates; and, also, matters connected (#)

References - none.

Author - (全譯) Lien Fang 聯芳 and Ch'ing Ch'ang 慶常.

Edition - the "T'ung-wên-kuan" 同文館 based upon the "Chü-chên-
pan" 聚珍版; (title-page) dated Kuang-Hsü 2/1876. Blocks;
"fên" paper.

Index - a detailed table of contents for 3 chüan or 14 章 ;續卷
1 chüan.

Bound in 1 t'ao 4 ts'ê.

Remarks - an ordinary edition; complete and in very good condition.
(#) with the presenting of credentials and other forms of documents.

Accession No.   116   Index No. - 149-bljh

Title   " Ting ê tsa lu "
                 訂 譌 雜 録

Classification - C-308 雜家 - 雜文

Subject - a work that treats of the erroneous usages and incorrect
  pronunciations of certain characters and expressions; mostly
  selected from old works, but amplified with the personal views
  of the author.

References - 160-1j 031-bgld 13/15 163-ggcz 10/5 012-zafk 12/22
  031-bgdf 119/26.

Author - (撰) Hu Ming-yü 胡 鳴 玉.

Edition - the "Ch'i-chên-shu-wu" 戢 戡 書 屋; dated Ch'ien-Lung
  4/1739. Blocks; bamboo paper.

Index- detailed table of contents for 10 chüan.

Bound in 1 t'ao 4 ts'ê; doubly interleaved.

Remarks - a fair edition; apparently complete and in good condition.

Accession No.   117 (a)   Index No. - 085-hgh

Title   Ch'ing i lu "

清異錄

Classification - C-368 小説家

Subject - a general collection of historical anecdotes and minor incidents from T'ang 唐 dynasty down to the Epoch of the Five Dynasties 五代 ; under 37 classes.

References - 160-1j 031-bgld 14/41 167-mhfm 17/25 012-zafk 14/16 031-bgdf 142/46.

Author - (撰) T'ao Ku 陶穀.

Edition - the "Ch'ên-shih-Yung-hsien-chai" 陳氏庸閒齋; (title-page) dated Kuang-Hsü "i-hai" 1/1875. Blocks; "mao-pien" paper.

Index - a general list of the 37 classes with the number of incidents under each class; the work itself in 2 chüan 上 下.

Bound in 2 ts'ê in 1 t'ao with (b).

Remarks - an ordinary edition; complete but with a few worm-holes.

Accession No.   117 (b)   Index No. - 145-cgh

Title   " Piao i lu "
                         表 異 録

Classification - C-348 類書

Subject - a work of an encyclopaedic character; classified into 20
    main divisions.

References - 012-zafk 13/26.

Author - (撰) Wang Chih-chien. 王 志 堅.

Edition - the "Ch'ên-shih-Yung-hsien-chai" 陳氏庸閒齋; (title-
    page) dated Kuang-Hsü "ping-tzŭ" 2/1876. Blocks; "mao-pien"
    paper.

Index - a general table of contents for 20 chüan.

Bound in 4 ts'ê in 1 t'ao with (a).

Remarks - an ordinary edition; the item is complete and in good
    condition.

Accession No.   118   Index No. - 032-1z

Title   " Mo-tzǔ "
                             墨子

Classification - C-308 雜家 — 雜文

Subject - the writings of the philosopher Mo Ti 墨翟 , on moral and
   political subjects, as well as certain matters of a military
   nature.

References - Wylie's Notes page 157   160-1j   163-ggcz 10/1   031-bgld
   13/1   030-iaff 18/13   106-gdkn 55/1   012-zafk 12/13   031-bgdf
   117/3.

Author - original work - Mo Ti 墨翟. See 160-1j Giles B D 1537.
   this work - (注).- Wang K'ai-yün 王 閻 運.

Edition - the "Chiang-hsi-kuan-shu-chü" 江西官書局; (title-page)
   dated Kuang-Hsü "chia-ch'ên" 30/1904. Blocks; "mao-pien" paper.

Index - none; in 3 chüan 上中下 or 71 篇.

Bound in 1 t'ao 3 ts'ê.

Remarks - an ordinary edition; the item is complete and without defects.
   certain parts of the work are printed white on black; and the
   reasons for such distinction are clearly stated in the postscriptum
   at the end of the work.

———•———

Accession No. 119   **Index No. –** 085-bzh

Title   " Ch'iu chi lu "
                求 己 錄

Classification – C-328 雜家 — 雜纂

Subject – a collection of excerpts from the Tso Chuan and Ch'un Ch'iu
and works of famous scholars of the Sung dynasty; mainly of a political character.

References – 012-zafk 13/11.

Author – (撰) T'ao Pao-lien 陶 葆 廉·

Edition – no notation; (preface) dated Kuang-Hsü 22/1896. Blocks;
"mao-pien" paper.

Index – a table of contents for 3 chüan.

Bound in 1 t'ao 3 ts'ê.

Remarks – an ordinary edition; in good condition and the item is
complete. The political situation of China during of late Ch'ing
period is largely the cause of the compilation of this work.

Accession No.   120   Index No. - 140-ickz

Title   " Lo-fan-lou wên chi "
                         落 帆 樓 文 集

Classification - D-43 別集一文
Subject- an individual collection of prose.

References - none.

Author - Shên Yao 沈 垚．

Edition - the "Chia-yeh-t'ang" 嘉 業 堂 ; (preface) dated "mou-wu"
    1918. Blocks; "mao-pien" paper.

Index - a detailed table of contents for 24 chüan;補遺 1 chüan.

Bound in 1 t'ao 8 ts'ê.

Remarks - an ordinary edition; the item is complete and in good
    condition.

Accession No.　　121　　Index No. - 009-hzib

Title　　　　" Wo Wên-tuan kung i shu "
　　　　　　　倭 文 端 公 遺 書

Classification - D-43 別集 一文

Subject - an individual collection of literary compositions,- prose.

References - 012-zafk 18/33.

Author - (輯) Wo Jên-kung 倭 仁 恭.

Edition - the "Han-yüan-lou" 翰 元 樓 ; (title-page) dated Kuang-Hsü 3/1877. Blocks; "fên" paper.

Index - a detailed table of contents for 12 chüan.

Bound in 1 t'ao 6 ts'ê.

Remarks - an ordinary edition; complete and without defects.

Accession No. 122   Index No. - 169-gzd

Title   " Lang-fêng chi "
                         閬　風　集

Classification - D-33 別集 － 詩文

Subject - an individual collection of prose and poetry, mostly
          the latter.

References - 031-bgld 16/26   106-gdkn 92/9   030-iaff 32/7
          012-zafk 15/32   031-bgdf 165/11.

Author - (撰) Shu Yüeh-hsiang 舒 岳 祥.

Edition - the "Chia-yeh-t'ang"嘉 業 堂; (preface) dated "i-mao"
          1915.   Blocks; "mao-pien" paper.

Index - a general table of contents for 12 chüan.

Bound in 1 t'ao 2 ts'ê.

Remarks - the edition is an ordinary one; and the item appears
          to be complete, but has a slight defect on page 13 in
          chüan 6.

Accession No. 123   Index No. - 132-zki

Title   " <u>Tzǔ ching pien</u> "
                 自   鏡   編

Classification - C-328 雜家一雜纂

Subject - selections of short essays from writings of famous
    philosophers and renowned scholars; mainly of a preceptive
    character; and consisting of principles, and examples on
    man's training along the lines of morality and ethics.

References - none.

Author - （編輯） <u>Yang Ch'i-lieh</u> 楊 其 烈.

Edition - no notation; (postscriptum) dated Tao-Kuang "ting-yu"
    17/1837.   Blocks; "fên" paper.

Index - none; in 4 chüán.

Bound in 1 t'ao 2 ts'ê.

Remarks - an ordinary edition; the item is stained but has no other
    defects.

Accession No. 124   **Index No. -** 067-zdg(zb)

Title   " Wên fang ssŭ k'ao t'u shuo "
文 房 肆 考 圖 説

Classification - C-266 譜錄 - 文房四寶

Subject - an illustrated handbook on the equipment of a Chinese
study,- inkslabs, paper, ink, brushes, etc.,- together
with additional matter treating of literary composition,
painting, and related subjects.

References - none.

Author - (纂) T'ang Ping-chün 唐 秉 鈞.

Edition - no particular notation; (preface) dated Ch'ien-Lung
"ping-shên" 41/1776.   Blocks; "fên" paper.

Index - a general table of contents for 8 chüan; separate list
at the beginning of each chüan.

Bound in 1 t'ao 8 ts'ê; doubly interleaved.

Remarks - this is a very fine edition; the item is complete and,
with the exception of some water stains; in generally good
condition.   An interesting point is the inclusion of the
subject of "ginseng"; the explanation of the author for this
being the lack of works on that subject for which reason he
included a short chapter with regard to it.

The University of Toronto Chinese Library

Accession No. 125   Index No. — 030-bnh(zb)

Title   " Ku ch'ou suan k'ao shih "
               古　籌　算　考　釋

Classification — C-138 天文算法－算書

Subject — a treatise on mathematics based upon old formulas.

References — none.

Author — Lao Nai-hsüan 勞乃宣.

Edition — the "Wan-hsien kuan-shê" 完縣官舍; (title-page)
dated Kuang-Hsü 12/1886.   Blocks; "fên" paper.

Index — a general table of contents for 6 chüan.

Bound in 1 t'ao 6 ts'ê.

Remarks — a good edition; complete and in good condition.

Accession No.   126   Index No. - 198-zfed

Title   " Lu-chou ch'u chi "
                     鹿　洲　初　集

Classification - D-43 別集一文
Subject - an individual literary collection,- prose; with "running"
    commentary.

References - 163-ggcz 15/12   031-bgld 18/41   012-zafk 17/20
    031-bgdf 173/51.

Author - (著) Lan Ting-yüan 藍 鼎 元 (評) K'uang Min-pên
    曠 敏 本 ·

Edition - privately published; (preface) dated Yung-Chêng "jên-tzŭ"
    10/1732.   Blocks; "fên" paper.

Index - a detailed table of contents for 20 chüan; arranged according
    to classes of writings and chronologically.

Bound in 1 t'ao 8 ts'ê.

Remarks - this item is complete and in very good condition.

140

Accession No.   127 (a)   Index No. - 198-zffg

Title   " Lu-chou tsou su "
                        鹿 洲 奏 疏

Classification - B-62 詔令奏議 — 奏議
Subject - a collection of memorials.

References - none.

Author - Lan Ting-yüan 藍 鼎 元.

Edition - privately published; no date.   Blocks; "fên" paper.

Index - none.

Bound in 1/2 ts'ê in 1' t'ao with (b).

Remarks - an ordinary edition; without defects.

The University of Toronto Chinese Library

Accession No. 127 (b)   Index No. - 198-zfbf

Title   " Lu-chou kung an "
                鹿 洲 公 案

Classification - B-107 傳記一獨録

Subject - a series of memoranda by Lan Ting-yüan regarding his
    official duties as district magistrate of P'u-ning 普寧 ,
    towards the close of last century (Wylie).

References - Wylie's Notes page 37 O12-zafk 5/25   O31-bgdf 64/26.

Author - (著) Lan Ting-yüan 藍 鼎 元·

Edition - privately published; (preface) dated Yung-Chêng "ohi-yu"
    7/1729.   Blocks; "fên" paper.

Index - a table of contents for 2 chüan 上 下 .

Bound in 1 1/2 ts'ê in 1 t'ao with (a).

Remarks - as under (a).

142

Accession No. 128   Index No. - 051-bhcf   075-ded

Title   " P'ing t'ai chi lüeh "
                        平　臺　紀　略
                      " Tung chêng chi "
                        東　征　集

Classification - B-32 紀事本末

Subject - (a) an historical record of the punitive expedition

against the formosan rebels, during the year 1721-1723;

(b) correspondence and proclamations issued during the

above period.

References - 012-zafk 4/13   031-bgdf 49/33.

Author - (著) Lan Ting-yüan 藍 鼎 元 · (評) Wang Chê-fu

王 者 輔 .

Edition - privately published; (preface) dated Yung-Chêng 10/1732.

Blocks; "fên" paper.

Index - (平 臺 紀 略) none; in 1 chüan; (東 征 集) a detailed

table of contents for 6 chüan.

Bound in 1 t'ao 4 ts'ê.

Remarks - an ordinary edition; complete and without defects.

Accession No.   129   Index No. – 009-hbff

Title   " Hsiu shih shih pi "

修 史 試 筆

Classification – B-117 傳記一總録

Subject – collected biographies of famous officials and scholars

of the T'ang 唐 dynasty with "running" commentary.

References – 012-zafk 5/16   031-bgdf 63/21.

Author – (纂) Lan Ting-yüan 藍 鼎 元 (評) K'uang Min-pên

曠 敏 本·

Edition – privately published; (preface) dated Yung-Chêng "mou-shên"

6/1728.   Blocks; "fên" paper.

Index – a list of names in 2 chüan 上 下 ·

Bound in 1 t'ao 2 ts'ê.

Remarks – an ordinary edition, in perfect condition.

Accession No. 130   **Index No.** - 030-bzzi

Title   " <u>Ssŭ-ma Ch'ang-ch'ing chi</u> "

司 馬 長 卿 集

Classification - D-43 別 集 一 文

Subject - an individual collection of prose.

References - 012-zafk 15/2

Author - (著) <u>Ssŭ-ma Hsiang-ju</u> 司馬 相 如 (校) <u>Weng Shih-hsien</u>

汪 士 賢 .

Edition - no particular notation; (preface) dated T'ien-Ch'i "ping-yin"

6/1626.   Blocks; bamboo paper.

Index - a table of contents arranged according to classes of writing;

not divided into chüan.

Bound in 1 t'ao 1 ts'ê; doubly interleaved.

Remarks - this is a very good edition; and the item is complete

and has no defects except the last page, a portion of which

is repaired.

Accession No.　131　　　　　Index No. - 072-dhzb

Title　　" I-t'ang shih san tzŭ wên hsüan "
易　堂　十　三　子　文　選

Classification - D-73　總集一文
Subject - a general collection of prose by thirteen authors.

References - none.

Author - (選) Wang Ch'uan-chih 王泉之.

Edition - the "Chêng-yü-shu-wu" 政餘書屋 ; (title-page) dated
Tao-Kuang 8/1828.　　Blocks; "mao-pien" paper.

Index - a detailed table of contents for 4 chüan with the names of
the authors.

Bound in 1 t'ao 2 ts'ê.

Remarks - the item is complete and in good condition.

Accession No.   132   Index No. - 012-eebf

Title   " Ping fa shih lüeh hsüeh "
               兵 法 史 略 學

Classification - C-33 兵家
Subject - a short treatise on the history of military affairs;
    mainly based upon the military situations during the
    period of Ch'un Ch'iu 春秋 ; prepared for use as a
    textbook.

References - none.

Author - (纂) Ch'ên Ch'ing-nien 陳慶年 ·

Edition - the "Chêng-hsüeh-t'ang" 正 學 堂 ; (title-page) dated
    Kuang-Hsü 25/1899.   Blocks; "mao-pien" paper.

Index - detailed table of contents for 2 chüan.

Bound in 1 t'ao 2 ts'ê.

Remarks - an ordinary modern edition; complete and without any
    defects.

Accession No. 133   Index No. - 147-dgze

Title   " Kuei chia jih i pien "
規　家　日　益　編

Classification - C-328 雜家 — 雜纂

Subject - a collection of short passages mostly selected from the
writings or sayings of famous philosophers and scholars;
consisting in the main of precepts and maxims to be adopted
by man in his conduct as well as in the ruling of a family;
a basic work on "ethics".

References - none.

Author - (纂) Yao T'i-chieh 姚 體 傑 .

Edition - no notation; no date.   Blocks; bamboo paper.

Index - separate lists of contents for 2 "chi" 前 後 .

Bound in 1 t'ao 2 ts'ê.

Remarks - this is a good edition; and the item appears to be complete
and in generally good condition. This work seems to have been
published during the period of Ch'ien-Lung, but no exact date
can be traced.

Accession No. 134   Index No. - 067-zbgg

Title   " Wên shih t'ung i "
                         文　史　通　義

Classification - D-43 別集－文
Subject – an individual collection of critical compositions on a
          variety of literary and classical subjects; divided into
          "nei p'ien" 內篇 and "wai p'ien" 外篇.

References - 012-zafk 18/8.

Author – (撰) Chang Hsüeh-ch'êng 章　學　誠·

Edition – the "Ching-hua-ko" 菁華閣; (title-page) dated
          Kuang-Hsü "kuei-ssǔ" 19/1893.   Blocks; "mao-pien" paper.

Index – 3 separate lists of contents,- (內篇) - 5 chüan
        (外篇) - 3 chüan (校讐通義) - 3 chüan.

Bound in 1 t'ao 10 ts'ê.

Remarks – an ordinary edition; the item is new.   The supplement
          to this work is entitled:-
                   " Chiao ch'ou t'ung i "
                     校　讐　通　義   075-fpgg

149

Accession No. 135   Index No. - 075-dedh

Title   " Tung Chou lieh kuo chih "
               東 周 列 國 志

Classification - C-368 小 說 家

Subject - (Wylie) "----- written in the form of a novel, differs
    less from authentic history probably than any other in the
    same category. It embraces the period when China was divided
    into a great many tributary states, and extends from the 8th
    to the 3rd century B. C. when the Tsin dynasty was established."

References - Wylie's Notes page 203. Giles' "Chinese Literature"
    page 310.

Author - of the original work, not known; (評 點) Ts'ai Hao 蔡昴

Edition - the "Shanghai-shu-chü" 上 海 書 局 ; (preface) dated
    Ch'ien-Lung 17/1752; lithographed on "fên" paper.

Index - a detailed table of contents for 27 chüan or 108 sections.

Bound in 1 t'ao 8 ts'ê.

Remarks - a very ordinary edition; the item has no defects and is
    complete. There are a few illustrations at the beginning
    of each chüan.

Accession No.   136   Index No. - 111-cbh

Title   " Chih ku lu "
                          知 古 錄

Classification - C-33 兵家

Subject - treats of military administration and tactics; the various
essentials of the subject being illustrated by a series of
historical notes giving the actual methods of ancient generals
in dealing with problems with which they were confronted.

References - none.

Author - (纂輯) Hêng Ling 恒玲; (叅閱) Yü Fu 毓孚:

Edition - published by the "Pi-jo-wo" 避熱窩; (title-page)
dated T'ung-Chih 2/1863.   Blocks; "mao-pien" paper.

Index - a table of contents for 3 chüan; 附 錄 1 chüan.

Bound in 1 t'ao 3 ts'ê; doubly interleaved.

Remarks - a fair edition; in good condition and the item is complete.

The University of Toronto Chinese Library

Accession No. 137   Index No. - 072-dbzg

Title   " <u>Ming</u> <u>wu</u> <u>ta</u> <u>chia</u> <u>chi</u> "
                明　五　大　家　集

Classification - D-43 別集 一文

Subject - a collection of literary compositions,- prose, by five
          famous writers of the <u>Ming</u> 明 dynasty. (separate notes
          follows)

References - see under the several works.

Author - see under the several works; (選) <u>Chang Ju-hu</u> 張汝瑚

Edition - see under the several works.

Index - see under the several works.

Bound in 2 t'ao 20 ts'ě (8-12).

Remarks - a fair edition; the item is complete and in generally
          good condition with the exception of some worm-holes.

Accession No. 137 (a)   **Index No.** - 040-dzld   040-dzld

Title   " Sung Wên-hsien hsien-shêng chi "
宋 文 憲 先 生 集
" Sung Wên-hsien chi "
宋 文 憲 集

Classification - D-43 別集 一文
Subject - an individual collection of prose.

References - none to this particular edition; but see 012-zafk 16/10
031-bgdf 169/2   163-ggcz 15/1.

Author - (著) Sung Lien 宋 濂 ; (選) Chang Ju-hu 張 汝 瑚·

Edition - the "Wên-ling-shu-lin" 溫 陵 書 林; (title-page) dated
K'ang-Hsi 21/1682.   Blocks; bamboo paper.

Index - a detailed classified table of contents for 11 chüan.

Bound in 4 ts'ê in 1 t'ao with (b).

Remarks - as under # 137.

Accession No. 137 (b)   **Index No.** - 070-zamd   077-amd

Title   " Fang Chêng-hsüeh hsien-shêng chi "

方 正 學 先 生 集

" Chêng-hsüeh chi "

正 學 集

Classification - D-43 別 集 一 文

Subject - an individual collection of prose.

References - none to this particular edition; but see 012-zafk 16/14.

Author - (著) Fang Hsiao-ju 方 孝 儒 ; (選) Chang Ju-hu

張 汝 瑚 .

Edition - the "Shih-ku-t'ang" 視 古 堂 ; no notation as to the
date; but undoubtedly same as that of (a).   Blocks;
bamboo paper.

Index - a detailed classified table of contents for 13 chüan.

Bound in 4 ts'ê in 1 t'ao with (a).

Remarks - as under # 137.

Accession No. 137 (c)   Index No. - 096-zltd   162-ltd

Title   " Wang Tsun-yen hsien-shêng chi "
        王　遵　巖　先　生　集
        " Tsun-yen chi "
        遵　巖　集

Classification - D-43 別集一文
Subject - an individual collection of prose.

References - none to this particular edition; but see 012-zafk 16/25
    031-bgdf 172/13   031-bgld 18/27.

Author - (著) Wang Shên-chung 王 慎 中; (選) Chang Ju-hu
    張　汝　瑚.

Edition - the "Ying-hsüeh-shu-lin" 郢 雪 書 林; (preface) dated
    K'ang-Hsi "jên-hsü" 21/1682.   Blocks; bamboo paper.

Index - a detailed classified table of contents for 10 chüan.

Bound in 4 ts'ê in 1 t'ao with (d) and (e).

Remarks - as under # 137.

Accession No. 137 (d)   Index No. - 030-gfzd   140-fzd

Title   " T'ang Ching-ch'uan hsien-shêng chi "
             唐 荆 川 先 生 集
             " Ching-ch'uan chi "
             荆 川 集

Classification - D-43 別集一文
Subject - an individual collection of prose.

References - none to this particular edition; but see 012-zafk 16/25
        031-bgld 18/28   031-bgdf   172/18   163-ggcz 15/8.

Author - (著) T'ang Shun-chih 唐順之 (選) Chang Ju-hu
        張汝瑚.

Edition - the "Ying-hsüeh-shu-lin" 郢雪書林; (preface) dated
        K'ang-Hsi "hsin-yu" 20/1681.   Blocks; bamboo paper.

Index - a detailed classified table of contents for 6 chüan.

Bound in 4 ts'ê in 1 t'ao with (c) and (e).

Remarks - as under # 137.

Accession No. 137 (e)   **Index No.** - 077-ngzd   173-gzd

Title   " Kuei Chên-ch'uan hsien-shêng chi "

歸 震 川 先 生 集

" Chên-ch'uan chi "

震 川 集

Classification - D-43 別集一文

Subject - an individual collection of prose.

References - none to this particular edition; but see 012-zafk 16/29

031-bgdf 172/44   031-bgld 18/21   163-ggcz 15/9.

Author - (著) Kuei Yu-kuang 歸 有 光 ; (選) Chang Ju-hu

張 汝 瑚.

Edition - the "Ying-hsüeh-shu-lin" 郢 雪 書 林 ; (preface) dated

K'ang-Hsi "jên-hsü" 21/1682.   Blocks; bamboo paper.

Index - a detailed classified table of contents for 10 chüan.

Bound in 4 ts'ê in 1 t'ao with (c) and (d).

Remarks - as under # 137; but with a few bad defects at the end of

last ts'ê.

Accession No. 138   Index No. - 018-dz   015-dfeg

Title   " Lieh-tzǔ "
                            列 子
                      " Ch'ung-hsü-chên-ching "
                         冲 虛 真 經

Classification - C-731 道家

Subject - a work on metaphysical philosophy; one of the principal

   works of the Taoist gospel; with commentaries and explanations.

References - Wylie's Notes page 217 160-1j   012-zafk 14/32

   031-bgdf 146/18. The above are general references and
   not to this particular edition.

Author - reputed to be Lieh Yü-k'ou 列 禦 寇, but the actual

   existence of such a person is somewhat doubtful. (註)

   Chu Tê-chih 朱 得 之.

Edition - the "Hao-jan-chai" 浩 然 齋 ; no notation as to the date;

   but apparently a Ming edition.   Blocks; "mien" paper.

Index - a detailed table of contents for 8 chüan.

Bound in 1 t'ao 6 ts'ê.

Remarks - this is a very good edition; and the item is complete and

   in very good condition.

Accession No. 139   **Index No.** - 154-ibha   120-f1d

Title   " Lai-ku-t'ang ch'ih tu hsin ch'ao san hsüan chieh lin chi "
賴 古 堂 尺 牘 新 鈔 三 選 結 隣 集
" Chieh lin chi "
結 隣 集

Classification - D-73 總集一文
Subject - a general collection of extracts taken from the letters of
more than 200 scholars; with marginal notes.

References - 012-zafk 19/19.

Author - (編) Chou Tsai-chün 周 在 浚 .

Edition - the "Lai-ku-t'ang" 賴 古 堂 ; (preface) dated Tao-Kuang
6/1826.   Blocks; "fên" paper.

Index - a detailed list of authors with their native districts for
15 chüan (see remarks).

Bound in 1 t'ao 8 ts'ê.

Remarks - an ordinary edition; the item is complete and in good
condition.   This work itself is in 16 chüan; but the last
is not given in the index.

Accession No. 140   Index No. - 154-ibha   140-ned

Title   " Lai-ku-t'ang ch'ih tu hsin ch'ao êrh hsüan ts'ang chü chi "
          賴 古 堂 尺 牘 新 鈔 二 選 藏 弆 集
                " Ts'ang chü chi "
                藏 弆 集

Classification - D-73 總 集 一 文

Subject - a general collection of extracts taken from the letters

    of more than 200 scholars.

References - 012-zafk 19/19.

Author - (編) Chou Tsai-chün 周 在 浚 .

Edition - the "Lai-ku-t'ang" 賴 古 堂 ; (title-page) dated Tao-Kuang

    19/1839.   Blocks; "fên" paper.

Index - a detailed list of authors with native districts for 16 chüan.

Bound in 1 t'ao 6 ts'ê.

Remarks - an ordinary edition; the item is complete and without

    defects.

160

The University of Toronto Chinese Library

Accession No.   141   Index No. - 001-bhck   118-ezzz

Title   " San kuo chih yen i "
                   三 國 志 演 義
                   " Ti i ts'ai tzŭ shu "
                   第 一 才 子 書

Classification - C-368 小 説 家

Subject - an historical novel relating to the period of the three
    Kingdoms,- Wei 魏 , Shu 蜀 , and Wu 吳 ; in 120 chapters;
    with illustrations and portraits at the beginning of the
    first chüan.

References - Wylie's Notes page 202 160-1j.

Author - Lo Kuan-chung 羅 貫 中 (評) Mao Tsung-kang 毛 宗 崗.

Edition - the "Ching-lun-t'ang" 經 綸 堂; (preface) dated
    Shun-Chih "chia-shên 1/1644.   Blocks; bamboo paper.

Index - detailed table of contents for 51 chüan or 120 hui 回 .

Bound in 2 t'ao 20 ts'ê (10 each).

Remarks - an ordinary edition; the item has no defects and is complete.

Accession No. 142   Index No. - 072-diz

Title   " Ch'ang tao yen "
                    昌   道   言

Classification - C-13 儒家

Subject - a collection of short notes on a variety of subjects of
         a philosophical character.

References - none.

Author - (著) Hu Fei-ying 胡 蜚 英.

Edition - the "Hu-shuang-kuei-hsüan" 胡 雙 桂 軒; (title-page)
         dated Tao-Kuang "chia-wu" 14/1834.   Blocks; "fên" paper.

Index - a detailed table of contents for 5 chüan.

Bound in 1 t'ao 2 ts'ê; doubly interleaved.

Remarks - the item is complete and in generally good condition.

Accession No. 143   Index No. - 140-pzbh

Title   " Su Ch'ang-kung ch'i hsüan "
                蘇　長　公　啓　選

Classification - D-43 別集一文

Subject - selected extracts from the correspondence and writings of

    Su Shih 蘇軾 of the Sung 宋 dynasty.

References - none.

Author - (同選) Chung Hsing 鐘惺 and T'an Yüan-ch'un 譚元春.

Edition - a Ming edition; no notation as to the date.   Blocks;

    bamboo paper.

Index - a list of 83 items; in 2 chüan 上　下 .

Bound in 1 t'ao 2 ts'ê; doubly interleaved.

Remarks - a fairly good edition; the item has no defects and is in

    very good condition.

Accession No. 144   Index No. - 184-zlfe

Title   " Shih hsien hung pi "
               食 憲 鴻 秘

Classification - C-270 譜録 一 食譜
Subject - a comprehensive treatise on Chinese gastronomy under a
     .number of classifications.

References - none.

Author - Nien Hsi-yao 年希尭 .

Edition - no notation; (preface) dated Yung-Chêng 9/1731.
     Blocks; bamboo paper.

Index - a detailed classified table of contents for 2 chüan 上 下 .

Bound in 1 t'ao 4 ts'ê; doubly interleaved with leaves from some
     old books.
Remarks - a fair edition; complete but stained in places.

Accession No.   145   Index No. - 033-zdoc

Title   " Shih lin i hsün "
                         士　林　彝　訓

Classification - C-328 雜家 － 雜纂
Subject - a collection of notes of a homiletical character taken
    from various standard works; with annotations by the
    compiler.

References - none.

Author - (述) Kuan Huei 關　槐 .

Edition - the "Tuan-hsi-shu-yüan" 端　溪　書　院; (preface) dated
    Chien-Lung 54/1789.   Blocks; "fên" paper.

Index - a table of contents for 8 chüan.

Bound in 1 t'ao 4 ts'ê.

Remarks - a good edition; the item is complete and in good condition.

Accession No. 146   Index No. - 064-hah

Title   " T'an pên lu "
                          探   本   録

Classification - C-308 雜家 — 雜文

Subject - miscellaneous notes and expositions on a variety of
    subjects mostly in connection with the conduct and social
    environment of "man".

References - none.

Author - (著) Yün Mao-ch'i 雲茂琦.

Edition - privately published; (title-page) dated Hsien-Fêng 1/1851.
    Blocks; "mao-pien" paper.

Index - a table of contents for 23 chüan.

Bound in 1 t'ao 6 ts'ê.

Remarks - a fair edition; the item is complete, but has a few
    repaired defects,- worm-holes.

— ● —

Accession No. 147   **Index No.** – 077-jccz

Title   " Li-tai ming jên hua p'u "
            歷 代 名 人 畫 譜

Classification – C-223 藝術一書畫

Subject – a collection of paintings by famous artists during the
period from the Chin 晉 down to the Ch'ing 清 dynasty;
together with biographical notes of the artists.

References – 012-zafk 11/20.

Author – (撰) Ku Ping 顧 炳 .

Edition – the "Hung-wên-shu-chü" 鴻 文 書 局 ; (title-page) dated
Kuang-Hsü "mou-tzŭ" 14/1888.   Lithographed on "fên" paper.

Index – a list of the artists for 4 ts'ê; arranged dynastically.

Bound in 1 t'ao 4 ts'ê; doubly interleaved with margins.

Remarks – the item is complete and as if new.

Accession No.   148   Index No. - 031-bd1d

Title   " Ssŭ chung i chi "
                    四　忠　遺　集

Classification - D-33 別集 - 詩文
Subject - a collection of literary compositions,- prose and poetry,
   by 4 loyal officials. (see separate notes that follows)

References - see under the several works.

Author - see under the several works.

Edition - the "Ch'u-li-chü-k'uei-shu-ko" 楚醴聚奎書閣; (title-
   page) dated T'ung-Chih 10/1871.   Blocks; "fên" paper.

Index - see under the several works.

Bound in 2 t'ao 24 ts'ê (10ᵣ14).

Remarks - a modern edition; the item is new.

Accession No.   148 (a)   **Index No.** - 149-iied   149-iidg

Title   " <u>Chu-ko</u> <u>ch'êng</u> <u>hsiang</u> <u>chi</u> "
　　　　　　諸　葛　丞　相　集
　　　　　　" <u>Chu-ko</u> <u>wu</u> <u>hou</u> <u>chi</u> "
　　　　　　諸　葛　武　侯　集

Classification - D-33 別集－詩文
Subject - an individual collection of literary compositions, prose
　　　　and poetry.

References - 012-zafk 15/3.   031-bgdf 174/1.

Author - (撰) <u>Chu-ko Liang</u> 諸葛亮 ; (編) <u>Chu Lin</u> 朱璘.

Edition - the "<u>Ch'u-li-ching-lai-shu-shih</u>" 楚醴景萊書室;
　　　(title-page) dated T'ung-Chih 7/1868.   Blocks; "fên" paper.

Index - a general table of contents for 4 chüan; 卷 首 1 chüan.

Bound in 4 ts'ê in 1 t'ao with (b) and (c).

Remarks - as under # 148.

Accession No. 148 (b) Index No. - 075-idid

Title " Yang Chung-min chi "
楊 忠 愍 集

Classification - D-33 別集一詩文
Subject - an individual miscellaneous collection,- prose and poetry.

References - 012-zafk 16/27 163-ggcz 15/8 031-bgld 18/29
031-bgdf 172/28.

Author - (撰) Yang Chi-shêng 楊 繼 盛.

Edition - as under (a).

Index - a general table of contents for 6 chüan; 卷 首 1 chüan.

Bound in 3 ts'ê in 1 t'ao with (a) and (c).

Remarks - as under # 148.

Accession No. 148 (c)   Index No. - 030-bdab

Title   " Shih Chung-chêng kung chi "
                 史   忠   正   公   集

Classification - D-33 別集 一 詩文

Subject - an individual collection of prose and poetry.

References - 012-zafk 16/39.

Author - (撰) Shih K'o-fa 史 可 法.

Edition - as under (a).

Index - a general table of contents for 5 chüan; 卷 首 1 chüan.

Bound in 3 ts'ê in 1 t'ao with (a) and (b).

Remarks - as under # 148.

171

Accession No. 148 (d)　　　　**Index No.** - 067-zzd　　067-zghb

Title　　　　　" Wên-shan chi "
　　　　　　　　文　山　集

　　　　　　　" Wên Hsin-kuo kung chi "
　　　　　　　文　信　國　公　集

Classification - D-33 別集 – 詩文

Subject - an individual comprehensive collection of prose and poetry.

References - 012-zafk 15/31　　031-bgdf 164/27　　031-bgld 16/34.

Author - (撰) Wên T'ien-hsiang 文　天　祥.

Edition - as under (a).

Index - a general table of contents for 21 chüan.

Bound in 1 t'ao 14 ts'ê.

Remarks - as、under # 148.

Accession No. 149   Index No. - 075-dnzd

Title   " Sung yin wên chi "
                    松 隱 文 集

Classification - D-33 別集 — 詩文
Subject - an individual literary collection of prose and poetic
          writings.

References - 029-pffz 498   012-zafk 15/20   031-bgdf 156/21
            031-bgld 16/3.
Author - (著) Ts'ao Hsün 曹 勛 .

Edition - the "Chia-yeh-t'ang" 嘉 業 堂 ; (postscriptum) dated
          "kêng-shên" 1920.   Blocks; "mao-pien" paper.

Index - none; in 40 chüan.

Bound in 1 t'ao 4 ts'ê.

Remarks - an ordinary modern edition; complete and without defects.

Accession No. 150   Index No. - 060-iecd

Title   " Fu-ch'u-chai chi wai shih "
               復 初 齋 集 外 詩

Classification - D-33 別集 － 詩文
Subject - an individual collection of literary compositions,- prose
     and poetry.

References - 012-zafk 17/40   029-pffz 498/

Author - (撰) Weng Fang-kang 翁 方 網 ·

Edition - the "Chia-yeh-t'ang" 嘉 業 堂 ; no date.   Blocks;
     "mao-pien" paper.

Index - (外 詩) - none; in 24 chüan; (外 文) - a detailed table
     of contents for 4 chüan.

Bound in 1 t'ao 10 ts'è.

Remarks - a modern edition; the item is new.

Accession No. 151   Index No. - 026-dald

Title   " Wei T'ai-p'u chi "
危 太 樸 集

Classification - D-33 別集 一 詩文
Subject - an individual literary collection,- prose and poetry.

References - 029-pffz 498.

Author - (著) Wei Su 危 素 .

Edition - the "Chia-yeh-t'ang" 嘉 業 堂 ; no date.   Blocks;
          "mao-pien" paper.

Index - (詩集) - none; in 2 chüan; (文 集) - detailed table
        of contents for 10 chüan; (續 集) detailed table of contents
        for 10 chüan.
Bound in 1 t'ao 6 ts'ê.

Remarks - a modern edition; apparently complete and without defects.

Accession No.   152   Index No. - 160-imd

Title   " Pien hsüeh chi "
                         辨　學　集

Classification - C-513 釋　家　C-731 道　家
Subject - discussions by various scholars on Buddhist and Taoist
    works, including "Lao-tzǔ", "Chuang-tzǔ", etc.

References - none.

Author - (撰) Tsêng Ho-jui 曾　和　瑞.

Edition - privately published; dated Kuang-Hsü "chia-shên" 10/1884.
    Blocks; "mao-pien" paper.

Index - a general list of works on front of title-page; not divided
    into chüan; separate lists for the first two works.

Bound in 1 t'ao 8 ts'ê.

Remarks - the item is complete and in fairly good condition.

Accession No. 153   Index No. - 050-zgn

Title   " Chin ching tsuan "
                            巾   經   纂

Classification - C-328 雜家 一 雜纂
Subject - an historical miscellany classified into 20 headings;
        together with criticisms by the author.

References - none.

Author - (著) Sung Tsung-yüan 宋 宗 元.

Edition - privately published; (preface) dated Ch'ien-Lung "hsin-wei"
        16/1751.   Blocks; bamboo paper.

Index - a general table of contents; in 20 chüan.

Bound in 1 t'ao 8 ts'ê; doubly interleaved.

Remarks - this is a good edition; and the item appears to be complete
        and in very fine condition.

Accession No. 154   Index No. - 075-chzl

Title   " Li Kang-chi i chi "
                李 剛 己 遺 集

Classification - D-33 別集一詩文

Subject - an individual collection of prose and poetical writings.

References - none.

Author - (著) Li Kang-chi 李 剛 己.

Edition - no notation; dated Min-Kuo 6/1917.   Blocks; "mao-pien"
         paper.

Index - a general table of contents for 5 chüan; separate lists
        for each chüan.

Bound in - 1 t'ao 4 ts'ê.

Remarks - an ordinary good edition; the item is as new.

178

The University of Toronto Chinese Library

Accession No. 155   **Index No.** - 002-cffe

Title   " Chung shu tien ku hui chi "
　　　　　　　中　書　典　故　彙　紀

Classification - B-257 職官

Subject - extracts dealing with the duties and functions of the

"Chung-shu" (中 書),- an old title equivalent to

"prime-minister", - taken from the several dynastic histories.

References - 160-1j (中 書)   029-pffz 498.

Author - (輯) Wang Chêng-kung 王 正 功.

Edition - the "Chia-yeh-t'ang" 嘉 業 堂 ; (postscriptum) dated

"ping-ch'ên" 1916.   Blocks; "mao-pien" paper.

Index - a general table of contents for 8 chüan.

Bound in 1 t'ao 4 ts'ê.

Remarks - an ordinary modern edition; the item is new.

Accession No.　156　　　　Index No. － 030-bgzz

Title　　　　　　" <u>Chü</u> <u>yü</u> <u>t'u</u> <u>yin</u> <u>pu</u> <u>chu</u> "
　　　　　　　　句　餘　土　音　補　注

Classification － D-33 別集一詩文

Subject － an individual collection of prose and poetic writings of
　　　various styles; with commentaries and explanations.

References － 029-pffz 498　012-zafk 17/26.

Author － (著) <u>Chüan Tsu-wang</u> 全 祖 望 ; (補 注) <u>Ch'ên Ming-hai</u>
　　　陳 銘 海 .

Edition － the "<u>Chia-yeh-t'ang</u>" 嘉 業 堂 ; (postscriptum) dated
　　　"jên-hsü" 1922.　　Blocks; "mao-pien" paper.

Index － none; in 6 chüan.

Bound in 1 t'ao 4 ts'ê.

Remarks － an ordinary modern edition; the item is new.

The University of Toronto Chinese Library

Accession No.   157   Index No. - 181-jdjg

Title   " Lei lin tsa shuo "
                    類 林 雜 說

Classification - C-348 類書

Subject - a work of an encyclopaedic character under numerous

    headings; with historical anecdotes of ancient worthies

    as well as extracts from famous works introduced to illustrate

    the items under discussion.

References - 029-pffz 498.

Author .- (編) Wang P'êng-shou 王 朋 壽.

Edition - the "Chia-yeh-t'ang" 嘉 業 堂 ; (postscriptum) dated

    "kêng-shên" 1920.   Blocks; "mao-pien" paper.

Index - a list of "classes" for 15 chüan.

Bound in 1 t'ao 2 ts'ê.

Remarks - an ordinary modern edition; the item is as new.

Accession No. 158 (a)   Index No. - 075-eczc

Title   " Ch'a T'o-shan nien p'u "
               查 他 山 年 譜

Classification - B-107 傳記一獨録

Subject - the biographical record of Ch'a Shên-hsing 查 慎 行.

References - 029-pffz 498.

Author - (撰) Ch'en Ching-chang 陳 敬 璋.

Edition - the "Chia-yeh-t'ang" 嘉 業 堂 ; no date.   Blocks;
        "mao-pien" paper.

Index - none; in 1 chüan.

Bound in 1 ts'ê in 1 t'ao with (b) (c) and (d).

Remarks - an ordinary modern edition; the item is new.

Accession No.   158 (b)   Index No. - 109-mzad

Title   " Ch'ü Mu-fu hsien-shêng tzǔ ting nien p'u "
           瞿 木 夫 先 生 自 訂 年 譜

Classification - B-107 傳記一獨録
Subject - the autobiography of Ch'ü Chung-jung 瞿 中 溶.

References - 029-pffz 498.

Author - Ch'u Chung-jung 瞿 中 溶.

Edition - the "Chia-yeh-t'ang" 嘉 業 堂 ; dated "kuei-ch'ou" 1913.
          Blocks; "mao-pien" paper.

Index - none; in 1 chüan.

Bound in 1 ts'ê in 1 t'ao with (a) (c) and (d).

Remarks - as under (a).

Accession No. 158 (c)   Index No. - 060-gkhc

Title   " Hsü Shou-tsang nien p'u "

徐　壽　臧　年　譜

Classification - B-107 傳記 一 獨録

Subject - the biographical record of Hsü T'ung-po 徐 同 柏.

References - 029-pffz 498.

Author - Hsü Shih-yen 徐 士 燕.

Edition - uniform with (b).

Index - none; in 1 chüan.

Bound in 1 ts'ê in 1 t'ao with (a) (b) and (d).

Remarks - as under (a).

The University of Toronto Chinese Library

Accession No. 158 (d) **Index No.** – 075-czdc

Title   " Li Shên-ch'i nien p'u "

李 申 耆 年 譜

Classification – B-107 傳記 — 獨録

Subject – the biographical record of Li Chao-lo 李 兆 洛 .

References – 029-pffz 498.

Author – (撰) Chiang T'ung 蔣 彤 .

Edition – uniform with (b).

Index – none; in 3 chüan.

Bound in 1 ts'ê in 1 t'ao with (a) (b) and (c).

Remarks – as under (a).

Accession No.   159   Index No. - 162-dehg

Title   " Chin ssǔ lu fa ming "
               近　思　録　發　明

Classification - C-13 儒家

Subject - selected extracts from the works of various famous
    philosophers; with additions and commentaries.

References - none to this particular work; for 近　思　録, see 160-1j
    031-bgld 9/10   012-zafk 10/3   031-bgdf 92/20.

Author - (纂註) Shih Huang 施　璜 .

Edition - the "T'ung-ch'êng-li-chi-hung-t'ang" 桐城 李寄鴻堂;
    (preface) dated K'ang-Hsi "i-yu" 44/1705.   Blocks; bamboo
    paper.

Index - a general table of contents for 14 chüan.

Bound in 1 t'ao 6 ts'ê.

Remarks - a fairly good edition; the item is complete and in good
    condition.

Accession No. 160   Index No. - 185-ziqg

Title   " Shou lêng yen ching chih chih "
                首 楞 嚴 經 直 指

Classification - C-513 釋家

Subject - an explanation of a Buddhist sutra.

References - Wylie's Notes page 205.

Author - (譯) Pan-la-mi-ti 般刺密諦.

Edition - published by Fu Hung-lieh 傅弘烈 ; no date.
         Blocks; "mao-pien" paper.

Index - none; in 10 chüan.

Bound in 1 t'ao 5 ts'ê.

Remarks - a good edition; complete and in perfect condition.

Accession No. 161   Index No. - 102-zzzz

Title   " Yu-li-shan-jên chü p'u "
由 里 山 人 菊 譜

Classification - C-223 藝術 － 書畫
Subject - a collection of paintings of various kinds of chrysanthemums.

References - none.

Author - Miao Ku-ying 繆谷瑛.

Edition - the "Chung-hua-shu-chü" 中華書局 ; dated "chia-tzǔ"
1924.   Lithographed on "fên" paper.

Index - a table of contents for 5 classifications.

Bound in 1 t'ao 2 ts'ê.

Remarks -- a good modern edition; the item is new.

Accession No.   162   Index No. - 172-dzhp

Title   " Ya yü t'ang ts'ung shu "
                    雅　雨　堂　叢　書

Classification - C-338 叢書
Subject - a collection of reprints of 12 works.

References - 029-pffz 396   012-zafk 13/14.

Author - (校刊) Lu Chien-tsêng 盧見曾．

Edition - the "Ya-yü-t'ang" 雅雨堂 ; dated Ch'ien-Lung "ping-tzǔ"
        21/1756.   Blocks; bamboo paper.

Index - none for the whole collection.

Bound in 4 t'ao 20 ts'ê (6-4-4-6).

Remarks - a good edition; the item is complete and in generally very
        good condition.

Accession No.   163   Index No. - 036-kgj

Title   " Mêng ch'uang kao "
                    夢 窗 稿

Classification — D-113 詞曲 一 詞集

Subject — a collection of lyrical compositions. or a state,

as well as of other institutions and questions connected

with foreign relations.

References — 163-ggcz 16/16   012-zafk 20/15   031-bgld 20/16

    031-bgdf 199/1.

Author — (撰) Wu Wên-ying 吳 文 英．

Edition — the "Ssŭ-yin-chai" 四 印 齋; (preface) dated Kuang-Hsü

    "chi-hai" 25/1899.   Blocks; "fên" paper.

Index — detailed table of contents for 4 chüan; 補 遺 1 chüan.

    (小 篇) 2 chüan 上 下．

Bound in 1 t'ao 4 ts'ê; doubly interleaved.

Remarks — a good modern edition; the item is new.

190

Accession No.   164   Index No. - 053-hf

Title   " Yung shu "
                          庸　書

Classification - B-277 政書 — 通制
Subject - a treatise on internal administration of a state,
        as well as of other institutions and questions connected
        with foreign relations.

References - none.

Author - Sung Yü-jên 宋育仁.

Edition - no notation; (preface) dated Kuang-Hsü 22/1896.
        Blocks; "fên" paper.

Index - (內篇) a table of contents for 2 chüan 上 下 ;
        (外篇) 2 chüan 上 下 .

Bound in 1 t'ao 4 ts'ê.

Remarks - a modern edition; complete and without defects.

Accession No. 165.   **Index No.** - 162-1hhh

Title   " Tao yüan ching sui "
          道 原 精 萃

Classification - C-973 基 督 教

Subject - a collection of works on Roman Catholicism.

References - none.

Author - (述) Jules Aleni 艾 儒 畧.

Edition - the "Tz'ŭ-mu-t'ang" 慈 母 堂 ; dated Kuang-Hsü 13/1887.
     Blocks; foreign paper.

Index - 3 separate lists of contents among the 6 works.

Bound in 1 t'ao 6 ts'ê.

Remarks - a very fine edition; the item is complete and in good
     condition.

Accession No. 166   Index No. - 012-bcez

Title   " Liu-ju chü-shih ch'üan chi "
六 如 居 士 全 集

Classification - D-33 別 集 一 詩 文

Subject - an individual literary collection,- prose and poetry; with
supplement.

References - 012-zafk 16/25.

Author - (撰) T'ang Yin 唐 寅.

Edition - the "Kuo-k'o-shan-fang" 果 克 山 房; (preface) dated
Chia-Ch'ing 6/1801.   Blocks; bamboo paper.

Index - (全 集) a table of contents for 7 chüan; 外 集 6 chüan;
制 義 1 chüan; 畫 譜 3 chüan.

Bound in 2 t'ao 8 ts'ê (4-4); doubly interleaved.

Remarks - this is a good edition; and the item appears to be complete
and in good condition with the exception of two or three
repaired defects.   The following is the supplement :-

" Hua wu lien yin "
花 鴉 聯 吟
4 chüan (140-djkd)

—◆—

Accession No. 167   **Index No.** - 170-hbic

Title   " T'ao Yüan-hui chung ch'êng i chi "
陶 元 暉 中 丞 遺 集

Classification - D-33 別集一詩文

Subject - an individual collection of literary compositions,-
prose and poetry.

References - none.

Author - （著） T'ao Lang-hsien 陶 朗 先.

Edition - the "Chü-chên-fang-sung-yin-shu-chü" 聚 珍 倣 宋 印 書 局;
(postscriptum) dated "chi-wei" 1919.   Blocks; "fên" paper.

Index - a detailed table of contents for 3 chüan; 附 錄 1 chüan.

Bound in 1 t'ao 4 ts'ê; doubly interleaved.

Remarks - a good edition; the item is new.

The University of Toronto Chinese Library

Accession No. 168   Index No. - 106-zdeg

Title   " Po mei ku shih "
               白 眉 故 事

Classification - C-348 類書

Subject - a classified encyclopaedia; the items of which being
          explained by selected notes from various standard works.

References - none.

Author - (集) Hsü I-chung 許 以 忠.

Edition - the "Chü-chin-t'ang" 聚 錦 堂 ; dated K'ang-Hsi "jên-wu"
          41/1702.   Blocks; bamboo paper.

Index - a classified table of contents for 10 chüan.

Bound in 1 t'ao 4 ts'ê.

Remarks - an ordinary edition; complete and without defects.

Accession No. 169   Index No. - 069-iilm   085-hg

Title   " Hsin pien fan-i Ch'ing yü "
                 新 編 繙 譯 清 語
                     " Ch'ing yü "
                     清   語

Classification - A-161 小 學 一 字 書

Subject - a Chinese-Manchu glossary; arranged under 33 classifications
         similar to the usual headings of an encyclopaedia.

References - none.

Author - not stated.

Edition - a manuscript written on "k'ai-hua" paper; undated.

Index - 2 separate lists of classifications.

Bound in 1 t'ao 2 ts'ê; singly interleaved.

Remarks - a very good manuscript; the item appears to be complete
         (pages not numbered) and in very fine condition except for
         some stains.

The University of Toronto Chinese Library

Accession No. 170   **Index No.** ~ 196-fcci   015-nzff

Title   " Hung hsüeh yin yüan t'u chi "

鴻　雪　因　緣　圖　記

" Ning-hsiang-shih Hung hsüeh yin yüan "

凝　香　室　鴻　雪　因　緣

Classification - C-368 小説家

Subject - an illustrated collection of miscellaneous notes and

writings.

References - none.

Author - (著) Lin Ch'ing 麟慶.

Edition - no particular notation; dated Tao-Kuang "ting-wei" 27/1847.

Blocks; "fên" paper.

Index - a general table of contents for 3 "chi", with separate lists

at the beginning of each "chi".

Bound in 1 t'ao 6 ts'ê.

Remarks - a very good edition; the item is in good condition and

appears to be complete (pages not numbered).

Accession No. 171   Index No. - 196-fcci   015-nzff

Title   " Hung hsüeh yin yüan t'u chi "
鴻　雪　因　緣　圖　記
" Ning-hsiang-shih Hung hsüeh yin yüan "
凝　香　室　鴻　雪　因　緣

Classification - C-368 小 說 家

Subject - a collection of miscellaneous notes and writings.

References - none.

Author - (著) Lin Ch'ing 麟 慶.

Edition - the "Yün-yin-t'ang" 雲 蔭 堂 ; dated "mou-hsü" 1898.
Blocks; "fên" paper.

Index - separate lists of contents for 2 chüan.

Bound in 1 t'ao 2 ts'ê.

Remarks - a good edition; complete and in excellent condition.

198

Accession No. 172   Index No. - 030-gfba

Title   " T'ang shih san pai shou chu shih "
               唐 詩 三 百 首 註 釋

Classification - D-68 總集一詩
Subject - a general collection of some 300 poems written by famous
         poets of the T'ang 唐 dynasty; with notes and explanations.

References - none.

Author - (手編) Hêng T'ang T'ui Shih 蘅 塘 退 士; (註)
         Chang Hsieh 章 燮.

Edition - the "Wên-pao-t'ang-shu-fang" 文 寶 堂 書 坊; dated
         Kuang-Hsü 15/1889.   Blocks; "mao-pien" paper.

Index - a general table of contents for 6 chüan.

Bound in 1 t'ao 8 ts'ê.

Remarks - a poor edition; the item has no defects.   The following
         is a supplement to this work:-
               " T'ang shih san pai shou hsü hsüan "
               唐 詩 三 百 首 續 選   (030-gfba)
               by Yü Ch'ing-yüan 于 慶 元.

The University of Toronto Chinese Library

Accession No. 173   **Index No.** – 061-cgii   102-ghzd

Title   " <u>Chih i hsin pien</u> "
                        志 異 新 編
                    " <u>I yü chu chih tz'ǔ</u> "
                    異 域 竹 枝 詞

Classification – D-38 別集一詩

Subject – an individual collection of poetical writings.

References – 012-zafk 17/13.

Author – (著) <u>Fu Ch'ing</u> 福 慶 .

Edition – no notation; (preface) dated Chia-Ch'ing 4/1799.

    Blocks; "fên" paper.

Index – none; in 4 chüan.

Bound in 1 t'ao 2 ts'ê; doubly interleaved.

Remarks – a good edition; the item appears to be complete and has

    water stains as well as repaired defects in many places.

The University of Toronto Chinese Library

Accession No. 174   Index No. – 075-cded

Title   " Li Chung-ting chi hsüan "
                李　忠　定　集　選

Classification – D-33 別集 — 詩文

Subject – an individual comprehensive literary collection,– prose
     and poetry.

References – 031-bgdf 174/40.

Author – (撰) Li Kang 李　綱.

Edition – no notation; (preface) dated K'ang-Hsi "i-yu" 44/1705.
     Blocks; bamboo paper.

Index – a detailed classified table of contents for 44 chüan
     (in 2 parts).

Bound in 2 t'ao 16 ts'ê (8-8).

Remarks – a fair edition; the item is complete and in generally
     good condition with the exception of a number of repaired
     worm-holes.

Accession No. 175   **Index No.** – 046-hdml

Title   " Ts'ui Tung-pi i shu "

崔 東 壁 遺 書

Classification – C-338 叢書

Subject – a collection of reprints of 19 works related to history and government.

References – 029-pffz 377   012-zafk 13/14.

Author – (撰) Ts'ui Shu 崔 述 .

Edition – the "Ku-shu-liu-t'ung-ch'u" 古 書 流 通 處; dated "chia-tzŭ" 1924.   Blocks; foreign paper.

Index – a general table of the 19 works with separate lists for each.

Bound in 2 t'ao 20 ts'ê (10 each).

Remarks – a very ordinary edition; the item is complete and in perfect condition.

Accession No. 176   Index No. - 144-czcc   149-cgj

Title   " K'an-shih-chai chi shih kao "
           衍 石 齋 記 事 稾
           " Chi shih kao "
           記 事 稾

Classification - D-43 別集一文

Subject - an individual collection of literary writings,- prefaces,
          postscripts etc.

References - none.

Author - Ch'ien I-chi 錢 儀 吉.

Edition - no notation; (preface) dated Tao-Kuang "chia-wu" 14/1834.
          Blocks; "mao-pien" paper.

Index - a table of contents for 10 chüan; 續 稾 10 chüan.

Bound in 1 t'ao 10 ts'ê.

Remarks - the item is in perfect condition and complete.

Accession No. 177   Index No. - 077-1001

Title   " Li-tai ming yüan t'u shuo "
              歷 代 名 媛 圖 説

Classification - B-117 傳記一總録

Subject - collected biographies of distinguished women of all

    dynasties; with sketches.

References - none.

Author - not stated.

Edition - the "Tien-shih-chai" 點石齋; dated Kuang-Hsü 5/1879.

    Blocks; "fên" paper. lithograph.

Index - 2 separate lists of names for 2 chüan.

Bound in 1 t'ao 2 ts'ê.

Remarks - an ordinary edition; the item is complete; page 21 in

    chüan 2 is torn and missing.

Accession No. 178   Index No. - 167-zhde   167-zhg

Title   " Chin-kang pan-jo-po-lo-mi ching "
             金 剛 般 若 波 羅 蜜 經
             " Chin-kang ching "
             金 剛 經

Classification - C-513 釋家
Subject - the so-called "Diamond Sutra"; in Sanscrit Vadjra tchedika,
    being a condensation of the Pradjnâ pâramitâ.

References - Wylie's Notes page 205. 012-zafk 14/21.

Author - (譯) Chiu-mo-lo-shih 鳩摩羅什· (註) Ta-ch'ien
    大 謙 ·

Edition - no notation as to the edition or date; but apparently of
    the Ming period.   Blocks; bamboo paper.

Index - none; in 1 chüan.

Bound in 1 t'ao 2 ts'ê; doubly interleaved.

Remarks - a very good edition; the item is stained on top margins
    but is without serious defects.

205

Accession No. 179 (a)   Index No. - 096-zg

Title   " Yü hai "
             玉 海

Classification - C-348 類書

Subject - an encyclopaedia of broad scope, including extracts and
    references from works covering almost the whole field of
    Chinese literature.   (see remarks)

References - Wylie's Notes page 184   160-lj   163-ggcz 10/14
    031-bgld 14/11   167-mhfm 17/9   030-iaff 20/10 106-gdkn 61/1
    012-zafk 13/22   031-bgdf 135/48.

Author - Wang Yin-lin 王 應 麟.

Edition - a Yüan edition; exact date unknown (see remarks).
    Blocks; bamboo paper.

Index - none; see "remarks".

Bound in 1 ts'e in 1 t'ao with (b); 蝴 蝶 裝.

Remarks - this item consists of only chüan 111 of the whole set,
    which is in 204 chüan according to the catalogues.   It is
    in generally good condition and contains 45 pages.

Accession No.   179 (b)   Index No. - 146-zzez   149-ofc

Title   " Hsi-shan Chên-wên-kung tu shu chi "
西 山 真 文 公 讀 書 記
" Tu shu chi "
讀 書 記

Classification - C-13 儒家

Subject - [Wylie] "It treats chiefly of mental philosophy, and the
character and doings of eminent ministers from the Hëa down
to the time of the Five Dynasties."   (see remarks)

References - Wylie's Notes page 86   160-1j   163-ggcz 7/5   031-bgld
9/14   037-ahhg (hsü) 5/9   167-mhfm 13/12   030-iaff 15/14
106-gdkn 40/18   012-zafk 10/4   031-bgdf 92/42.

Author - (撰) Chên Tê-hsiu 真 德 秀 .

Edition - Yüan Dynasty reprint, mainly from the original Sung
Dynasty blocks, with a few deficiencies made good by new
blocks cut Yen-Yu 5/1318. Blocks; "ma-sha" paper.

Index - none; see "remarks".

Bound in   1 ts'ê in 1 t'ao with (a); 蝴 蝶 裝 ; doubly interleaved.

Remarks - this item contains only 19 pages of chüan 35,- page 2-20;
8 pages of chüan 37,-1-8; and 1 page of chüan (?); all of 甲集 .
The whole work is in 59 chüan according to 037-ahhg. An
exceedingly good edition in very good condition.

207

The University of Toronto Chinese Library

Accession No. 180   Index No. - 018-ebcp

Title   " Pieh-hsia chai ts'ung shu "

別 下 齋 叢 書

Classification - C-338 叢書

Subject - a collection of reprints of 28 miscellaneous works.

References - 029-pffz 239   012-zafk 13/17.

Author - (編) Chiang Kuang-hsü 蔣 光 煦.

Edition - the "Chu-chien-chai" 竹 簡 齋; dated Tao-Kuang "ting-yu"
27/1847.   Blocks; "fên" paper.

Index - a general table of contents for 28 works.

Bound in 2 t'ao 24 ts'ê (12 each).

Remarks - the item is complete and as new.

The University of Toronto Chinese Library

Accession No. 181   Index No. - 085-ghgl

Title   " Shê wên tzǔ chiu "
              涉 聞 梓 舊

Classification - C-338 叢書

Subject - a collection of reprints of 25 miscellaneous standard
    works.

References - 029-pffz 346 012-zafk 13/17.

Author - (編) Chiang Kuang-hsü 蔣 光 煦.

Edition - the "Chiang-shih-I-nien-t'ang" 蔣 氏 宜 年 堂 ; dated
    Hsien-Fêng 1/1851.   Blocks; "fên" paper.

Index - a general table of contents for 25 works.

Bound in 2 t'ao 24 ts'ê (12 each).

Remarks - the item is complete and as new.

Accession No. 182   Index No. - 163-lghl   184-fedf

Title   " Têng Hou-an i shu "
                     鄧 厚 巷 遺 書
             " Yang hsing hsien pi yü lu chai yao "
                     養 性 閒 筆 語 錄 摘 要

Classification - C-328 雜家 一 雜纂
Subject - a miscellaneous collection of notes and discussions on
         certain parts of the "Four Books"; the nature of man; and
         other related subjects.

References - 012-zafk 13/10.

Author - Têng Fêng-kuang 鄧 逢 光.

Edition - no notation; dated Tao-Kuang 30/1850.   Blocks; "fên"
         paper.

Index - 4 separate lists of contents; not divided into chüan.

Bound in 1 t'ao 4 ts'ê.

Remarks - an ordinary edition; the item is complete and without
         defects.

The University of Toronto Chinese Library

Accession No. 183   Index No. - 163-lghl   184-fedf

Title

" Têng Hou-an i shu "

鄧 厚 菴 遺 書

" Yang hsing hsien pi yü lu chai yao "

養 性 間 筆 語 録 摘 要

Classification - C-328 雜 家 一 雜 纂

Subject - a miscellaneous collection of notes and discussions on
    certain parts of the "Four Books"; the nature of man; and
    other related subjects.

References - 012-zafk 13/10.

Author - Têng Fêng-kuang 鄧 逢 光.

Edition - no notation; dated Tao-Kuang 30/1850.   Blocks; "fên"
    paper.

Index - 4 separate lists of contents; not divided into chüan.

Bound in 1 t'ao 4 ts'ê.

Remarks - an ordinary edition; the item is complete and without
    defects.

Accession No. 184   Index No. - 033-kifz

Title   " Shou ch'in yang lao hsin shu "

壽　親　養　老　新　書

Classification - C-120 醫學療法衛生

Subject - a general treatise on the preservation of health; the
treatment of common medical cases; the selection of nutritious
food materials for aged persons; and a collection of prescriptions.

References - 031-bgdf 103/26   012-zafk 10/23   163-ggcz 8/3
031-bgld 10/10/

Author - (chüan 1) Ch'ên Chih 陳直 ; (chüan 2-4) Tsou Hsüan 鄒鉉 .

Edition - no notation (preface) dated T'ung-Chih 9/1870.   Blocks;
"fên" paper.

Index - a detailed table of contents for 4 chüan; separate list for
chüan 1.

Bound in 1 t'ao 4 ts'ê.

Remarks - an ordinary edition; the item is in perfect condition and
complete.

Accession No.   185   Index No. - 149-ofh

Title   " Tu   shu   lu "
                        讀 書 録

Classification - C-13 儒家

Subject - miscellaneous notes consisting of references to and

extracts from various philosophical works as well as

discussions upon the same.

References - 160-1j   163-ggcz 7/5   031-bgld 9/18 012-zafk 10/5

031-bgdf 93/8.

Author - (撰) Hsüeh Hsüan 薛瑄 .

Edition - no notation; apparently of the Ch'ing period; no date.

Blocks; bamboo paper.

Index - none; main work,- 11 chüan; supplement,- 12 chüan.

Bound in 1 t'ao 6 ts'ê.

Remarks - the item is in generally good condition, and appears to

be complete.

Accession No.   186   Index No. - 037-abim

Title   " T'ai-shang kan ying p'ien t'u shuo "
          太 上 感 應 篇 圖 說

Classification - C-731 道家

Subject - [Wylie] - "This treatise which is composed in a style easy
     of comprehension, has for its object to elucidate the doctrine
     of future retribution."   This item is with illustrations.

References - Wylie's Notes page 223 160-1j.

Author - (輯) Chu Jih-fêng 朱 日 豐.

Edition - the "Lan-chou-kuan-shu" 蘭 州 官 署 ; dated T'ung-Chih
     13/1874.   Blocks; "fên" paper.

Index - none.

Bound in   2 t'ao 12 ts'ê (6-6).

Remarks - an ordinary edition; complete and without defects.

———•———

Accession No.   187   Index No. - 147-rbhf   073-fzpf

Title   " Kuan-ku-t'ang Shu mu ts'ung k'o "
               觀 古 堂 書 目 叢 刻
               " Shu mu ts'ung k'o "
               書 目 叢 刻

Classification - C-338 雜家 - 叢書

Subject - a collection of reprints of 15 catalogues.

References - none; but see 029-pffz 586.

Author - composed by Yeh Tê-hui 葉 德 輝.

Edition - the "Kuan-ku-t'ang" 觀 古 堂 ; dated Kuang-Hsü "kuei-mao"
         29/1903.   Blocks; "mao-pien" paper.

Index - a list of the 15 catalogues.

Bound in 2 t'ao 20 ts'ê (10 each).

Remarks - the item is complete and as if new.

Accession No. 188   Index No. - 149-hgzg

Title   " Lun yü ta i "
               論 語 大 義

Classification - A-134 四書 一 論語

Subject - an explanatory commentary on "The Analects".

References - none to this particular work.

Author - (撰) T'ang Wên-chih 唐 文 治.

Edition - published by Shih Chao-tsêng 施 肇 曾 ; dated "chia-tzǔ"
         1924.   Blocks; "mao-pien" paper.

Index - none.

Bound in 1 t'ao 3 ts'ê.

Remarks - this is a new edition.

Accession No.   189   Index No. - 149-ofzc

Title   " Tu shu jih chi "
                          讀 書 日 記

Classification - C-13 儒家
Subject - a collection of short essays of a philosophical nature.

References - 031-bgdf 98/6.

Author - (撰) Liu Yüan-lu 劉 源 渌.

Edition - no notation; (preface) dated Yung-Chêng 11/1733.
     Blocks; bamboo paper.

Index - a general table of contents for 6 chüan; "pu pien" 補 編
     2 chüan.

Bound in 1 t'ao 4 ts'ê.

Remarks - this is a fairly good edition; and the item is complete
     and without any defects.

The University of Toronto Chinese Library

Title   " I-shan wên ts'un "
                         一 山 文 存

Classification - D-43 別集一文

Subject - an individual literary collection,- prose.

References - none.

Author - Chang Shên 章 梫 .

Edition - no notation; (preface) dated Hsüan-T'ung "mou-wu" 1918.
    Blocks; "mao-pien" paper.

Index - a detailed table of contents for 12 chüan.

Bound in 1 t'ao 4 ts'ê.

Remarks - an ordinary modern edition; the item is new.

Accession No. 191   Index No. - 140-hfl

Title   " Ts'ai kên t'an "
                          菜 根 譚

Classification - C-328 雜家－雜纂

Subject - a comprehensive collection of short notes or jottings
    treating of the principles of the affairs of the universe,
    both psychologically and practically; the principles of
    "cause and effect" etc.

References - 012-zafk 13/6.

Author - (撰) Hung Ying-ming 洪 應 明.

Edition - no particular notation; (title-page) dated Tao-Kuang
    "i-wei" 15/1835.   Blocks; "fên" paper.

Index - none; in 1 chüan.

Bound in 1 t'ao 2 ts'ê; doubly interleaved.

Remarks - this is a fair edition; and the item is complete but
    with 2 or 3 repaired defects as well as some water stains.

Accession No. 192   Index No. - 042-zzzd

Title   " Hsiao shih shan fang ts'ung shu "
小　石　山　房　叢　書

Classification - C-338 叢書

Subject - a collection of reprints of 41 general works.

References - 029-pffz 121   012-zafk 13/16.

Author - (編) Ku Hsiang 顧　湘.

Edition - published by "Yü-shan-Ku-shih" 虞 山 顧 氏; dated
     T'ung-Chih "chia-hsü" 13/1874.   Blocks; "mao-pien" paper.

Index - a general table of the 41 works.

Bound in 2 t'ao 16 ts'ê (8-8).

Remarks - a very ordinary edition; the item is complete and without
     defects.

220

The University of Toronto Chinese Library

Accession No. 193   **Index No.** – 167-fzic

Title   " <u>T'ung jên chên chiu ching</u> "
銅　人　鍼　灸　經

Classification – C-112 醫 家 － 針 法

Subject – a treatise on acupuncture, based upon the methods of the
"T'ung-jên" 銅 人 ,– a copper model of the human body with
markings to illustrate the principles of acupuncture and
points for puncturing; with numerous illustrations.

References – Wylie's Notes page 101 160-1j   163-ggcz 8/2
031-bgld 10/9   012-zafk 10/22   031-bgdf 103/21.

Author – (編 修) <u>Wang Wei-i</u> 王　惟　一 .

Edition – based upon the Sung edition; dated "hsin-ch'ou" 1901.
Blocks; "fên" paper.

Index – a detailed table of contents for 5 chüan.

Bound in 1 t'ao 4 ts'ê.

Remarks – this is a very fine edition; and the work is in good
condition, complete and printed in red ink.

Accession No. 194 (a)   Index No. - 009-jece

Title   " Pei chi chiu fa "
              備   急   灸   法

Classification - C-113 醫家 一 灸法
Subject - a treatise on cauterization with moxa.

References - none.

Author - Chang Jui 張 銳 .

Edition - the "Shih-pan-t'ung-hsin-lan-shih" 十 瓣 同 心 蘭室;
         (preface) dated Kuang-Hsü 16/1890.   Blocks; "k'ai-hua"
         paper.

Index - none; but a list of part of the contents on the 1st page
       of the work.

Bound in 1 ts'ê in 1 t'ao with (b); doubly interleaved.

Remarks - a very fine edition; appears to be complete and in very
         good condition.

222

Accession No.   194 (b)   Index No. - 167-icmz

Title   " <u>Chên chiu tsê jih pien chi</u> "
               鍼　灸　擇　日　編　集

Classification - C-112 醫 家 — 針 法 C-113 醫 家 — 灸 法

Subject - the selection of "lucky days" upon which to employ
    acupuncture and moxa cauterization Treatment.

References - 012-zafk 10/26.

Author - 012-zafk gives <u>Chin Li-mêng</u> 金 禮 蒙 ,- the writer of a
    preface,- as the author.

Edition - uniform with (a).

Index - none.

Bound in 1 ts'ê in 1 t'ao with (a); doubly interleaved.

Remarks - as under (a).

Accession No. 195   Index No. - 146-zic   118-ebzz

Title   " Hsi hsiang chi "
西 廂 記
" Ti liu ts'ai tzǔ shu "
第 六 才 子 書

Classification - D-143 戲本

Subject - (Giles' Chinese Literature) " Of all the plays of the
Mongol dynasty, the one which will best repay reading is
undoubtedly the Hsi Hsiang Chi, or Story of the Western
Pavilion, in sixteen scenes. It is by Wang Shih-fu, of whom
nothing seems to be known except that he flourished in the (#)

References - 160-1j 012-zafk 20/33.

Author - Wang Shih-fu 王 實 甫 .

Edition - probably the "Ch'êng-yü-t'ang" 成 裕 堂 ; (preface)
dated Yung-Chêng "kuei-ch'ou" 11/1733.   Blocks; "fên" paper.

Index - a general table of contents for 8 chüan.

Bound in 2 t'ao 12 ts'ê; doubly interleaved with margins.

Remarks - a very good edition of a small size; the item is in good
condition and complete.

(#)   thirteenth century, and wrote thirteen plays, all of
which are included in the collection mentioned above. " The
dialogue of this play," says a Chinese cirtic, "deals largely
with wind, flowers, snow, and moonlight," which is simply a
euphemismtic way of stating that the story is one of passion
and intrigue. It is popular with the educated classes, by
whom it is regarded more as a novel than as a play.

225

Accession No. 196   Index No. - 106-ahfh

Title   " Po hua shih chien p'u "
百　華　詩　箋　譜

Classification - C-223 藝術 - 書畫

Subject - a collection of 100 coloured paintings of various kinds
of flowers.

References - none.

Author - possibly Chang Chao-hsiang 張　兆　祥; but not quite
sure.

Edition - the "Wên-mei-chai" 文美齋; dated Hsüan-T'ung 3/1911.
Blocks; "hsüan" paper.

Index - none.

Bound in 1 t'ao 2 ts'ê.

Remarks - this is a beautiful work; the item is complete and as
new.

226

Accession No. 197   Index No. - 085-zkk   118-ebzz

Title   " <u>Shui hu chuan</u> "
                        水 滸 傳
                   " <u>Ti wu ts'ai tzǔ shu</u> "
                      第 五 才 子 書

Classification - C-387 通 俗 小 說

Subject - a tale of brigandage in 70 chapters; with illustrations.

References - Wylie's Notes page 203 160-1j.

Author - <u>Shih Nai-an</u> 施 耐 卷.

Edition - the "<u>Kuang-po-sung-chai</u>" 廣 百 宋 齋; dated Kuang-Hsü
    "hsin-ch'ou" 17/1891.   Blocks; foreign paper.

Index - a table of contents for 70 hui 回 .

Bound in 1 t'ao 10 ts'ê.

Remarks - an ordinary cheap edition; no defects.

Accession No. 198   Index No. – 060-hid

Title   " Ts'ung yu chi "
                             從   游   集

Classification – D-73 總 集 一 詩

Subject – a general collection of poetic writings by some thirty

   pupils of Ch'ên Hu 陳 瑚 ; by whom an article is written

   in praise of each of them

References – none.

Author – (輯) Ch'ên Hu 陳 瑚 .   1613-75

Edition – the "Ch'iao-fan-lou" 峭 帆 樓; (postscriptum) dated

   "kuei-ch'ou" 1913.   Blocks; "mao-pien" paper.

Index – a list of names in 2 chüan.

Bound in 1 t'ao 2 ts'ê.

Remarks – a modern edition; the item is new.

Accession No. 199   Index No. - 009-fdd

Title   " Shih ch'ien chi "
                     使   黔   集

Classification - D-38 別集一詩
Subject - an individual collection of poetry.

References - 012-zafk 17/18.

Author - (撰) T'ang Yu-tsêng 湯 右 曾.   1656-1722

Edition - privately published; (preface) dated K'ang-Hsi "ting-ch'ou"
    36/1697.   Blocks; bamboo paper.

Index - none; in 2 chüan.

Bound in 1 t'ao 2 ts'ê; doubly interleaved with margins.

Remarks - this is a fairly good edition; the item appears to be
    complete and in very good condition.

Accession No. 200   Index No. - 037-eekz

Title   " Ch'i ku ch'ing wên chi "
               奇 觚 賡 文 集

Classification - D-43 別 集 一 文

Subject - an individual collection of literary compositions,-

          prefaces, postscripts, etc.

References - none.

Author - Yeh Ch'ang-chih 葉 昌 熾．

Edition - no notation; dated "hsin-yu" 1921.   Blocks; "mao-t'ai"

          paper.

Index - a detailed table of contents for 2 chüan 上　下 ; "wai chi"

          外　集　1 chüan.

Bound in 1 t'ao 2 ts'ê.

Remarks - an ordinary modern edition; complete and in good condition.

Accession No.　201　　　　　　Index No. - 030-bmjn

Title　　　　　" Ku hsüeh hui tsuan "
　　　　　　　古　學　彙　纂

Classification - C-348 類書

Subject - an encyclopaedic work classified under 10 main headings;
each with a number of subdivisions; the discussions of which
consist of extracts from standard works of all classes of
literature.

References - none.

Author - (輯) Chou Shih-yung 周昔雍.

Edition - the "Ai-jih-chai" 愛 日 齋; dated Ch'ung-Chêng "jên-wu"
15/1642.　　Blocks; bamboo paper.

Index - a general table of contents for 10 chüan; with separate
detailed lists.

Bound in 2 t'ao 14 ts's (7-7).

Remarks - this is an ordinary edition; and the item is complete,
but there are some bad defects, - worm-holes.

Accession No. 202   Index No. - 170-hjzk

Title   " Yin chih wên t'u shuo "
　　　　　　陰　隲　文　圖　説

Classification - C-308 雜家 一 雜文

Subject - an illustrated collection of fables setting forth examples

　　of retribution in connection with man's good or bad conduct.

References - none.

Author - (纂輯) Huang Chêng-yüan 黃 正 元.

Edition - the "Chin-wên-chai" 晉 文 齋 ; dated Tao-Kuang "ting-yu"

　　17/1837.　　Blocks; bamboo paper.

Index - none.

Bound in 1 t'ao 8 ts'ê.

Remarks - a fairly good edition; complete and in good condition.

　　This item includes the followings of a similar nature:-

　　　　" Yü hai tz'ŭ hang "
　　　　慈　海　慈　航　　　　　　　　(061-kgjd)
　　　" Hsing t'ien chên ching "
　　　　性　天　真　境　　　　　　　　(061-ea

　　(#)

232

" **Ti** **chün** **chieh** **shih** tzǔ **wên** "

帝　君　戒　士　子　文　　　　　　(050-fdcz)

" **Yü** **hsü** **chieh** **kung** **kuo** **ko** "

御　虛　階　功　過　格　　　　　　(060-hfic)

233

Accession No. 203   Index No. - 039-defd   162-ilg

Title   " Fu-yu-ti-chün ch'ien chu Tao-tê-ching "
         孚 佑 帝 君 淺 註 道 德 經

Classification - C-731 道家

Subject - a commentary on "Tao-tê-ching",- "the so-called 'Canon of
    Reason and Virtue'; a basic work of the Taoist gospel."

References - 160-1j Wylie's Notes page 216 012-zafk 14/30
    031-bgdf 146/5. The above are general references and not to this
    particular edition.

Author - (淺 註) Fu-yu-ti-chün 孚 佑 帝 君 .

Edition - the "Yung-shêng-chai" 永 盛 齋 ; (preface) dated "ting-ssü"
    1917.   Blocks; "fên" paper.

Index - a general table of contents for 2 chüan 上 下 .

Bound in 1 t'ao 2 ts'ê.

Remarks - an ordinary modern edition; complete and in good condition.

234

———•———

Accession No.   204   Index No. — 002-cg

Title   " Chung shuo "
                          中 說

Classification — C-13 儒家

Subject — a philosophical work of a political nature, on somewhat
    the same lines as the "Lun-Yü" 論 語 ; with annotations.

References — 160-1j   163-ggcz 7/2   031-bgld 9/5   106-gdkm 39/10
    012-zafk 10/2   031-bgdf 91/24.

Author — Wang T'ung 王 通 ; (注) Yüan I 阮 逸 .

Edition — a reproduction based upon the Sung edition; dated Kuang-Hsü
    16/1890.   Blocks; "mao-pien" paper.

Index — none; in 10 "p'ien" 篇 .

Bound in 1 t'ao 2 ts's.

Remarks — a fairly good edition; in excellent condition and the
    item is complete.

Accession No. 205   Index No. – 147–rdzh

Title   " Kuan shih yin p'u-sa ta pei hsin t'o-lo-ni ching "

觀 世 音 菩 薩 大 悲 心 陀 羅 尼 經

Classification – C–515 釋家

Subject – a standard Buddhist work.

References – Wylie's Notes page 206.

Author – (譯) Ch'ieh-fan-ta-mo 伽 梵 達 摩.

Edition – the "Hui-wên-chai" 會 文 齋; dated Hsien-Fêng 1/1851.
     Blocks; "fên" paper.

Index – none.

Bound in 1 t'ao 1 ts'ê.

Remarks – the item is complete and in good condition.

————— • • —————

Accession No. 206   Index No. - 085-gdbb

Title   " Hai Chung-chieh kung chi "
               海   忠   介   公   集

Classification - D-43 別集一文

Subject - an individual collection of literary compositions,- prose,-
   preceded by a biographical sketch.

References - none.   ⟶

Author - (著) Hai Jui 海 瑞 ; (評次) Huang Ping-shih 黃 秉 石.

Edition - no notation; dated T'ien-Ch'i "chia-tzǔ" 4/1624.
   Blocks; bamboo paper.

Index - none; a list of contents for the "chuan" 傳 .

Bound in 1 t'ao 5 ts's.

Remarks - this is a fairly good edition; the item is apparently
   complete and in very good condition.

The University of Toronto Chinese Library

Accession No. 207   Index No. - 021-ojog

Title   " Pei-hsi tzŭ i "
北 溪 字 義

Classification - C-13 儒家

Subject - an explanation of the meanings and the sources of certain characters and expressions picked out from the "Four Books".

References - 160-lj 163-ggoz 7/5   031-bgld 9/16   106-gdkn 41/4
167-mhfm 13/12   012-zafk 10/4   031-bgdf 92/49.

Author - (著) Ch'ên Shun 陳淳 ; (集 編) Wang Chien 王 雋 .

Edition - the "Wei-tao-yü-hsüan" 味 道 腴 軒 ; dated Kuang-Hsü "i-wei" 21/1895.   Blocks; "mao-pien" paper.

Index - a table of contents for 2 chüan 上 下 .

Bound in 1 t'ao 2 ts'ê.

Remarks - a fairly good edition; complete and without any defects.

Accession No. 208   Index No. — 154-hikg

Title   " <u>Hsien</u> <u>yüan</u> <u>t'u</u> <u>shuo</u> "
          賢 媛 圖 説

<u>Classification</u> — C-368 小 説 家

<u>Subject</u> — an illustrated collection of famous women showing examples
     of filial piety; virtue; etc.

<u>References</u> — none.

<u>Author</u> — not stated.

<u>Edition</u> — the "<u>Yen-ku-chai</u>" 延 古 齋; dated Kuang-Hsü "ping-wu"
     32/1906.   Blocks; "fên" paper.

<u>Index</u> — a general table of contents; in 1 chüan.

<u>Bound in</u> 1 t'ao 1 ts'ê.

<u>Remarks</u> — an ordinary edition; the item appears to be complete
     and without defects.

Accession No. 209　　　Index No. - 162-ilgb　　125-zzil

Title　　　" Tao-tê-ching k'ao i "

道 德 經 攷 異

" Lao-tzǔ Tao-tê-ching K'ao i "

老 子 道 德 經 攷 異

Classification - C-731 道家

Subject - an examination of the purity (? accuracy) of "Tao-tê-ching",-
"the so-called 'Canon of Reason and Virtue'; a basic work of the
Taoist gospel."

References - Wylie's Notes page 217　012-zafk 14/31.

Author - (撰) Pi Yüan 畢 沅 .

Edition - the "Ching-hsün-t'ang" 經 訓 堂; dated Ch'ien-Lung
"kuei-mao" 48/1783.　　Blocks; bamboo paper.

Index - none; in 2 chüan 上 下 .

Bound in 1 t'ao 2 ts'ê; doubly interleaved with some old book-leaves.

Remarks - a very ordinary edition; the item is complete and without
defects.

Accession No. 210   Index No. - 125-zzb1   125-zz1

Title   " Lao-tzŭ yüan i "
老 子 元 翼
" Lao-tzŭ i "
老 子 翼

Classification - C-731 道家

Subject - a collection of commentaries by various scholars upon the
"Tao-tê-ching",- "the so-called 'Canon of Reason and Virtue';
a basic work of the Taoist gospel."

References - 163-ggcz 11/10   031-bgld 14/46   012-zafk 14/31
031-bgdf 146/12.

Author - (原 輯) Chiao Hung 焦 竑 .

Edition - the "San-to-chai" 三 多 齋 ; (preface) dated Ch'ien-Lung
"kêng-shên" 5/1740.   Blocks; bamboo paper.

Index - a general table of contents for 2 chüan 上 下 .

Bound in 1 t'ao 4 ts'ê; doubly interleaved.

Remarks - this edition is a fairly good one; and the item is complete
and in very good condition.

The University of Toronto Chinese Library

Accession No. **211**   Index No. - **120-okkk**

Title   " Hung lou mêng t'u yung "

紅　樓　夢　圖　詠

Classification - C-368 小説家

Subject - a collection of sketches and poems illustrating the famous
characters of the "Hung lou mêng" 紅 樓 夢 .- " a popular
tale containing a picture of Chinese domestic life."

References - none.

Author - various.

Edition - no partiéular notation; dated Kuang-Hsü "chi-mao" 5/1879.
Blocks; "fên" paper.

Index - at the beginning of each of 4 ts's.

Bound in 1 t'ao 4 ts's; singly interleaved.

Remarks - a very fine work; the item is as new.

Accession No. 213   Index No. - 044-efze

Title   " Ch'ü Chia wên ho pien "

屈 賈 文 合 編

Classification - C-338 叢書

Subject - a collection of reprints of 4 literary works.

References - 039-pffz 279.

Author - (校 刊) Hsia Hsien-yün 夏 獻 雲.

Edition - the "Ch'angsha-Hsia-shih" 長 沙 夏 氏; dated Kuang-Hsü "ting-ch'ou" 3/1877.   Blocks; "fên" paper.

Index - separate list of contents for each work.

Bound in 1 t'ao 8 ts'ê.

Remarks - a very fine modern edition; the item is almost new.

Accession No. 213   Index No. – 060-ihld

Title   " Fu-an i chi "
              復庵遺集

Classification – D-33 別集一詩文
Subject – an individual literary collection,– prose and poetry.

References – none.

Author – Hsü Chüeh 許珏.

Edition – no notation; (postscriptum) dated "jên-hsü" 1922.
    Blocks; "fên" paper.

Index – a general table of contents for 24 chüan.

Bound in 1 t'ao 8 ts'ê.

Remarks – this is a new work.

244

Accession No. 214   Index No. – 086-ihzn

Title   " Hsi ch'ao jên chien "
　　　　　　　熙　朝　人　鑒

Classification – C-508 雜家 一 雜文

Subject – a collection of historical narratives giving account of
those notables, of the Ch'ing dynasty, to whom blessings
accrued through their performance of meritorious works.

References – none.

Author – Chang Chih-wan 張 之 萬.

Edition – no notation; dated Kuang-Hsü "ting-hai" 13/1887.   Blocks;
"mao-pien" paper.

Index – (上 集) detailed table of contents for 4 chüan; (下 集)
same for 4 chüan.

Bound in 1 t'ao 8 ts'ê.

Remarks – the item is complete and in good condition.

Accession No. 215   Index No. - 030-bzza

Title   " Ssŭ-ma Wên-chêng kung chi "
                 司 馬 文 正 公 集

Classification - D-33 別集－詩文

Subject - an individual miscellaneous collection of writings,- prose
    and poetry.

References - none.

Author - Ssŭ-ma Kuang 司 馬 光；(重鐫) Liu Tsu-tsêng 劉 組 曾.

Edition - the "Po-lu-t'ang" 百 禄 堂; dated Ch'ien-Lung "chia-tzŭ"
    9/1744.   Blocks; bamboo paper.

Index - a classified table of contents for 82 chüan.

Bound in 2 t'ao 20 ts's (10 each).

Remarks - a fairly good edition; in perfect condition and complete.

Accession No. 216   Index No. - 077-joz

Title   " Li-tai ming ch'ên yen hsing lu "
         歷 代 名 臣 言 行 録

Classification - B-117 傳記 - 總錄

Subject - a collection of short biographical notes relating to the
deeds of eminent ministers of the period from the Ch'in 秦
down to the Ming 明 dynasty.

References - 012-zafk 5/19.

Author - .(編-輯) Chu Huan 朱 桓 .

Edition - the "Wei-chai" 蔚 齋 ; dated Chia-Ch'ing "ting-ssŭ" 2/1797.
Blocks; "fên" paper.

Index - a general table of contents for 24 chüan with separate list
for each dynasty.

Bound in 4 t'ao 32 ts'ê (8 each).

Remarks - an ordinary edition; the item is apparently complete and
in good condition.

The University of Toronto Chinese Library

Accession No. 217 (a)   Index No. — 162-gncg

Title   " T'ung chien chi shih pên mo "
通 鑑 紀 事 本 末

Classification — B-32 紀事本末

Subject — a rearrangement of the historical narratives of the
"T'ung Chien" 通 鑑 of Ssŭ-ma Kuang 司 馬 光; which
embraces a period from the 4th century down to the end of
the Five Dynasties 五 代 .

References — Wylie's Notes page 27 163-ggcz 4/10   031-bgld 5/26
106-gdkn 22/11   012-zafk 4/11   031-bgdf 49/1   Gest No. 403.

Author — (編 輯) Yüan Shu 袁 樞; (論 正) Chang P'u 張 溥 .

Edition — the "Ssŭ-hsien-shu-chü" 思 賢 書 局; dated Kuang-Hsü
"mou-hsü" 24/1898.   Blocks; "mao-pien" paper.

Index — a general table of contents for 239 chüan.

Bound in 8 t'ao 64 ts's (8 each).

Remarks — an ordinary edition; the item is complete and in generally
good condition, with the exception of a few repaired defects
and some blurs as a result of careless printing.

Accession No. 217 (b)   Index No. - 048-bkog

Title   " Tso Chuan chi shih pên mo "
             左 傳 紀 事 本 末

Classification - B-32 紀 事 本 末

Subject - a collection of historical narratives based upon the
    "Tso Chuan" 左 傳 .

References - 163-ggoz 4/11   031-bgld 5/29   012-zafk 4/13
    031-bgdf 49/32   Gest No. 851.

Author - Kao Shih-ch'i 高 士 奇 .

Edition - uniform with (a).

Index - a general table of contents for 53 chüan.

Bound in 2 t'ao 12 ts's (8-4); 2nd. t'ao with (c).

Remarks - uniform with (a); but without blurs.

Accession No. 217 (c)   Index No. - 040-dbog

Title   " Sung shih chi shih pên mo "
                宋 史 紀 事 本 末

Classification - B-32 紀事本末

Subject - a collection of historical narratives of the Sung dynasty.

References - Wylie's Notes page 28   165-ggoz 4/10   031-bgld 5/27

     050-iaff 7/19   012-zafk 4/12   031-bgdf 49/8   Gest No. 851.

Author - (編) Fêng Ch'i 馮 琦 ; (增訂) Ch'ên Pang-chan
     陳 邦 瞻

Edition - uniform with (a).

Index - a general table of contents for 109 chüan.

Bound in 3 t'ao 20 ts's (4-8-8); 1st t'ao with (b).

Remarks - uniform with (a); but without blurs.

Accession No. 217 (d)   Index No. - 010-bbcg

Title   " Yüan shih chi shih pên mo "
             元　史　紀　事　本　末

Classification - B-32 紀事本末
Subject - a collection of historical narratives of the Yüan dynasty.

References - Wylie's Notes page 28   163-ggcz 4/10   031-bgld 5/27

    030-iaff 7/19   012-zafk 4/12   031-bgdf 49/9   Gest No. 851.

Author - (編　輯) Ch'ên Pang-chan 陳　邦　瞻；(論　正) Chang P'u
    張　溥 .

Edition - uniform with (a).

Index - a general table of contents for 27 chüan.

Bound in 4 ts'ê in 1 t'ao with (e).

Remarks - uniform with (a); but without blurs.

The University of Toronto Chinese Library

Accession No. 217 (e)   Index No. – 072-dbcg

Title   " Ming shih chi shih pên mo "
　　　　　　　明　史　紀　事　本　末

Classification – B-32 紀事本末

Subject – a collection of historical narratives of the Ming dynasty.

References – Wylie's Notes page 23   165-ggcz 4/10   031-bgld 5/29

　　012-zafk 4/13   031-bgdf 49/30   Gest No. 851.

Author – (編輯) Ku Ying-t'ai 谷 應 泰 .

Edition – uniform with (a).

Index – a general table of contents for 80 chüan.

Bound in 4 t'ao 20 ts's (2-6-6-6); 1st t'ao with (d).

Remarks – uniform with (a); but without blurs.

———•———

Accession No. 218   Index No. — 060-hdgn   162-gnio

Title   " Yü p'i t'ung chien chi lan "
          御 批 通 鑑 輯 覽
          " T'ung chien chi lan "
          通 鑑 輯 覽

Classification — B-22 編年

Subject — compilation of the important events of history, covering
    all dynasties from the time of Emperor Fu-Hsi 伏羲 through
    the Ming Dynasty, with commentaries.

References — 160-1j   163-ggoz 4/9   051-bgld 5/24   012-zafk 4/11
    051-bgdf 47/57   Gest No. 905.

Author — compiled on order of Emperor Ch'ien-Lung by a Board of
    Editors, headed by Fu Hêng 傅 恆 .

Edition — a palace edition; (preface) dated Ch'ien-Lung "ting-hai"
    32/1767.   Blocks; bamboo paper.

Index — a general table of contents for 120 chüan.

Bound in 8 t'ao 60 ts'ê (8-8-8-6-6-8-8-8).

Remarks — this is a fairly good edition; and the item is complete
    but stained in places.

253

Accession No. 219   Index No. - 037-zdzf   072-dzfc

Title   " Ta Ming i t'ung chih "
                大 明 一 統 志

Classification - B-187 地 理 一 總 志
Subject - Geography and Topography under the Ming Dynasty, with
        maps and illustrations.

References - 163-ggoz 5/10   051-bgld 7/5   012-zafk 6/1
        051-bgdf 68/11   Gest No. 2037.

Author - compiled by a commission headed by Li Hsien 李 賢 .

Edition - a Ming edition; (preface) dated T'ien-Shun 5/1461.
        Blocks; "mien" paper.

Index - a general table of contents for 90 chüan.

Bound in   5 t'ao 30 ts'è (6 each); singly interleaved.

Remarks - this is a very good edition; and the item appears to be
        complete.   There are quite a number of defects,- torn pages,
        worm-holes and stains.

folios
needs
dated

254

The University of Toronto Chinese Library

Accession No. **220**   Index No.- 024-gdgf

Title   " Nan hsün shêng tien "

南　巡　盛　典

Classification - B-237 政書－典禮

Subject - a detailed description of inspection tours made by the
Emperor Ch'ien-Lung in the South between 1751-1765.

References - Wylie's Notes page 71 160-1j 163-ggcz 6/4 031-bgld 8/12
012-zafk 9/7 031-bgdf 82/23 Gest No. 1057.

Author - Kao Chin 高晉 and others.

Edition - a palace edition; (preface) dated Ch'ien-Lung "hsin-mao"
36/1771.   Blocks; "fên" paper.

Index - a general table of contents for 120 chüan.

Bound in 4 t'ao 48 ts's. (12 each).

Remarks - a very good edition; complete and in good condition.

Accession No. 221 (a)   Index No. - 018-gkf   085-kf

Title   " Ch'ien Han shu "
                    前　漢　書

Classification - B-12 正史

Subject - a history of China covering the period from 206 B. C.
    to A. D. 24, - that of the "Han Dynasty"; also known under
    the designations (前) "Former Han" and (西) "Western Han".
    The officially recognized standard history of this period.

References - Wylie's Notes page 17 160-1j 163-ggoz 4/2 031-bgld 5/5
    106-gdkn 18/5   012-zafk 4/1   031-bgdf 45/18   Gest No. 1708.

Author - begun by Pan Ku 班 固 and completed by his sister Pan Chao
    班 昭 ; (注) Yen Shih-ku 顏 師 古 .

Edition - the "Chin-ling-shu-chü" 金 陵 書 局; dated T'ung-Chih
    8/1869.   Blocks; "mao-pien" paper.

Index - a general table of contents for 100 chüan.

Bound in 2 t'ao 16 ts's (8-8).

Remarks - a good edition; the item is complete and in good condition.

Accession No. 221 (b)   Index No. – 060-fkf

Title   " Hou Han shu "
                         後 漢 書

Classification – B-12 正史

Subject – a history of China covering the period from A.D. 25 to
    220,– that of the "Later Han Dynasty"; also known under the
    designations "Eastern Han".   The officially recognized
    standard history of this period.

References – Wylie's Notes page 17 160-1j 163-ggcz 4/3 031-bgld 5/7
    106-gdkn 18/6 012-zafk 4/2 031-bgdf 45/23 Gest No. 1710.

Author – of the 帝紀 and 列傳,– Fan Yeh 范 曄; （注）
    Chang Huai t'ai-tzŭ 章 懷 太子; of the 志,– Ssŭ-ma Piao
    司 馬 彪;（注）Liu Chao 劉 昭.

Edition – uniform with (a).

Index – a general table of contents for 130 chüan.

Bound in 2 t'ao 16 ts'ê (8-8).

Remarks – as under (a).

Accession No. 222   Index No. - 075-oddm   086-mgec

Title   " Li Ming-chung ying tsao fa shih "
            李 明 仲 營 造 法 式

Classification -- B-307 政書－考工

Subject - a work on Architecture, with Descriptions of the Building
    of Palaces, their Exteriors and Interiors, Decorations, Plans,
    etc., with many illustrations in black and white and colour
    plates.

References - 163-ggcz 6/5   031-bgld 8/16   167-mhfm 12/13
    012-zafk 9/14   031-bgdf 82/51   Gest No. 305.

Author - Li Chieh 李 誡 .

Edition - a reproduction based upon the Sung edition; dated Min-Kuo
    "i-ch'ou" 14/1925.   Blocks; "fên" paper.

Index - detailed table of contents for 34 chüan.

Bound in 1 t'ao 8 ts's.

Remarks - this is a very fine edition; and the item is new.

258

Accession No. 223   Index No. - 037-abmc

Title   " T'ai p'ing huan yü chi "
                 太 平 寰 宇 記

Classification - B-187 地 理 一 總 志

Subject - general statistical and descriptive view of the Chinese
    empire during the period T'ai-ping-hsing-kuo 太 平 興 國
    (A.D. 976-983).

References - Wylie's Notes page 44   160-1j   163-ggcz 5/9
    031-bgld 7/4   012-zafk 6/1   031-bgdf 68/6   Gest No. 819.

Author - (撰) Lo Shih 樂 史 .

Edition - the "Chin-ling-shu-chü" 金 陵 書 局; dated Kuang-Hsü
    8/1882.   Blocks; "mao-pien" paper.

Index - a general table of contents in 2 sections for 192 chüan
    (originally 200 chüan, chüan 4 and 113 to 119 being lost).

Bound in 4 t'ao 36 ts's (9 each).

Remarks - a modern edition; the item is in perfect condition.

Accession No. 224   Index No. - 120-hndc   044-azhh

Title   " (Ch'ih-mu-t'ang) Kang chien i chih lu "
尺 木 堂 綱 鑑 易 知 録

Classification - B-22 編年

Subject - (Gest No. 1442) - "a history covering the period from the
legendary "Three Emperors" down to the end of the Yüan Dynasty."

References -- Wylie's Notes page 27   012-zafk 4/11.

Author - Wu Ch'êng-ch'üan 吳 乘 權 and others.

Edition - the "Ch'ih-mu-t'ang" 尺 木 堂; (preface) dated K'ang-Hsi
50/1711.   Blocks; "fên" paper.

Index - a table of dynasties and reigns; arranged in chronological
order for 92 chüan; 明 紀 綱 目 20 chüan.

Bound in 8 t'ao 48 ts's (6 each).

Remarks - an ordinary edition; in generally good condition; but
the impression is not very good. Page 23 in chüan 33 is torn
and missing.   A supplement to this work, being the annals of
the Ming Dynasty, is entitled:-
    " Yü-chuan Ming chi kang mu "
    御 撰 明 紀 綱 目   (060-hldc)
    by Chang T'ing-yü 張 廷 玉 and others.

The University of Toronto Chinese Library

Accession No. 225   Index No. - 018-dzk

Title   " Lieh nü chuan "
                     列　女　傳

Classification - B-117 傳記 — 總録

Subject - biographies of famous women in ancient times; with
   illustrations.

References - none.

Author - （輯）Wang-shih 汪 氏；（繪圖）Ch'ou Ying-shih
   仇 英 實

Edition - the "Chih-pu-tsu-chai" 知 不 足 齋；(preface) dated
   Ch'ien-Lung 44/1779.   Blocks; "fēn" paper.

Index - a general table of names in 16 chüan.

Bound in 4 T'ao 24 ts'ê (6 each); doubly interleaved.

Remarks - this is a very fine edition; the item is complete and in
   very good condition.   The impression seems to have been printed
   from Ming blocks; but this is somewhat doubtful.

Accession No. 226   Index No. - 030-fhkc

Title   " Hsien-Shun Lin-an chih "
                   咸 淳 臨 安 志

Classification - B-192 地 理 一 省 志

Subject - "Gazeteer of the city of Hangchow in Chekiang province,
        its old name being Lin-an , capital of the Southern Sung
        Dynasty -----" (Gest No. 883).

References - 163-ggcz 5/11   031-bgld 7/10   012-zafk 6/4
        031-bgdf 68/28   Gest No. 883.

Author - (撰) Ch'ien Shuo-yu 潛 說 友.

Edition - the "Chên-ch'i-t'ang" 振 綺 堂 ; dated Tao-Kuang
        "kêng-yin" 10/1830.   Blocks; "mao-pien" paper.

Index - a table of contents for 96 chüan (originally 100 chüan;
        chüan 90-98-99-100 being lost); 札 記 3 chüan.

Bound in 4 t'ao 24 ts's (6 each).

Remarks - a good edition; in good condition except for a few
        worm-holes.

262

Accession No.   227   Index No. - 120-mb

Title   " I shih "
                        繹   史

Classification - B-32 紀事本末

Subject - (Gest No. 671),- "complete records of Chinese history
    from the remotest times to the end of the Ch'in Dynasty
    (206 B.C.)-------."

References - Wylie's Notes page 28 163-ggcz 4/11   031-bgld 5/29
    012-zafk 4/13   031-bgdf 49/31   Gest No. 671.

Author - Ma Su 馬驌.

Edition - no notation; (preface) dated K'ang-Hsi 9/1670.   Blocks;
    "mao-pien" paper.

Index - a general table of contents for 160 chüan.

Bound in 6 t'ao 50 ts's.

Remarks - a modern edition; the item is as new.

Accession No. 228   Index No. - 031-bgld

Title   " Ssǔ k'u chien ming mu lu piao chu "

四 庫 簡 明 目 錄 標 注

Classification - B-342 目錄一經籍

Subject - (Gest No. 947).-"Abridged edition of the Catalogue of
the Imperial Library during the reign of Emperor Ch'ien-Lung
(1736-1796), with additional notes and remarks----."

References - Gest No. 947.

Author - Shao I-ch'ên 邵 懿 辰.

Edition - no notation; dated Hsüan-T'ung 3/1911.   Blocks; "mao-pien"
paper.

Index - none; in 20 chüan arranged according to the usual 4 main
classifications of Chinese literature.

Bound in 1 t'ao 6 ts'ê.

Remarks - a fairly good modern edition; the item is new.

Accession No. **229**   Index No. — 072-ofgd

Title   " <u>Pao-shu-t'ing chi</u> "
                          曝　書　亭　集

Classification — D-33 別集 － 詩文

Subject — a miscellaneous individual collection of literary
compositions,— prose and poetry.

References — 163-ggcz 15/11   031-bgld 18/39   012-zafk 17/14
031-bgdf 173/25.

Author — (撰) <u>Chu I-tsun</u> 朱　彝　尊．

Edition — no notation; no date; possibly K'ang-Hsi.   Blocks;
bamboo paper.

Index — detailed table of contents for 80 chüan; 附　録　1 chüan;
笛　漁　小　豪 10 chüan.

Bound in 2 t'ao 20 ts'é (10 each).

Remarks — a fairly good edition; the item has no defects and is
apparently complete.   A supplement to this work, consisting
of poetical writings, is entitled :-
                " <u>Ti　yü　hsiao　kao</u> "
                笛　漁　小　豪   (118-ekzj)

265

———•———

Accession No. 230   Index No. - 145-gioz

Title   " Pu-kuo-chai wên tu "
　　　　　　　補　過　齋　文　牘

Classification — B-77 詔令奏議 － 公文

Subject — a miscellaneous collection of official documents,-
　　circulars, announcements, reports etc.,- written and
　　issued by the author during his governorship of Hsinkiang
　　at the beginning of the Chinese Republic.

References — none.

Author — Yang Tsêng-hsin 楊 增 新.

Edition — privately published; (preface) dated Min-Kuo 10/1921.
　　Blocks; "mao-pien" paper.

Index — separate lists of contents for each subdivision of the 10
　　main divisions.

Bound in 4 t'ao 32 ts'ê.

Remarks — a good modern edition; the item is in perfect condition.

Accession No. 251   Index No. – 040-hlgd   030-gdzh

Title   " (Yü-hsüan) T'ang-Sung wên shun "

御　選　唐　宋　文　醇

Classification – D-73 總集－文

Subject – an anthology of prose compositions of the T'ang and Sung
periods.

References – 163-ggoz 16/10   031-bgld 19/33   012-zafk 19/15
031-bgdf 190/13.

Author – various; prose selected under the direction of the Emperor
Ch'ien-Lung 乾隆.

Edition – the "Chê-chiang-shu-chü" 浙江書局; dated Kuang-Hsü
3/1877.   Blocks; "mao-pien" paper.

Index – a detailed table of contents for 58 chüan; separate list
for each chüan.

Bound in 2 t'ao 20 ts's (10 each).

Remarks – a rather ordinary edition; but complete and without
defects.   The impression in general is not very good.

267

Accession No. 232   Index No. - 146-zic

Title   " Hsi hu chih "
                 西 湖 志

Classification - B-297 地 理 — 山 川

Subject - (Gest No. 1532) - "a general topography of the "West Lake"
    region near Hangchow; including chapters on the scenery;
    sea-walls; bridges; gardens and pavilions; monasteries and
    temples; shrines; monuments; antiquities; famous men; literature;
    paintings; etc.; etc. (illustrated)".

References - Wylie's Notes page 55   051-bgld 7/23   012-zafk 8/8
    051-bgdf 76/40   Gest No. 1532.

Author - (總 修) Fu Wang-lu 傅 王 露.

Edition - the "Chê-kiang-shu-chü" 浙 江 書 局; dated Kuang-Hsü
    4/1878.   Blocks; "fên" paper.

Index - a table of contents for 48 chüan; arranged according to
    subject matter.

Bound in 2 t'ao 20 ts's (10 each).

Remarks - the item is complete and in very good condition.

The University of Toronto Chinese Library

Accession No.　233　　　　　Index No. - 149-oczf

Title　　　　　　" Tu Tu hsin chieh "
　　　　　　　　　讀　杜　心　解

Classification - D-38 別集－詩

Subject - a collection of some 1500 poems written by the famous
　　　poet Tu Fu 杜 甫 ; classified, rearranged and with annotations
　　　and explanations.

References - 012-zafk 15/6　031-bgdf 147/14　Toronto No. 72.

Author - (講 解) P'u Ch'i-lung 浦 起 龍.

Edition - the "Ning-6-chai" 寧 我 齋; (preface) dated Yung-Chêng
　　　2/1724.　　　Blocks; bamboo paper.

Index - a general table of contents for 6 chüan; with detailed lists
　　　for each subdivision of the 6 chüan.

Bound in 2 t'ao 12 ts's (6 each).

Remarks - this is a good edition; the item is in good condition
　　　with the exception of some stains.

Accession No. 234   Index No. - 060-h1gd   030-gdfh

Title   " (Yü-hsüan) T'ang-Sung shih shun "
               御 選 唐 宋 詩 醇

Classification - D-68 總集一詩

Subject - (Gest No. 1704)- "an anthology of poems of the T'ang and
          Sung periods.

References - 163-ggsz 16/10   031-bgld 19/33   012-zafk 19/15
          031-bgdf 190/14   Gest No. 1704.

Author - various; poems selected under the direction of the Emperor
          Ch'ien-Lung 乾 隆.

Edition - the "Chá-kiang-shu-chü" 浙 江 書 局; dated Kuang-Hsü
          7/1881.   Blocks; "mao-pien" paper.

Index - a detailed list of poems; 47 chüan.   Separate list at the
          beginning of each chüan.

Bound in 2 t'ao 20 ts's (10 each).

Remarks - the item is in good condition and complete.

270

Accession No. 235   Index No. - 085-kfd

Title   " Han shu ch'ao "

漢 書 鈔

Classification - B-137 史鈔

Subject - (Gest No. 767) - "The historical work Han Shu, or 'History of the Former Han Dynasty' by Pan Ku 班 固 rewritten on the basis of information derived from the Shih Chi of Ssŭ-ma Ch'ien 司 馬 遷 and other personal studies------."

References - 012-zafk 5/23   Gest No. 767.

Author - by Mao K'un 茅 坤.

Edition - privately published; (preface) dated Ch'ung-Chêng "i-hai" 8/1635.   Blocks; bamboo paper.

Index - a general table of contents for 93 chüan.

Bound in 4 t'ao 22 ts's (5-5-6-6).

Remarks - a good edition; the item is complete and has practically no defects except 2 or 3 repaired worm-holes.

The University of Toronto Chinese Library

Accession No. 236   Index No. - 170-ezeb

Title   " A-wên-ch'êng kung nien p'u "

阿 文 成 公 年 譜

Classification - B-107 傳記一獨録

Subject - biography and chronological record of Chang-chia Ai-kuei

章 佳 阿 桂.

References - 012-zafk 5/7   160-1j   Gest No. 1128.

Author - compiled by a board of editors headed by Na Yen-ch'êng

那 彥 成.

Edition - privately published; dated Chia-Ch'ing "kuei-yu" 18/1813.

Blocks; "fên" paper.

Index - none; in 16 chüan.

Bound in 2 t'ao 16 ts'ê (8-8).

Remarks - this item is incomplete.   012-zafk gives the number of

chüan as 24.

The University of Toronto Chinese Library

Title " T'ieh ch'in t'ung chien lou ts'ang shu mu lu "

鐵 琴 銅 劍 樓 藏 書 目 錄

Classification - B-342 目錄 一經籍

Subject - (Gest No. 986) - "catalogue of books antedating the Ming dynasty period-----."

References - 012-zafk 9/10 Gest No. 986.

Author - compiled by Ch'ü Yung 瞿 鏞.

Edition - the "Ku-li-chia-shu" 邑 里 家 塾; (preface) dated "ting-ssŭ" 1917. Blocks; "mao-pien" paper.

Index - a general table of classifications in 24 chüan.

Bound in 1 t'ao 10 ts'e.

Remarks - a good modern edition; in very good condition.

Accession No. 238 (a)   Index No. - 050-gio

Title   " T'ang hui yao "

唐 會 要

Classification - B-282 政書一通制

Subject - a treatise on governmental affairs of the T'ang 唐
dynasty; and consisting of classified details of all state
matters during the different reigns.

References - Wylie's Notes page 69   031-bgld 3/5   012-zafk 9/4
031-bgdf 31/4.

Author - Wang P'u 王溥.

Edition - the "Chiang-su-shu-chü" 江 蘇 書 局 ; dated Kuang-Hsü
"chia-shên" 10/1884.   Blocks; "mao-pien" paper.

Index - a table of contents for 100 chüan.

Bound in 4 t'ao 24 ts's (6 each).

Remarks - this is a good modern edition; and the item is complete
and has no defects.

Accession No.   238 (b)   Index No. - 007-bc1c

Title   " Wu-tai hui yao "

五 代 會 要

Classification - B-232 政書一通制

Subject - a treatise on governmental affairs of the Five Dynasties

五 代 ; and consisting of classified details of all state

matters during the different reigns.

References - Wylie's Notes page 69   031-bgld 3/5   012-zafk 9/4

031-bgdf 31/5.

Author - Wang P'u 王 溥 .

Edition - as under (a); but dated Kuang-Hsü "ping-hsü" 12/1886.

Index - a table of contents for 30 chüan.

Bound in 1 t'ao 6 ts's.

Remarks - as under (a).

Accession No. 258 (c)   Index No. - 146-zkic

Title   " Hsi-Han hui yao "
                    西 漢 會 要

Classification - B-282 政書－通制

Subject - a summary of events during the Western 西 or the Former Han
     前 漢 dynasty; the material being taken from Pan Ku's history.

References - Wylie's Notes page 70   051-bgld 8/6   012-zafk 9/4
     051-bgdf 81/10.

Author - Hsü T'ien-lin 徐 天 麟.

Edition - as under (a).

Index - a general table of contents for 70 chüan.

Bound in 1 t'ao 10 ts's.

Remarks - as under (a).

Accession No.   238 (d)   Index No. - 075-dkic

Title   " **Tung-Han hui yao** "
                   東　漢　會　要

Classification - B-282 政書 —通制

Subject - a summary of events during the <u>Eastern</u> 東 or the
          <u>Later Han</u> 後 漢 dynasty; together with a discussion of
          various problems of that period.

References - Wylie's Notes page 70   031-bgld 8/6   012-zafk 9/4
          031-bgdf 81/11.

Author - <u>Hsü T'ien-lin</u> 徐 天 麟 .

Edition - as under (a).

Index - a table of contents for 40 chüan.

Bound in 1 t'ao 8 ts's.

Remarks - as under (a).

Accession No. 259   Index No. - 051-edgf

Title   " Hsing Lu shêng tien "
                幸 魯 盛 典

Classification - B-287 政書－典禮

Subject - (Gest No. 1736) - "Record of a visit of Emperor K'ang-Hsi
    in the 23rd year of his reign in A.D. 1684 to the Temple and
    Tomb of Confucius at Ch'ü-fu and its neighborhood to observe
    the proper rites and ceremonies in honour of the Sage and his
    teachings."

References - 165-ggcz 6/4   051-bgld 8/12   012-zafk 9/7
    051-bgdf 82/18   Gest No. 1736.

Author - by K'ung Yü-ch'i 孔 毓 圻 and K'ung Yü-yen 孔 毓 埏；
    and an Imperial commission headed by Chin Chü-ching 金 居 敬．

Edition - a palace edition; (preface) dated K'ang-Hsi 28/1689.
    Blocks; "k'ai-hua" paper.

Index - none; 40 chüan.

Bound in 1 t'ao 20 ts's.

Remarks - this is a very good edition; and the item is complete and
    in very good condition, with the exception of a few worm-holes
    in the 1st ts's and some slight stains in the last ts's.

The University of Toronto Chinese Library

Accession No. 240   Index No. - 007-bcb   069-ibcb

Title   " (Hsin) Wu-tai shih "

新 五 代 史

Classification - B-12 正史

Subject - (Gest No. 1719) - "a history of China covering the period
from A. D. 907 to 959,- that of the "Epoch of the Five Dynasties".
The officially recognized (new) standard history of this period."

References - Wylie's Notes page 22   160-1j   163-ggcz 4/5
031-bgld 5/13   030-iaff 6/17   012-zafk 4/6   031-bgdf 46/11
Gest No. 1719.

Author - Ou-yang Hsiu 歐 陽 修; （注）Hsü Wu-tang 徐 無 黨;
（評）Yang Shên 楊 慎.

Edition - the "Ts'un-ku-chai" 存 古 齋; no date; but of the
Ming period.   Blocks; bamboo paper.

Index - a table of chapter headings for 74 chüan.

Bound in 1 t'ao 12 ts'ê.

Remarks - this item is stained to some extent around the margins;
having some slight defects,- repaired top and bottom margins
etc. Pages missing are as follows:- Chüan 6 pages 9, 10.
Chüan 39 page 11.

The University of Toronto Chinese Library

Accession No. 241 (a)   Index No. - 162-jmcz

Title   " Hsün-hsüeh-chai wên ch'ao "
               遜 學 齋 文 鈔

Classification - D-43 別集一文

Subject - a miscellaneous individual collection of prose.

References - Gest No. 1183   012-zafk 18/33.

Author - Sun I-yen 孫 衣 言 .

Edition - no notation; dated T'ung-Chih 12/1873; but this is for the
   original blocks and edition.   This item is a later impression
   as the text contains dates as late as Kuang-Hsü 17/1891.
   Blocks; "mao-pien" paper.

Index - a general table of contents for 12 chüan with separate table
   for each chüan; "supplement" 續 鈔 - 5 chüan in 5 separate
   lists.

Bound in 2 t'ao 8 ts's; second t'ao with (b).

Remarks - this is a rather poor edition; however, the item is
   complete.

280

Accession No. 241 (b)   Index No. - 162-jmof

Title   " Hsün-hsüeh-chai shih ch'ao "
遜　學　齋　詩　鈔

Classification - D-38 別集 — 詩

Subject - a miscellaneous individual collection of poems.

References - 012-zafk 18/33   Gest No. 1183.

Author - Sun I-yen 孫 衣 言.

Edition - uniform with (a), except the date of the blocks is
    T'ung-Chih 3/1864.

Index - none; in 10 chüan; "supplement" 續 鈔 5 chüan.

Bound in 1 t'ao 4 ts's with (a).

Remarks - as under (a).

Accession No. 242   Index No. - 212-zijc

Title   " Lung-yu hsien chih "
               龍 游 縣 志

Classification - B-194 地 理 一 別 志

Subject - a general topography of the district of Lung-yu (obsolete,
    now called Lo-shan 樂 山) in the province of Szechuan;
    including chapters on famous men and women; literature; etc.

References - none.

Author - Yü Shao-sung 余 紹 宋.

Edition - the "Ching-ch'êng-yin-shu-chü" 京 城 印 書 局 ; (preface)
    dated Min-Kuo 14/1925.   Blocks; "mao-pien" paper.

Index - a general table of chapter headings for 42 chüan.

Bound in 2 t'ao 16 ts'ê (8 each).

Remarks - the edition is new.

Accession No. 245   Index No. - 085-lpjz

Title   " Ch'êng-huai-yüan wên ts'un "
                澄 懷 園 文 存

Classification - D-43 別集 - 文

Subject - an individual miscellaneous collection of prose compositions.

References - none.

Author - by Chang T'ing-yü 張廷玉.

Edition - the "Yün-chien-kuan-shê" 雲間官舍 ; dated Kuang-Hsü
        17/1891.   Blocks; "mao-pien" paper.

Index - detailed table of contents for 15 chüan.

Bound in 1 t'ao 6 ts's.

Remarks - a very ordinary edition; complete and without any defects.

The University of Toronto Chinese Library

Accession No. 244   Index No. - 170-1gjc

Title   " <u>Yang-hsin hsien chih</u> "
　　　　　　陽　信　縣　志

Classification - B-194 地 理 一 別 志

Subject - a general topography of the <u>Yang-hsin</u> district in the
　　　province of <u>Shantung</u>; including chapters on education; famous
　　　men and women; literature; natural products; etc.

References - 012-zafk 6/19.

Author - originally by <u>Wang Yün-shên</u> 王 允 深 ; revised by a
　　　Board of Editors headed by <u>Chu Lan</u> 朱 蘭 ．

Edition - no notation; dated "ping-yin" 1926.   Blocks; Japanese
　　　paper.

Index - a general table of contents for 8 chüan, arranged according
　　　to subject matters.

Bound in 1 t'ao 8 ts's.

Remarks - this is a very fine new edition.

Accession No. **245**   Index No. **- 076-kijh**

Title   " <u>Ou yu tsa lu</u> "
               歐 游 雜 錄

<u>Classification</u> **- B-222** 地 理 一 游 記

<u>Subject</u> **-** record of a journey to the European countries, principally
     Germany and including England, France and other states passed
     on the way; made by <u>Hsü Chien-yin</u> in the 5th year of Kuang-Hsü
     under Imperial order.

<u>References</u> **- none.**

<u>Author</u> **- <u>Hsü Chien-yin</u>** 徐 建 寅 .

<u>Edition</u> **-** no notation; no date; but undoubtedly of the Kuang-Hsü
     period.   Blocks; "fēn" paper.

<u>Index</u> **-** none; 2 chüan 上 下 .

<u>Bound in</u> 1 t'ao 2 ts's.

<u>Remarks</u> **-** an ordinary edition; apparently complete and in good
     condition.

The University of Toronto Chinese Library

Accession No. 246   Index No. - 012-dck

Title   " Lieh hsien chuan "
列　仙　傳

Classification - C-721 道家

Subject - a collection of biographies of some sixty Taoist immortals;
together with portraits.

References - Wylie's Notes page 218   031-bgld 14/49   012-zafk 14/33
031-bgdf 146/32.

Author - reputed to be Liu Hsiang 劉向 ; (輯) Huan-ch'u-t'ao-jen
還 初 道 人.

Edition - the "Sao-yeh-shan-fang" 埽 葉 山 房 ; dated Kuang-Hsü
"ting-hai" 13/1887.   Blocks; "fên" paper.

Index - a general table of names for 4 chüan.

Bound in 1 t'ao 4 ts's; doubly interleaved.

Remarks - the item is in good condition and complete.

Accession No. 247   Index No. - 153-zgic

Title   " Chih-shêng pien nien shih chi "
          至 聖 編 年 世 紀

Classification - B-107 傳記 — 獨録

Subject - the memoirs of Confucius arranged chronologically with
         numerous references to other historical works of a similar
         character; and also an account of the proper rites and
         respects paid to the Sage by various emperors from the period
         of the death of Confucius down to the period of Ch'ien-Lung.

References - 031-bgdf 59/17.

Author - (仝 輯) Li Shuo 李 灼 and Huang Shêng 黄 晟 •

Edition - the "I-chêng-t'ang" 亦 政 堂 ; dated Ch'ien-Lung "hsin-wei"
         16/1751.   Blocks; "mao-pien" paper.

Index - a general table of contents for 24 chüan,- chüan 1 to 16
         arranged chronologically chüan 17 to 24 dynastically.

Bound in 2 t'ao 12 ts's (6 each).

Remarks - this edition is a fairly good one; and the item is complete
         and in perfect condition.

The University of Toronto Chinese Library

Accession No. 248   Index No. – 062-gage

Title   " Ch'i Shao-pao nien p'u ch'i pien "
          戚 少 保 年 譜 耆 編

Classification – B-107 傳記 – 獨録
Subject – the biography and chronological record of Ch'i Chi-kuang
          戚 繼 光．

References – none.

Author – by his son Ch'i Tsu-kuo 戚 祚 國 and others of his family.

Edition – the "Hsien-yu-ch'ung-hsün-tz'ŭ" 仙遊 崇 勳 祠 ; dated
          Tao-Kuang "ting-wei" 27/1847.   Blocks; "fên" paper.

Index – none; 12 chüan.

Bound in 1 t'ao 12 ts's.

Remarks – this edition is not a good one at all; but the item is
          complete.

Accession No. 249 (a)   Index No. - 030-bzag

Title   " Ssŭ-ma t'ai-shih-wên-kuo Wên-chêng kung nien p'u "
司 馬 太 師 溫 國 文 正 公 年 譜

Classification - B-107 傳記 — 獨録
Subject - the biography of Ssŭ-ma Kuang 司 馬 光.
王 安 石.

References - 029-pffz 241.

Author - (著) Ku Tung-kao 顧 棟 高.

Edition - the "Ch'iu-shu-chai" 求 恕 齋 ; dated "ting-ssŭ" 1917.
    Blocks; "mao-pien" paper.

Index - a general table of contents arranged chronologically;
    10 chüan.

Bound in 4 ts's in 1 t'ao with (b).

Remarks - the item is new.

————◆————

Accession No. **250**   Index No. - **077-nzee**   **149-eebc**

Title   " Kuei Fang p'ing tien Shih chi "

歸　方　評　點　史　記

" P'ing tien Shih chi "

評　點　史　記

Classification - **B-367** 史 評

Subject - (a) critical commentary on the Shih chi 史 記 of

Ssǔ-ma Ch'ien 司 馬 遷 by Kuei Yu-kuang; (b) a short

work of a similar character by Fang Pao.

References - to (a) - 012-zafk 9/28.

Author - Kuei Yu-kuang 歸 有 光 and Fang Pao 方 苞 .

Edition - published by "Chang Yü-chao" 張 裕 釗 ; dated Kuang-Hsü

2/1876.   Blocks; "fěn" paper.

Index - (a) a general table of contents for 130 chüan; (b) none;

4 chüan.

Bound in 2 t'ao 20 ts'ê (10 each).

Remarks - an ordinary good edition; the item has no defects and is

apparently complete.

Accession No.   251   Index No. - 067-zffg

Title   " Wên chang chih nan "
                 文　章　指　南

Classification - D-73 總集一文

Subject - " a general collection of literary compositions written
    by famous ancient scholars; classified into 5 general headings
    with subdivisions for each." (Toronto No. 68)

References - 031-bgdf 192/41 Toronto No. 68.

Author - (編) Kuei Yu-kuang 歸 有 光 ; (蒐輯) Hsü Hsiao-lien
    許 筱 蓮 .

Edition - the "Wan-chiang-chieh-shu" 皖 江 節 署 ; dated Kuang-Hsü
    2/1876. Blocks; "mao-pien" paper.

Index - a detailed table of contents for 5 集   , each consisting of
    a few subdivisions; separate lists for each subdivision.

Bound in 1 t'ao 4 ts's.

Remarks - this is an ordinary edition; in good condition and the
    item is complete.

The University of Toronto Chinese Library

Accession No. 252   Index No. - 106-ahkk

Title   " Po chiang t'u chuan "
                  百　將　圖　傳

Classification - B-117 傳記 一 總錄

Subject - a collection of short biographical notes, together with
    illustrations, of 100 generals noted for their distinguished
    deeds during the period dating from the Chou 周 to the Ming 明
    dynasty.

References - none.

Author - Ting Jih-chang 丁 日 昌 .

Edition - no notation; (preface) dated T'ung-Chih 9/1870.   Blocks;
    "fên" paper.

Index - 2 separate lists of names; in 2 chüan 上 下 .

Bound in 1 t'ao 6 ts'ê; doubly interleaved.

Remarks - this is a fairly good edition; and the item is in very
    fine condition.

Accession No. 253   Index No. - 154-fegn

Title   " <u>Tzŭ chih t'ung chien kang mu fa ming</u> "
          資 治 通 鑑 綱 目 發 明

Classification - B-367 史 評

Subject - an elucidation of the "<u>Tzŭ chih t'ung chien kang mu</u>" of
    <u>Chu Hsi</u> 朱熹 ,- " a reconstruction and condensation of the
    '<u>T'ung chien</u>' 通鑑 ".

References - Wylie's Notes page 25   163-ggcz 4/8   012-zafk 9/23
    Gest No. 643.

Author - <u>Yin Ch'i-hsin</u> 尹起莘 .

Edition - no notation; (preface) dated Chia-Ch'ing 8/1803.   Blocks;
    "mao-pien" paper.

Index - none; 59 chüan.

Bound in 1 t'ao 6 ts's.

Remarks - a good edition; the item is complete and in generally
    good condition with the exception of a few worm-holes and
    some slight stains.   In 163-ggcz and Wylie's Notes this
    work has been classified under B-22.

294

———•———

Accession No. 254   Index No. - 030-gn

Title   " T'ang chien "

唐　鑑

Classification - B-367 史 評

Subject - an explanation of matters of the T'ang period, and more
    particularly criminal affairs.

References - 163-ggoz 6/9   031-bgld 8/29   167-mhfm 12/19
    012-zafk 9/27   031-bgdf 88/5   Gest No. 917.

Author - (撰) Fan Tsu-yü 范 祖 禹 .

Edition - no notation; (preface) dated Yüan-Yu 1/1086; but this item
    appears to have been published during the Chia-Ch'ing period
    of the Ch'ing Dynasty.   Blocks; bamboo paper.

Index - none; 24 chüan.

Bound in 1 t'ao 4 ts's.

Remarks - this item is complete and has some slight defects,-
    worm-holes.

The University of Toronto Chinese Library

Accession No. 255   Index No. - 064-icci   021-cize

Title   " Yang-chou pei hu hsiao chih "
             揚 州 北 湖 小 志

Classification - B-207 地 理 — 山 川

Subject - (Gest No. 2334) - "a general description of the North Lake
    region of Yang-chou."

References - 012-zafk 8/9   Gest No. 2334.

Author - (著) Chiao Hsün 焦 循 .

Edition - no particular notation; (preface) dated Chia-Ch'ing
    "mou-ch'ên" 13/1808.   Blocks; "fên" paper.

Index - a detailed table of contents for 6 chüan.

Bound in 1 t'ao 4 ts'ê; doubly interleaved.

Remarks - this is a complete item with some repaired top margins.

The University of Toronto Chinese Library

Accession No. 256   **Index No.** - 030-bgga

Title
" Shih t'ung t'ung shih "
史   通   通   釋

Classification - B-367 史 評

Subject - an historical critique; being an elaboration of the
"Shih t'ung".

References - 160-1j   163-ggcz 6/9   031-bgld 8/28   012-zafk 9/27
031-bgdf 88/4   Gest No. 97.

Author - (撰) P'u Ch'i-lung 浦 起 龍 .

Edition - no notation; dated Kuang-Hsü "i-yu" 11/1885.   Blocks;
"fên" paper.

Index - a general table of contents for 20 chüan.

Bound in - 1 t'ao 6 ts'ê.

Remarks - an ordinary edition; complete and without defects.

Accession No. 257   Index No. - (a) 037-zgc   (b) 037-zgcf
                                             (c) 037-zgcg

Title   (a)   " Ta shih chi "
                      大   事   記

        (b)   " Ta shih chi chieh t'i "

        (#)   大   事   記   解   題

Classification - B-22 編年

Subject - "a series of historical criticisms; covering the period

    from (Chou) Ching-Wang （周） 敬 王 39/481 B.C. to

    (Han) Wu-Ti Chêng-Ho （漢） 武 帝 - 征 和 3/90 B.C."

    (Gest No. 1977).

References - 160-1; 163-ggcz 4/8   031-bgld 5/22   167-mhfm 9/10

    106-gdkn 20/19   012-zafk 4/9   031-bgdf 47/35   Gest No. 1977.

Author - (撰) Lü Tsu-ch'ien 呂 祖 謙.

Edition - the "Wu-ying-tien" 武 英 殿; dated Ch'ien-Lung 51/1786.

    Blocks; "fên" paper.

Index - none; (a) 12 chüan; (b) 12 chüan; (c) 3 chüan.

Bound in 2 t'ao 20 ts's; (10-10); doubly interleaved.

Remarks - a useful historical reference work.   The item is complete

    and has no defects except some slight stains.

    (#)   (c) " Ta shih chi t'ung shih "
              大   事   記   通   釋

The University of Toronto Chinese Library

Accession No.   258   Index No. - 018-mgk

Title   " Chien   hsieh   chuan "

劍　俠　傳

Classification - C-368 小説家

Subject - (Wylie) - "----- is a series of biographical notices of
remarkable swordsmen during the T'ang dynasty."

References - Wylie's Notes page 199   012-zafk 14/13   031-bgdf 144/3.

Author - not stated.

Edition - the "Yang-ho-t'ang" 敦 穌 堂 ; dated Hsien-Feng "mou-wu"
8/1858.   Blocks; "fan" paper.

Index - a table of contents for 4 chüan.

Bound in 1 t'ao 2 ts'e; doubly interleaved.

Remarks - a very good edition; the item is complete and in generally
good condition,- defects in last 3 pages of 2nd ts'e.

Accession No. 259   Index No. - 169-jzg

Title   " Ch'üeh-li chih "
                         闕　里　誌

Classification - B-107 傳記 一 獨録

Subject - a general description of Ch'üeh-li, a place in Ch'ü-fu,

    Shantung, where Confucius resided and started his teaching;

    together with chapters on the historical remains; the biography

    and chronological record of the Sage; his temple and grave; etc.

References - 012-zafk 5/1   031-bgdf 59/4.

Author - (撰) Ch'ên Hao 陳 鎬 .

Edition - reprinted from old Ming blocks; undated.   Blocks;

    "k'ai-hua" paper.

Index - a general table of contents for 24 chüan.

Bound in 1 t'ao 10 ts'ê.

Remarks - a fine edition; the item appears to be complete and in

    generally good condition,- some slight stains.

Accession No. 260   Index No. - 030-bggk

Title   " Shih t'ung hsiao fan "
                    史 通 削 繁

Classification - B-367 史 評
Subject - an historical critique; being an abridgment of the
     "Shih-t'ung".

References - 012-zafk 9/27.

Author - (撰) Chi Yün 紀 昀.

Edition - the "Liang-kuang-chieh-shu" 兩 廣 節 署 ; dated Tao-Kuang
     13/1833.   Blocks; "fên" paper.

Index - a general table of contents for 4 chüan.

Bound in 1 t'ao 4 ts's.

Remarks - a complete item in good condition.   This work is with
     punctuations and marginal notes in red.

Accession No.   261   Index No. - 012-zofz   167-zzga

Title   " Pa-ch'iung-shih Chin shih pu chêng "
             八 瓊 室 金 石 補 正

Classification - B-347 目錄一金石
Subject - a comprehensive description of inscriptions on stones and
    metals covering nearly all dynasties in Chinese history from
    the period of Chou downwards; written after the model of the
    "Chin shih sui pien" 金 石 萃 編 , and with additions and
    corrections.
References - none.

Author - (撰) Lu Tsêng-hsiang 陸 增 祥.

Edition - the "Hsi-ku-lou" 希 古 樓 ; (preface) dated "i-ch'ou"
    1925.   Blocks; "mao-pien" paper.

Index - a detailed list of "inscriptions" for 130 chüan arranged
    chronologically; the list itself in 3 sections.

Bound in 8 t'ao 64 ts'ê

Remarks - a useful reference work, very well arranged.   The item is
    almost new.   The following works are the supplements and of a
    similar character:-

    (#)

" **Chin shih cha chi** "

金 石 札 記

4 chüan (167-zzac)

" **Chin shih ch'ü wei** "

金 石 袪 僞

1 chüan (167-zzel)

" **Yüan chin shih ou ts'un** "

元 金 石 偶 存

1 chüan (010-bzzi)

The University of Toronto Chinese Library

Accession No. 262   Index No. - 075-cddm   086-mgec

Title   " Li Ming-chung ying tsao fa shih "
             李 明 仲 營 造 法 式

Classification - B-307 政書 一考工

Subject - a work on Architecture with Descriptions of the Building
    of Palaces, their Exteriors and Interiors, Decorations, Plans,
    etc., with many illustrations.

References - 163-ggcz 6/5   031-bgld 8/16   167-mhfm 12/13
    012-zafk 9/14   031-bgdf 82/51   Gest No. 305   Toronto No. 222.

Author - Li Chieh 李 誠 .

Edition - no notation; dated Min-Kuo 8/1917.   Lithographed on "fên"
    paper.

Index - a detailed table of contents for 34 chüan.

Bound in 1 t'ao 8 ts'ê.

Remarks - a very fine modern edition; the item is as new.   Toronto
    No. 222 is much superior to this item.

Accession No.   263 (a)   Index No. - 072-ddbk

Title   " Ming chuang yüan t'u k'ao "
                明 狀 元 圖 考

Classification - B-117 傳記 一 總錄

Subject - " a collection of illustrated notes regarding incidents in
    the lives of scholars who came out first at the triennial
    palace examinations during the Ming Dynasty." (Gest No. 3535-a)

References - 012-zafk 5/14 Gest No. 3534-a.

Author - (彙編) Ku Ting-ch'ên 顧 鼎 臣 . (see Remarks)

Edition - the "Fu-yüan-shu-shih" 福 元 書 室 ; dated Hsien-Fêng
    6/1856. Blocks; "fên" paper.

Index - a general table of contents for 3 chüan; covering the period
    from A.D. 1371-1607; detailed lists at the beginning of each
    chüan.

Bound in 6 ts'ê in 1 t'ao with (b); doubly interleaved.

Remarks - a very good edition; the item is complete and in very
    good condition.
        012-zafk gives the author as T'ang Pin-yin 湯 賓 尹 .

Accession No. 265 (b)　　　Index No. - 031-hhbb

Title　　　" Kuo ch'ao san yüan t'i yung "

國 朝 三 元 題 咏

Classification - D-68 總集一詩

Subject - "two collections of poems composed upon and for the
occasions of the Imperial banquets given in honor of the
"triple first" (三元) Ch'ien Ch'i 錢棨 (Chien-Lung
"hsin-ch'ou" 46/1781) and "quadruple first" (四元)
Ch'en Chi-ch'ang 陳繼昌 (Chia-Ch'ing "keng-ch'en"　(#)

References - 012-zafk 19/15.

Author - (編) Lu Hsi-hsiung 陸錫熊.

Edition - uniform with (a).

Index - a detailed table of contents at the beginning of each of
2 chüan.

Bound in 2 ts'e in 1 t'ao with (a); doubly interleaved.

Remarks - as under (a).

(#)　25/1820)."　　(Gest No. 3535-b).

The University of Toronto Chinese Library

Accession No. 264   Index No. - 062-1hf

Title   " Chan kuo ts'ê "
               戰 國 策

Classification - B-52 雜史

Subject - (Gest No. 298)-" Narrative of the Contending States
    (Ch'in, Ch'u, Ch'i, Yen, Han, Chao and Wei), contending
    for Empire during the last two centuries of the Chou Dynasty
    (B.C. 1122-255)----"

References - Wylie's Notes page 32   Gest No. 298.

Author - unknown; (合 評) Ch'ên Jên-hsi 陳 仁 錫 and Chung Hsing
    鍾 惺 .

Edition - no particular notation; (preface) dated Chih-Shun 4/1333,
    but this is a Ming edition.   Blocks; bamboo paper.

Index - a general table of contents for 12 chüan; separate list for
    each chüan.

Bound in 1 t'ao 4 ts'ê.

Remarks - a good edition; the item is complete and has no defects.

The University of Toronto Chinese Library

Accession No. 265   Index No. - 162-hef

Title   " I Chou shu "
                    逸   周   書

Classification - B-42 別史

Subject - a record of the Chou Dynasty.

References - Wylie's Notes page 29 160-1j 031-bgld 5/30 030-iaff

   7/19 012-zafk 4/14 031-bgdf 50/1 Gest No. 2326.

Author - (注) K'ung Chao 孔晁 .

Edition - a Ming edition; no date.   Blocks; bamboo paper.

Index - a general table of contents for 10 chüan (and supplements).

Bound in 1 t'ao 4 ts'é; doubly interleaved.

Remarks - this is a fairly good edition; and the item is complete

   and in generally good condition - last ts'é with repaired

   corners.

Accession No. 266   Index No. - 077-jooz

Title   " Li-tai ming jên nien p'u "
                歷 代 名 人 年 譜

Classification - B-117 傳記一總錄
Subject - (Gest No.99) - "Yearly record of important events and of
    birth and death of famous men of the dynasties from B.C. 206
    up to the year 1843 ----"

References - 012-zafk 5/19   Gest No. 99.

Author - Wu Jung-kuang 吳 榮 光.

Edition - the "Pao-ching-t'ang" 寶 經 堂 ; no date; see "Remarks".
    Blocks; "mao-t'ai" paper.

Index - none; 10 chüan.

Bound in 1 t'ao 10 ts'ê.

Remarks - this is a rather poor edition. Some pages seem to be
    missing from the first part of the work, hence the lack of
    date.

Accession No. 267 (a)   Index No. - 085-kfcz

Title   " Man-chou ming ch'ên chuan "
          滿 洲 名 臣 傳

Classification - B-117 傳記 一 總錄

Subject - (Gest No. 113-a)-" Biographies of Manchu ministers of note
    from the beginning of the Manchu dynasty up to the reign of
    emperor Ch'ien-Lung."

References - Wylie's Notes page 38   012-zafk 5/17   Gest No. 113-a

Author - not stated.

Edition - the "Kuo-shih-kuan" 國 史 館; undated.   Blocks;
    "mao-t'ai" paper.

Index - a general table of names; 48 chüan.

Bound in 6 t'ao 48 ts's (8 each).

Remarks - a rather poor edition of a small size; the item is complete.

Accession No.   267 (b)   Index No. — 085-kczk

Title   " Han ming ch'ên chuan "
                      漢　名　臣　傳

Classification — B-117 傳記 — 總錄
Subject — (Gest No. 113-b)- "Biographies of Chinese ministers of
    note from the beginning of the Manchu dynasty up to the
    reign of emperor Ch'ien-Lung."

References — Wylie's Notes page 38 012-zafk 5/17 Gest No. 113-b.

Author — not stated.

Edition — uniform with (a).

Index — a general table of names; 32 chüan.

Bound in 4 t'ao 32 ts'ê (8 each).

Remarks — as under (a).

Accession No. 268   Index No. - 115-jbh

Title   " Chi ku lu "
            稽 古 錄

Classification - B-22 編年

Subject - brief notes on historical events from the period of
Fu-hsi up to the year A.D. 1067; an abridgment of the
author's earlier historical annals.

References - Wylie's Notes page 25 160-1j 163-ggoz 4/7 031-bgld 5/20
012-zafk 4/8 031-bgdf 47/21 Gest No. 119.

Author - (撰) Ssŭ-ma Kuang 司 馬 光.

Edition - no notation; no date; but of the late Ch'ing period.
Blocks; "fên" paper.

Index - a general table of contents for 20 chüan arranged chronologically.

Bound in 1 t'ao 4 ts'ê.

Remarks - this is a very good edition; and the item is complete and
in good condition.

Accession No. 269   Index No. - 010-bb11

Title   " Yüan shih hsin pien "
                    元   史   新   編

Classification - B-42 別 史
Subject - a record of the Yüan Dynasty.

References - none.

Author - (重 修) Wei Yüan 魏 源 .

Edition - the "Shên-wei-t'ang" 慎 微 堂 ; dated Kuang-Hsü "i-ssŭ"
    31/1905.   Blocks; "fên" paper.

Index - a detailed table of contents for 95 chüan.

Bound in 4 t'ao 32 ts'ê (8 each).

Remarks - this is a very good modern edition; and the item is as new.

Accession No. 270   Index No. - 010-bheb

Title   " Yüan ch'ao pi shih "
             元   朝   祕   史

Classification - B-42 別史
Subject - a secret record of the Yüan period written in plain dialect.

References - 029-pffz 392   012-zafk 4/15.

Author - not stated.

Edition - the "Lien-yün-i-ts'ung-shu" 連 筠 簃 叢 書; dated
   Tao-Kuang 27/1847.   Blocks; bamboo paper.

Index - none; 15 chüan.

Bound in 1 t'ao 4 ts's; doubly interleaved.

Remarks - this is a fairly good edition; and the item is complete
   and in very good condition.

Accession No. 271   Index No. - 077-dgkd

Title   " Wu-shêng Kuan Chuang-mu i chi t'u chih "
武 聖 關 壯 繆 遺 蹟 圖 誌

Classification - B-107 傳記一獨錄

Subject - miscellaneous illustrated notes on the life of Kuan Yü
關 羽 ,- the most celebrated Chinese military hero and
canonized as the God of War; together with chapters on his
temple, grave etc.

References - none.

Author- not stated.

Edition- no notation; (preface) dated Min-Kuo 10/1921.   Blocks;
"fên" paper.

Index- a general table of contents for 10 chüan; separate lists
for each chüan.

Bound in¹ t'ao 4 ts'ê.

Remarks- this is a very good modern edition; and the item is complete
and in excellent condition.

Accession No. 272   Index No. - 032-khbz   030-bzkl

Title   " Shu k'o ku wên hui hsüan "
               塾 課 古 文 匯 選

Classification - D-73 總集一文

Subject - " a general collection of literary compositions,- prose,
   by ancient famous scholars and officials; many of which are
   of historical interest and importance." (Toronto No. 107)

References - Toronto No. 107.

Author - (評選) Wên Ch'êng-hui 溫 承 惠．

Edition - the "Pao-yang-tu-shu" 保 陽 督 署; dated Chia-Ch'ing
   "kuei-yu" 18/1813.   Blocks; "fên" paper.

Index - detailed table of contents for 8 chüan.

Bound in 1 t'ao 6 ts'ê.

Remarks - an incomplete item; the whole of chüan 6 and 7 being
   missing.

Accession No. 273   Index No. - 065-egn

Title   " Wên-chou ching chi chih "
             溫 州 經 籍 志

Classification - B-342 目録一經籍

Subject - a descriptive catalogue of books.

References - none.

Author - (編) Sun I-jang 孫詒讓.

Edition - the "Chekiang-kung-li-t'u-shu-kuan" 浙江公立圖書館 ;
    dated Min-Kuo 10/1921.   Blocks; "mao-pien" paper.

Index - a general table of contents for 36 chüan arranged according
    to the usual classifications of Chinese literature.

Bound in 2 t'ao 16 ts'ê (8 each).

Remarks - this is an ordinary modern edition; and the item is
    complete.

317

Accession No.   274　　　　　Index No. - 040-dbzg　　040-doge

Title　　　　　" Sung liu shih chia tz'ǔ "
　　　　　　　　宋 六 十 家 詞
　　　　　　　" Sung ming chia tz'ǔ "
　　　　　　　　宋 名 家 詞

Classification - D-118 詞曲 - 詞選
Subject - a general collection of selected lyrical compositions
　　of 61 famous scholars of the Sung period.

References - 012-zafk 20/27　　031-bgdf 200/17.

Author - (編) Mao Chin 毛晉 .

Edition - published by "Ch'ien-t'ang-Wang-shih" 錢塘 汪 氏 ;
　　dated Kuang-Hsü "mou-tzǔ" 14/1888.　　Blocks; "fên" paper.

Index - a general table of works of 61 authors; not divided into
　　chüan; separate lists for each of 61 works.

Bound in　4 t'ao 36 ts's (9-8-10-9).

Remarks - this edition is a very fine one; and the item is complete
　　and as if new.

The University of Toronto Chinese Library

Accession No. 275   Index No. - 037-ahfb

Title   " T'ien lu ko wai shih "
            天　祿　閣　外　史

Classification - C-308 雜家一雜文

Subject - a collection of miscellaneous notes and discussions;
    mainly of a political character.

References - 012-zafk 12/13   031-bgdf 124/2.

Author - (著) Huang Hsien 黃憲 .

Edition - no notation; (preface) dated Chia-Ching 2/1523.   Blocks;
    bamboo paper.

Index - a general table of contents for 8 chüan.

Bound in 1 t'ao 4 ts's; doubly interleaved.

Remarks - this is a very good edition; and the item is complete and
    in very good condition with the exception of some stains.

Accession No. 276   Index No. - 030-gzzk

Title   " T'ang ts'ai tzŭ chuan "
                唐　才　子　傳

Classification - B-117 傳記－總録

Subject - (Wylie) - "---- is a collection of 397 biographies of
    authors and authoresses, during the Tang and succeeding
    five dynasties----"

References - Wylie's Notes page 35 163-ggcz 5/4   031-bgld 6/14
    106-gdkn 29/17   030-iaff 9/14   012-zafk 5/11   031-bgdf 58/2.

Author - (撰) Hsin Wên-fang 辛 文 房．

Edition - the "Wên-hsüeh-shan-fang" 文 學 山 房；(postscriptum)
    dated "jên-hsü" 1921.   Blocks; "fên" paper.

Index - a table of names; 10 chüan.

Bound in 1 t'ao 4 ts'ê; doubly interleaved.

Remarks - a good edition; the item is complete and in very good
    condition.

The University of Toronto Chinese Library

Accession No. 277   **Index No.** – 072-dcko

Title   " I-chih chai yao lei pien "
　　　　　　　易 知 摘 要 類 編

Classification – C-348 類書

Subject – (Gest No. 3671) – "an historical classified encyclopaedia,
　covering the period from the legendary "Three Emperors" down
　to and including the Ming Dynasty."

References – Gest No. 3671.

Author – by Fu Chün 富俊.

Edition – the "Shao-i-t'ang" 紹 衣 堂 ; dated T'ung-Chih "chia-hsü"
　13/1874.   Blocks; "fên" paper.

Index – a general table of contents, arranged according to classes
　of subject matter, in 12 chüan.

Bound in 2 t'ao 12 ts'ê.

Remarks – this is a good edition; and the item is complete and in
　good condition.

The University of Toronto Chinese Library

Accession No. 278   Index No. - 189-zzk

Title   " Kao shih chuan "

高   士   傳

Classification - B-117 傳記一總録

Subject - (Gest No. 1294) - "a collection of biographies of ancient
worthies; with portraits."

References - Wylie's Notes page 35 160-1j 163-ggcz 5/4 031-bgld 6/11
167-mhfm 10/5   030-1aff 9/10   106-gdkn 27/7   012-zafk 5/10
031-bgdf 57/24   Gest No. 1294.

Author - Huang-fu Mi 皇 甫 謐.

Edition - the "Yang-ho-t'ang" 教 穌 堂 ; dated Hsien-Fêng "mou-wu"
8/1858.   Blocks; "fên" paper.

Index - a list of the "worthies"; in 3 chüan.

Bound in 1 t'ao 4 ts'ê; doubly interleaved.

Remarks - this is a very good edition; and the item is in very
good condition.

322

The University of Toronto Chinese Library

Accession No. 279   Index No. - 024-zzcf

Title   " Shih-chu-chai shu hua p'u "
十 竹 齋 書 畫 譜

Classification - C-223 藝術 - 書畫

Subject - a collection of polychromatic drawings; under eight
classifications.

References - Wylie's Notes page 155.

Author - Hu Chêng-yen 胡 正 言.

Edition - the "Sao-yeh-shan-fang" 掃 葉 山 房 ; dated Kuang-Hsü
"chi-mao" 5/1879.   Blocks; "fên" paper.

Index - none; a list of "classifications" on the title-page.

Bound in 1 t'ao 8 ts'ê.

Remarks - an ordinary edition; the item is in very good condition.
This work contains some very good specimens of Chinese painting.

Accession No. 280   Index No. - 024-zzof

Title   " Shih-chu-chai shu hua p'u "
十 竹 齋 書 畫 譜

Classification - C-223 藝術 一書畫
Subject - a collection of polychromatic drawings; under eight
classifications.

References - Wylie's Notes page 155   Toronto No. 279.

Author - Hu Chêng-yen 胡 正 言.

Edition - the "Shih-chu-chai" 十 竹 齋; (preface) dated "kuei-wei"
1883.   Blocks; "fên" paper.

Index - none.

Bound in 1 t'ao 16 ts's.

Remarks - this work is a duplicate of No. 279.   The edition is an
ordinary one; and the item is in very good condition.

The University of Toronto Chinese Library

Accession No. 281   Index No. - 002-cg

Title   " Chung   shuo "
                      中   説

Classification - C-13 儒家

Subject - a philosophical work of a political nature, on somewhat
    the same lines as the "Lün-Yü" 論 語 ; with annotations.

References - 160-1j 163-ggcz 7/2   031-bgdf 91/24   031-bgld 9/5
    106-gdkn 39/10   012-zafk 10/2   Toronto No. 204.

Author - Wang T'ung 王 通 ; (注) Yüan I 阮 逸 .

Edition - the "Ching-jèn-t'ang" 敬 忍 堂 ; no date; apparently
    printed from old Ming blocks during the Ch'ing period.
    Blocks; "fèn" paper.

Index - a table of contents; 10 chüan.

Bound in 1 t'ao 4 ts'è; doubly interleaved.

Remarks - this is a very good edition; and although the impression
    was from old blocks, the printing is almost as good as the
    original.   This item is a duplicate of No. 204.

The University of Toronto Chinese Library

Accession No. 282 (a)   Index No. - 162-1bcg

Title   " Liao shih chi shih pên mo "
           遼 史 紀 事 本 末

Classification - B-32 紀事本末
Subject - a history of the Liao Dynasty.

References - Gest No. 1644-a

Author - Li Yu-t'ang 李 有 棠.

Edition - the "Li-i-o-lou" 李 移 鄂 樓; dated Kuang-Hsü "kuei-mao"
          29/1903.   Blocks; "fên" paper.

Index - a list of chapter headings for 42 chüan,- 40 and a "shuo"
        and "mo".

Bound in 1 t'ao 8 ts'ê.

Remarks - an ordinary edition; the item is complete and in good
          condition.   The last chüan contains an extensive bibliography.

Accession No. 282 (b)   Index No. - 167-zbcg

Title   " Chin shih chi shih pên mo "
               金 史 紀 事 本 末

Classification - B-32 紀 事 本 末
Subject - a history of the Chin Dynasty.

References - Gest No. 1644-b.

Author - Li Yu-t'ang 李 有 棠 .

Edition - uniform with (a).

Index - a list of chapter headings for 54 chüan,- 52 and a "shou"
        and "mo".

Bound in 1 t'ao 12 ts's.

Remarks - as under (a).

Accession No. 283   Index No. - 030-gdzz   120-negd

Title   " T'ang Sung pa ta chia wên tu pên "
唐 宋 八 大 家 文 讀 本
" Tsuan p'ing T'ang Sung pa ta chia wên tu pên "
纂 評 唐 宋 八 大 家 文 讀 本

Classification - D-73 總 集 一 文

Subject - a general collection of prose compositions by 8 famous
authors of the T'ang and Sung dynasties; with commentaries
and marginal notes.

References - 012-zafk 19/23.

Author - (評 點) Shên Tê-ch'ien 沈 德 潛 ; (批 選) Wei Yüan
魏 源 ; (纂 評) Ishimura Teiichi 石 村 貞 一 .

Edition - the "Ni-sho-dō Tokyo" 東 京 弍 書 堂 ; (preface) dated
Meiji 12/1879.   Blocks; Japanese paper.

Index - a detailed table of contents for 8 chüan.

Bound in 1 t'ao 8 ts'ê.

Remarks - this is a very fine edition; and the item is complete
and in excellent condition.

The University of Toronto Chinese Library

Accession No. 284   **Index No.** - 076-hebb   030-bbpe

Title   " Ch'in-ting ku chin ch'u êrh chin chien "
　　　　　　欽　定　古　今　儲　貳　金　鑑

Classification - B-367 史 評

Subject - (Gest No. 1319)- "discusses the selection and appointment
of the Imperial Heir Apparent, with special reference to
historical examples."

References - 031-bgld 8/32   012-zafk 9/29   031-bgdf 88/27
Gest No. 1319.

Author - officially compiled.

Edition - official; dated Ch'ien-Lung 48/1783.   Blocks; bamboo
paper.

Index - a table of contents for 6 chüan, arranged chronologically.

Bound in 1 t'ao 4 ts'ê.

Remarks - this is a good edition; and the item is without defects
and complete.

329

Accession No. 285   Index No. - 031-bfzd

Title   " Ssŭ shu jên wu pei k'ao "
             四 書 人 物 備 考

Classification - A-131 四書

Subject - (Gest No. 1882) - "an explanation of persons, things, etc.,
    referred to in the Four Books; a guide and hand-book, or
    concordance to the Four Books."

References - Gest No. 1882.

Author - (增定) Ch'ên Jên-hsi 陳 仁 錫.

Edition - the "San-lo-chai" 三 樂 齋 ; dated Ch'ien-Lung 5/1740.
    Blocks; bamboo paper.

Index - a detailed table of contents for 12 chüan.

Bound in 1 t'ao 6 ts'ê.

Remarks - a rather poor edition; the item is complete and without
    defects.

The University of Toronto Chinese Library

Accession No. 286   Index No. - 077-jcon

Title   " <u>Li-tai ming ju chuan</u> "

歷 代 名 儒 傳

Classification - B-117 傳記－總録

Subject - collected biographies of noted scholars of the period

from the <u>Han</u> 漢 down to and including the <u>Yüan</u> 元 dynasty.

References - none.

Author - (仝 訂) <u>Chu Shih</u> 朱 軾 and <u>Ts'ai Shih-yüan</u> 蔡 世 遠 .

Edition - apparently official, as the title-page has the designation

"<u>Pĕn-ya-ts'ang-pan</u>" 本 衙 藏 板; (preface) dated Yung-Chĕng

7/1729.   Blocks; bamboo paper.

Index - a list of names, arranged chronologically; 8 chüan.

Bound in 1 t'ao 2 ts'ĕ.

Remarks - this is a good edition; and the item is complete and in

generally good condition.

Accession No. 287 (a)   Index No. - 077-jcnh

Title   " Li-tai chiang yü piao "
               歷 代 疆 域 表

Classification - B-187 地 理 一 總 志
Subject - a comprehensive collection of territorial tables; showing
    the locations of capitals; principal territories occupied, and
    other detailed matters during the various periods from the time
    of the Five Emperors down to and including the Ming Dynasty.

References - 012-zafk 6/2.

Author - (編 輯) Tuan Ch'ang-chi 段 長 基.

Edition - the "Wei-ku-shan-fang" 味 古 山 房; dated Chia-Ch'ing
    "i-hai" 20/1815.   Blocks; "fên" paper.

Index - a list of "periods" at the beginning of each of 3 chüan.

Bound in 4 ts's in 1 t'ao with (b).

Remarks - an important historical work.   The item is complete and
    in good condition; but the impression is defective in some
    places.

Accession No. 287 (b)   Index No. - 077-jcez

Title   " Li-tai yen ko piao "
               歷 代 沿 革 表

Classification - B-187 地 理 一 總 志

Subject - a comprehensive collection of tables showing the changes

in the names of the districts of the principal provinces in

China; together with other matter of historical interest;

during the period from the beginning of Chinese history

down to the end of the Ming Dynasty.

References - 012-zafk 6/2.

Author - (編 輯) Tuan Ch'ang-chi 段 長 基 .

Edition - uniform with (a).

Index - a list of provinces at the beginning of each of 3 chüan.

Bound in 6 ts's in 1 t'ao with (a).

Remarks - as under (a).

Accession No.   288   Index No. - 024-gcbl 024-gblz 021-cblz

Title   " Nan Pei shih shih hsiao lu "
               南　北　史　識　小　録

Classification - B-137 史钞
                              of
Subject - (a) a collection/selections taken from the "Nan shih"
         南 史 ; together with commentarial notes; (b) same from
         the "Pei shih" 北 史.

References - 160-1j 163-ggcz 5/6   031-bgld 6/19   012-zafk 5/29
         031-bgdf 65/4   Gest No. 94.

Author - (同 編) Shên Ming-sun 沈 名 蓀 and Chu K'un-t'ien
         朱 昆 田.

Edition - the "Wu's Ch'ing-lai-t'ang" 吳 氏 清 來 堂; dated
         T'ung-Chih "hsin-wei" 10/1871.   Blocks; "mao-pien" paper.

Index - (a) a general table of contents for 14 chüan; (b) same for
         14 chüan.

Bound in 1 t'ao 12 ts'e.

Remarks - an ordinary edition; the item is complete and without
         defects.

The University of Toronto Chinese Library

Accession No. 289   Index No. - 030-beji

Title   " Shih hsing yün pien "
　　　　　　　　史　　姓　　韻　　編

Classification - B-117 傳記 — 總録 C-348 類書

Subject - (Gest No. 91) - "Index of names of persons mentioned in the "Erh shih ssŭ shih" 二 十 四 史 ,- the twenty-four dynastic histories, arranged according to rhymes-----"

References - 073-fzfh 史目/29　Gest No. 91.

Author - (輯) Wang Hui-tsu 汪 輝 祖 ·

Edition - the "Kêng-yü-lou-shu-chü" 耕 餘 樓 書 局; dated Kuang-Hsü "chia-shên" 10/1884.　　Type; "fên" paper.

Index - a table of contents for 64 chüan.

Bound in 2 t'ao 16 ts's.

Remarks - a good edition; the item is complete and in good condition.

The University of Toronto Chinese Library

Accession No. 290   Index No. - 181-11zb

Title   " Ku Tuan-wên kung nien p'u "

顧 端 文 公 年 譜

Classification - B-107 傳記 － 獨録

Subject - the biography and chronological record of Ku Hsien-ch'êng

顧 憲 成.

References - 029-pffz 582   058-jffz (hsü) ping/12.

Author - (初 編) Ku Shu 顧 樞;(記 略) Ku Yü-mu 顧 興 沐.

Edition - privately published; dated Ch'ung-Chêng 2/1629.   Blocks;
    bamboo paper.

Index - none; 2 chüan.

Bound in 1 t'ao 2 ts'ê; doubly interleaved.

Remarks - a very fine edition; the item is complete and in perfect
    condition.

Accession No. 291   Index No. - 039-mb

Title   " Hsüeh shih "
                         學 史

Classification - B-367 史 評

Subject - critiques on Chinese history from the Chou 周 down
    to the Yüan 元 dynasty.

References - 165-ggcz 6/10   031-bgld 8/31   106-gdkn 38/18
    030-iaff 14/24   012-zafk 9/28   031-bgdf 88/21.

Author - (撰) Shao Pao 邵 寶 .

Edition - a manuscript written on bamboo paper; (preface) dated
    Chêng-Tê "mou-yin" 13/1518.

Index - a general table of contents for 15 chüan.

Bound in 1 t'ao 6 ts'ê; doubly interleaved.

Remarks - a very good manuscript; the item is complete and in good
    condition.

337

Accession No.   292   Index No. - 180-Jb

Title   " Yün shih "
                               韻 史

Classification - B-367 史 評

Subject - a brief historical account of China from the remotest
    times down to the end of the Sung Dynasty; written in rhymes
    and with notes and explanations.

References - 012-zafk 9/30.

Author - (撰) Hsü T'un-an 許 遯 庵.

Edition - no notation; no date.   Blocks; "mao-pien" paper.

Index - none; 2 chüan.

Bound in 1 t'ao 2 ts'ê; doubly interleaved.

Remarks - a fairly good edition; the item is complete and in
    generall good condition except the last page, which is
    somewhat damaged.   A supplement to this work, consisting
    of an historical account of the succeeding two dynasties, (⑤)

(#) **Yüan** and **Ming**,- is entitled :-

" **Yün shih pu** "

韻 史 補　　　　　 1 chüan (180-jbg)

by **Li Yü-ts'ên** 李 玉 岑 .

Classification -

Subject - a description of the

in the province of

References -

Author -

Edition -

Index -

Remarks -

Accession No. 293   Index No. - 024-gnij

Title   " Nan-yo tsung shêng chi "
               南 嶽 總 勝 集

Classification - B-207 地 理 一 山 川

Subject - a description of the Nan-yo,- the Hêng-shan Mountain 衡 山
     in the province of Hunan.

References - 012-zafk 8/6   029-pffz 572   Gest No. 2259.

Author - by Ch'ên T'ien-fu 陳 田 夫.

Edition - based upon the Sung edition; dated Kuang-Hsü "ping-wu"
     32/1906.   Blocks; "fên" paper.

Index - none; in 3 chüan.

Bound in 1 t'ao 3 ts'ê; doubly interleaved.

Remarks - a very good edition.   The item is new.

The University of Toronto Chinese Library

Accession No. 294   Index No. - 075-bzcm

Title   " Chu-tzŭ nien p'u "
                朱 子 年 譜

Classification - B-107 傳記一獨録

Subject - the biography and chronological record of Chu Hsi 朱熹 ；
    together with other related matters.

References - 163-ggcz 5/3   031-bgld 6/11   012-zafk 5/5
    031-bgdf 57/19   59/27   60/34.

Author - (原輯) Li Fang-tzŭ 李方子 ；(增修) Li Mo 李默.

Edition - no notation; (preface) dated Chia-Ching "jên-tzŭ" 31/1552,
    but this is a Ch'ing edition.   Blocks; bamboo paper.

Index - a general table of contents for 卷首 and 5 chüan.

Bound in 1 t'ao 2 ts'ê.

Remarks - a fairly good edition.   The item is complete and without
    defects.

Accession No. 295   Index No. - 077-jcbz   077-jcch

Title   " Li-tai nan ch'ih p'u "
歴 代 男 齒 譜
" Li-tai ming hsien ch'ih p'u "
歴 代 名 賢 齒 譜

Classification - C-343 類書

Subject - an encyclopaedic work consisting of notes and selections
from various historical works, mostly in regard to the
peculiarities in the lives of ancient worthies; arranged
according to ages.

References - none.

Author - (輯) I Tsung-t'un 易 宗 涒 .

Edition - the "Tz'ŭ-shu-t'ang" 賜 書 堂 ; (preface) dated K'ang-Hsi
55/1716.   Blocks; "fên" paper.

Index - a table of "ages"; 9 chüan.

Bound in 2 t'ao 18 ts'ê.

Remarks - this is a rather poor edition; and the item is complete.
Three pages at the end of last ts'ê are badly damaged.

Accession No. 296   Index No. – 106–dhlc

Title   " Huang ch'ing chih kung t'u "
                皇　清　職　貢　圖

Classification – B–192 地理一省志

Subject – an illustrated description of the various tributary states
    under the control of China, as well as those barbarian tribes
    residing in the mountainous regions in the western and south-
    western part of China, during the period of Ch'ien-Lung of the
    Manchu Dynasty.

References – 031-bgld 7/13   012-zafk 6/7   031-bgdf 71/21.

Author – compiled under Imperial order by a commission headed by
    Fu Hêng 傅　恒 .

Edition – a palace edition; dated Ch'ien-Lung "hsin-ssŭ" 26/1762.
    Blocks; "hsi-lien" paper.

Index – separate table of contents at the beginning of each of
    9 chüan.

Bound in 2 t'ao 12 ts'ê; singly interleaved (6-6).

Remarks – this is a very fine edition; and the item is complete and
    in perfect condition.

343

Accession No. 297   Index No. - 053-1chk

Title   " Kuang ming chiang chuan "
                       廣　名　將　傳

Classification - B-117 傳記一總録
Subject - a collection of biographies of famous generals during the
     period from the Chou down to the end of the Ming dynasty.

References - 029-pffz 325.

Author - (註斷) Huang Tao-chou 黃 道 周.

Edition - the "Hai-shan-hsien-kuan" 海 山 仙 館; dated Tao-Kuang
     27/1847.   Blocks; "fẽn" paper.

Index - a table of contents for 20 chüan, arranged dynastically.

Bound in 1 t'ao 6 ts'ẽ.

Remarks - a rather good edition; but the item has quite a few
     worm-holes, some of which are very serious.

Accession No. 298   Index No. - 085-kfcg

Title   " Han shu ti li chih chiao pên "
             漢 書 地 理 志 校 本

Classification - B-12 正史

Subject - a critical commentary on the "Ti li chih" 地 理 志 of
    "Han shu" 漢 書 ,- a chapter on Geography in the official
    history of the Han Dynasty.

References - 012-zafk 4/2.

Author - by Wang Yüan-sun 汪 遠 孫.

Edition - the "Chên-ch'i-t'ang" 振 綺 堂 ; dated Tao-Kuang
    "mou-shân" 28/1848.   Blocks; "fân" paper.

Index - none; 2 chüan.

Bound in 1 t'ao 2 ts'ê; doubly interleaved.

Remarks - a very good edition; the item is as if new.

Accession No. 299   Index No. - 169-jzzp

Title   " Ch'üeh-li wên hsien k'ao "
                  闕 里 文 獻 考

Classification- B-107 傳記 — 獨錄

Subject - a complete handbook on all details regarding the life of
     Confucius,- his biographical record; descendents up to the
     71st generation; temple and other historical remains; ritual
     and ceremonial observances; records of his disciples; and
     numerous related subjects.

References - 012-zafk 5/2.

Author - (敬 述) K'ung Chi-fên 孔 繼 汾.

Edition - no notation; (preface) dated Ch'ien-Lung 27/1762.
     Blocks; "mao-pien" paper.

Index - a detailed table of contents for 100 chüan.

Bound in 2 t'ao 12 ts's (6-6).

Remarks - a very useful reference book.   The item is complete and
     in very good condition.

The University of Toronto Chinese Library

Accession No.   300   **Index No.** - 169-jzzp

Title   " Ch'üeh-li wên hsien k'ao "

闕 里 文 獻 考

Classification - B-107 傳記一獨錄

Subject - (Toronto No. 299) - "a complete handbook on all details
regarding the life of Confucius,- his biographical record;
descendents up to the 71st generation; temple and other
historical remains; ritual and ceremonial observances;
records of his disciples; and numerous related subjects."

References - 012-zafk 5/2 Toronto No. 299.

Author - (敬述) K'ung Chi-fên 孔 繼 汾.

Edition - no notation; (preface) dated Ch'ien-Lung 27/1762.
Blocks; "mao-t'ai" paper.

Index - a detailed table of contents for 100 chüan.

Bound in - 2 t'ao 8 ts'ê (4-4).

Remarks - this is a duplicate of No. 299. More than 20 pages at
the end of last chüan are badly damaged.

Accession No. 301 (a)   Index No. - 046-zd(zb)b

Title   " Shan-tung k'ao ku lu "
                 山 東 考 古 録

Classification - B-217 地 理 一 雜 記

Subject - researches into historical remains, as well as topographical
    conditions of the province of Shantung.

References - 012-zafk 8/18   031-bgdf 77/24.

Author - (著) Ku Yen-wu 顧 炎 武．

Edition - the "Shan-tung-shu-chü" 山 東 書 局; dated Kuang-Hsü
    8/1882.   Blocks; "mao-pien" paper.

Index - none; in 1 chüan.

Bound in 1 ts'ê in 1 t'ao with (b).

Remarks - a fairly good edition; complete and in very good condition.

Accession No.   302   Index No. - 120-ozd(zb)

Title   " <u>Hsü Shan-tung k'ao ku lu</u> "
                 續　山　東　考　古　録

Classification - B-217 地理一雜記

Subject - (Toronto No. 301-b) - "a classified geographical treatise
    on the province of <u>Shantung</u>; with chapters on mountains, rivers,
    districts, historical changes etc; being a continuation and
    development of "<u>Shan-tung k'ao ku lu</u>" 山東考古録.

References - Toronto No. 301-b.

Author - (述) <u>Yeh Kuei-shou</u> 葉圭綬 .

Edition - the "<u>Kua-chiao-chien-lu</u>" 蝸角尖廬 ; dated Hsien-Fêng
    1/1851.   Blocks; "fên" paper.

Index - a table of contents for 32 chüan.

Bound in   1 t'ao 6 ts'ê.

Remarks - this is a fairly good edition; and the item is complete
    and in very good condition.

Accession No. 301 (b)   Index No. - 120-ozd(zb)

Title   " Hsü Shan-tung k'ao ku lu "

續 山 東 考 古 錄

Classification - B-217 地理 一雜記

Subject - a classified geographical treatise on the province of
Shantung; with chapters on mountains, rivers, districts,
historical changes etc; being a continuation and development
of "Shan-tung k'ao ku lu" 山 東 考 古 錄。

References - none.

Author - (述) Yeh Kuei-shou 葉 圭 綬。

Edition - uniform with (a).

Index - a table of contents for 32 chüan.

Bound in 6 ts'$ in 1 t'ao with (a).

Remarks - as under (a).

The University of Toronto Chinese Library

Accession No.   303   Index No. - 067-zzsg

Title   " **Wên-tzŭ tsuan i** "
                文 子 纘 義

Classification - C-731 道家

Subject - an ancient treatise on Taoism; based upon the doctrines
    of Lao-tzŭ; with commentaries.

References - Wylie's Notes page 218 (文子) 163-ggcz 11/11
    031-bgld 14/49   012-zafk 14/33   031-bgdf 146/30.

Author - of original - a disciple of Lao-tzŭ; exact name unknown.
    (合 註) Chu Pien 朱弁 and others. (評) Sun Kung 孫鑛.

Edition - no notation; no date.   Blocks; bamboo paper.

Index - a general table of contents for 12 chüan.

Bound in I t'ao 6 ts'ê; doubly interleaved.

Remarks - this is a good edition; and the item is complete and
    without defects.   031-bgld says that this item is an imitation
    of the work under description with changes in authorship, and
    is generally ignored by the catalogues.

351

Accession No. 304   Index No. - 108-jzc

Title   " Pan-shan chih "
                         盤　山　志

Classification - B-207 地 理 — 山 川

Subject - a description of the Pan-shan Mountain situated not far
   to the east of Peiping; including chapters on various
   topographical aspects of the mountain; temples and other
   constructions; literary compositions written by famous
   scholars of all dynasties; visits by previous emperors; etc.

References - none.

Author - (纂 輯) Chih P'u 智 朴 .

Edition - no notation; (preface) dated K'ang-Hsi 30/1691.   Blocks;
   "fên" paper.

Index - a detailed table of contents for 10 chüan; "pu-i" 補 遺
   4 chüan.

Bound in 1 t'ao 4 ts'ê.

Remarks - an ordinary edition; the item is complete and as if new.

Accession No. 305   Index No. - 042-sbh

Title   " Shang yu lu "
                        尚 友 錄

Classification - C-348 類書

Subject - a collection of biographical notes of ancient worthies;
    based upon selections from various standard works; the items
    being arranged according to rhymes.

References - 012-zafk 13/25   031-bgdf 138/27.

Author - (編纂) Liao Yung-hsien 廖 用 賢; (補輯)
    Chang Po-ts'ung 張 伯 琮.

Edition - the "T'ien-lu-chai" 天 禄 齋; (preface) dated K'ang-Hsi
    "ping-wu" 5/1666.   Blocks; bamboo paper.

Index - a list of surnames, arranged according to rhymes; 22 chüan.

Bound in 2 t'ao 12 ts'ê (6-6).

Remarks - this item is complete but with some repaired defects,-
    worm-holes, mostly at the beginning or end of each ts'ê.

Accession No. 306   Index No. - 001-b1c

Title   " San ch'ien chih "
                  三   遷   志

Classification - B-107 傳記 一 獨録

Subject - a work on Mencius; consisting of his biography and
    chronological record; record of his posterity and disciples;
    historical remains of his temple and grave; lessons from
    his mother; etc; etc.

References - 012-zafk 5/1   031-bgdf 59/16.

Author - (同 撰) Mêng Yen-t'ai 孟 衍 泰, Wang T'ê-hsüan 王 特選
    and Chung Yün-chin 仲 薀 錦.

Edition - no notation; (preface) dated Ch'ung-Chêng "mou-ch'ên"
    1/1628.   Blocks; "mao-pien" paper.

                青雷正版本

Index - a general table of contents for 12 chüan.

Bound in 1 t'ao 4 ts'ê.

Remarks - a very fine edition.   The item is complete and without
    defects.

354

Accession No.　307　　　　　Index No. - 041-kj

Title　　　　　　　　　" Tui lei "
　　　　　　　　　　　　對　類

Classification - C-348 類書

Subject - an encyclopaedia of antithetical phrases and couplets.

References - 012-zafk 13/25　　031-bgdf 138/35.

Author - not stated. (致註) Wu Mien-hsüeh 吳 勉 學.

Edition - an undated Ming edition.　　Blocks; bamboo paper.

Index - a general table of the main classifications; and a detailed
　　list of contents for 20 chüan.

Bound in 1 t'ao 12 ts'ê.

Remarks - a fair edition.　The item is complete and in generally
　　good condition with the exception of the last (20th) chüan
　　which contains several defective pages.

Accession No. 308 (a)   Index No. - 038-ezij

Title   " Hsing shih hsün yüan "
               姓 氏 尋 源

Classification - C-348 類書

Subject - an encyclopaedia of researches into the origins of
         Chinese family names, arranged according to rhymes.

References - none.

Author - (纂) Chang Chu 張澍.

Edition - the "Tsao-hua-shu-wu" 棗 華 書 屋; (preface) dated
         Tao-Kuang "mou-hsü" 18/1838.   Blocks; "mao-pien" paper.

Index - none; 45 chüan.

Bound in 3 t'ao 18 ts'ê (6 each); doubly interleaved.

Remarks - this is a very fine edition; and the item is complete and
         as if new.   The last ts'ê is slightly stained.

Accession No. 308 (b)   Index No. - 038-ezng

Title   " Hsing shih pien wu "
                       姓   氏   辯   誤

Classification - C-348 類書

Subject - an encyclopaedia embracing mistakes of family names,
    as appearing in various works; together with explanations
    and authoritative corrections; the items being arranged
    according to rhymes.

References - none.

Author - (纂) Chang Chu 張 澍 .

Edition - uniform with (a).

Index - none; 30 chüan.

Bound in 1 t'ao 8 ts'ê; doubly interleaved.

Remarks - as under (a).

Accession No. 309   Index No. - 010-bbmz

Title   " Yüan shih i wên chêng pu "
               元 史 譯 文 證 補

Classification - B-12 正 史

Subject - a revised history of the Yüan Dynasty with corrections

   and additions.

References - 160-1j.

Author - (撰) Hung Chün 洪 鈞 .

Edition - no notation; dated Kuang-Hsü "ting-yu" 23/1897.

   Blocks; "mao-t'ai" paper.

Index - a general table of contents for 30 chüan; of which 9 chüan

   are missing.

Bound in 1 t'ao 4 ts'ê.

Remarks - a fairly good edition in very good condition.

358

The University of Toronto Chinese Library

Accession No. 310   Index No. - 149-obzf

Title   " <u>Tu shih ta lüeh</u> "
                    讀 史 大 略

<u>Classification</u> - B-367 史 評

<u>Subject</u> - critiques upon Chinese history from the remotest times
       down to the end of the <u>Yüan Dynasty</u>; with a short supplement
       of one chapter.

<u>References</u> - 012-zafk 9/31.

<u>Author</u> - (撰) <u>Sha Chang-po</u> 沙 張 白 。

<u>Edition</u> - no particular designation; dated Tao-Kuang "ping-wu"
       26/1846.   Blocks; "fên" paper.

<u>Index</u> - a general table of contents for 60 chüan and a supplement.

<u>Bound in</u> 2 t'ao 16 ts'ê (8-8).

<u>Remarks</u> - this is a fairly good edition; and the item is complete
       and without defects except some stains.   This work is
       punctuated and with hand-written marginal notes in black and
       red.

Accession No. 311   Index No. - 030-cdck   075-ckfb

Title   " Ho-fei Li Ch'in-k'o kung chêng shu "
           合 肥 李 勤 恪 公 政 書
           " Li Ch'in-k'o kung chêng shu "
           李 勤 恪 公 政 書

Classification - B-72 詔令奏議一奏議

Subject - a collection of memorials and other official documents

     of Li Han-chang 李 瀚 章.

References - none.

Author - by Li Han-chang 李 瀚 章 ; (編 輯) Li Ching-yü 李 經 畬
     and others of his family.

Edition - no notation; (Imperial edict) dated Kuang-Hsü 25/1899.
     Lithographed on "fên" paper.

Index - separate lists of contents at the beginning of 卷 首 and
     each of the 10 chüan.

Bound in 1 t'ao 10 ts'ê.

Remarks - this is a good modern edition.   The item is new.

360

Accession No. 312 (a)   Index No. - 120-iekc

Title   " Lien ping shih chi "
               練 兵 實 紀

Classification - C-33 兵 家

Subject - a treatise on military training.

References - Wylie's Notes page 91   160-1j   163-ggcz 7/9
       031-bgld 9/28   012-zafk 10/14   031-bgdf 99/22.

Author - (撰) Ch'i Chi-kuang 戚 繼 光.

Edition - the "Pao-lin-t'ang" 寶 林 堂; dated Kuang-Hsü "i-hai"
       1/1875.   Blocks; bamboo paper.

Index - a general table of contents for 9 chüan; 雜 集 6 chüan.

Bound in 1 t'ao 6 ts'ê.

Remarks - an ordinary edition.   The item is complete and without
       defects.

Accession No. 312 (b)   Index No. - 120-cfif

Title   " Chi hsiao hsin shu "
                   紀   效   新   書

Classification - C-33 兵 家

Subject - a treatise on military training and related matters;
    together with a short chapter on marines.

References - Wylie's Notes page 91 160-1j 163-ggcz 7/9
    031-bgld 9/28   012-zafk 10/14   031-bgdf 99/23.

Author - (撰) Ch'i Chi-kuang 戚 繼 光.

Edition - uniform with (a).

Index - a general table of contents for 卷 首 and 18 chüan.

Bound in 1 t'ao 6 ts'ê.

Remarks - as under (a).

362

Accession No. 313   Index No. - 149-obcf

Title   " Tu shih chi lüeh "
               讀 史 紀 畧

Classification - C-367 史 評

Subject - (Gest No. 3592) - "a digest of history, from ancient
    times down to and including the Ming Dynasty."

References - Gest No. 3592.

Author - (纂輯) Hsiao Chün 蕭 濬 .

Edition - the "Jan-ching-chai" 澹 靜 齋 ; dated Tao-Kuang 20/1840.
    Blocks; bamboo paper.

Index - a general table of contents for 4 chüan.

Bound in 1 t'ao 4 ts'ê; doubly interleaved.

Remarks - a fairly good edition; the item is complete and in very
    good condition.

Accession No. 314   Index No. - 076-hejb   140-jbjf

Title   " Ch'in-ting Mêng-ku yüan liu "
               欽　定　蒙　古　源　流
               " Mêng-ku yüan liu "
               蒙　古　源　流

Classification - B-52 雜史

Subject - a history of Mongolia.

References - 160-1j 012-zafk 4/24 031-bgdf 51/29.

Author - translated from the Mongolian text under imperial order of
    emperor Ch'ien-Lung 乾　隆 .

Edition - officially published; dated Ch'ien-Lung 55/1790.   Blocks;
    "fên" paper.

Index - none; in 8 chüan.

Bound in 1 t'ao 4 ts'ê :

Remarks - a modern edition; the item is complete and in good condition.

Accession No. 315   Index No. - 128-gh11

Title   " Shêng hsien hsiang tsan "
                    聖   賢   像   贊

Classification - B-117 傳 記 一 總 錄

Subject - a general collection of eulogies written by the emperors
    and noted scholars of various periods in praise of ancient
    sages and famous philosophers; together with portraits.

References - 012-zafk 5/1   Gest No. 1082.

Author - unknown.

Edition - no notation; (preface) dated Ch'ung-Chêng "jên-shên"
    5/1632.   Blocks; "fên" paper.

Index - a detailed table of contents for 3 ts'ê or chüan.

Bound in 1 t'ao 4 ts'ê.

Remarks - an ordinary edition; in generally good condition and
    complete.

Accession No. 316   Index No. - 118-eddd

Title   " Li-wêng ch'üan chi "
                      笠   翁   全   集

Classification - D-33 别集 – 詩文

Subject - an individual comprehensive collection of literary

   compositions,- prose and poetry.

References - 012-zafk 17/13   Gest No. 2339.

Author - (著) Li Yü 李 漁 .

Edition - the "Chieh-tzŭ-yüan" 芥 子 園 ; (preface) dated

   Yung-Chêng 8/1730.   Blocks; bamboo paper.

Index - a general table of contents for 16 chüan; detailed tables

   at the beginning of each chüan.

Bound in 2 t'ao.24 ts'ê (12 each).

Remarks - an ordinary edition; the item is in generally good

   condition.

Accession No. 317   Index No. - 212-zzzd

Title   " <u>Lung-ch'uan wên chi</u> "
        龍 川 文 集

<u>Classification</u> - D-33 別集一詩文

<u>Subject</u> - an individual collection of prose and poetry, mostly the
    former.

<u>References</u> - 160-1j 163-ggoz 13/17 031-bgld 16/26 106-gdkn 88/12
    030-iaff 31/1 167-mhfm 21/22 012-zafk 15/28 031-bgdf 162/10
    Gest No. 406.

<u>Author</u> - (著) <u>Ch'ên Liang</u> 陳亮 ‧ † 1192

<u>Edition</u> - no notation; (preface) dated Ch'ung-Chêng "kuei-yu" 6/1633.
    Blocks; bamboo paper.

<u>Index</u> - a detailed table of contents for 30 chüan.

<u>Bound in</u> 1 t'ao 6 ts'ê.

<u>Remarks</u> - a very good edition; the item is complete and in very
    good condition.

Accession No. 318   Index No. - 120-glgo

Title   " Ching Liao su tu "
                   經 遼 疏 牘

Classification - B-72 詔令奏議 一奏議

Subject - a collection of memorials and other official correspondence.

References - none.

Author - (著) Hsiung T'ing-pi 熊 廷 弼.

Edition - reprinted by the "Hu-pei-t'ung-chih-chü" 湖北通志局;
    (original preface) dated T'ai-Ch'ang 泰昌 1/1620.   Blocks;
    "fên" paper.

Index - a table of contents for 9 chüan; a separate list for 10th
    chüan.

Bound in 1 t'ao 10 ts'ê.

Remarks - this is a good modern edition; and the item is complete
    and almost new.

Accession No. 319   Index No. - 055-azbi   007-zzzb

Title   " <u>Nien-êrh</u> <u>shih</u> <u>kan</u> <u>ying</u> <u>lu</u> "
               廿　二　史　感　應　録

               " <u>Erh-shih-êrh</u> <u>shih</u> <u>kan</u> <u>ying</u> <u>lu</u> "
               二　十　二　史　感　應　録

<u>Classification</u> - C-328 雜家 - 雜纂

<u>Subject</u> - selected notes from the twenty-two dynastic histories,
     illustrative of and mainly in connection with secret rewards
     and punishments meted out to individuals according to their
     moral and ethical conduct.

<u>References</u> - 012-zafk 13/9.

<u>Author</u> - (輯) <u>P'êng Hsi-su</u> 彭 希 涑.

<u>Edition</u> - no notation; dated Hsüan-T'ung 1/1909.   Blocks; "fên"
     paper.

<u>Index</u> - none; 2 chüan.

<u>Bound in</u> 1 t'ao 2 ts'ê.

<u>Remarks</u> - this is a fairly good modern edition; and the item is
     complete and in very good condition.

Accession No. 320   Index No. - 072-dcza   075-czab

Title   " Ming Li Wên-chêng kung nien p'u "
               明 李 文 正 公 年 譜
               " Li Wên-chêng kung nien p'u "
               李 文 正 公 年 譜

Classification - B-107 傳記 — 獨録

Subject - the biography and chronological record of Li Tung-yang
         李 東 陽.

References - none.

Author - (纂輯) Fa Shih-shen 法 式 善 ; (增補) T'ang Chung-mien
         唐 仲 晃.

Edition - privately published; (preface) dated Chia-Ch'ing "kuei-hai"
         8/1803.   Blocks; bamboo paper.

Index - none; in 7 chüan.

Bound in 1 t'ao 2 ts'ê.

Remarks - a fairly good edition.   The item is complete and in
         generally good condition.

Accession No. 321   Index No. - 120-ghcf

Title   " Sui k'ou chi lüeh "
             綏 寇 紀 畧

Classification - B-32 紀事本末

Subject - (Gest No. 1343) - "a detailed account of brigandage by
    roving bands towards the end of the Ming dynasty, and its
    suppression; together with a chapter on calamities and
    strange events."

References - 160-1j 163-ggcz 4/10 031-bgld 5/29 012-zafk 4/13
    031-bgdf 49/28   Gest No. 1343.

Author - (纂 輯) Wu Wei-yeh 吳 偉 業 .

Edition - the "Chao-k'uang-ko" 照 曠 閣 ; (postscriptum) dated
    Chia-Ch'ing "chia-tzǔ" 9/1804.   Blocks; bamboo paper.

Index - a general table of contents for 12 chüan; supplement in 3
    chüan.

Bound in 1 t'ao 8 ts'ê.

Remarks - a good edition.   The item is complete and without defects
    except some stains.

Accession No. 322   Index No. - 040-dbla

Title   " Sung Yüan chiu pên shu ching yen lu "
　　　　　宋　元　舊　本　書　經　眼　録

Classification - B-342 目 録 一 經 籍

Subject - a catalogue of Sung and Yüan works; with descriptions.

References - Gest No. 983.

Author - by Mo Yu-chih 莫 友 之 .

Edition - privately published; (index) dated T'ung-Chih "kuei-yu"
　　12/1873.   Blocks; "fên" paper.

Index - a detailed list for 2 chüan; with 2 supplements.

Bound in 1 t'ao 2 ts'ê.

Remarks - a modern edition.   The item is almost new.

Accession No. 323   Index No. - 112-izh

Title   " Pi   hsüeh   lu "
                         碧   血   録

Classification - B-117 傳記一總録

Subject - a collection of short biographies of famous men of the
    period from the Ch'in 秦 down to the Ming 明 dynasty; with
    illustrations.

References - 012-zafk 5/21.

Author - (著 論) Chuang Chung-fang 莊 仲 方 ; (繪 圖)
    Hsia Luan-hsiang 夏 鸞 翔 .

Edition - the "T'ung-wên-shu-chü" 同 文 書 局 ; dated Kuang-Hsü
    8/1882.   Lithographed on "fên" paper.

Index - a detailed list of names in 5 chüan, arranged chronologically.

Bound in 1 t'ao 5 ts'ê; singly interleaved.

Remarks - this edition is a very good one; and the item is complete
    and in very good condition.

Accession No. 324   Index No. - 120-gdcf

Title   " Ching shih yao lüeh "
                     經　世　要　畧

Classification - B-117 傳記一總録

Subject - biographical records of prominent ministers and famous
    generals of the period from the Ch'in 秦 down to and
    including the Sung 宋 dynasty.

References - none.

Author - (編輯) Wan T'ing-yen 萬 廷 言.

Edition - apparently original; (preface) dated Wan-Li "kêng-hsü"
    38/1610.   Blocks; bamboo paper.

Index - a table of names; 20 chüan.

Bound in 1 t'ao 10 ts'ê.

Remarks - this is a very fine edition; and the item is complete
    and in generally good condition with the exception of a few
    repaired defects in the 1st ts'ê.

The University of Toronto Chinese Library

Accession No. 325   Index No. - 096-zjzc

Title   " Yŭ-ch'i-shêng nien p'u hui chien "
玉 谿 生 年 譜 會 箋

Classification - B-107 傳記一獨錄

Subject - the biography and chronological record of Li Shang-yin

李 商 隱.

References - none.

Author - (編纂) Chang Ts'ai-t'ien 張 采 田; (參 校)
Liu Ch'êng-kan 劉 承 幹.

Edition - the "Ch'iu-shu-chai" 求 恕 齋; dated "ting-ssŭ" 6/1917.
Blocks; "mao-pien" paper.

Index - none; 4 chüan.

Bound in 1 t'ao 4 ts'ê.

Remarks - an ordinary edition. The item is complete.

Accession No. 326   Index No. - 101-zbd

Title   " Yung-liu chi "
                    用 六 集

Classification - D-43 別集一文
Subject - an individual collection of literary compositions,- prose.

References - 012-zafk 17/3   031-bgdf 181/2.

Author - (著) Tiao Pao 刁包 . 1603-1669

Edition - the "Shun-chi-lou" 順 積 樓 ; dated K'ang-Hsi "chia-ch'ên"
    3/1664.   Blocks; bamboo paper.

Index - a classified table of contents for 12 chüan.

Bound in 1 t'ao 6 ts'ê.

Remarks - this is not a good edition.   The impression is blurred
    in many places.

—— ◆ ——

Accession No.   327   **Index No.** - 173-chhb

Title   " Hsüeh-an ch'ing shih "
                    雪 巷 清 史

·

Classification - C-308 雜家－雜文

Subject - a collection of miscellaneous writings and expositions.

References - 031-bgdf 128/24.

Author - (著) Lo Ch'un 樂 純 .

Edition - the "Chin-ling-shu-lin" 金 陵 書 林 ; (preface) dated
Wan-Li "chia-yin" 42/1614.   Blocks; bamboo paper.

Index - a detailed table of contents for 5 chüan.

Bound in n 1 t'ao 4 ts'ê.

Remarks - this is a fairly good edition. The item is complete and
in generally good condition.

Accession No.   328   Index No. - 030-gdzz

Title   " T'ang Sung pa ta chia wên ch'ao "
             唐 宋 八 大 家 文 鈔

Classification - D-73 總集 - 文

Subject - a general collection of literary compositions, mainly
   prose, written by 8 famous authors of the T'ang and Sung
   periods.

References - 160-1j 163-ggcz 16/8 031-bgld 19/27 030-iaff 39/19
   029-pffz 320 012-zafk 19/11 031-bgdf 189/28 Gest No. 915.

Author - (批 評) Mao K'un 茅 坤 .

Edition - a Ming edition; dated Wan-Li "chi-mao" 7/1579.   Blocks;
   bamboo paper.

Index - separate list of contents for each individual collection.

Bound in 8 t'ao 44 ts'ê (5-3-12-4-8-5-5-2).

Remarks - a fairly good edition; the item appears to be complete
   and in generally good condition,- some worm-holes. The 4th
   work is a hand-written replacement.

   (#)

378

(#)

(1)   " Han Wên kung wên ch'ao "
韓 文 公 文 鈔
                              (178-hzbz)

by Han Yu 韓 愈 16 chüan.

(2)   " Liu Liu-chou wên ch'ao "
柳 柳 州 文 鈔
                              (075-eecz)

by Liu Tsung-yüan 柳 宗 元 12 chüan.

(3)   " Ou-yang Wên-chung kung wên ch'ao "
歐 陽 文 忠 公 文 鈔
                              (076-kizd)

by Ou-yang Hsiu 歐 陽 修 52 chüan.

(4)   " Su Wên kung wên ch'ao "
蘇 文 公 文 鈔
                              (140-pzbz)

by Su Hsün 蘇 洵 10 chüan.

(5)   " Su Wên-chung kung wên ch'ao "
蘇 文 忠 公 文 鈔
                              (140-pzdb)

by Su Shih 蘇 軾 28 chüan.

(6)   " Su Wên-ting kung wên ch'ao "
蘇 文 定 公 文 鈔
                              (140-pzeb)

by Su Ch'ê 蘇 轍 20 chüan.

(7)   " Wang Wên kung wên ch'ao "
王 文 公 文 鈔
                              (096-zzbz)

by Wang An-shih 王 安 石 16 chüan.

(8)   " Tsêng Wên-ting kung wên ch'ao "
曾 文 定 公 文 鈔
                              (073-hzeb)

by Tsêng Kung 曾 鞏 10 chüan.

Accession No.   329   Index No. - 076-hehn   053-hnh

Title   " Ch'in-ting k'ang chi lu "
                 欽 定 康 濟 錄
                 " K'ang chi lu "
                 康 濟 錄

Classification - B-292 政書一邦計

Subject - a treatise on the problems of political economy; especially
    at the time of famine or flood; with a section on relief works
    during the previous dynasties of Chinese history.

References - 160-1j 163-ggcz 6/4   031-bgld 8/14   012-zafk 9/11
    031-bgdf 82/38.

Author - (撰) Ni Kuo-lien 倪 國 璉.

Edition - no notation; dated Ch'ien-Lung 5/1740.   Blocks;
    "mao-pien" paper.

Index - a table of contents for 4 chüan.

Bound in 1 t'ao 6 ts'ê.

Remarks - a very good edition; complete and in perfect condition.

Accession No. 330 (a)   Index No. - 073-fzfh

Title   " Shu mu ta wên "
                書　目　答　問

Classification - B-342 目録 一 經籍

Subject - a catalogue of books; with a list of authors of the

Ch'ing Dynasty.

References - 012-zafk 9/19   Gest No. 427.

Author - (撰) Chang Chih-tung 張 之 洞.

Edition - privately published; (preface) dated Kuang-Hsü 1/1875.

Blocks; "fên" paper.

Index - a table of contents, classified under the usual four

headings of Chinese literature, with 2 additions.

Bound in 1 ts'ê in 1 t'ao with (b).

Remarks - an ordinary modern edition; the item is complete and

without defects.

Accession No. 330 (b)　　　Index No. - 159-icg

Title　　　　　" Yu hsüan yü "
　　　　　　　輶　軒　語

Classification - C-328 雜家－雜纂

Subject - a collection of articles under 7 classes; chiefly dealing
　　with the education of a man,- his moral training, necessary
　　works to be studied, principles of writing compositions,
　　rules of Imperial examinations, etc.

References - 012-zafk 13/11.

Author - (撰) Chang Chih-tung 張 之 洞.

Edition - uniform with (a).

Index - a list of 7 chapter headings.

Bound in 1 ts'ê in 1 t'ao with (a).

Remarks - same as under (a).

Accession No. 331   Index No. - 085-hbfe

Title   " Shun-Hua ko t'ieh shih wên "
               淳 化 閣 帖 釋 文

Classification - B-347 目錄 一金石.

Subject - explanatory notes on the Shun-Hua specimens of handwriting.

References - 012-zafk 9/22.

Author - (校定) Chu Chia-piao 朱 家 標.

Edition - the "Ch'iung-chin-t'ang" 絧 錦 堂 ; (preface) dated
   K'ang-Hsi "kuei-hai" 22/1683.   Blocks; bamboo paper.

Index - a detailed table of contents for 10 chüan.

Bound in 1 t'ao 2 ts'ê; doubly interleaved.

Remarks - a fairly good edition; the item is complete and in very
   good condition.

———•—•———

Accession No. 332   Index No. - 029-bdzn   029-bdzj

Title   " Yu lin i kao "
                友 林 乙 藁 (稿)

Classification - D-33 別集一詩文
Subject - an individual literary collection,- prose and poetry.

References - 163-ggoz 13/19   031-bgld 16/30   167-mhfm 21/24

    012-zafk 15/29   031-bgdf 163/3.

Author - by Shih Mi-ning 史 彌 寧.

Edition - a manuscript facsimile of the Sung edition, written on

    thin Japanese paper.

Index - a detailed table of contents; not divided into chüan.

Bound in 1 t'ao 1 ts'ê; doubly interleaved.

Remarks - a very fine manuscript; the item is complete and very neat.

The University of Toronto Chinese Library

Accession No. 333   Index No. - 040-cdzc

Title   " Shou Pien jih chih "
守　汴　日　志

Classification - B-52 雜史

Subject - a journal of the defence of the city of K'ai-fêng in Honan by Li Kuang-tien, while it was besieged by the insurgent Li Tzŭ-ch'êng 李 自 成 at the end of the Ming dynasty.

References - Wylie's Notes page 33 012-zafk 4/23 031-bgdf 54/21.

Author - (撰) Li Kuang-tien 李 光 壁 .

Edition - no notation; dated Kuang-Hsü 24/1899.　　Blocks; "fên" paper.

Index - none; in 1 chüan.

Bound in 1 t'ao 4 ts'ê; doubly interleaved.

Remarks - an ordinary edition; the item is in good condition and appears to be complete.

The University of Toronto Chinese Library

Accession No. 334   Index No. - 031-bfcm

Title   " Ssǔ Hung nien p'u "
四 洪 年 譜

Classification - B-117 傳記一總錄

Subject - the biographies and chronological records of Hung Hao
洪 皓 and his sons,- Hung Kua 洪 适 , Hung Tsun 洪 遵
and Hung Man 洪 邁 .

References - 029-pffz 159.

Author - of the 1st and 3rd works - Hung Ju-k'uei 洪 汝 奎 ; of
the 2nd and 4th works - Ch'ien Ta-hsin 錢 大 昕 .

Edition - the "Hui-mu-chai" 晦 木 齋; dated Hsüan-T'ung 1/1909.
Blocks; "fên" paper.

Index - none; 4 chüan.

Bound in 1 t'ao 4 ts'ê.

Remarks - a good modern edition; the item is almost new.

Accession No. 335   Index No. - 037-zgmf

Title   " Ta i chio mi lu "
                   大 義 覺 迷 錄

Classification - B-302 政書-法令 B-67 詔令奏議-奏議

Subject - (Gest No. 2081) - "a collection of Imperial edicts on the
    subject of rebellious subjects in general, and especially with
    reference to Lü Liu-liang 呂 留 良 ; issued as a result of
    Tsêng Ching's 曾 靜 comments on certain of Lü's writings;
    together with related matter, including a judicial interrogation
    (#)

References - Gest No. 2081.

Author - the Emperor Yung-Chêng 雍 正 .

Edition - no notation; probably official; not dated.   Blocks;
    bamboo paper.

Index - none; 4 chüan.

Bound in 1 t'ao 8 ts'ê; doubly interleaved.

Remarks - the item is in generally good condition and appears
    to be complete.

    (#) of Tsêng Ching on a charge of high treason and malfeasance
    in office; etc., etc."

—— • ——

Accession No.　336　　　　Index No. – 010-been

Title　　　　　　" Yüan-Ho　hsing　tsuan "
　　　　　　　　　元　和　姓　纂

Classification – C-348 類書

Subject – an encyclopaedia of Chinese family names, their origins, etc; arranged according to rhymes.

References – 160-1j　163-ggcz 10/12　031-bgld 14/3　012-zafk 13/20 031-bgdf 135/11.

Author – (撰) Lin Pao 林寶 .

Edition – the "Chin-ling-shu-chü" 金陵書局; dated Kuang-Hsü 6/1880.　Blocks; "mao-pien" paper.

Index – none; 10 chüan.

Bound in 1 t'ao 4 ts'ê.

Remarks – this item is complete and in good condition.

Accession No. 337   Index No. - 154-hag

Title   " Chih K'ung shuo "
                    質   孔   説

Classification - C-13 儒家

Subject - a collection of short essays on the doctrine of Confucius
    and other related subjects.

References - none.

Author - (輯) Chou Mêng-yen 周 夢 顏 .

Edition - privately published; (preface) dated Ch'ien-Lung "i-ch'ou"
    10/1745.   Blocks; bamboo paper.

Index - at the beginning of each of 2 chüan.

Bound in 1 t'ao 2 ts'ê; doubly interleaved.

Remarks - an ordinary edition; the item is complete and without
    defects.

———•———

Accession No. 338   **Index No.** - 085-hgkd

Title   " Ch'ing yü chai ch'ao "
清　語　摘　鈔

Classification - A-161 小學一字書

Subject - a classified Chinese-Manchu dictionary of official terms
and phrases.

References - none.

Author - not stated.

Edition - the "Chü-chên-t'ang" 聚珍堂 ; dated Kuang-Hsü 15/1889.
Blocks; "mao-t'ai" paper.

Index - none.

Bound in 1 t'ao 4 ts'ê.

Remarks - this is one of the cheap editions, and the item is complete
and in good condition.

Accession No. 339   Index No. - 170-hhdd

Title   " T'ao Yüan-ming chi "
               陶　淵　明　集

Classification - D-33 別集 — 詩文

Subject - an individual literary collection,- poetry and prose.

References - 160-1j 163-ggcz 12/2 031-bgld 15/4 167-mhfm 19/6
     031-bgdf 148/32 012-zafk 15/3   Gest No. 1556.

Author - T'ao Ch'ien 陶　潛 .

Edition - a facsimile of the original edition of Su 蘇 style
     handwriting; dated Kuang-Hsü "chi-mao" 5/1879.   Blocks;
     "hsüan" paper.

Index - a table of contents for 10 chüan.

Bound in 1 t'ao 3 ts'ê.

Remarks - this is a very fine edition; and the item is complete and
     in very good condition.

Accession No. 340   **Index No.** - 036-kefn

Title   " Mêng-p'o-shih huo ku ts'ung pien "
夢 坡 室 獲 古 叢 編

Classification - C-260 譜錄－器物

Subject - a descriptive and classified catalogue of photo-litho
reproductions of ancient bronze objects in possession of
Chou Ch'ing-yün 周 慶 雲 .

References - none.

Author - (藏器) Chou Ch'ing-yün 周 慶 雲 ; (編次)
Tsou Shou-ch'i 鄒 壽 祺 .

Edition - the "Chou's-Mêng-p'o-shih" 周 氏 夢 坡 室; dated "ting-mao"
1927.   Lithographed on "fên" paper.

Index - a list of 8 sections; separate list of objects for each
section.

Bound in 1 t'ao 12 ts'ê.

Remarks - a very fine modern work.   The item is new.

392

The University of Toronto Chinese Library

Accession No. 341   **Index No.** - 120-obzl

Title   " Hsü ku wên tz'ŭ lei tsuan "

續 古 文 辭 類 纂

Classification - D-63 總集－詩文

Subject - a general collection of prose with some poetic writings
under 10 classifications, being supplementary to "Ku wên tz'ŭ
lei tsuan" 古文辭類纂.

References - Toronto Nos. 11(b), 12(b).

Author - (纂集) Wang Hsien-ch'ien 王 先 謙.

Edition - the "Hsü-shou-t'ang" 虛 受 堂; dated Kuang-Hsü "jên-wu"
8/1882.   Blocks; "mao-pien" paper.

Index - a general table of contents for 34 chüan with compiler's
notes at the end.

Bound in 1 t'ao 8 ts'ê.

Remarks - this is an ordinary modern edition; and the item is
complete and in very good condition.

Accession No.   342   Index No. - 002-cczd

Title   " Chung-chou jên wu k'ao "
                 中 州 人 物 考

Classification - B-117 傳記－總録

Subject - biographical sketches of renowned persons of Honan province
during the Ming Dynasty; under seven groups arranged according to
their characteristics and positions.

References - 163-ggcz 5/5   031-bgld 6/17   160-1j   012-zafk 5/15
031-bgdf 58/22.

Author - (輯) Sun Ch'i-fêng 孫奇逢 .

Edition - possibly privately published; (preface) dated Tao-Kuang
"chia-ch'ên" 24/1844.   Blocks; "t'u-fên" paper.

Index - separate at the beginning of each of 8 chüan.

Bound in 2 t'ao 8 ts'ê.

Remarks - this is not a good edition at all.   The item is, however,
in good condition.

———— •◆• ————

Accession No. 343   **Index No.** – 061-hef

Title   " Hui ti shu "
惠　迪　書

Classification – C-328 雜家 – 雜纂

Subject – a collection of notes taken from some Taoist and other
    individual works, chiefly consisting of rules, commandments,
    etc governing the conduct of man as well as chapters on the
    importance of performing meritorious and virtuous works.

References – none.

Author – (著錄) Ta-yüan-shih 大 原 氏.

Edition – privately published; dated Kuang-Hsü 10/1884.   Blocks;
    "mao-pien" paper.

Index – a general table of contents for 6 chüan,– "nei p'ien" 內篇
    3 chüan and "wai p'ien" 外 篇 3 chüan.

Bound in 1 t'ao 2 ts'ê.

Remarks – the item is complete and in good condition.

Accession No. 344   Index No. - 163-fjof

Title   " Hsi-yüan tu shu chih "
         郋 園 讀 書 志

Classification - B-342 目錄 － 經籍
Subject - a descriptive catalogue of books.

References - none.

Author - (撰) Yeh Te-hui 葉 德 輝 .

Edition - the "Shanghai Tan-yüan" 上 海 澹 園 ; dated "mou-ch'ên"
         1928.   Type; "fên" paper.

Index - a general list of the 4 main divisions of Chinese literature
        in 16 chüan; separate detailed table at the beginning of each
        chüan.
Bound in 2 t'ao 16 ts'ê.

Remarks - a modern edition; the item is new.

Accession No. 345   Index No. - 102-gmld   036-kaeg

Title   " Hua hsüeh chien ming "
                畫   學   簡   明
         " Mêng-huan-chü hua hsüeh chien ming "
          夢 幻 居 畫 學 簡 明

Classification - C-223 藝 術 一 書 畫
Subject - a concise treatise on Chinese paintings with supplements
      (illustrated).

References - none.

Author - (著) Chêng Chi 鄭 績 .

Edition - the "Mêng-huan-chü" 夢 幻 居 ; (preface) dated T'ung-Chih
     "chia-tzŭ" 3/1864.   Blocks; "fên" paper.

Index - a general table of contents for 5 chüan (with supplements).

Bound in 1 t'ao 10 ts'ê.

Remarks - this is a good work; and the item is in very good condition.

Accession No. 346   Index No. - 170-hjzk

Title   " Yin chih wên t'u shuo "
               陰 騭 文 圖 說

Classification - C-308 雜家 — 雜文

Subject - (Toronto No. 202) - "an illustrated collection of fables
    setting forth examples of retribution in connection with good
    or bad conduct."

References - Toronto No. 202.

Author - Ch'ing Chu 清 柱 .

Edition - the "Yu-yüeh-chai" 有 櫂 齋 ; dated Chia-Ch'ing "hsin-yu"
    6/1801.   Blocks; bamboo paper.

Index - none; in 4 chüan.

Bound in 1 t'ao 4 ts'ê; doubly interleaved with margins.

Remarks - this item is a duplicate of No. 202; but the edition is
    a much better one.   A few pages are repaired.

Accession No.   347   Index No. - 041-kzdj

Title   " Tui-shan yin kao "
                     對 山 印 稿

Classification - C-233 藝術 - 篆刻
Subject - an extensive collection of seal impressions in red.

References - none.

Author - (鐫) Yang Hsieh 楊 燮 .

Edition - the "Shih-ch'ao-shu-chai" 嗜鈔書齋; (preface) dated
     Tao-Kuang 9/1829.   Blocks; "fên" paper.

Index - a general table of contents in 10 ts'ê.

Bound in 1 t'ao 8 ts'ê; doubly interleaved.

Remarks - this is a fine edition; and the item is in very good
     condition.   This item does not contain the last 2 ts'ê
     (9-10) as given in the index; probably because they were
     proposed and not published.

Accession No. 348   Index No. - 118-nni

Title   " Ch'ou chi pien "
                   籌　濟　編

Classification - B-292 政書一邦計

Subject - (Gest No. 1321) - "calamities and relief in their
    principal aspects."

References - 012-zafk 9/13   Gest No. 1321.

Author - (輯) Yang Ching-jên 楊 景 仁.

Edition - no notation; (preface) dated Tao-Kuang 9/1829.   Blocks;
    "fên" paper.

Index - a general table of contents for a leading chapter and 32
    chüan.

Bound in 2 t'ao 8 ts'ê.

Remarks - this item is complete and in good condition.

Accession No. 349   Index No. - 096-gmek

Title   " Li hsüeh tsung chuan "
                理   學   宗   傳

Classification - B-117 傳記 - 總錄

Subject - a collection of biographies of noted scholars of the
period from the Han 漢 down to and including the Ming 明
dynasty.   宋 seu H 672

References - 012-zafk 5/15.

Author - (輯) Sun Ch'i-fêng 孫奇逢．

Edition - no notation; (preface) dated K'ang-Hsi 6/1669.   Blocks;
bamboo paper.

Index - a general table of names for 26 chüan arranged dynastically.

Bound in 1 t'ao 8 ts'ê.

Remarks - a fairly good edition; the item is complete and without
defects.

Accession No.   350   Index No. - 075-defd

Title   " Tung-p'o shih chi chu "
東 坡 詩 集 註

Classification - D-38 別集一詩

Subject - a commentary on poems of Su Shih 蘇軾 .

References - none to this particular edition.

Author - (輯註) Ch'ien Ta-hsin 錢大昕; (纂) Hung Liang-chi
洪 亮 吉 ; (分 編) Li Hsi-kung 李錫恭 .

Edition - the "Wên-wei-t'ang" 文 蔚 堂 ; dated Ch'ien-Lung
"jên-yin" 47/1782. Blocks; bamboo paper.

Index - a detailed table of contents for 32 chüan.

Bound in 2 t'ao 12 ts'ê.

Remarks - this item is complete and has no defects except some
worm-holes.

Accession No. 351   Index No. - 030-bbje   124-jeoh

Title   " Ku chin han yüan ch'iung chü "

古 今 翰 苑 瓊 琚

" Han yüan ch'iung chü "

翰 苑 瓊 琚

Classification - D-73 總集一文

Subject - a collection of selected masterpieces of prose compositions
by famous authors from ancient times down to and including the
Ming Dynasty.

References - 012-zafk 19/8   031-bgdf 192/14.

Author - (選) Yang Shên 楊 慎 ; (評) Sun K'uang 孫 鑛 ;
(校) Ch'ên Yüan-su 陳 元 素 .

Edition - no particular notation; (preface) dated T'ien-Ch'i 1/1621.
Blocks; bamboo paper.

Index - a general table of contents for 12 chüan; separate list at
the beginning of each chüan.

Bound in 2 t'ao 12 ts'ê; doubly interleaved.

Remarks - this is a very good edition; and the item appears to be
complete and is in perfect condition.

403

Accession No. 352   Index No. - 030-bchz

Title   " Shih chi lun wên "
                    史 記 論 文

Classification - B-367 史 評

Subject - a commentary on the "Shih chi" 史 記 of Ssŭ-ma Ch'ien
            司 馬 遷.

References - 012-zafk 9/30.

Author - (評 點) Wu Chien-ssŭ 吳 見 思 ; (參 訂) Wu Hsing-tsu
            吳 興 祚.

Edition - the "Ch'ih-mu-t'ang" 尺 木 堂 ; (preface) dated K'ang-Hsi
            "ting-mao" 26/1687.   Blocks; bamboo paper.

Index - a general table of contents for 130 chüan.

Bound in 2 t'ao 20 ts'ê.

Remarks - the item appears to be complete and in generally good
            condition.

404

Accession No. 353   Index No. - 001-dgig

Title   " <u>Shih</u> <u>shuo</u> <u>hsin</u> <u>yü</u> <u>pu</u> "

世　說　新　語　補

<u>Classification</u> - C-368 小 說 家

<u>Subject</u> - appendix to a collection of minor incidents from the <u>Han</u> 漢

to the <u>Chin</u> 晉 dynasty inclusive.

<u>References</u> - Wylie's Notes page 189 012-zafk 14/8 031-bgdf 143/31

Gest No. 618 Toronto No. 80.

<u>Author</u> - <u>Ho Liang-chün</u> 何 良 俊 .

<u>Edition</u> - a Ming edition; (preface) dated Chia-Ching "i-wei" 14/1535.

Blocks; bamboo paper.

<u>Index</u> - a general table of contents for 20 chüan.

<u>Bound in</u> 1 t'ao 6 ts'ê.

<u>Remarks</u> - a good edition; the item is without defects. The

impression in general is not very good.

Accession No. 354   Index No. - 144-jngc

Title   " Wei-Tsang t'ung chih "
　　　　　　　　衛　藏　通　志

Classification - B-227 地理 — 外記

Subject - a general description of Tibet,- its territory; topography;

　　religion; money and commerce; inhabitants; defenses; etc.

References - 012-zafk 8/27.

Author - not stated.

Edition - the "Chien-hsi-ts'un-shê" 漸　西　村舍; dated Kuang-Hsü

　　22/1896.　　Blocks; "mao-pien" paper.

Index - a general table of contents for a leading chapter and

　　16 chüan.

Bound in 1 t'ao 8 ts'ê.

Remarks - the item is complete and without defects.

Accession No.   355   Index No. - 102-elh

Title   " Hsü tê lu "
                              畜 德 録

Classification - C-328 雜家 一 雜纂
Subject - a collection of writings and sayings of famous philosophers
    and scholars from the Chou 周 down to the end of the Ming 明
    dynasty; all of which being of a moral and ethical character.

References - 012-zafk 13/7   031-bgdf 133/9.

Author - (纂輯) Hsi Ch'i-t'u 席啓圖 .

Edition - the "Ch'ien-hsin-ssǔ" 懺 心 寺 ; dated T'ung-Chih
    "ting-mao" 6/1867.   Blocks; "mao-pien" paper.

Index - a general table of chapter headings for 20 chüan.

Bound in 1 t'ao 10 ts'ê.

Remarks - this is an ordinary edition; and the item is complete and
    in perfect condition.

Accession No. 356   Index No. - 030-dgch

Title   " Wu-chün ming hsien t'u chuan tsan "
          吳 郡 名 賢 圖 傳 贊

Classification - B-117 傳記－總錄

Subject - woodcuts of ancient worthies of the Su-chow 蘇 州 region,
    formerly known under the designation Wu-chün; with eulogies and
    biographical notes.

References - 012-zafk 5/20.

Author - (輯) Ku Yüan 顧 沅.

Edition - that of the author; (preface) dated Tao-Kuang 9/1829.
    Blocks; "fên" paper.

Index - a list of names in 20 chüan.

Bound in 1 t'ao 8 ts'ê.

Remarks - a fairly good edition; the item is complete and in very
    good condition.

Accession No. 357   Index No. - 061-fghd

Title   " En-sung-t'ang chi "
　　　　　　　　恩　誦　堂　集

Classification - D-33 别集 - 詩文
Subject - an individual literary collection,- prose and poetry.

References - none.

Author - by Li Shang-ti 李 尚 迪.

Edition - privately published; (preface) dated Tao-Kuang "ting-wei"
　　27/1847.　　Blocks; "fên" paper.

Index - (詩) a general table of contents for 10 chüan; (文)
　　same for 2 chüan.

Bound in 1 t'ao 2 ts'ê.

Remarks - the item is complete and in very good condition.

Accession No.   358   Index No. - 144-jphb

Title   " Hêng-lu-ching-shê ts'ang kao "
                 衡 廬 精 舍 藏 稿

Classification - D-33 別集一詩文
Subject - an individual miscellaneous collection of prose and poetry.

References - 163-ggcz 15/9   031-bgld 18/31   012-zafk 16/28
      031-bgdf 172/39.

Author - (著) Hu Chih 胡 直 .

Edition - the "Ch'i-ssǔ-shu-shu" 齊 思 書 塾 ; dated Kuang-Hsü
      "kuei-mao" 29/1903.   Blocks; "mao-t'ai" paper.

Index - a detailed classified table of contents for 30 chŭan; 續稿
      11 chŭan.

Bound in 1 t'ao 12 ts'ê.

Remarks - one of the cheap modern editions; the item is complete
      and without defects.

410

The University of Toronto Chinese Library

Accession No.　359　　　　Index No. - 030-chg1

Title　　　　" <u>Ming hsien hua hsiang chuan</u> "
　　　　　　名　賢　畫　像　傳

<u>Classification</u> - B-117 傳記一總録

<u>Subject</u> - a collection of biographies of some of the most eminent
　　worthies of all periods in Chinese history; with portraits.

<u>References</u> - none.

<u>Author</u> - <u>Wang Hui-tien</u> 王　會　典 .

<u>Edition</u> - the "<u>Kuo-ch'ün-chu-i-shê</u>" 國 羣 鑄 一 社 ; dated Min-Kuo
　　3/1914.　　Lithographed on foreign paper.

<u>Index</u> - a table of names arranged chronologically; in 1 chüan.

<u>Bound in</u> 1 t'ao 2 ts'ê.

<u>Remarks</u> - a modern cheap edition; complete and without defects.

Accession No.　360 (a)　　　Index No. - 070-eepf

Title　　　　　" Shih　chu　su　shih "
　　　　　　　　施　注　蘇　詩

Classification - D-38 別集一詩

Subject - a commentary on the poems of Su Shih 蘇軾 .

References - Wylie's Notes page 229　163-ggcz 13/6　012-zafk 15/15

　　031-bgdf 154/4　Gest No. 2018.

Author - (注) Shih Yüan-chih 施 元 之 ; (閱定) Sung Lo 宋犖

　　and Chang Jung-tuan 張 榕 端 ; (刪補) Shao Ch'ang-hêng

　　邵 長 蘅 ; Ku Ssǔ-li 顧 嗣 立 ; and Sung Chih 宋 至 .

Edition - the "Chin-ch'ang-pu-yüeh-lou" 金 閶 步 月 樓 ; (preface)

　　dated K'ang-Hsi "chi-mao" 38/1699.　　Blocks; bamboo paper.

Index - a detailed table of contents for 42 chüan.

Bound in 2 t'ao 11 ts'ê with (b).

Remarks - this item is complete, but with serious defects in many

　　places,- worm-holes which have been repaired.

412

Accession No. 360 (b)   Index No. - 140-pfog

Title   " Su shih hsü pu i "
               蘇 詩 續 補 遺

Classification - D-38 別 集 - 詩

Subject - a supplement to (a).

References - as under (a).

Author - (補註) Fêng Ching 馮 景 .

Edition - uniform with (a).

Index - a detailed table of contents for 2 chüan.

Bound in 1 ts'ê in 2d t'ao with (a).

Remarks - as under (a).

———•———

Accession No. 361   Index No. - 029-pffz

Title   " Ts'ung shu shu mu hui pien "
                叢   書   書   目   彙   編

Classification - B-342 目錄 一 經籍

Subject - (Gest No. 1096) - "a list giving the contents of 2279
    collections of reprints arranged in the order of the number
    of strokes in the first character of the title."

References - Gest No. 1096.

Author - compiled by Shên Ch'ien-i 沈 乾 一 .

Edition - the "I-hsüeh-shu-chü" of Shanghai 上海醫學書局 ; dated
    Min-Kuo 17/1928.   Type; foreign paper.

Index - arranged according to the number of strokes in the first
    character of the title.

Bound in 1 t'ao 4 ts'ê.

Remarks - a modern edition; complete and without defects.   As to
    the value of this work the following is quoted from the Gest
    Library Catalogue:- "This is not a work of any literary merit
    and its accuracy is more than doubtful."

Accession No.　362　　　　Index No. - 085-gebf

Title　　　　　" Hai-tai shih lüeh "
　　　　　　　　海 岱 史 略

Classification - B-117 傳記-總錄

Subject - a classified collection of biographies, taken from the official dynastic histories of China, of noted officials and scholars, natives of Eastern Shantung,- formerly known under the designation Hai-tai; covering a period from the Han 漢 down to and including the Ming 明 dynasty.

References -none.

Author - (編) Wang Yü-ch'ao 王 馭 超 .

Edition - privately published, and possibly by the author; (preface) dated Chia-Ch'ing 23/1818.　Blocks; "mao-pien" paper.

Index - 12 separate lists of contents at the beginning of each dynastic section with successive number of chüan; 140 chüan in all.

Bound in　4 t'ao 24 ts'ê.

Remarks - the item is complete and in very good condition except for some slight stains.

415

Accession No. 363   Index No. - 102-eeme

Title   " Liu ch'ên p'u ch'u pien "
留 真 譜 初 編

Classification - B-342 目録 一 經籍

Subject - (Gest No. 1095)- "a collection of reproductions of specimen
pages from old printed and manuscript works found in Japan."

References - Gest No. 1095.

Author - edited by Yang Shou-ching 楊 守 敬.

Edition - privately published; (preface) dated Kuang-Hsü "hsin-ch'ou"
27/1901.   Blocks; "fên" paper.

Index - none; in 12 chüan.

Bound in 1 t'ao 12 ts'ê.

Remarks - the work is a very useful one.   It is apparently complete
and has no defects.

The University of Toronto Chinese Library

Accession No. 364   Index No. - 152-1fdh

Title   " <u>Yü chang hsien hsien chiu chia nien p'u</u> "
豫 章 先 賢 九 家 年 譜

Classification - B-117 傳記－總錄

Subject - a collection of biographies and chronological records of nine ancient famous scholars.

References - 012-zafk 5/22.

Author - (編) <u>Yang Hsi-min</u> 揚 希 閔．

Edition - no notation; (preface) dated Kuang-Hsü 3/1877.   Blocks; "fên" paper.

Index - a general list of 9 works.

Bound in 1 t'ao 12 ts'ê.

Remarks - a very ordinary edition; the item is in generally good condition.

Accession No. 365   Index No. - 031-bahg

Title   " <u>Ssŭ-pên-t'ang tso yu pien</u> "
                    四 本 堂 座 右 編

Classification - C-328 雜家－雜纂
Subject - a general miscellany on morality and ethics.

References - 031-bgdf 133/10.

Author - (輯) <u>Han-shan-tzŭ</u> 韓 山 子 i.e., <u>Chu Ch'ao-yüan</u>
         朱 潮 遠

Edition - privately published; (preface) dated K'ang-Hsi 3/1664.
         Blocks; bamboo paper.

Index - (main work) a general table of contents for 24 chüan under
        4 main headings; (2d "chi") a similar index.

Bound in 1 t'ao 8 ts'ê.

Remarks - a fairly good edition. The item has no defects and is
          complete. Certain parts of the work are with punctuations in
          red.

The University of Toronto Chinese Library

Accession No. 366   Index No. - 212-zbzc

Title   " Lung-hu-shan   chih "
龍 虎 山 志

Classification - B-207 地理一山川

Subject - a description of the Lung-hu Mountains, situated to the
south-west of the Kuei-hsi 貴溪 district in the province of
Kiangsi; with chapters on topography; historical remains;
famous persons; monasteries; literature; etc.

References - none.

Author - (輯) Miao-chêng-chên-jên 妙 正 真 人 i.e., Lou Chin-yüan
婁 近 垣 .

Edition - the "T'ai-shang-ch'ing-kung" 太 上 清 宮 ; dated Ch'ien-Lung
"kêng-shên" 5/1740.   Blocks; bamboo paper.

Index - a general table of contents for 16 chüan.

Bound in 1 t'ao 6 ts'ê.

Remarks - the item is complete, but has some defects,- worm-holes
and stains.

Accession No. 367   Index No. - 077-aozp   067-zpg(zb)

Title   " Chêng   hsü   Wên   hsien   t'ung   k'ao   shih   ta   pien "
                正   續   文   獻   通   考   識   大   編
               " Wên   hsien   t'ung   k'ao   shih   ta   pien "
                文   獻   通   考   識   大   編

Classification - B-282 政書一通制

Subject - miscellaneous notes on and extracts from the "Wên hsien
    t'ung k'ao",- a general encyclopaedia on matters relating to
    government.

References - none.

Author - of original - Ma Tuan-lin 馬 端 臨 and Wang Ch'i 王圻
    of this work - (編) Fang Jo-t'ing 方 若 珽 .

Edition - privately published; (preface) dated K'ang-Hsi "i-ch'ou"
    24/1685.   Blocks; bamboo paper.

Index - a general table of contents; 24 chüan.

Bound in 2 t'ao 10 ts'ê (5-5).

Remarks - 4 pages at the beginning of chüan 20 and 1 page at the
    end of chüan 24 are torn and missing.   The item is otherwise
    in fairly good condition.

420

The University of Toronto Chinese Library

Accession No.   368   **Index No.** - 055-azbc   007-zzzb

Title   " <u>Nien-i   shih   yüeh   pien</u> "
     廿 一 史 約 編

     " <u>Erh-shih-i   shih   yüeh   pien</u> "
     二 十 一 史 約 編

Classification - B-137 史鈔

Subject - a condensed version of the twenty-one official dynastic
  histories of China; that is, from ancient times up to the end
  of the <u>Yüan Dynasty</u>; together with an additional chapter on
  matters of the <u>Ming Dynasty</u>.

References - 012-zafk 5/29.

Author - (述) <u>Chêng Yüan-ch'ing</u> 鄭 元 慶 ; (鑒定)
<u>Ch'ên Ch'ü-shih</u> 陳 瞿 石 .

Edition - the "<u>Yü-chi-t'ing</u>" 魚 計 亭 ; (preface) dated "ping-tzǔ"
  (? Ch'ien-Lung 21/1756).   Blocks; "mao-t'ai" paper.

Index - a general table of contents for a leading chüan and 8 "pu" 部

Bound in 1 t'ao 8 ts'ê.

Remarks - a useful historical reference work. Certain parts of the
  impression are blurred, and 1 page is missing at the end of the
  6th ts'ê.

421

—— • ——

Accession No. 369   Index No. - 064-fhcn

Title   " Ch'ih-ching-chai ts'ang shu chi yao "
             持 靜 齋 藏 書 記 要

Classification - B-342 目録 一 經籍

Subject - (Gest No. 999)- "Catalogue of books, printed and in

   manuscript, in a private library,-----"

References - Gest Nos. 999 and 1935.

Author - by Mo Yu-chih 莫 友 芝.

Edition - the "Wên-hsüeh-shan-fang" 文 學 山 房 ; (preface) dated

   "kêng-wu" 1870 (?).   Blocks; "fên" paper.

Index - none; 2 chüan.

Bound in 1 t'ao 2 ts'ê; doubly interleaved.

Remarks - a good edition; complete and without defects.

Accession No. 370 (a)   Index No. - 103-ich

Title   " I nien lu "
                 疑 年 録

Classification - B-117 傳記 － 總録

Subject - vital records of prominent persons,- dates of birth and
    death.

References - 012-zafk 5/17.

Author - (編) Ch'ien Ta-hsin 錢 大 昕 ; (校) Wu Hsiu 吳 修 .

Edition - no notation; (preface) dated Chia-Ch'ing 18/1813.   Blocks;
    "mao-pien" paper.

Index - none; 4 chüan.

Bound in 1 ts'ê in 1 t'ao with (b).

Remarks - an ordinary edition; complete and without defects.

Accession No. 370 (b)   Index No. - 120-oich

Title   " Hsü i nien lu "
                         續 疑 年 録

Classification - B-117 傳記一總録
Subject - a supplement to (a).

References - 012-zafk 5/18.

Author - (編) Wu Hsiu 吳 修 .

Edition - uniform with (a).

Index - none; 4 chüan.

Bound in 1 ts'ê in 1 t'ao with (a).

Remarks - as under (a).

Accession No. 371   Index No. - 103-ichj

Title   " I nien lu hui pien "

疑 年 録 彙 編

Classification - B-117 傳記－總録

Subject - (Gest No. 1358) - "vital statistics of prominent persons,-
dates of birth and death,- being a compilation of numerous
similar works published previously under the same general
title."

References - Gest No. 1358.

Author - (增 輯) Chang Wei-hsiang 張 惟 驤.

Edition - the "Hsiao-shuang-chi-an" 小 雙 寂 庵 ; dated "i-ch'ou"
1925.   Blocks; "mao-pien" paper.

Index - none; 16 chüan and an index.

Bound in 1 t'ao 8 ts'ê.

Remarks - a useful reference work.   The item is complete and
without defects.

425

Accession No. 372   Index No. - 061-fcnf

Title   " Hsi-chai ts'ang shu "
                      息　齋　藏　書

Classification - C-308 雜家 - 雜說

Subject - a general classified collection of extracts taken from
    standard philosophical works as well as literary writings
    of renowned scholars.

References - 012-zafk 125/42.

Author - (撰) P'ei Hsi-tu 裴希度.

Edition - privately published; (preface) dated K'ang-Hsi 2/1663.
    Blocks; bamboo paper.

Index - a detailed table of contents for 12 chüan.

Bound in 1 t'ao 8 ts'ê; doubly interleaved with margins.

Remarks - this is a very good edition; and the item is complete
    and in excellent condition with the exception of a few stained
    pages.

The University of Toronto Chinese Library

Accession No. 373   Index No. - 030-bffg

Title   " Shih shih tsai pu "
               史　拾　載　補

Classification - B-367 史評

Subject - a commentary on the section Pa shu 八書 ,- the "eight
treatises",- and on certain parts of the section Lieh chuan
列傳 ,- the "narratives",- of the "Shih chi" of Ssǔ Ma-ch'ien.

References - 012-zafk 9/29   031-bgdf 90/13.

Author - (鑒) Ch'ên Tzǔ-lung 陳于龍 ;(箋) Wu Hung-chi 吳弘基

Edition - no notation; no date, but apparently of the Ming period.
Blocks; bamboo paper.

Index - a general table of the 4 works; separate detailed lists at
the beginning of each section of the 4 works; contents not
arranged under chüan.

Bound in 4 t'ao 18 ts'ê; doubly interleaved with margins.

Remarks - this is a very fine edition; and the item is complete and
in very good condition.   The following works are included in
this item:-
(#)

427

(#)
        " <u>Shih</u> <u>shih</u> <u>i</u> <u>wên</u> "
        史   拾   遺   聞   (030-bflh)

      " <u>Shih</u> <u>shih</u> <u>kuang</u> <u>lan</u> "
      史   拾   廣   覽   (030-bflo)

     " <u>Shih</u> <u>shih</u> <u>chung</u> <u>tuan</u> "
     史   拾   眾   斷   (030-bffn)

428

The University of Toronto Chinese Library

Accession No. 374   **Index No.** - 001-blc

Title   " San ch'ien chih "
　　　　　　　　　 三　　遷　　志

Classification - B-107 傳記一獨録

Subject - (Toronto No. 306) - "a work on Mencius; consisting of his
　　biography and chronological record; record of his posterity
　　and disciples; historical remains of his temple and grave;
　　lessons from his mother; etc; etc."

References - 012-zafk 5/1　　031-bgdf 59/12　　Toronto No. 306.

Author - by Shih Ê 史鶡 .

Edition - no notation, but apparently original; (preface) dated
　　Chia-Ching "jên-tzǔ" 31/1552.　　Blocks; "mien" paper.

Index - a table of contents for 6 chüan.

Bound in 1 t'ao 4 ts'ê; doubly interleaved.

Remarks - This is a very fine edition; and the item is in very good
　　condition and complete with the exception of 2 pages which are
　　missing as follows:- Chüan 2 pages 10 and 13.　　This item is
　　not an exact duplicate of No. 306; the latter being a revised
　　edition by different authors with additions and modifications.

The University of Toronto Chinese Library

Accession No. 375   Index No. - 031-hhej

Title   " Kuo-ch'ao jou yüan chi "
               國 朝 柔 遠 記

Classification - B-282 政書－通制

Subject - a treatise on Sino-Foreign diplomatic relations from the
    first reign (Shun-Chih) of the Ch'ing Dynasty down to and
    including the T'ung-Chih period; together with related matter.

References - none.

Author - (編) Wang Chih-ch'un 王 之 春 . (H818 f (1934)

Edition - the "Kuang-ya-shu-chü" 廣 雅 書 局 ; dated Kuang-Hsü
    17/1891.   Blocks; "mao-t'ai" paper.

Index - a table of the various "reigns" arranged in successive order
    for 18 chüan; a separate list for 2 chüan for the supplement 附編

Bound in 1 t'ao 10 ts'ê.

Remarks - this is a very ordinary edition; and the item is complete
    and without defects except some stains.

430

— · —

Accession No. 376   **Index No.** - 049-afzj

Title   " <u>Pa-na-ma sai hui Chih-li kuan hui ts'ung pien</u> "

巴 拿 馬 賽 會 直 隸 觀 會 叢 編

Classification - B-227 地理 - 外記

Subject - a collection of 20 works in connection with the International Industrial and Fine Arts Exhibition held in 1915 at
the city of San Francisco in commemoration of the opening of the
Panama Canal.

References - none.

Author - by a group of authors headed by <u>Yen Chih-i</u> 嚴 智 怡
under the auspices of the Industrial Bureau of Chihli.

Edition - published by the "<u>Industrial Bureau of Chihli</u>" 直隸實業廳;
(preface) dated Min-Kuo 10/1921.   Type; "mao-pien" paper.

Index - a list of the 20 works and their authors in 2 "pien" 上 下.

Bound in 2 t'ao 16 ts'ê (8.8).

Remarks - a very interesting work.   The item is complete and
as new.

431

Accession No. 377   Index No. - 108-jzc

Title   " P'an-shan chih "
                          盤 山 志

Classification - B-207 地理 - 山川

Subject - (Toronto No. 304)- "a description of the Pan-shan Mountain
    situated not far to the east of Peiping; including chapters on
    various topographical aspects of the mountain; temples and
    other constructions; literary compositions written by famous
    scholars of all dynasties; visits by previous emperors; etc."

References - Toronto No. 304.

Author - (纂輯) Chih P'u 智朴.

Edition - no notation; (postscriptum) dated T'ung-Chih 11/1872.
    Blocks; "fên" paper.

Index - a detailed table of contents for 10 chüan; "pu i" 補遺
    4 chüan.

Bound in 1 t'ao 4 ts'ê.

Remarks - a duplicate of No. 304.   The item is in good condition and
    complete.

432

The University of Toronto Chinese Library

Accession No. 378   **Index No.** - 067-zpg(zb)

Title   " Wên hsien t'ung k'ao chi yao "

文 獻 通 考 紀 要

Classification - B-282 政書一通制

Subject - a collection of some 400 poems embracing the important features of the "Wên hsien t'ung k'ao",- generally known as an encyclopaedia on matters relating to government; together with explanatory notes.

References - none.

Author - not stated.

Edition - no particular notation; undated.   Blocks; bamboo paper.

Index - 2 separate detailed tables of contents; 2 chüan 上 下 .

Bound in 1 t'ao 2 ts'ê.

Remarks - the item is complete and in fairly good condition. There are a few worm-holes, and those in important places have been repaired.

The University of Toronto Chinese Library

Accession No. 379   Index No. - 102-zzic

Title   " Chia-tzǔ hui chi "
                 甲　子　會　紀

Classification - B-22 編年

Subject - a table of 71 Chinese Cycles (of 60 years each, as
    designated by the method of the 10 stems and 12 branches),
    beginning with the 8th year of Huang-Ti and ending with the
    42d year of Chia-Ching; together with significant historical
    features included under the respective years as well as an (#)

References - 012-zafk 4/10   031-bgdf 48/14.

Author - (編集) Hsüeh Ying-ch'i 薛　應　旂 .

Edition - no notation; (preface) dated Chia-Ching "chi-wei" 38/1559.
    Blocks; bamboo paper.

Index - detailed table of contents for 5 chüan.

Bound in 1 t'ao 4 ts'ê.

Remarks - a useful reference work. The item is complete and in
    very good condition.

    (#) additional chapter on miscellaneous related matters.

Accession No. 380   Index No. - 201-zdib

Title   " Huang Chung-tuan kung nien p'u "
               黃   忠   端   公   年   譜

Classification - B-107 傳記－獨録

Subject - the biography and chronological record of Huang Tao-chou
黃 道 周 .

References - none.

Author - (編) Chuang Ch'i-ch'ou 莊 起 儔 ; (校) Ts'ai Shih-yüan
蔡 世 遠.

Edition - no notation; (preface) dated Tao-Kuang 9/1829.   Blocks;
    "fên" paper.

Index - none; 4 chüan (and supplement).

Bound in 1 t'ao 2 ts'ŝ.

Remarks - an ordinary edition; the item is complete and without
    defects.

Accession No. 381   Index No. - 128-ggbc

Title   " S̲h̲ê̲n̲g̲ c̲h̲i̲a̲o̲ s̲h̲i̲h̲ c̲h̲i̲ "

聖　教　史　紀

Classification - C-971 基督教

Subject - a record of Christianity during ancient times i.e. the
   period A. D. 1 - 600.

References - none.

Author - H̲s̲i̲e̲h̲ W̲e̲i̲-̲l̲o̲u̲ 謝　衛　樓.

Edition - no special designation; (preface) dated Kuang-Hsü 16/1890.
   Blocks; "fên" paper.

Index - a table of contents for 3 chüan in 5 sections.

Bound in 1 t'ao 4 ts'ê.

Remarks - this item is not a translation of any particular work in
   a European language; and the materials are selected from several
   standard works on Christian history. A good edition; the item
   is with punctuations and marks for proper names, thereby making
   the text easy of comprehension.

The University of Toronto Chinese Library

Accession No. 382   Index No. - 053-pzzc

Title   " Lu-shan hsiao chih "

　　　　　　　盧　山　小　志

Classification - B-207 地理 - 山川

Subject - a description of the Lu-shan Mountain situated to the south
of Chiu-chiang District in the province of Kiangsi; with sketches
illustrating the various aspects of the mountain, and a collection
of poems written during various dynasties with regard thereto.

References - 012-zafk 8/10.

Author - (撰) Ts'ai Ying 蔡 瀛 .

Edition - the "Lang-hsüan-pieh-kuan" 嫏 嬛 別 館 ; dated Tao-Kuang
4/1824.　　Blocks; "fên" paper.

Index - a general table of contents for 卷 首 and 24 chüan.

Bound in 1 t'ao 6 ts'ê.

Remarks - the item is complete and in very good condition.

The University of Toronto Chinese Library

Accession No. 383   Index No. - 149-obcf

Title   " Tu shih chi lüeh "

讀 史 紀 畧

Classification - B-367 史評

Subject - (Gest No. 3592) - "a digest of history, from ancient times down to and including the Ming Dynasty."

References - Gest No. 3592.   Toronto No. 313.

Author - (纂輯) Hsiao Chün 蕭潯 .

Edition - the "Tan-ching-chai" 澹靜齋 ; dated Tao-Kuang 20/1840. Blocks; bamboo paper.

Index - a general table of contents for 4 chüan.

Bound in 1 t'ao 4 ts'ê; doubly interleaved.

Remarks - this item is a duplicate of No. 313; and the edition is also the same. Pages at the beginning of the 1st ts'ê - those of the prefaces - are with repaired corners. The work is complete.

Accession No. 384   Index No. - 120-gdmm

Title   " Ching shih huan ying pien "
經　世　環　應　編

Classification - C-328 雜家 - 雜纂

Subject - selections, from historical works, of notes and incidents
mainly illustrating the efficiency of momentary acuteness and
versatility.

References - 031-bgdf 132/18.

Author - (輯) Ch'ien Chi-têng 錢　鑸　登.

Edition - a Ming edition; no date.   Blocks; bamboo paper.

Index - a table of chapter headings for 8 chüan.

Bound in 2 t'ao 10 ts'ê (5-5); doubly interleaved.

Remarks - a good edition; the item appears to be complete, but there
are worm-holes on many of the top margins.   Chüan 5 does not
seem to be complete; but there is no detailed table of contents
to aid in ascertaining this point.

Accession No. 385   Index No. - 072-eccz

Title   " Chao-tai ming jên ch'ih-tu hsiao chuan "
         昭 代 名 人 尺 牘 小 傳

Classification - B-117 傳記一總錄

Subject - a collection of some 600 short biographical notes of noted
       officials and scholars of the Ch'ing Dynasty; together with the
       titles of works they have written.

References - 012-zafk 5/18.

Author - (采 輯) Wu Hsiu 吳 修 .

Edition - privately published; (preface) dated Tao-Kuang 6/1826.
       Blocks; "fên" paper.

Index - a list of names; 24 chüan.

Bound in 1 t'ao 2 ts'ê; doubly interleaved.

Remarks - as a catalogue, this work seems to be a useful one for
       reference in case of doubt as to the real authorship of any
       particular book.   An ordinary edition; the item is complete
       but with a few reparied defects, mostly on the corners and
       edges.

Accession No. 386   Index No. - 085-khzi

Title   " Han pei wên fan "
                 漢 碑 文 範

Classification - B-347 目錄 一金石

Subject - a series of readings of inscriptions on ancient stone
    tablets of the Han Dynasty.

References - none.

Author - (纂) Wu K'ai-shêng 吳 闓 生.

Edition - no notation; (preface) dated "chia-tzǔ" 1924.   Blocks;
    "fên" paper.

Index - a detailed list of contents for 4 chüan.

Bound in 1 t'ao 2 ts'ê.

Remarks - a very fine modern edition printed in red; the item is
    new.

Accession No. 387   Index No. - 069-1mle   077-1chh

Title " Hsin-chien tsêng-ting Li-tai chieh lu ch'üan pien "
新 鐫 增 定 歷 代 捷 録 全 編
" Li-tai chieh lu ch'üan pien "
歷 代 捷 録 全 編

Classification - B-367 史評

Subject - critical discussions on Chinese history from the remotest
times down to the period of Wan-Li of the Ming Dynasty.

References - none.

Author - various; (訂) Ch'ên Chi-ju 陳 繼 儒.

Edition - the "Ts'un-ya-chai" 存 雅 齋 ; (preface) dated T'ien-Ch'i
"ping-yin" 6/1626.   Blocks; bamboo paper.

Index - a detailed table of contents for 8 chüan.

Bound in 1 t'ao 4 ts'ê.

Remarks - the item appears to be complete and is in good condition.

442

The University of Toronto Chinese Library

Accession No. 388   Index No. - 120-ckkk

Title   " Hung lou mêng t'u yung "
                  紅　樓　夢　圖　詠

Classification - C-368 小説家

Subject - (Toronto No. 211) - "a collection of sketches and poems
   illustrating the famous characters of the "Hung lou mêng"
   紅 樓 夢 ,- a popular tale containing a picture of Chinese
   domestic life.

References - Toronto No. 211.

Author - various.

Edition - no notation; dated Kuang-Hsü 10/1884.   Blocks; "fên" paper.

Index - at the beginning of each of 4 ts'ê.

Bound in 1 t'ao 4 ts'ê; doubly interleaved.

Remarks - a duplicate of No. 211.   The edition is very good; and
   the item is almost new.

443

Accession No. 389   Index No. - 120-izcz   120-izdg

Title

" Lien-ch'uan ming jên hua hsiang "
練 川 名 人 畫 象

" Lien-ch'uan hsien chê hua hsiang "
練 川 先 哲 畫 象

Classification - B-117 傳記一總録

Subject - woodcuts of worthies of the Lien-ch'uan region,- now known
as the District of Chia-ting 嘉 定 in Kiangsu Province; of
the period from the Sung down to and including the Ch'ing
Dynasty; together with biographical notes.

References - none.

Author - (編次) Ch'êng Tsu-ch'ing 程 祖 慶 .

Edition - that of the author; (preface) dated Tao-Kuang 28/1848.
Blocks; "fên" paper.

Index - a detailed list of names for 4 chüan; 附 卷 2 chüan;
separate list for 3 chüan for the 續 編 .

Bound in 1 t'ao 8 ts'ê; doubly interleaved.

Remarks - this is a very fine edition; and the item is complete
and in very good condition.

2
sel
288

Accession No. 390   **Index No.** - 024-gcbl 024-gblz 021-cblz

Title   " <u>Nan</u> <u>Pei</u> <u>shih</u> <u>shih</u> <u>hsiao</u> <u>lu</u> "
南　北　史　識　小　錄

Classification - B-137 史鈔

Subject - (Toronto No. 288) - "(a) a collection of selections taken
from the "<u>Nan shih</u>" 南史 ; together with commentarial notes;
(b) same from the "<u>Pei shih</u>" 北史 ."

References - 160-lj 163-ggcz 5/6 031-bgld 6/19 012-zafk 5/29
031-bgdf 65/4 Gest No. 94 Toronto No. 288.

Author - (同編) <u>Shên Ming-sun</u> 沈 名 蓀 and <u>Chu K'un-t'ien</u>
朱 昆 田 .

Edition - "<u>Wu's Ch'ing-lai-t'ang</u>" 吳 氏 清 來 堂 ; dated T'ung-Chih
"hsin-wei" 10/1871.   Blocks; "mao-t'ai" paper.

Index - (a) a general table of contents for 14 chüan; (b) none; 14
chüan.

Bound in 2 t'ao 12 ts'ê.

Remarks - a very ordinary edition; the item is complete and in good
condition with the exception of a defective page at the end of
14th chüan of (b).

445

———— ● ————

Accession No. 391   Index No. - 067-zfbi

Title   " Wên chang kuei fan "
                文   章   軌   範

Classification - D-73 總集 - 文

Subject - a general collection of 69 prose compositions by some of
    the most famous ancient scholars of the Han, Chin, T'ang and
    Sung periods; with punctuations and commentarial notes in red.

References - 160-1j 163-ggcz 16/5 031-bgld 19/16 030-iaff 38/22
    106-gdkn 114/16 012-zafk 19/4 031-bgdf 187/34.

Author - (編) Hsieh Fang-tê 謝 枋 得。

Edition - the "T'ung-yin-shu-wu" 桐 陰 書 屋; dated Kuang-Hsü
    "kuei-wei" 9/1883.   Blocks; "fên" paper.

Index - a detailed table of contents for 7 chüan.

Bound in 1 t'ao 2 ts'ê.

Remarks - a fair edition; the item is in good condition.   One or
    two pages (most probably one) are missing at the end of the
    work; as the last composition does not seem to be complete.

446

The University of Toronto Chinese Library

Accession No. 392   Index No. - 024-gkmd

Title   " Nan-fêng Liu hsien-shêng wên chi "
南 豐 劉 先 生 文 集

Classification - D-43 別 集 - 文

Subject - an individual collection of prose compositions.

References - none.

Author - by Liu Fu-ching 劉 孚 京 .

Edition - the "Chü-chên-fang-sung-yin-shu-chü" of Shanghai 上 海 聚 珍
做 宋 印 書 局; dated "chi-wei" 1919.   Blocks; "mao-pien"
paper.

Index - a detailed table of contents for 4 chüan; 補 遺 1 chüan.

Bound in 1 t'ao 4 ts'ê.

Remarks - a good modern edition; the item is almost new.

Accession No. 393   Index No. - 035-gfgc

Title   " Hsia Shih-lang nien p'u "

夏 侍 郎 年 譜

Classification - B-107 傳記 -獨錄   1831-1880

Subject - the biography and chronological record of Hsia T'ung-shan

夏 同 善 ; together with a short biography of his wife who

was born in the family of T'u 屠 .

References - none.

Author - by his sons,- Hsia Kêng-fu 夏庚復 ; Hsia Tun-fu 夏敦復

and Hsia Hsieh-fu 夏偕復 .

Edition - privately published by the Hsia family; (postscriptum) dated

Min-Kuo 9/1920.   Blocks; "fên" paper.

Index - none; 年譜 1 chüan; 碑銘 1 chüan; 墓銘 1 chüan;

屠夫人行狀 1 chüan.

Bound in 1 t'ao 1 ts'ê.

Remarks - a very fine clear-cut edition; the item is new.

The University of Toronto Chinese Library

Accession No.   394   Index No. - 053-1dzk

Title   " Kuang lieh nü chuan "
                     廣 列 女 傳

Classification - B-117 傳記－總錄

Subject - a collection of biographies of famous women of ancient
    times.

References - 012-zafk 5/22.

Author - (纂) Liu K'ai 劉 開 .

Edition - reprinted by "Yü Yüeh" 俞 樾 ; dated Kuang-Hsü 10/1884.
    Blocks; "fên" paper.

Index - a general table of classification headings in 20 chüan.

Bound in 1 t'ao 6 ts'ê.

Remarks - an ordinary edition; the item appears to be complete and
    in generally good condition.

Accession No.   395   Index No. - 007-zzbf

Title   " Ễrh-shih shih shuo jun piao "
               二 十 史 朔 閏 表

Classification - B-157 時 令   C-133 天文算法 - 推步

Subject - (Gest No. 1722) - "a calendar for the 60 year cycles

   covering the period from the beginning of the Han Dynasty

   206 B C -, down to the 29th year of Min-Kuo - A D 1940;

   with corresponding years according to the Roman, Christian,

   and Mohammedan eras; together with miscellaneous tables."

References - Gest No. 1722.

Author - by Ch'ên Yüan 陳 垣.

Edition - the "Pei-ching-ta-hsüeh" 北 京 大 學; or the "Li-yün

   shu-wu" 勵 耘 書 屋; dated Min-Kuo 14/1925.   Lithographed

   on "fên" paper.

Index - none.

Bound in 1 t'ao 1 ts'ê.

Remarks - a useful reference work.   The item is new.

450

Accession No. 396   Index No. - 061-izer

Title   " I-ta-li ts'an shu "
               意 大 利 蠶 書

Classification - C-53 農家

Subject - a treatise on the rearing of silkworms in Italy.

References - none.

Author - (著) Tan T'u-lu 丹 吐 魯 .

Edition - no notation; no date.   Blocks; "mao-pien" paper.

Index - a general table of contents for 15 章 .

Bound in 1 t'ao 2 ts'ê; doubly interleaved.

Remarks - a fairly good modern edition; the item is complete and
    in good condition.

Accession No. 397   Index No. - 192-shfl

Title   " Yü-hua-ko i chi "
                     鬱 華 閣 遺 集   .

Classification - D-38 別集一詩
Subject - an individual collection of poems; with a chapter on

lyrical compositions.

References - none.

Author - (撰) Shêng Yü 盛 昱 .

Edition - privately published; (preface) dated Kuang-Hsü 31/1905.

Blocks; "hsüan" paper.

Index - none; in 4 chüan.

Bound in 1 t'ao 1 ts'ê.

Remarks - a fairly good modern edition; the item is apparently

complete and in very good condition.

The University of Toronto Chinese Library

Accession No. 398   Index No. - 039-azgg

Title   " K'ung-tzŭ chia yü " .
               孔 子 家 語

Classification - C-13 儒家

Subject - (Wylie) - "Traditional words of Confucius"; with commentary.

References - Wylie's Notes page 82 160-1j   163-ggcz 7/1
      031-bgld 9/1   037-ahhg 9/1; (hsü) 5/3; (hsü) 16/2   (#)

Author - of the commentary - Wang Su 王 肅 .

Edition - the "Shu-yeh-t'ang" 書 業 堂 ; dated Ch'ien-Lung
      "hsin-ch'ou" 46/1781.   Blocks; bamboo paper.

Index - a general table of contents for 10 chüan.

Bound in 1 t'ao 2 ts'ê.

Remarks - this is a fairly good edition; and the item is complete
      and in good condition.

      (#) 167-mhfm 13/1   012-zafk 10/1   031-bgdf 91/3.

The University of Toronto Chinese Library

Accession No. 399   Index No. - 112-1zh

Title   " Pi hsüeh lu "
                          碧   血   錄

Classification – B-117 傳記一總錄

Subject – (Toronto No. 323) – "a collection of short biographies of
famous men of the period from the Ch'in 秦 down to the Ming 明
dynasty; with illustrations."

References – 012-zafk 5/21   Toronto No. 323.

Author – (著 論) Chuang Chung-fang 莊 仲 方 ; (繪 圖)
Hsia Luan-hsiang 夏 鸞 翔 .

Edition – the "T'ung-wên-shu-chü" 同 文 書 局 ; dated Kuang-Hsü
8/1882.   Lithographed on "fên" paper.

Index – a detailed table of names in 5 chüan, arranged chronologically.

Bound in 1 t'ao 5 ts'ê.

Remarks – this item is complete and in good condition; being an exact
duplicate of No. 323.

Accession No. 400   Index No. - 210-zcck

Title   " Ch'i ming chi shu "
                    齊 名 紀 數

Classification - C-348 類書
Subject - lists of historical personages grouped in numerical
    categories.

References - 012-zafk. 13/29.

Author - (輯) Wang Ch'êng-lieh 王 承 烈.

Edition - the "Huan-shan-lou" 環 山 樓 ; dated Chia-Ch'ing "kuei-yu"
    18/1813.   Blocks; bamboo paper.

Index - a general table of numerical categories; 12 chüan.

Bound in 1 t'ao 6 ts'ê; doubly interleaved.

Remarks - this is a fairly good edition; and the item is complete
    and in very good condition.

Accession No. 401   Index No. - 195-dzjc

Title   " Lu-shan hsien chih "
魯 山 縣 志

Classification - B-194 地理-別志

Subject - topography of the Lu-shan 魯 山 district in Honan; with

chapters on government and administration; historical remains;

mountains and rivers; biographies; literature; etc.

References - none.

Author - (纂) Wu I 武 億 and Tung Tso-tung 董 作 棟.

Edition - no notation; (preface) dated Chia-Ch'ing 1/1796.   Blocks;

"t'u-fên" paper.

Index - a general table of contents for 26 chüan.

Bound in 1 t'ao 6 ts'ê.

Remarks - this is a very ordinary edition; and the item is complete

and in generally good condition.

The University of Toronto Chinese Library

Accession No. 402   Index No. - 166-dc

Title   " <u>Yeh   chi</u> "
                          野   記

<u>Classification</u> - C-368 小說家

<u>Subject</u> - a collection of notes and jottings of a miscellaneous
    character.

<u>References</u> - 031-bgdf 143/19.

<u>Author</u> - (纂) <u>Chu Yün-ming</u> 祝 允 明.

<u>Edition</u> - published by "<u>Chu-shih</u>" 祝 氏 ; dated T'ung-Chih "chia-hsü"
    13/1874.   Blocks; "mao-pien" paper.

<u>Index</u> - none; 4 chüan.

<u>Bound in</u> 1 t'ao 2 ts'ê; doubly interleaved.

<u>Remarks</u> - the item is complete and without defects.

Accession No. 403   Index No. - 113-he

Title   " <u>Chin   pien</u> "
                            禁   扁

Classification - B-194 地理－別志

Subject - (Wylie) - "----- containing a detail of the imperial
    residences, during the preceding succession of dynasties."

References - Wylie's Notes page 43 163-ggcz 5/9   031-bgld 7/3
    012-zafk 6/1   031-bgdf 68/2.

Author - (纂次) <u>Wang Shih-tien</u> 王 士 黙 .

Edition - the "<u>Yang-chou-shih-yüan</u>" 揚 州 使 院 reprint; dated
    "ping-hsü" (? Ch'ien-Lung 31/1766.)   Blocks; bamboo paper.

Index - a table of contents for 5 sections designated by the 1st 5
    of the 10 stems.

Bound in 1 t'ao 4 ts'ê; doubly interleaved.

Remarks - a very good edition; the item is complete and in very
    fine condition.

Accession No. 404   Index No. - 075-elzd

Title   " Jou-ch'iao wên ch'ao "

　　　　　　　柔　橋　文　鈔

Classification - D-43 别集 一文

Subject - an individual collection of prose compositions.

References - none.

Author - by Wang Fên 王棻 .

Edition - the "Kuo-kuang-shu-chü" 國光書局 ; dated "chia-yin"

　　1914.　　Lithographed on foreign paper.

Index - a detailed table of contents for 16 chüan.

Bound in 1 t'ao 8 ts'ê.

Remarks - an ordinary cheap edition; the item is complete and in

　　good condition.

Accession No.   405   Index No. - 056-cbhd

Title   " Shih-ku-t'ang chi "
                           式　古　壺　集

Classification - D-43 別集 -文
Subject - an individual literary collection,- prose.

References - none.

Author - (著) Chang Yün-i 張雲翼 .

Edition - no notation; dated Ch'ien-Lung "ting-yu" 42/1777.

   Blocks; "fên" paper.

Index - none.

Bound in 1 t'ao 4 ts'ê; quadruply interleaved with old book-leaves.

Remarks - a very good edition; the item is in good condition, but
   there is no table of contents to aid in ascertaining whether
   the text is complete or not, though it appears to be.

Accession No.　　406　　　　Index No. - 040-ogof

Title　　　　" An-nan　chih　lüeh "

安　南　志　畧

Classification - B-147 載記

Subject - "a narrative account of Annam."

References - Wylie's Notes page 41　163-ggcz 5/8　031-bgld 6/24

012-zafk 5/30　031-bgdf 66/27.

Author - (編) Li Tsê 黎 則 .

Edition - the "Lo-shan-t'ang" 樂 善 堂 of Shanghai; dated "chia-
shên" 1884.　Type; "mao-pien" paper.

Index - a general table of contents for 20 chüan.

Bound in 1 t'ao 4 ts'ê.

Remarks - a very ordinary edition; the item is complete and in
good condition.

Accession No.   407   Index No. - 154-hecb

Title   " Shang-ch'i hsüan ssǔ chung ho pien "
             賣 奇 軒 四 種 合 編

Classification - C-328 雜家-雜纂

Subject - (Wylie) - "----- is a collection of four treatises, i.e.,
    the 無 雙 譜 Woo shwang poo, a series of portraits of
    illustrious ancient worthies, with brief descriptive details;
    the 東 坡 遺 意 Tung p'o ê e, fac-similes of autographs of
    the poet Soo Tung-p'o; the 二 妙 Urh meaou, drawings of   (#)

References - Wylie's Notes page 154.

Author - not stated.

Edition - no notation; (anonymous postscriptum) dated "kêng-tzǔ"
    (?) 1900.   Blocks; "fên" paper.

Index - none.

Bound in 1 t'ao 4 ts'ê; doubly interleaved.

Remarks - this is a very fine edition; and the item appears to be
    complete and is in very good condition.

    (##)

462

(#) the bamboo; and the 官子譜 Kwan tsze poo, a book of
diagrams of the Chinese game of drafts, 圍棊 Wei k'e."

(##) " <u>Wu</u> <u>shuang</u> <u>p'u</u> "   B-117   (086-hjm)
      無　雙　譜

      " <u>Tung-p'o</u> <u>i</u> <u>i</u> "   C-223   (075-deli)
      東　坡　遺　意

      " <u>Erh</u> <u>miao</u> "   C-223   (007-zd)
      二　妙

      " <u>Kuan</u> <u>tzŭ</u> <u>p'u</u> "   C-238   (040-ezm)
      官　子　譜

Accession No.   408   Index No. - 085-akzz   012-zzg

Title   " Yung-chia pa mien fêng "
                 永 嘉 八 面 鋒

                 " Pa mien fêng "
                   八 面 鋒

Classification - C-348 類書

Subject - a collection of notes and expositions on a variety of
    subjects.

References - 163-ggcz 10/13   031-bgld 14/8   012-zafk 13/21
    031-bgdf 135/34.

Author - not stated.   See under "Remarks".

Edition - the "Hu-hai-lou" 湖 海 樓 ; (postscriptum) dated
    Chia-Ch'ing "chi-mao" 24/1819.   Blocks; "mao-pien" paper.

Index - a detailed table of contents for 13 chüan.

Bound in 1 t'ao 4 ts'ê; doubly interleaved.

Remarks - a good edition; complete and without defects.   There is
    no trace as to the authorship of this work.   031-bgdf states
    that owing to the similarity in their special names,- 永 嘉 ,-
    this work has been credited by some to Ch'ên Fu-liang 陳 傅 良
    or Yeh Shih 葉 適 ; but this is extremely doubtful.

Accession No. 409   Index No. - 011-blao

Title   " Nei chien ch'ih tu pien chu "
               內 簡 尺 牘 編 註

Classification - D-43 別集一文

Subject - a individual collection of letters; with explanatory notes.

References - 163-ggcz 13/11   012-zafk 15/21   031-bgdf 157/16.

Author - (撰) Sun Ti 孫覿 ; (編注) Li Tsu-yao 李 祖 堯.

Edition - published by "Shêng's Ssŭ-hui-chai"盛氏思惠齋 ;
     dated Kuang-Hsü "ping-shên" 22/1896.   Blocks; "fên" paper.

Index - a detailed table of contents for 10 chüan.

Bound in 1 t'ao 2 ts'ê.

Remarks - a very fine clear-cut edition printed in red; the item
     has no defects and is complete.

Accession No. 410   Index No. - 031-hhkm

Title   " Kuo-ch'ao han hsüeh shih ch'êng chi "
             國 朝 漢 學 師 承 記

Classification - B-117 傳記一總録

Subject - a collection of biographies of famous Ch'ing Dynasty
    scholars, writers on ancient Chinese literature.

References - 012-zafk 5/18.

Author - (纂) Chiang Fan 江 藩 .

Edition - the "Chü-chên-pan" 聚 珍 板; dated Kuang-Hsü 2/1876.
    Blocks; "mao-pien" paper.

Index - a table of contents (i.e. names) for 8 chüan.

Bound in 1 t'ao 2 ts'ê.

Remarks - an ordinary edition; complete and in good condition.
    There is a short supplement to this work entitled:-

        " Kuo-ch'ao ching shih ching i "
          國 朝 經 師 經 義
                                    (031-hhgg)

Accession No. 411   Index No. - 075-drkc

Title   " Tung-kuan Han chi "
                             東　觀　漢　記

Classification - B-42 別史
Subject - a record of the Later Han 後漢 or Estern Han 東漢
        dynasty.

References - 160-1j   012-zafk 4/15   031-bgld 5/30   031-bgdf 50/4.

Author - (撰) Liu Chên 劉珍 according to "Sui-shu ching chi chih"
         隋書經籍志.

Edition - the "Sao-yeh-shan-fang" 掃葉山房 ; dated Ch'ien-Lung
         42/1777.   Blocks; bamboo paper.

Index - a detailed classified table of contents for 24 chüan.

Bound in 1 t'ao 4 ts'ê.

Remarks - a fair edition; the item is complete and in good condition.

467

Accession No. 412   Index No. - 149-ofiz

Title   " Tu shu tso jên p'u "

讀 書 做 人 譜

Classification - C-328 雜家－雜纂

Subject - a treatise on "man", along moral and ethical lines; together with quotations from various standard works.

References - 012-zafk 13/10.

Author - (輯) Lung Ping-yüan 龍 炳 垣 .

Edition - a manuscript written on "mao-t'ai" paper; dated T'ung-Chih 11/1872.

Index - a general table of subject headings; not divided into chüan.

Bound in 1 t'ao 2 ts'ê; doubly interleaved with leaves of some old books.

Remarks - an ordinary manuscript. The item is in good condition; but as the pages are not numbered, it is difficult to tell whether the text is complete or not, though it appears to be.

Accession No. 413   Index No. - 075-kfcf

Title   " <u>Shu yüan chi lüeh</u> "

樞　垣　紀　略

Classification - B-52 雜史

Subject - miscellaneous records of the Court in Peking from the
    period of Ch'ien-Lung to that of T'ung-Chih; including
    chapters on Imperial Edicts; appointments; extension of
    bounties; lists of officials etc.

References - none.

Author - of original <u>Liang Chang-chü</u> 梁章鉅 of this work -
    <u>The Imperial Prince I Hsin</u> 奕訢 .

Edition - no notation; (preface) dated Kuang-Hsü 1/1875.   Blocks;
    "fên" paper.

Index - none; 28 chüan.

Bound in 1 t'ao 6 ts'ê.

Remarks - a very fine neat edition; the item appears to be complete.
    Chüan 24 and 25 contain pages with repaired worm-holes.   The
    work is otherwise in very good condition.

Accession No.   414   Index No. - 001-dazn

Title   " Ping Ting kuei chien "
                    丙 丁 龜 鑑

Classification - C-188 術數 - 陰陽五行

Subject - containing incidents that occurred in all the "ping-wu" 丙午
    and "ting-wei" 丁未 years in the 60-year cycles from the
    period of the Ch'in 秦 to the end of the Five Dynasties;
    showing, by the method of tortoise-shell divination, that
    all such years are those of distress; together with a   (#)

References - 031-bgdf 111/39.

Author - (撰) Ch'ai Wang 柴望 . of the supplement - unknown.

Edition - apparently a later Ch'ing Dynasty reprint (preface) dated
    Chih-Chêng 至正 23/1363.   Blocks; bamboo paper.

Index - none; 5 chüan; 續錄 2 chüan (6-7).

Bound in 1 t'ao 2 ts'ê.

Remarks - a work of very little value. The edition is an ordinary
    one; and the item is complete and in good condition. It is of
    interest to note that the author was imprisoned on Imperial
    order owing the compilation of this work; but was later
    released.

(#) supplement by later authors embracing the two succeeding
Sung and Yüan Dynasties.

Accession No.   415   Index No. - 167-zihh

Title   " Chin hu ching sui "
                 金 壺 精 粹

Classification - A-161 小學-字書
Subject - explanations of a collection of Chinese couplets grouped
     under 4 general headings; together with an additional chapter
     on couplets composed of 2 similar characters.

References - none.

Author - (增訂) Hao Tsai-t'ien 郝 在 田 and Chang Yang-shan
     張 仰 山 . (The latter is apparently a courtesy name).

Edition - the "Sung-chu-chai" 松 竹 齋 ; dated Kuang-Hsü "ping-tzǔ"
     2/1876.   Blocks; "fên" paper.

Index - none.

Bound in 1 t'ao 2 ts'ê.

Remarks - a very useful reference work.   The edition is very good;
     and the item is almost new.   On the lower page-edges are given
     the names of those who calligraphed the text for the cutting of
     the blocks.   One of them is Lu Jun-hsiang 陸 潤 庠 ,- one of
     the most famous calligraphists toward the close of the Ch'ing
     Dynasty.

The University of Toronto Chinese Library

———•———

Accession No. 416   Index No. - 075-ikpf

Title   " Ying-lien ts'ung hua "
                 楹   聯   叢   話

Classification - C-348 類書

Subject - an encyclopaedia of antithetical phrases; with explanatory
  notes.

References - 012-zafk 13/29.

Author - (輯) Liang Chang-chü 梁 章 鉅 .

Edition - the "Kuei-lin-shu-chai" 桂 林 署 齋 ; dated Tao-Kuang
  "kêng-tzǔ" 20/1840.   Blocks; "mao-t'ai" paper.

Index - none; 12 chüan; 續 話 4 chüan.

Bound in 1 t'ao 6 ts'ê.

Remarks - the item has no defects and is apparently complete.

473

Accession No. 417   Index No. - 149-gg

Title   " <u>Shuo</u> <u>fu</u> "
                          說 郛

Classification - C-328 雜家 - 雜纂

Subject - a collection of reprints of 13 works on "tea",- being a
    small part (item 93) of the voluminous work entitled "<u>Shuo fu</u>",-
    [Gest No. 898] - "collection of copious extracts from works on
    all four classes of literature from more than 2,000 works ----"

References - Wylie's Notes page 170   160-1j   031-bgdf 123/21
    163-ggcz 10/11   031-bgld 13/30   029-pffz 473   058-iffz 13/45
    Gest No. 898.
Author - of the whole work - (纂) <u>T'ao Tsung-i</u> 陶 宗 儀 ;
    (重 輯) <u>T'ao T'ing</u> 陶 珽 .

Edition - the 說 郛 本 ; no date.   Blocks; bamboo paper.

Index - none.

Bound in 1 t'ao 4 ts'ê; doubly interleaved.

Remarks - as noted above, this is only a small part (but a complete
    separate item) of the work under discussion.   This item
    includes the following 13 works :-

    (#)

474

(#) 1. " <u>Ch'a</u> <u>ching</u> "　　　(140-fg)　3 chüan
　　　茶　經　　　　　by <u>Lu Yü</u> 陸羽

2. " <u>Ch'a</u> <u>lu</u> "　　　　(140-fh)　1 chüan
　　　茶　錄　　　　　by <u>Ts'ai Hsiang</u> 蔡襄

3. " <u>Shih</u> ch'a <u>lu</u> "　　(149-ffh)　1 chüan
　　　試　茶　錄　　　by <u>Sung Tzŭ-an</u> 宋子安

4. " <u>Ta</u> <u>kuan</u> ch'a <u>lun</u> "　(037-zrfh)　1 chüan
　　大　觀　茶　論　　by <u>Hui Tsung</u> 徽宗

5. " <u>Pei</u> <u>yüan</u> ch'a <u>lu</u> "　(021-cefh)　1 chüan
　　北　苑　茶　錄　　by <u>Hsiung Fan</u> 熊蕃

6. " <u>Pei</u> <u>yüan</u> pieh <u>lu</u> "　(021-ceeh)　1 chüan
　　北　苑　別　錄　　by <u>Chao Ju-li</u> 趙汝礪

7. " <u>P'in</u> ch'a <u>yao</u> <u>lu</u> "　(030-ffch)　1 chüan
　　品　茶　要　錄　　by <u>Huang Ju</u> 黃儒

8. " <u>Pên</u> ch'ao ch'a <u>fa</u> "　(075-ahfe)　1 chüan
　　本　朝　茶　法　　by <u>Sung Kua</u> 宋括

9. " <u>Chien</u> ch'a shui <u>chi</u> "　(086-ifzc)　1 chüan
　　煎　茶　水　記　　by Chang Yu-hsin 張又新

10. " <u>Shih-liu</u> t'ang p'in "　(024-zbif)　1 chüan
　　十　六　湯　品　　by <u>Su I</u> 蘇廙

11. " <u>Shu</u> chu ch'a hsiao p'in "　(162-eifz)　1 chüan
　　述　煮　茶　小　品　by <u>Yeh Ch'ing-ch'ên</u> 葉清臣

12. " <u>Tou</u> ch'a chi "　　　(191-nfc)　1 chüan
　　鬪　茶　記　　　　by <u>T'ang Kêng</u> 唐庚

13. " <u>Ts'ai</u> ch'a <u>lu</u> "　　(064-hfh)
　　採　茶　錄　　　　by <u>Wên T'ing-yün</u> 溫庭筠

————•◦•————

Accession No. 418 **Index No. –** 167-hh

Title " Ch'ien lu "

錢 録

Classification – C-263 譜録一錢幣

Subject – [Gest No. 1738] – "a description of Chinese coins and medals, principally the ancient ones."

References – Wylie's Notes page 147 160-1j 163-ggcz 9/9 031-bgld 12/15 012-zafk 12/3 031-bgdf 115/25 Gest Nos. 1072(b) and 1738.

Author – prepared by an Imperial commission.

Edition – a palace edition; (preface) dated Ch'ien-Lung "hsin-wei" 16/1751. Blocks; "k'ai-hua" paper.

Index – a general table of contents for 16 chüan, arranged chronologically.

Bound in 1 t'ao 4 ts'ê; doubly interleaved.

Remarks – this is indeed a very fine edition; but pages 2,3 and 4 in chüan 16 are missing. It is strange to notice that all the page-edges in the first 2 ts'ê have been cut, repaired and handwritten characters filled in; while the last 2 ts'ê; being (#)

(#)   apparently of a similar edition, are with printed titles
       etc on the page-edges.   After careful consideration, it
       appears that this is no more than a mere correction of
       mistakes made in the cutting of the blocks.

Accession No. 419   Index No. - 167-zzkg

Title   " Chin Shih t'u shuo "
　　　　　　金　石　圖　説

Classification - B-347 目録 - 金石

Subject - a collection of ancient inscriptions on stones and metals.

References - 031-bgdf 87/28   Gest No. 1073.

Author - (集説) Niu Yün-chên 牛運震 ; (撫圖) Ch'u Hsün 褚峻 ;
　　　(編補) Liu Shih-hêng 劉世珩.

Edition - the "Chü-hsüeh-hsüan" 聚學軒 ; dated Kuang-Hsü "i-wei"
　　　21/1895.   Blocks; "mien" paper.

Index - a general table of contents in 4 parts.

Bound in 1 t'ao 4 ts'ê.

Remarks - this is a very good edition; and the item appears to be
　　　complete and is in very good condition.

Accession No.   420   Index No. - 167-zzkg

Title   " Chin   Shih   t'u   shuo "
                          金   石   圖   說

Classification - B-347 目錄 - 金石

Subject - a collection of ancient inscriptions on stones and metals.

References - 031-bgdf 87/28   Gest No. 1073   Toronto No. 419.

Author - (集說) Niu Yün-chên 牛運震 ; (撫圖) Ch'u Hsün 褚峻 ;
         (編補) Liu Shih-hêng 劉世珩 .

Edition - the "Chü-hsüeh-hsüan" 聚學軒 ; dated Kuang-Hsü "i-wei"
         21/1895.   Blocks; "fên" paper.

Index - a general table of contents in 4 parts.

Bound in 1 t'ao 4 ts'ê; singly interleaved.

Remarks - this is a duplicate of No. 419; but the edition was
         apparently printed from different blocks.   The item is
         complete and in very good condition.

Accession No. 421   Index No. - 055-azbc   007-zzzb

Title   " Nien-i shih yüeh pien "
               廿 一 史 約 編

               " Erh-shih-i shih yüeh pien "
               二 十 一 史 約 編

Classification – B-137 史鈔

Subject – a condensed version of the twenty-one official dynastic

   histories of China; that is, from ancient times up to the end

   of the Yüan Dynasty; together with an additional chapter on

   matters of the Ming Dynasty.

References – 012-zafk 5/29   Toronto No. 368.

Author – (述) Chêng Yüan-ch'ing 鄭 元 慶 ; (鑒定)

   Ch'ên Ch'ü-shih 陳 瞿 石 .

Edition – the "Shan-ch'êng-t'ang" 善 成 堂 ; (preface) dated

   "ping-tzǔ" (? Ch'ien-Lung 21/1756), but this is a modern

   reprint.   Blocks; "mao-t'ai" paper.

Index – a general table of contents for a leading chüan and 8 "pu" 部 .

Bound in 1 t'ao 8 ts'ê.

Remarks – a duplicate of No. 368.   The edition is a very ordinary

   one; but the item appears to be complete and is without defects.

Accession No. 422   Index No. - 085-hkcz   061-zhi

Title   " Ch'ing-wu-chai hsin shang pien "
               清 窩 齋 心 賞 編
                  " Hsin shang pien "
                  心   賞   編

Classification – C-328 雜家 一雜纂

Subject – a collection of extracts taken from various works; mainly
     treating of the problems of life and preservation of health.

References – 012-zafk 13/5   031-bgdf 132/14.

Author – (輯) Wang Hsiang-chin 王 象 晉 .

Edition – privately published; (preface) dated "kuei-yu" (? Ch'ung-Chêng
     6/1633).   Blocks; bamboo paper.

Index – a list of 6 subject headings; complete in 1 chüan.

Bound in 1 t'ao 2 ts'ê; doubly interleaved with margins.

Remarks – a fairly good edition; the item is without defects other
     than repaired worm-holes.   The following pages are missing,-
     20, 25, 26, 28.

———◆———

Accession No. 423   Index No. - 113-fdco

Title   " Hsiang hsing yao lan "
                 祥　刑　要　覽

Classification - C-43 法家
Subject - a general treatise on jurisprudence.

References - 012-zafk 10/13   031-bgdf 101/18.

Author - (編纂) Wu No 吳訥 ; (附錄) Ch'ên Ch'a 陳察 .

Edition - the "Yüeh-tung-fu-shu" 粵東撫署; dated Tao-Kuang
    "chia-wu" 14/1834.   Blocks; bamboo paper.

Index - a detailed table of contents for 4 chüan.

Bound in 1 t'ao 2 ts'ê.

Remarks - the item is in good condition and complete with the
    exception that page 8 in chüan 2 is missing.

Accession No. 424   Index No. - 128-gh11

Title

" Shêng hsien hsiang tsan "

聖　賢　像　贊

Classification - B-117 傳記 一 總錄

Subject - (Toronto No. 315) - "a general collection of eulogies
written by the emperors and noted scholars of various periods
in praise of ancient sages and famous philosophers; together
with portraits."

References - 012-zafk 5/1   Gest No. 1082   Toronto No. 315.

Author - not given.

Edition - the "Hui-wên-t'ang" of Ch'ü-fu 曲阜會文堂; dated
Kuang-Hsü 4/1878.   Blocks; "mao-pien" paper.

Index - a detailed table of contents for 3 ts'ê or chüan.

Bound in 1 t'ao 4 ts'ê.

Remarks - a duplicate of No. 315; but the edition is a better one.
The item has no defects and is complete.

Accession No. 425   Index No.- 181-fccb   031-bgcm

Title   " I-chih-chai ssŭ p'u "
               頤　志　齋　四　譜
               " Ssŭ chia nien p'u "
               四　家　年　譜

Classification - B-117 傳記－總錄

Subject - a collection of four biographies and chronological records.

References - 012-zafk 5/21.

Author - (編) Ting Yen 丁晏 .

Edition - the "I-chih-chai" 頤 志 齋 ; dated Tao-Kuang "kuei-mao"
     23/1843.   Blocks; "mao-pien" paper.

Index - none.

Bound in 1 t'ao 2 ts'ê; doubly interleaved.

Remarks - an ordinary edition; complete and without defects.
     The 4 works are as follows :-
     (#)

(#)　" Chêng Chün nien p'u "
　　　鄭　君　年　譜　　　　　　　　(163-1dcm)

　　　" Ch'ên Ssŭ-wang nien p'u "
　　　陳　思　王　年　譜　　　　　　(170-hezo)

　　　" T'ao Ching-chieh nien p'u "
　　　陶　靖　節　年　譜　　　　　　(170-heic)

　　　" Lu Hsüan-kung nien p'u "
　　　陸　宣　公　年　譜　　　　　　(170-hfbc)

485

Accession No. 426 (a)   Index No. - 031-hbha

Title   " <u>Kuo shih hsien liang tz'ŭ-wang ta-ch'ên hsiao chuan</u> "
          國　史　賢　良　祠　王　大　臣　小　傳

Classification - B-117 傳記一總録

Subject - a collection of biographies of loyal officials and Imperial
     princes of the <u>Ch'ing Dynasty</u>.

References - 012-zafk 5/17.

Author - not stated.

Edition - official; no date.   Blocks; "fên" paper.

Index - separate lists of contents (names and official titles) for
     each of 2 chüan 上　下 .

Bound in 1 ts'ê in 1 t'ao with (b) (c) and (d).

Remarks - the item is complete, but with some slight worm-holes
     which have been repaired.

———•———

Accession No. 426 (b)   Index No. - 031-hbnd

Title   " Kuo shih ju-lin chuan "
             國　史　儒　林　傳

Classification - B-117 傳記 － 總録

Subject - a collection of biographies of famous scholars of the
    Ch'ing Dynasty.

References - none; but see 012-zafk 5/18.

Author - (?) by Yüan Yüan 阮　元 .

Edition - uniform with (a).

Index - separate lists of contents (names) for each of 2 chüan 上　下 .

Bound in 1 ts'ê in 1 t'ao with (a) (c) and (d).

Remarks - as under (a), but without defects.   012-zafk 5/18 has
    a work with the title,- 國朝 儒 林 文 苑 傳 which seems to be
    a combined work of (b) and (c).   Further evidences are
    unavailable to ascertain whether this is true or not.

————•—•————

Accession No. 426 (c)   Index No. - 031-hbze

Title   " Kuo shih wên-yüan chüan "
                國   史   文   苑   傳

Classification - B-117 傳記－總録
Subject - a collection of biographies of famous scholars of the
    Ch'ing Dynasty; especially their activities and teachings.

References - none; but see 012-zafk 5/18.

Author - (?) by Yüan Yüan 阮 元 .

Edition - uniform with (a).

Index - separate lists of contents (names) for each of 2 chüan 上 下 .

Bound in 1 ts'ê in 1 t'ao with (a) (b) and (d).

Remarks - as under (b).

Accession No. 426 (d)   Index No. - 031-hbic

Title   " Kuo shih hsün-li chuan "
                       國　史　循　吏　傳

Classification - B-117 傳記 - 總録
Subject - a collection of biographies of loyal officials of the
  Ch'ing Dynasty.

References - none.

Author - not stated.

Edition - as under (a).

Index - a list of names; 1 chüan.

Bound in 1 ts'ê in 1 t'ao with (b) (c) and (d).

Remarks - as under (a).

489

Accession No. 427   Index No. - 077-lcia   077-jcia

Title   " Li-tai hsün-liang nêng-li lieh-chuan hui ch'ao "
           歷 代 循 良 能 吏 列 傳 彙 鈔

Classification - B-117 傳記-總錄   B-137 史鈔
Subject - a collection of biographies of loyal officials of all
         dynasties, from the beginning of Chinese history down to the
         end of the Ming Dynasty; mainly extracted from the official
         dynastic histories of the above period.

References - none.

Author - by Ch'iao Yung-ch'ien 喬 用 遷.

Edition - the "Yu-hêng-chai" 有 恒 齋 ; dated Tao-Kuang "chia-ch'ên"
         24/1844.   Blocks; "fên" paper.

Index - a detailed table of contents (names) arranged chronologically;
        not divided into chüan.

Bound in 1 t'ao 4 ts'ê.

Remarks - the item appears to be complete and is in good condition.

The University of Toronto Chinese Library

Accession No. 428   Index No. - 075-dddk

Title   " Tung-lin lieh chuan "
                              東　林　列　傳

Classification - B-117 傳記一總録

Subject - a collection of some 180 biographies of noted scholars
    toward the close of the Ming Dynasty; all of whom were members
    of the Tung-lin-tang 東　林　黨 ,- organized by Ku Yen-wu 顧炎武
    and others for the purpose of teaching and lecturing, at a place
    called Tung-lin-shu-yüan 東　林　書　院(location: Wu-hsi, (#)

References - 160-1j 163-ggcz 5/5 031-bgld 6/17 012-zafk 5/15
    031-bgdf 58/23.

Author - (撰) Ch'ên Ting 陳鼎．

Edition - the "T'ieh-chien-shu-wu" 鐵 肩 書 屋; dated K'ang-Hsi
    "hsin-mao" 50/1711.   Blocks; bamboo paper.

Index - a detailed table of contents (names) for 24 chüan; 卷末
    2 chüan 上 下．

Bound in 1 t'ao 10 ts'ê.

Remarks - a fairly good edition; the item is apparently complete
    but with many repaired pages, mostly in the last ts'ê which
    must have reached the worst of its condition before repairs
    were undertaken.

(#) Kiangsu), formerly in use by <u>Yang Shih</u> (Sung period) for similar purposes and was later reconstructed by <u>Ku</u> and others.

Accession No. 429   Index No. - 118-obed

Title   " Chou-ch'ing shu lin "
　　　　　　　　籀　高　述　林

Classification - C-308 雜家一雜文

Subject - a collection of discussions and disquisitions on a
variety of unrelated subjects.

References - none.

Author - by Sun I-jang 孫詒讓 . 18??-1708

Edition - no notation; dated "ping-ch'ên" 1916.   Blocks; "mao-t'ai"
paper.

Index - none; 10 chüan.

Bound in 1 t'ao 4 ts'ê.

Remarks - an ordinary edition; the item is complete and almost new.

Accession No. 430   Index No. - 118-obed

Title   " Chou-ch'ing shu lin "
                 籀 高 述 林

Classification - C-308 雜家一雜文

Subject - a collection of discussions and disquisitions on a
    variety of unrelated subjects.

References - Toronto No. 429.

Author - by Sun I-jang 孫 詒 讓.

Edition - no notation; dated "ping-ch'ên" 1916.   Blocks; "mao-t'ai"
    paper.

Index - none; 10 chüan.

Bound in 1 t'ao 4 ts'ê.

Remarks - a duplicate of No. 429; and apparently printed from the
    same blocks.   The item is complete and in very good condition.

Accession No. 431   Index No. - 018-bjao   044-aojo

Title   " Fên-lei ch'ih-tu pei lan "
             分 類 尺 牘 備 覽
             " Ch'ih-tu pei lan "
             尺 牘 備 覽

Classification - D-73 總集一文
Subject - a collection of classified correspondence.

References - none.

Author - compiled by Wang Hu-pang 王虎榜.

Edition - the "Chên-i-shu-chü" 珍藝書局; dated Kuang-Hsü
     "kêng-yin" 16/1890.   Type; foreign paper.

Index - a detailed classified table of contents for 30 chüan.

Bound in 1 t'ao 6 ts'ê.

Remarks - an ordinary cheap edition.   The item is complete and
     without defects.   This work is of the nature of a "ready
     letter-writer."

Accession No. 432   Index No. - 201-mg1g

Title   " Hung-kung ching shih lu "
               黌 宮 敬 事 錄

Classification - B-287 政書 一典禮

Subject - a general treatise on proper ceremonies observed on the
    occasions of sacrifice to Confucius and Kuan-ti 關帝 ,-
    the God of War; with illustrations of sacrificial utensils,
    musical instruments etc.

References - none.

Author - (輯) Kuei Liang 桂良 .

Edition - possibly official; dated T'ung-Chih "jên-shên" 11/1872.
    Blocks; "fên" paper.

Index - a general table of contents for 6 chüan; separate detailed
    list for each chüan.

Bound in 1 t'ao 4 ts'ê.

Remarks - this is a very good edition; and the item is complete
    and in very fine condition.

496

Accession No. 433   Index No. - 087-hedd

Title   " Wei chêng chung kao "
                為 政 忠 告

Classification - B-277 職官

Subject - a collection of 3 works treating of the principal duties
    of officials, together with homiletical advice to them on
    loyalty and benevolence.

References - none to the collective title.   To 牧民忠告
    012-zafk 9/3   031-bgdf 80/20.

Author - (撰) Chang Yang-hao 張養浩 .

Edition - the "Pi-hsien-chai" 碧鮮齋 ; (preface) dated Chih-Chêng
    至 正 15/1355, but this item is a reprint of the late Ch'ing
    period.   Blocks; bamboo paper.

Index - separate for each work.

Bound in 1 t'ao 2 ts'ê; doubly interleaved.

Remarks - a very good edition; complete and in perfect condition.
    The 3 works are :-
            " Mu min chung kao "   (093-dadd)
              牧 民 忠 告
            " Fêng hsien chung kao "   (182-zldd)
              風 憲 忠 告
            " Miao t'ang chung kao "   (053-lhdd)
              廟 堂 忠 告

Accession No. 434   Index No. - 140-qfqh

Title   " Lan-kuei pao lu "
                         蘭 閨 寶 録

Classification - B-117 傳記－總録

Subject - a collection of biographies of distinguished women,
    covering the period from the Han 漢 down to and including
    the Ch'ing Dynasty.

References - none.

Author - (編次) Yün Chu 惲 珠.

Edition - the "Hung-hsiang-kuan" 紅 香 館 ; dated Tao-Kuang
    11/1831.   Blocks; "fên" paper.

Index - a general table of "classification" headings for 6 chüan;
    detailed lists of names for each of 6 chüan.

Bound in 1 t'ao 8 ts'ê; doubly interleaved with margins.

Remarks - this is a fairly good edition; and the item is complete
    and in very good condition with the exception of chüan 3, a
    part of which are stained, and with some slight defects on
    the edges.

The University of Toronto Chinese Library

Accession No. 435   Index No. - 140-jifh

Title   " Jung-hu-ts'ao-t'ang tsêng yen lu "
          蓉 湖 草 堂 贈 言 錄

Classification - B-107 傳記-獨錄

Subject - a collection of eulogistic writings,- such as biographical
    notes, funeral orations, inscriptions on stone tablets, etc,-
    written in praise of Miss Yün Chu 惲 珠 (Mrs. Lin T'ing-lu
    麟 廷 鏐) by friends and relatives after her death.
                    1771- 1833

References - none.

Author - compiled by her first son Lin Ch'ing 麟 慶 .

Edition - apparently the author's family edition; dated Tao-Kuang
    "ping-shên" 16/1836.   Blocks; "mao-pien" paper.

Index - a general table of 12 "classification" headings with
    compiler's notes.

Bound in 1 t'ao 4 ts'ê; doubly interleaved.

Remarks - a very fine edition; the item is complete and in perfect
    condition.

Accession No.　436　　　　Index No.　140-jifh

Title　　" Jung-hu-ts'ao-t'ang tsêng yen lu "
　　　　　蓉　湖　草　堂　贈　言　録

Classification – B-107 傳記一獨録

Subject – a collection of eulogistic writings,- such as biographical
　　notes, funeral orations, inscriptions on stone tablets, etc,-
　　written in praise of Miss Yün Chu 惲珠 (Mrs Lin T'ing-lu
　　麟 廷 鋯) by friends and relatives after her death.

References – Toronto No. 435.

Author – compiled by her first son Lin Ch'ing 麟 慶 .

Edition – apparently the author's family edition; dated Tao-Kuang
　　"ping-shên" 16/1836.　　Blocks; "fên" paper.

Index – a general table of 12 "classification" headings with
　　compiler's notes.

Bound in　1 t'ao 2 ts'ê; singly interleaved.

Remarks – a duplicate of No. 435.　The item is complete and in
　　very good condition, with the exception of one repaired page
　　at the end.

500

Accession No. 437   Index No. - 061-zkl

Title   " Hsin ching pien "
                          心   鏡   編

Classification - C-328 雜家 - 雜纂
Subject - selected short passages from various standard works;
    chiefly of a moral and ethical character.

References - 031-bgdf 133/19.

Author - (韓) T'an Wên-kuang 譚 文 光 .

Edition - no particular notation; (preface) dated Ch'ien-Lung 12/1747.
    Blocks; bamboo paper.

Index - a general table of contents for 10 chüan.

Bound in 1 t'ao 2 ts'ê.

Remarks - the item is complete and in fairly good condition.
    Owing to age dryness, the paper is rather fragile.

Accession No. 438   Index No. - 162-moof

Title   " Huan-tu-ê-shu-shih lao-jên shou ting nien p'u "
            還 讀 我 書 室 老 人 手 訂 年 譜

Classification - B-107 傳記 - 獨録

Subject - the autobiography and chronological record of Tung Hsün

董 恂 .

References - none.

Author - Tung Hsün 董 恂 .

Edition - privately published; (Imperial Edict) dated Kuang-Hsü
    18/1892.   Blocks; "mao-pien" paper.

Index - none; 2 chüan.

Bound in 1 t'ao 2 ts'ê.

Remarks - the item is complete and almost new.

Accession No.   439   Index No. - 106-adzl

Title   " Po-sung-i-ch'an fu "
                百宋一廛(廛) 賦

Classification - D-38 別集一詩

Subject - a verse of 2640 characters written in the "fu" (賦)
      style in description of a private library of Sung works;
      with annotations.

References - none.

Author - (撰) Ku Kuang-ch'i 顧廣圻; (注) Huang P'ei-lieh
      黃玉烈.

Edition - privately published; dated Kuang-Hsü 3/1877.   Blocks;
      "mien" paper.

Index - none; complete in 1 chüan.

Bound in 1 t'ao 1 ts'ê; doubly interleaved.

Remarks - a complete item in perfect condition.

Accession No. 440   Index No. - 115-dldh

Title   " Ch'iu-hui-yin-kuan shih ch'ao "
                秋 蟪 吟 館 詩 鈔

Classification - D-33 别集 - 詩文
Subject - an individual collection of poetry; with 2 supplementary
     chapters on lyrical writings and prose compositions.

References - none.

Author - (撰) Chin Ho 金 和 .

Edition - no notation; (preface) dated "chia-yin" 1914.   Type;
     foreign paper.

Index - none; 詩 鈔 6 chüan; 來雲閣詞鈔 1 chüan; 文鈔 1 chüan.

Bound in 1 t'ao 6 ts'ê.

Remarks - the item is new.

504

Accession No. 441 (a)   Index No. - 039-azcm

Title   " <u>K'ung-tzŭ</u> <u>nien</u> <u>p'u</u> <u>kang</u> <u>mu</u> "
             孔 子 年 譜 綱 目

Classification - B-107 傳記一獨録

Subject - the biography and chronological record of <u>Confucius</u>.

References - 031-bgdf 59/14.

Author - (編輯) <u>Hsia Hung-chi</u> 夏 洪 基 .

Edition - a Ming edition; (preface) dated Ch'ung-Chêng "chia-shên"
    1644.   Blocks; bamboo paper.

Index - none; 1 chüan.

Bound in 1 ts'ê in 1 t'ao with (b) (c) and (d).

Remarks - this is a fairly good edition; and the item is complete
    and without defects.

Accession No. 441 (b)   Index No. - 039-azdz

Title   " K'ung mên ti-tzŭ chuan lüeh "

孔 門 弟 子 傳 略

Classification - B-117 傳記一總錄

Subject - a collection of biographies of the disciples of Confucius.

References - 031-bgdf 59/14.

Author - (編輯) Hsia Hung-chi 夏 洪 基 .

Edition - uniform with (a).

Index - a list of names for 2 chüan.

Bound in 2 ts'ê in 1 t'ao with (a) (c) and (d).

Remarks - as under (a).

Accession No. 441 (c)   Index No. - 077-lcfz   077-jcfz

Title   " Li-tai ti-wang t'ung hsi "
                 歷 代 帝 王 統 系

Classification - B-117 傳記 -總錄

Subject - a list of emperors of all dynasties in Chinese history
    up to the end of the Ming period; arranged chronologically
    and with brief notes,- years in reign, age, etc - under each.

References - none.

Author - (彙纂) Hsia Hung-chi 夏 洪 基 .

Edition - uniform with (a); except (preface) dated Ch'ung-Chêng
    "kuei-wei" 16/1643.

Index - a table of dynastic names in 2 chüan.

Bound in 2 ts'ê in 1 t'ao with (a) (b) and (d).

Remarks - as under (a).

—— • —— • ——

Accession No. 441 (d)   Index No. - 077-lczz   077-jczz

Title   " <u>Li-tai chia-tzǔ pien-nien ch'üan t'u</u> "
           歷 代 甲 子 編 年 全 圖

Classification - B-22 編 年   B-137 時 令

Subject - a table of the Chinese 60-year cycles beginning with
         the first year of <u>Huang-Ti</u> and ending in the last year of
         <u>Ch'ung-Chêng</u>.

References - none.

Author - (編 定) <u>Hsia Hung-chi</u> 夏 洪 基 .

Edition - uniform with (a); except (preface) dated Ch'ung-Chêng
         "kuei-wei" 16/1643.

Index - a table of 73 "chia-tzǔ",- the first year of each cycle.

Bound in 1 ts'ê in 1 t'ao with (a) (b) and (c).

Remarks - as under (a).

Accession No.   442   Index No. - 128-glcf

Title   " Shêng-miao chi tien t'u k'ao "
            聖　廟　祀　典　圖　效

Classification - B-117 傳記一總録

Subject - biographies of Confucius and his disciples and followers;
    with illustrations; places occupied in the Confucian Temple;
    and eulogies of various emperors.

References - none.

Author - (敬輯) Ku Yüan 顧 沅 .

Edition - no notation; (preface) dated Tao-Kuang "ping-hsü" 6/1826.
    Blocks; "fên" paper.

Index - a general table of contents for a leading chapter and 5 chüan;
    崇 聖 祠 效 1 chüan; 聖 蹟 圖 1 chüan; 孟子聖蹟圖
    1 chüan.
Bound in 1 t'ao 6 ts'ê.

Remarks - a very good edition; the item is complete and in good
    condition except that the first page of the last ts'ê is torn
    and part missing.

Accession No. 443　　　　　Index No. - 060-gzzb　　031-bkj

Title　　　　" Hsü Wên-ch'ang Ssŭ shêng yüan "
　　　　　　徐 文 長　四　聲　猿

　　　　　　　" Ssŭ shêng yüan "
　　　　　　四　聲　猿

Classification - D-143 詞曲—戲本

Subject - a collection of 4 plays of a miscellaneous character.

References - none.

Author - by Hsü Wên-ch'ang 徐 文 長 ; (評 點) Yüan Hung-tao
袁 宏 道 .

Edition - no notation; no date.　　Blocks; bamboo paper.

Index - a list of the 4 plays.

Bound in 1 t'ao 1 ts'ê; doubly interleaved.

Remarks - this edition is not one of the best; and the impression
　　is blurred and difficult to read in many places.　The item is
　　complete and in very good condition.　Page 73 and the preface
　　are handwritten.

Accession No. 444 (a)   Index No. - 009-kgc

Title   " Ch'uan Ching piao "
                          傳　　經　　表

Classification - B-117 傳記－總錄

Subject - a table showing by whom and the manner in which the
    "Five Classics", and their interpretation, have been passed
    down from scholar to scholar; beginning with Confucius
    himself and ending with scholars of the Wei Dynasty; with
    brief notes under the names.

References - 012-zafk 5/18.

Author - (撰) Pi Yüan 畢 沅 .

Edition - the "Hung-ta-t'ang" 宏 達 堂 ; dated Kuang-Hsü 5/1879.
    Blocks; "mao-pien" paper.

Index - none; 1 chüan.

Bound in 1 ts'ê in 1 t'ao with (b).

Remarks - an ordinary edition; the item is complete and in very
    good condition.

Accession No.   444 (b)   Index No. - 162-ggc

Title   " T'ung   Ching   piao "
                          通   經   表

Classification – B-117 傳記一總錄

Subject – a five-column table listing a group of ancient scholars
    well-versed in "The Classics"; with brief notes under each
    name.

References – 012-zafk 5/18.

Author – (撰) Pi Yüan 畢 沅 .

Edition – Uniform with (a).

Index – none; 1 chüan.

Bound in 1 ts'ê in 1 t'ao with (a).

Remarks – as under (a).

Accession No. 445   Index No. - 096-klhh

Title   " Hsüan-chi sui chin "
                  璇   璣   碎   錦

Classification - D-38 別集 - 詩

Subject - an individual collection of poetic writings of various
    styles; with illustrations of the objects described; and on
    each object the particular poem or poems reproduced and
    dissected; together with explanations as to the method of
    reading.

References - 012-zafk 17/12   031-bgdf 183/3.

Author - (著) Wan Shu 萬 樹 .

Edition - the "Ssŭ-ching-chai" 似 靜 齋 ; dated Kuang-Hsü "mou-tzŭ"
    14/1888.   Blocks; "fên" paper.

Index - 2 separate lists of contents for 2 chüan 上 下 .

Bound in 1 t'ao 2 ts'ê.

Remarks - this work is a combination of both art and literature,
    and an outcome of much time and energy; although there is
    very little to indicate its being of any use. A very good
    modern edition; complete and as if new.

The University of Toronto Chinese Library

Accession No. 446   Index No. - 009-ejzj

Title   " Ho Po-shih pei lun "
何 博 士 備 論

Classification - C-33 兵家

Subject - a collection of discussions on military affairs of the
ancient time.

References - 163-ggoz 7/9   031-bgld 9/27   106-gdkn 42/6   167-mhfm 13/16
012-zafk 10/14   031-bgdf 99/16.

Author - (撰) Ho Ch'ü-fei 何 去 非.

Edition - the "liu-hsiang-shih" 留 香 室 ; no date.   Blocks;
Korean paper.

Index - none; in 1 chüan or 26 "p'ien" 篇 .

Bound in 1 t'ao 2 ts'ê; doubly interleaved.

Remarks - the item is complete and in very good condition.

514

Accession No. 447   Index No. - 140-idzj

Title   " Wan shih yü hêng lu "
                    萬   世   玉   衡   錄

Classification - C-13 儒家

Subject - a collection of notes on political philosophy under 64
    main headings; the materials and examplifications being
    selected from historical records of the period from the time
    of the Five Emperors 五 帝 down to and including the Ming 明
    dynasty.

References - 031-bgdf 97/30.

Author - (編 輯) Chiang I 蔣 伊 .

Edition - no notation; (author's memorial) dated Ch'ien-Lung 2/1737.
    Blocks; bamboo paper.

Index - a detailed table of contents for 4 chüan.

Bound in 1 t'ao 4 ts'ê.

Remarks - a fairly good edition; the item appears to be complete
    and is in good condition with the exception of a few repaired
    worm-holes at the end of 4th ts'ê.

Accession No. 448   Index No. - 167-mlkj

Title   " Tieh-ch'iao man kao "
                鐵　橋　漫　稿

Classification - D-33別集一詩文

Subject - an individual miscellaneous collection of prose and poetry.

References - 012-zafk 18/3.

Author - （撰）Yen K'o-chün 嚴 可 均.

Edition - that of "Chiang-shih" 蔣 氏 ; dated Kuang-Hsü "i-yu"
          11/1885.   Blocks; "fên" paper.

Index - none; 8 chüan.

Bound in 1 t'ao 4 ts'ê.

Remarks - an ordinary edition; the item is complete.

Accession No. 449   Index No. - 196-jffz   135-fzgm

Title   " Hao-ch'êng Shu-shih tsu p'u "
                鶴　城　舒　氏　族　譜

Classification - B-117 傳記一總錄
Subject - a genealogical record of the Shu 舒 family of Hao-ch'êng.

References - none.

Author - compiled by Shu Liang-pi 舒 良 弼．

Edition - privately published by the Shu family; dated Kuang-Hsü
        "kuei-mao" 29/1903.   Blocks; "fên" paper.

Index - a general table of contents; 1 chüan.

Bound in 1 t'ao 1 ts'ê.

Remarks - a very good edition; the item is complete, but stained
        at the top margins.

Accession No. 450   Index No. - 167-zihh

Title   " Chin hu ching sui "
                  金   壺   精   粹

Classification - A-161 小學 一字書

Subject - explanations of a collection of Chinese couplets grouped
        under 4 general headings; together with an additional chapter
        on couplets composed of 2 similar characters.

References - Toronto No. 415.

Author - (增訂) Hao Tsai-t'ien 郝 在 田 and Chang Yang-shan
        張 仰 山 . (The latter is apparently a courtesy name)

Edition - the "Sung-chu-chai" 松 竹 齋 ; dated Kuang-Hsü "ping-tzǔ"
        2/1876.   Blocks; "fên" paper.

Index - none.

Bound in 1 t'ao 2 ts'ê.

Remarks - this is an exact duplicate of No. 415.   The item is
        complete and in fairly good condition.

Accession No.   451   Index No. - 067-zeeh

Title   " Wên yüan ying hua "

文 苑 英 華

Classification - D-63 總集 - 詩文

Subject - (Gest No. 602) - "Collection of all specimens of polite
    literature subsequent to the Liang dynasty of authors of the
    T'ang dynasty (nine-tenths of the work) and the preceding
    lesser dynasties,-----."

References - Wylie's Notes page 240   160-lj   163-ggcz 16/2   031-bgld
    19/8   037-ahhg (hsü) 19/16   167-mhfm 23/7   030-iaff 38/9   (#)

Author - Li Fang 李 昉 and others.   See Wylie's Notes page 183
    Giles B. D. 1122.

Edition - dated Lung-Ch'ing 1/1567.   Blocks; "mien" paper.

Index- a general classified table of contents for 1000 chüan;
    detailed table of contents at the beginning of each chüan.

Bound in 20 t'ao 150 ts'ê (1st 10 t'ao 8 each; 2d 10 t'ao 7 each).

Remarks - a part of this item seems to be from the original
    Lung-Ch'ing blocks; and the rest is made up of later impressions
    either from old blocks or blocks cut at the time the impression
    was undertaken; and on various kinds of paper.

      (##)

(#)   106-gdkn 112/15   012-zafk 19/3   031-bgdf 186/30
       Gest Nos. 602 and 1526.

(##)   The item appears to be complete, but there are
       quite a few repaired defects; worm-holes, etc throughout
       the work.   Pages handwritten are - 1/1-2; 60/6-9;
       132/3,4,9; 281/1; 321/1-9; 450/11-13; 465/6; whole of
       671 and 672 except 2 pages; 677/5; 680/9-13; 690/8-17;
       720/9-12; 741/13-16.

The University of Toronto Chinese Library

Accession No. 452   **Index No.** - 018-mzff   196-ff

Title   " Liu-shih   Hung   shu "

劉 氏 鴻 書

Classification - C-348 類書

Subject - a general classified encyclopaedia; the descriptions of
the items being mainly selected from various standard works.

References - 012-zafk 13/25   031-bgdf 138/23   Gest No. 727.

Author - (纂輯) Liu Chung-ta 劉 仲 達 ; (刪正) T'ang Pin-yin
湯 賓 尹.

Edition - a Ming edition; (preface) dated Wan-Li "hsin-hai" 39/1611.
Blocks; bamboo paper.

Index - a table of the 24 "classifications"; a detailed table of
contents for 108 chüan; separate list for each chüan.

Bound in 8 t'ao 56 ts'ê (7 each); doubly interleaved.

Remarks - this item appears to have been very well preserved by the
former owner (or owners); and despite its age, it is still in
perfect condition. A very good edition; complete; and the
impression is clear and easy to read.

The University of Toronto Chinese Library

Accession No. 453   Index No. - 037-acc

Title   " T'ien chung chi "
                               天   中   記

Classification - C-348 類書

Subject - (Gest No. 370) - "Encyclopaedia of all kinds of Subjects

    pertaining to all four Classes of Literature,-----."

References - 160-1j 163-ggcz 10/16   031-bgld 14/15   012-zafk 13/25

    031-bgdf 136/10   Gest No. 370.

Author - (纂) Ch'ên Yao-wên 陳 耀 光 ; (校) T'u Lung 屠 隆 .

Edition - Ch'ing Dynasty reprint of the original Ming edition;

    (original preface) dated Wen-Li "i-wei" 23/1595.   Blocks;

    "t'u-fên" paper.

Index - a detailed table of contents for 60 chüan.

Bound in 6 t'ao 60 ts'ê (10 each).

Remarks - an ordinary good edition; the item is complete, and

    practically without defects except a few minor ones.

Accession No.　454　　　　　Index No. - 203-ezcg

Title　　　　　" Tien-shih-chai　hua　pao "
　　　　　　　　點　石　齋　畫　報

Classification - C-368 小說家

Subject - (Gest No. 1489) - "an illustrated magazine of current events
　　in China and elsewhere about the year 1884 (?); together with
　　pictures of fabulous and strange events."

References - Gest No. 1489.

Author - numerous.

Edition - no notation; (preface) dated Kuang-Hsü 10/1884.
　　Lithographed on "fên" paper.

Index - lists of pictures at the beginning of each of 30 "chi".

Bound in 10 t'ao 60 ts'ê (6 each); doubly interleaved.

Remarks - a very interesting and amusing collection of pictures.

The University of Toronto Chinese Library

Accession No. 455   Index No. - 149-cnhg

Title   " Chi tsuan yüan hai "
                  記　纂　淵　海

Classification - C-348 類書

Subject - (Gest No. 560) - "Encyclopaedic work embracing articles

　　on all Four Classes of Literature,-----"

References - 163-ggcz 10/13 C31-bgld 14/9 106-gdkn 60/3 030-iaff

　　20/7 167-mhfm 17/5 Gest No. 560 012-zafk 13/21 031-bgdf

　　135/38.

Author - (纂集) P'an Tzŭ-mu 潘　自　牧 ; (補遺) Wan Chia-pin

　　王　嘉　賓.

Edition - no notation; dated Wan-Li "chi-mao" 7/1579.   Blocks;

　　"mien" paper.

Index - a detailed classified table of contents for 100 chüan.

Bound in 6 t'ao 48 ts'ê (8 each).

Remarks - this is a very fine edition; and the item is apparently

　　complete and, with the exception of a few repaired defects and

　　stains, it is in perfect condition.   A part of the preface is

　　missing.

Accession No. 456   Index No. - 096-zzcb   096-zzcd

Title   " Wang Wên-ch'êng kung ch'üan shu "
             王 文 成 公 全 書
             " Wang Wên-ch'êng ch'üan shu "
             王 文 成 全 書

Classification - D-33 別集一詩文

Subject - an individual collection of prose and poetry.

References - 163-ggcz 15/7   031-bgld 18/23   012-zafk 16/20

    031-bgdf 171/33   Gest No. 405.

Author - (撰) Wang Shou-jên 王 守 仁.

Edition - no notation; (preface) dated Wan-Li "ping-shên" 24/1596.

    Blocks; "mien" paper.

Index - a detailed table of contents for 38 chüan.

Bound in 4 t'ao 20 ts'ê (5 each).

Remarks - this item is made up of two or three copies of the same

    work.   Different kinds of paper and varied size of blocks

    were noticed on going over the work; but there is no doubt

    that the whole item was printed in the Ming period.

        Manuscript pages - 3/49; whole of chüan 31.

The University of Toronto Chinese Library

Accession No. 457   Index No. - 073-hzab   067-zabd

Title   " Tsêng Wên-chêng kung ch'üan chi "
           曾　文　正　公　全　集

Classification - D-33 別集－詩文 B-72 詔令奏議－奏議 B-107 傳記－獨錄
Subject - (Gest No. 450) - "Collection of works on Prose, Poetry,
     Government Affairs, Politics, Letters, Diaries etc."

References - 012-zafk 4/32 5/9 18/31   Gest Nos. 450 and 1664.

Author - Tsêng Kuo-fan 曾 國 藩 .   See 160-1j   Giles B. D. 2021.

Edition - the "Chuan-chung-shu-chü" 傳忠書局 ; dated Kuang-Hsü
     2/1876.   Blocks; "fên" paper.

Index - a table of contents for an introductory chapter.   a general
     table of contents for 156 chüan. separate tables at the beginning
     of most of the chüan.
Bound in 12 t'ao 128 ts'ê (10-10-11-12-12-12-10-10-10-10-10-11).

Remarks - this is an ordinary but clear cut edition; and the item
     is complete and as new.   The blocks of the individual works
     were cut at different times and in 3 different places.   The
     following 4 works do not agree with the general table of
     contents in the numbers of chüan:-

                    (#)

526

(#) 1. 詩集 4 chüan (table of contents - 3)
    2. 文集 4 chüan (table of contents - 3)
    3. 雜著 4 chüan (table of contents - 2)
    4. 讀書録 10 chüan (table of contents - 4)

There is also a work not listed in the table of contents,- the
"Mêng-tzǔ-yao-lüeh" 孟子要畧, in 5 chüan.

Accession No. 458 (a)   **Index No.** - 075-afhz

Title

" Pên ts'ao kang mu "
本 草 綱 目

Classification - C-117 醫家 - 藥料

Subject - (Gest No. 524) - "The Chinese Materia Medica, the nucleus
of which is the small work in 3 chüan, ascribed to the ancient
Shên-Nung 神農 , arranged in 16 classifications with 62 subdivisions, with 1880 different medicaments, selected from
upwards of 800 preceding authors,-----"

References - Wylie's Notes page 100 160-1j 163-ggcz 8/6
031-bgld 10/21 012-zafk 10/28 031-bgdf 104/32 Gest No. 524.

Author - (編輯) Li Shih-chên 李 時 珍 ; (校梓) Chang Shao-t'ang
張 紹 棠 .

Edition - a reprint by "Chang's Wei-ku-chai" 張氏味古齋 ; dated
Kuang-Hsü "i-yu" 11/1885.   Blocks; "fên" paper.

Index - a general classified table of contents for 52 chüan.

Bound in 6 t'ao 34 ts'ê; 6th t'ao with (b) and (c).

Remarks - a good edition; the item is complete and in very good
condition.

Accession No. 458 (b)   Index No. – 075-afhz   140-ofkz

Title   " Pên-ts'ao-kang-mu yao p'in tsung mu "
本 草 網 目 藥 品 總 目

Classification – C-117醫家－藥料

Subject – (Gest No. 524-a) – "Index of the drugs described in the
Pên ts'ao kang mu 本 草 網 目,-----"

References – 012-zafk 10/33   Gest No. 524-a.

Author – (輯) Ts'ai Lieh-hsien 蔡 烈 先 .

Edition – uniform with (a).

Index – none; 1 chüan.

Bound in 1/2 ts'ê in 6th t'ao of (a).

Remarks – as under (a).

Accession No. 458 (c)   Index No. - 075-afhz

Title   " Pên-ts'ao-kang-mu t'u "
                本 草 網 目 圖

Classification - C-117 醫家 - 藥料

Subject - a classified collection of some 1100 cuts illustrating
    the principal sources of the materials entering into Chinese
    drugs and medicines.

References - Gest No. 524-b.

Author - (審定) Chang Shih-yü 張 士 瑜 and Chang Shih-hêng
        張 士 珩 .

Edition - uniform with (a).

Index - none; 3 chüan.

Bound in 1 1/2 ts's in 6th t'ao of (a).

Remarks - as under (a).

————◆————

Accession No. 458 (d)　　　　Index No. - 140-1z11

Title　　　　　　" Wan fang chên hsien "

萬　方　鍼　線

Classification - C-117 醫家 - 藥料

Subject - (Gest No. 524-e) - "Compilation of the prescriptions
contained in the Pên ts'ao kang mu 本草綱目 classified
according to diseases,-----."

References - 012-zafk 10/33　Gest No. 524-e.

Author - (輯) Ts'ai Lieh-hsien 蔡烈先 .

Edition - the "Yeh-shan-chu-chü" of Chin-ling 金陵冶山竹屋 ;
undated.　　Blocks; "fên" paper.

Index - a table of "classifications" for 8 chüan.

Bound in 3 ts'ê in 1 t'ao with (e) and (f).

Remarks - as under (a).

Accession No.　　458 (e)　　　　Index No. - 037-sgzf

Title　　　　　" Ch'i ching pa mo k'ao "

奇　經　八　脈　攷

Classification - C-101 醫家 – 診脈

Subject - (Gest No. 524-c) - "Eight treatises on eight different
kinds of pulse and how to detect disease by the pulse and
variations of same due to different diseases, compiled with
original material ------."

References - 160-1j　163-ggoz 8/6　031-bgld 10/21　012-zafk 10/28
031-bgdf 104/33　Gest No. 524-c.

Author - (輯) Li Shih-chên 李 時 珍.

Edition - no notation; but apparently uniform with (a).

Index - none; 1 chüan.

Bound in 1/2 ts'ê with (f); in 1 t'ao with (d); (f) and (g).

Remarks - as under (a).

532

———•———

Accession No. 458 (f)   Index No. - 085-pifm

Title   " Pin-hu mo hsüeh "
                 瀕 湖 脈 學

Classification - C-101 醫家 一診脈

Subject - (Gest No. 524-d) - "Work on the pulse with commentaries,
    ending with a 4-character rhyme on the function, importance,
    etc. of pulse, compiled with original material,-----."

References - 160-1j   163-ggcz 8/6   031-bgld 10/21   012-zafk 10/28
    031-bgdf 104/33   Gest No. 524-d.

Author - (撰) Li Shih-chên 李 時 珍 .

Edition - no notation; but apparently uniform with (a).

Index - none; 1 chüan.

Bound in 1/2 ts'ê with (e); in 1 t'ao with (d); (e) and (g).

Remarks - as under (a).

Accession No. 458 (g)   Index No. - 075-afhz

Title   " Pên-ts'ao-kang-mu shih i "
               本 草 綱 目 拾 遺

Classification - C-117 醫家 - 藥料

Subject - (Gest No. 524-f) - "Supplement to the Pên ts'ao kang mu,
    adding two classifications and correcting errors in the
    original,-----."

References - 163-ggcz 8/6   012-zafk 10/34   Gest No. 524-f.

Author - (韓) Chao Hsüeh-min 趙 學 敏.

Edition - uniform with (a).

Index - a table of "classifications" for 10 chüan; separate lists
    for each chüan.

Bound in 2 t'ao 8 ts'ê; 1st t'ao with (d); (e) and (f).

Remarks - as under (a).

534

Accession No. 459   Index No. - 146-zejj

Title   " Hsi-pei lei kao "
                          西 陂 類 稿

Classification - D-33 別集一詩文

Subject - an individual comprehensive and classified collection of
     miscellaneous prose and poetry.

References - 031-bgld 18/40   012-zafk 17/16   031-bgdf 173/35
     Gest No. 928.

Author - (撰) Sung Lo 宋 犖 .
                     Lao
                     此34 — 1713

Edition - no notation; (preface) dated K'ang-Hsi 50/1711.   Blocks;
     "mao-pien" paper.

Index - a detailed classified table of contents for 50 chüan (and
     supplements).

Bound in 4 t'ao 20 ts'ê.

Remarks - this is a very good edition; and the item is complete
     and in perfect condition with the exception of a few repaired
     worm-holes in the last ts'ê.

Accession No. 460   Index No. - 060-hhbj   018-bjch

Title   " Yü-chih Fên lei tzŭ chin "
           御   製   分   類   字   錦
           " Fên lei tzŭ chin "
           分   類   字   錦

Classification - C-348 類書

Subject - (Gest No. 900) - "Compilation of words and phrases of
    two to four characters, taken from works on all four classes
    of literature and novels expressing beautiful ideas, classified
    according to subjects into 40 divisions, with 618 sub-divisions,
    -----."

References - 160-1j 163-ggcz 10/16   031-bgld 14/17   012-zafk 13/26
    031-bgdf 136/20   Gest No. 900.

Author - compiled on order of Emperor K'ang-Hsi by a Commission
    headed by Chang T'ing-yü 張 廷 玉 .

Edition - a palace edition; dated K'ang-Hsi 61/1722.   Blocks;
    "mao-pien" paper.

Index - a classified table of contents for 64 chüan.

Bound in 8 t'ao 64 ts'ê (8 each).

Remarks - a very fine edition.   The item is complete and in very
    good condition.

Accession No. 461   Index No. - 053-phki   076-kizd   067-zdd

Title   " Lu-ling Ou-yang Wên-chung kung ch'üan chi "
          盧 陵 歐 陽 文 忠 公 全 集
          " Ou-yang Wên-chung kung ch'üan chi "
          歐 陽 文 忠 公 全 集

Classification - D-33 別集－詩文
Subject - an individual literary collection,- prose and poetry.

References - Wylie's Notes page 230   160-lj   163-ggcz 13/4
     031-bgld 15/39   037-ahhg 6/28   10/15 (hsü) 11/5 18/14
     167-mhfm 20/16 030-iaff 27/8 106-gdkn 76/1 012-zafk 15/15 (#)
Author - Ou-yang Hsiu 歐 陽 修。

Edition - the "Hsiao-ssŭ-t'ang" 孝 思 堂 ; dated Ch'ien-Lung
     "ping-yin" 11/1746. Blocks; "mao-pien" paper.

Index - a general table of contents for 153 chüan, arranged
     according to classes of writings; 附 錄 5 chüan.

Bound in 4 t'ao 24 ts'ê (6 each).

Remarks - this is a fairly good edition; and the item is complete
     and in very good condition.

     (#) 031-bgdf 153/35   Gest Nos. 706, 838 and 1558.

537

Accession No.   462   Index No. - 075-izgd

Title   " Yang Wên-jo hsien-shêng chi "
              楊 文 弱 先 生 集

Classification - D-33别集－詩文
Subject - an individual literary collection,- prose and poetry.

References - 085-hohm 3/50.

Author - (著) Yang Ssŭ-ch'ang 楊 嗣 昌 .

Edition - no notation; but of the Ming period; undated. Blocks;
    bamboo paper.

Index - none; 57 chüan.

Bound in 4 t'ao 32 ts'ê; doubly interleaved.

Remarks - this item is among those prohibited during the
    Ch'ing Dynasty.   It was apparently printed about the close
    of the Ming Dynasty.   This work is in generally good condi-
    tion,- defects not being numerous.

The University of Toronto Chinese Library

Accession No. 463   **Index No.** - 115-hg

Title   " <u>Pai hai</u> "
                        稗 海

Classification - C-338 雜家-叢書

Subject - (Gest No. 729) - "Collection of Reprints of 70 works
   by different authors, dealing with historical events -------"

References - Wylie's Notes page 262 160-1j 031-bgld 13/32
   012-zafk 13/12 029-pffz 451 Gest Nos. 729 and 2231.

Author - compiled and edited by <u>Shang Chün</u> 商 濬 .

Edition - possibly a later impression from the original Ming
   blocks; undated. Blocks; "mao-t'ai" paper.

Index - a table of the 70 works.

Bound in 10 t'ao 80 ts'ê (8 each).

Remarks - the item is complete and with but a few slight defects.
   (#)

(#) Manuscript pages:-

"Shih i chi" - whole of chüan 1 and 2; chüan 4/5-6; chüan 6/6

"Ta T'ang hsin yü" - chüan 1/3-6

"Lêng chai yeh hua" - 8/1-2

"Hsü Yen-chou shih hua" - preface page

"Kuei-hsin tsa shih ch'ien chi" - page 15.

Accession No.   464   Index No. - 061-hhcp

Title   " Hsi-yin-hsüan ts'ung shu "
                惜 陰 軒 叢 書

Classification - C-338 雜家 一叢書
Subject - a collection of reprints of 34 general works.

References - 012-zafk 13/16 029-pffz 378.

Author - (輯) Li Hsi-ling 李錫齡.

Edition - the "Hung-tao-shu-yüan" 宏道書院; (preface) dated
      Tao-Kuang "ping-wu" 26/1846.   Blocks; "mao-pien" paper.

Index - a table of the 34 works.

Bound in 16 t'ao 114 ts'ê (8-6-7-6-8-8-8-6-7-8-10-6-6-8-6-6).

Remarks - the item is complete and in very good condition.

Accession No.   465   Index No. - 106-agjn

Title   " Po Chia lei tsuan "
                  百 家 類 纂

Classification - C-328 雜家-雜纂

Subject - a collection of selected portions from the writings
    of famous philosophers of the period from the Chou Dynasty
    down to and including a part of the Ming Dynasty.

References - 031-bgdf 131/25 Gest No. 772.

Author - (纂輯) Shên Chin 沈 津 .

Edition - no notation; (preface) dated Lung-Ch'ing 1/1567.
    Blocks; "mien" paper.

Index - a classified table of contents (titles) for 40 chüan.

Bound in 4 t'ao 16 ts'è (4 each).

Remarks - the edition is a very good one; and the item is
    practically complete, but with a few repaired defects.
    The following parts are handwritten:-
        chüan 1 and preface and index; chüan 17-39-40.

Accession No.   466   **Index No.** - 007-zcgg   123-gdm

Title   " Êrh-ju-t'ing Ch'ün fang p'u "
             二 如 亭 群 芳 譜
             " Ch'ün fang p'u "
             群   芳   譜

Classification - C-283 譜錄一草木

Subject - a herbarium under 12 heads,-the Heavens, the Year, Grains,
    Vegetables, Fruits, Tea and Bamboo, Mulberry, Hemp and
    Grass-cloth Plants, Medicinal Plants, Trees, Flowers,
    Shrubs, and Birds and Fishes; the chief portion of which
    consists of extracts from preceding authors, ancient and (#)

References - Wylie's Notes page 152 160-1j 012-zafk 12/10
    031-bgdf 116/38 Gest No. 863.

Author - (撰) Wang Hsiang-chin 王 象 晋 .

Edition - no notation; (preface) dated Ch'ung-Chêng 2/1629.
    Blocks; "fên" paper.

Index - a general table of "classifications" with the number of
    chüan for each; separate lists for each ts'ê.

Bound in - 2 t'ao 28 ts'ê (14-14).

Remarks - this is a fairly good edition; and the item is complete
    and in very good condition,- some slight stains.

    (#) modern, regarding the various productions of the garden
    and field; and the details relate mainly to the medicinal
    virtues of the different objects.

Accession No.　　467 (a)　　Index No. – 111-cczc

Title　　" Chih-pu-tsu-chai ts'ung shu "
　　　　知　不　足　齋　叢　書

Classification – C-338雜家-叢書

Subject – a collection of reprints of 200 works of all classes of
　　Chinese literature.

References – Wylie's Notes page 262　160-1j　012-zafk 13/14
　　Gest No. 543.

Author – (編) Pao T'ing-po 鮑 廷 博.

Edition – the "Chih-pu-tsu-chai"知 不 足 齋 ; (preface) dated
　　Ch'ien-Lung 41/1776.　Blocks; "fên" paper.

Index – separate lists of contents for each of 30 "chi" with
　　the exception of the 6th.

Bound in　30 t'ao 240 ts'ê (8 each).

Remarks – this is a very fine small edition; and the item is com-
　　plete and in fairly good condition,- some stains and one or
　　two defects.　This item is apparently made up of 3 copies
　　of the same work; because the ts'ê are in 3 different
　　sizes (slightly different).　But they appear to have been
　　printed from one set of blocks.

Accession No.   467 (b)   **Index No.** - 120-occz

Title   " Hsü Chih-pu-tsu-chai ts'ung shu "
　　　　　　　　　　續　知　不　足　齋　叢　書

Classification - C-338 雜家－叢書

Subject - a supplement to (a); and consisting of 17 works.

References - 029-pffz 275.

Author - (刊) Kao Ch'êng-hsün 高 承 勳 ．

Edition - published by the author; no date.   Blocks; "fên" paper.

Index - separate lists for the 2 "chi".

Bound in 4 t'ao 16 ts'ê.

Remarks - a very good small edition; the item is complete and
　　　in good condition.

545

Accession No.　468　　　　　　Index No. - 037-aqfp

Title　　　　" T'ien-jang-ko ts'ung shu "
　　　　　　　天　壤　閣　叢　書

Classification - C-338 雜家 －叢書

Subject - a collection of reprints of 23 works (including additions)
　　on various subjects.

References - 012-zafk 13/19　029-pffz 142　Gest Nos. 992 and 2076.

Author - (編) Wang I-jung 王　懿　榮 .

Edition - the "I-yün-ching-shê" 一 雲 精 舍 ; dated "ting-mou" 1917.
　　Blocks; "fên" paper.

Index - a list of the 23 works.

Bound in 4 t'ao 28 ts'ê (6-7-7-8).

Remarks - this is a very good modern edition; and the item is new.

The University of Toronto Chinese Library

Accession No.   469   **Index No. –** 118-hz

Title   " <u>Kuan-tzŭ</u> "

           管 子

Classification – C-43 法家

Subject – (Gest No. 3614) "a treatise on political philosophy,

legislation, and related subjects."

References – Wylie's Notes page 92   160-lj   163-ggcz 7/9

     031-bgld 10/1   037-ahhg (hsü) 16/3   167-mhfm 14/1   030-iaff 16/1

     106-gdkn 42/10   012-zafk 10/17   031-bgdf 101/1   Gest No. 3614.

Author – attributed to <u>Kuan Chung</u> 管仲 , also known as

<u>Kuan I-wu</u> 管夷吾 , but doubtful.   See 160-lj   Giles B.D. 1006.

(註 釋) <u>Fang Hsüan-ling</u> 房 玄 齡 .

Edition – the "<u>Chü-wên-t'ang</u>" 聚 文 堂 ; dated Chia-Ch'ing "chia-tzŭ"

9/1804.   Blocks; "fên" paper.

Index – a general table of contents for 86 sections in 24 chüan.

Bound in   2 t'ao 10 ts'ê; doubly interleaved.

Remarks – a fairly good edition; the item is complete and in

generally good condition.

The University of Toronto Chinese Library

Accession No. 470   **Index No.** - 118-hz

Title   " Kuan-tzŭ "
                              管 子

Classification - C-43 法家

Subject - (Gest No. 3614) "a treatise on political philosophy,
    legislation, and related subjects."

References - Wylie's Notes page 92   160-lj   163-ggcz 7/9   031-bgld 10/1
    037-ahhg (hsü) 16/3   167-mhfm 14/1   030-iaff 16/1   106-gdkn 42/10
    012-zafk 10/17   031-bgdf 101/1   Gest No. 3614   Toronto No. 469.

Author - attributed to <u>Kuan Chung</u> 管 仲 , also known as <u>Kuan I-wu</u>
    管 夷 吾 , but doubtful. See 160-lj   Giles B.D. 1006.
    (註) <u>Fang Hsüan-ling</u> 房 玄 齡 .

Edition - no notation; no date. Blocks; bamboo paper.

Index - a general table of contents for 86 sections in 24 chüan.

Bound in 2 t'ao 12 ts'e; doubly interleaved with old book-leaves.

Remarks - this item is complete and in good condition with the
    exceptions of some slight defects and 3 pages missing from
    the beginning of chüan 14.

————•————

Accession No.   471   Index No. - 060-hezb   039-zbhh

Title   " Yü-ting Tzŭ shih ching hua "
             御 定 子 史 精 華
             " Tzŭ shih ching hua "
             子 史 精 華

Classification - C-348 類書

Subject - an encyclopaedia of selected phrases from various
    philosophical and historical works under 30 main classifi-
    cations and about 280 sub-divisions.

References - Wylie's Notes page 188   160-1j   163-ggcz 10/16
    031-bgld 14/17   012-zafk 13/26   031-bgdf 136/21   Gest No. 291.

Author - compiled on order of Emperor K'ang-Hsi by an Imperial
    Commission headed by two Imperial princes Yün-lu 允 祿 and
    Yün-li 允 禮 , and Chang T'ing-yü 張 廷 玉 .

Edition - published by Wang Ching-huan 王 景 桓; (postscriptum)
    dated Ch'ien-Lung 55/1790.   Blocks; "fên" paper.

Index - a general table of contents for 160 chüan.

Bound in 6 t'ao 48 ts'ê (8 each).

Remarks - this is a fair edition; and the item is complete but
    with quite a few worm-holes.

Accession No. 472   Index No. - 046-nglf

Title   " Ling-nan i shu "
                          嶺 南 遺 書

Classification - C-338 雜家 一 叢書

Subject - a collection of reprints of 59 works on a variety of
    subjects.

References - 012-zafk 13/16   029-pffz 559   Gest No. 562.

Author - (輯) Wu Yüan-wei 伍 元 薇 .

Edition - published by "Wu-shih" of Nan-hai 南 海 伍 氏 ; dated
    Tao-Kuang "hsin-mao" 11/1831.   Blocks; "mao-pien" paper.

Index - a general table of the 59 works divided into 6 "chi".

Bound in 12 t'ao 80 ts'ê (6-8-4-10-7-5-7-7-6-6-6-8).

Remarks - an ordinary but clear cut edition; the item is complete
    and in good condition.

Accession No. 473   Index No. - 072-dkgz   201-zdib   201-zkgd

Title   " Ming Chang-p'u Huang Chung-tuan kung ch'üan chi "
明 漳 浦 黃 忠 端 公 全 集
" Huang Chung-tuan kung chi "
黃 忠 端 公 集

(#)

Classification - D-33 別集 - 詩文

Subject - an individual collection of prose and poetry.

References - 012-zafk 16/39.

Author - (撰) Huang Tao-chou 黃 道 周 ; (重 編) Ch'ên Shou-ch'i
陳 壽 祺 .

Edition - no notation; dated Tao-Kuang "chi-ch'ou" 9/1829.

Blocks; bamboo paper.

Index - a detailed table of contents for 50 chüan; a separate
table for 卷 首 .

Bound in 4 t'ao 24 ts'ê (6 each).

Remarks - an ordinary edition; the item is complete and in good
condition with the exception of a few worm-holes, at the end
of the work.   More than ten pages in chüan 26 are defective
but have been very well repaired.

(#)   " Huang Chang-p'u chi "
黃 漳 浦 集

Accession No. 474   Index No. - 001-bzdc

Title   " San-ch'ang-wu-chai ts'ung shu "
               三 長 物 齋 叢 書

Classification - C-338 雜家 - 叢書

Subject - a collection of reprints of 25 general works.

References - 012-zafk 13/16   058-jffz 7/61.

Author - (編) Huang Pên-chi 黃 本 驥 .

Edition - the "San-ch'ang-wu-chai" 三 長 物 齋 ; dated Tao-Kuang
          27/1847.   Blocks; "mao-t'ai" paper.

Index - a table of the 25 works.

Bound in 8 t'ao 78 ts'ê (10-10-10-8-10-10-10-10).

Remarks - a very ordinary edition; the item is complete and with no
          defects other than a few pages which are torn and parts missing.

Accession No. 475   **Index No.** - 007-zzzz

Title   " Êrh-shih-êrh tzŭ "
                          二 十 二 子

Classification - C-338 雜家 - 叢書

Subject - a collection of reprints of 22 works on philosophy,
    Taoism, and other subjects.

References - 160-1j   029-pffz page 6   058-jffz (hsü) ping/9.

Author - not stated.

Edition - the "Chêkiang-shu-chü" 浙 江 書 局 ; dated Kuang-Hsü
    1/1875.   Blocks; "mao-t'ai" paper.

Index - a list of the 22 works with the number of ts'ê for each.

Bound in 8 t'ao 83 ts'ê (11-12-11-10-7-10-11-11).

Remarks - a very ordinary edition; the item is apparently complete
    and in good condition.

————— • —————

Accession No.   476   **Index No.** - 149-ofjc

Title   " <u>Tu</u> <u>shu</u> <u>tsa</u> <u>chih</u> "
                     讀　書　雜　志

Classification - C-308 雜家 - 雜說

Subject - a collection of disquisitions and commentaries on ten
      standard philosophical and historical works.

References - 012-zafk 12/23.

Author - (撰) <u>Wang Nien-sun</u> 王 念 孫 .

Edition - no notation; no date. Blocks; "fên" paper.

Index - a general table of the 10 works; 餘編 2 chüan.

Bound in 4 t'ao 24 ts'ê.

Remarks - a good **modern** edition; the item is complete and in
      good condition.

554

- - - • - - -

Accession No. 477　　　　　Index No. - 077-ddhe

Title　　　　" Wu lin chang ku ts'ung pien "
　　　　　　武 林 掌 故 叢 編

Classification - C-338 雜家 - 叢書

Subject - a collection of reprints of 187 works mainly on prose and
　　　poetry.

References - 029-pffz 257　012-zafk 13/19　Gest No. 567.

Author - (編) Ting Ping 丁 丙 .

Edition - published by "Ting-shih" of "Chia-hui-t'ang" 嘉 惠 堂 丁 氏;
　　　dated "kuei-wei"　1883.　　Blocks; "mao-t'ai" paper.

Index - separate lists of works for each of 26 "chi".

Bound in 26 t'ao 208 ts'ê (8 each).

Remarks - an ordinary edition; the item is complete and in good
　　　condition.　012-zafk gives the author of this work as
　　　Ting Shên 丁 申 .

Accession No. 478   Index No. - 170-hzd   163-gzdb

Title   " Ling-ch'uan chi "
                              陵   川   集

              " Ho Wên-chung kung Ling-ch'uan wên chi "
                郝 文 忠 公 陵   川 文 集

Classification - D-33 別集 - 詩文

Subject - a miscellaneous individual literary collection,- prose
    and poetry.

References - 160-1j 163-ggcz 14/1   031-bgld 17/2   167-mhfm 22/2
    106-gdkn 95/1   012-zafk 16/1   031-bgdf 166/11   Gest No. 1613.

Author - Ho Ching 郝 經 .

Edition - privately published; (preface) dated Chia-Ch'ing "mou-wu"
    3/1798.   Blocks; "fên" paper.

Index - a detailed table of contents for 39 chüan.

Bound in 1 t'ao 10 ts'ê.

Remarks - this is a very fine edition; complete and in perfect
    condition.   The impression is clear and easy to read.

The University of Toronto Chinese Library

Accession No. 479   Index No. - 189-zzlf

Title   " Kao-tzŭ i shu "
高 子 遺 書

Classification – D-33 別集 - 詩文

Subject - an individual collection of prose and poetry, grouped
under 12 classifications.

References - 163-ggcz 15/9   012-zafk 16/32   031-bgdf 172/53
Toronto No. 49.

Author - (撰) Kao P'an-lung 高 攀 龍 .

Edition - no notation; (preface) dated Ch'ung-Chêng 1/1628.
Blocks; bamboo paper.

Index - a detailed table of contents for 12 chüan.

Bound in 1 t'ao 8 ts'ê.

Remarks - a fairly good edition; the item is complete and in good
condition,- last page slightly defective.

—— • ——

Accession No. 480   Index No. - 072-zchd

Title
              " Jih chih lu chi shih "
               日　知　録　集　釋

Classification - C-308 雜家 - 雜說

Subject - a collection of miscellaneous notes and writings on
    various subjects; with commentaries.

References - 012-zafk 12/21.

Author - (著) Ku Yen-wu 顧 炎 武 ; (集釋) Huang Ju-ch'êng
         黄 汝 成 .

Edition - reprinted by "Huang's Hsi-ch'i-ts'ao-lu" 黄氏西谿草廬 ;
    dated Tao-Kuang 14/1834.   Blocks; "mao-pien" paper.

Index - a detailed table of contents for 32 chüan; 刊 誤 2 chüan.

Bound in 2 t'ao 16 ts'ê.

Remarks - the item is complete and in practically perfect condition.

Accession No. 481   Index No. - 024-zifk

Title   " Shih-wan-chüan-lou ts'ung shu "
十 萬 卷 樓 叢 書

Classification - C-338 雜家一叢書
Subject - a collection of reprints of 51 works.

References - 160-1j 012-zafk 13/19 029-pffz 15 Gest No. 2344.

Author - compiled by Lu Hsin-yüan 陸 心 源.

Edition - of the compiler; dated (一 集) Kuang-Hsü "chi-mao"
    5/1879. (二 集) Kuang-Hsü 8/1882. (三 集) Kuang-Hsü
    "jên-ch'ên" 18/1892.   Blocks; "mao-t'ai" paper.

Index - a list of the works, with the authors. 1st "chi" 16 works;
    2d "chi" 21; 3d "chi" 14.

Bound in 14 t'ao 112 ts'ê (8 each).

Remarks - an ordinary good edition; the item is complete and as new.

Accession No. 482   Index No. - 037-ablc

Title   " T'ai-p'ing kuang chi "
                         太 平 廣 記

Classification - C-368 小 説 家

Subject - (Gest No. 1048) - "an encyclopaedia of supernatural,
    mysterious, strange, and peculiar matters."

References - 160-1j   163-ggcz 11/6   031-bgld 14/38   012-zafk 14/14
    031-bgdf 142/32   Gest No. 1048.

Author - (編) Li Fang 李 昉 and others.

Edition - the "San-jang-Mu-chi" 三 讓 睦 記; dated Tao-Kuang
    "ping-wu" 26/1846.   Blocks; "mao-t'ai" paper.

Index - a general table of contents for 500 chüan.

Bound in 8 t'ao 48 ts'ê (6 each).

Remarks - an ordinary "pocket" edition; the item is complete and
    in very good condition.

Accession No. 483   Index No. - 120-oabl

Title   " Hsü T'ai-p'ing kuang chi "
               續　太　平　廣　記

Classification - C-368 小 説 家
Subject - a supplement to "T'ai-p'ing kuang chi" 太平廣記

   (No. 482).

References - none.

Author - (集) Lu Shou-ming 陸壽名 .

Edition - the "yün-wai-lou" 雲 外 樓 ; dated Tao-Kuang 3/1823.

   Blocks; "mao-t'ai" paper.

Index - separate general tables of contents arranged under 18 "pu".

Bound in 1 t'ao 8 ts'ê.

Remarks - an ordinary edition; the item is complete and without

   defects.

Accession No. 484   Index No. - 149-ofcp

Title   " Tu-hua-chai ts'ung shu "
                          讀 畫 齋 叢 書

Classification - C-338 雜家 - 叢書
Subject - a collection of reprints of 45 miscellaneous works.

References - 058-jffz 6/2.

Author - (編 輯) Ku Hsiu 顧 修 .

Edition - apparently privately published; (preface) dated
    Chia-Ch'ing 4/1799.   Blocks; "fên" paper.

Index - separate lists of works for each of 8 "chi" except the 乙 集 .

Bound in 8 t'ao 64 ts'ê (8-9-7-8-9-7-9-7).

Remarks - a modern edition; the item is new.

562

Accession No. 485   Index No. - 140-nhhp

Title   " Ts'ang-hsiu-t'ang ts'ung shu "
                藏 修 堂 叢 書

Classification - C-338 雜家 - 叢書

Subject - a collection of reprints of 37 works on history, painting,
          medicine and other general subjects.

References - none.

Author - (?) compiled by Liu Wan-jung 劉 晚 榮 .

Edition - the "Ts'ang-hsiu-shu-wu" 藏 修 書 屋 ; (preface) dated
          Kuang-Hsü "kêng-yin" 16/1890.   Blocks; "fên" paper.

Index - a general list of the 37 works divided into 6 "chi";
        separate lists for each "chi" except the first one.

Bound in 6 t'ao 54 ts'ê (8-8-10-11-8-9).

Remarks - a fairly good "pocket" edition; the item is as new.

Accession No. 486   Index No. - 002-cihf

Title   " Chung hsing chiang shuai pieh chuan "
             中   興   將   帥   別   傳

Classification - B-117 傳記一總錄

Subject - a collection of biographies of generals who participated
    in the campaigns of the T'aip'ing Rebellion, during the period
    between Tao-Kuang and T'ung-Chih.

References - none.

Author - (撰) Chu K'ung-chang 朱孔彰.

Edition - no notation; dated Kuang-Hsü "ting-yu" 23/1897.   Blocks;
    "mao-pien" paper.

Index - a detailed table of names for 30 chüan.

Bound in 1 t'ao 10 ts'ê.

Remarks - an ordinary edition; the item is complete and without
    defects.

Accession No. 487   Index No. - 053-1zee   001-bobz

Title   " Kuang wên yüan ying hua "
              廣　文　苑　英　華
              " San hsü ku wên ch'i shang "
              三　續　古　文　奇　賞

Classification - D-63 總集 - 詩文

Subject - a general collection of prose and poetry of ancient
         scholars prior to the Ming Dynasty; with marginal notes.

References - 012-zafk 19/14   031-bgdf 193/37.

Author - (評選) Ch'ên Jên-hsi 陳　仁　錫 .

Edition - the "Ch'i-shang-chai" 奇　賞　齋 ; (preface) dated T'ien-Ch'i
         "chia-tzŭ" 4/1624.   Blocks; bamboo paper.

Index - a detailed classified table of contents for 26 chüan.

Bound in 2 t'ao 16 ts'ê (8-8).

Remarks - a good edition; the item is complete, but with repaired
         worm-holes here and there.

Accession No.   488   Index No. - 178-hzz   178-hz

Title

" Han   Fei-tzŭ "
韓   非   子

" Han-tzŭ "
韓   子

Classification - C-43 法家

Subject - (Gest No. 1559) - "a collection of 55 miscellaneous essays
on a variety of subjects, very few of which can properly be
considered as pertaining to law or legislation, and some are
closely related to Taoism and allied matters."

References - Wylie's Notes page 92 160-1j 163-ggcz 7/10 031-bgld 10/2
030-iaff 16/2 106-gdkn 42/12 167-mhfm 14/9 012-zafk 10/17
031-bgdf 101/7 Gest No. 1559.

Author - Han Fei 韓 非 .

Edition - a Ming edition; (preface) dated Wa -Li 6/1578.   Blocks;
"mien" paper.

Index - a table of contents for 20 chüan.

Bound in 1 t'ao 6 ts'ê.

Remarks - this is a very fine and clear impression; and the item is
complete and in very good condition.   Whole of chüan 6, 7, and
8 are hand-written.

Accession No. 489   Index No. - 128-gilf

Title   " Shêng yü hsiang chieh "
聖　諭　像　解

Classification - C-13 儒家

Subject - explanation of the "Sacred Edict", with numerous
illustrations of ancient worthies noted for their good
reputation and virtuous conduct.

References - Wylie's Notes page 87 160-1j Toronto Nos. 6, 7 and 8.

Author - Liang Yen-nien 梁 廷 年 .

Edition - a reprint by "Fu-ch'u-t'ang" 復 初 堂 ; (postscriptum)
dated Kuang-Hsü 7/1881.   Blocks; "fên" paper.

Index - separate tables of contents at the beginning of each of 20
chüan.

Bound in 1 t'ao 10 ts'ê.

Remarks - a very fine clear-cut edition; the item is complete and as
new.

Accession No. 490   Index No. - 067-zf

Title   " Wên   lüeh "
                           文   略

Classification - D-73 總集一文

Subject - a general collection of prose of ancient scholars.

References - none.

Author - (選) Liu Kuang-shêng 劉 廣 生 .

Edition - a Ming edition; (preface) dated Wan-Li "mou-wu" 46/1618.

    Blocks; "mien" paper.

Index - separate tables of contents at the beginning of each of 2

    chüan.

Bound in 1 t'ao 8 ts'ê.

Remarks - a very good edition; the item is complete and in very

    good condition,- a few worm-holes.

Accession No. 491   Index No. - 096-zzcb   096-zzcd

Title   " Wang Wên-ch'êng kung ch'üan shu "
                 王 文 成 公 全 書

               " Wang Wên-ch'êng ch'üan shu "
                 王 文 成 全 書

Classification - D-33 別集 - 詩文
Subject - an individual collection of prose and poetry.

References - 163-ggcz 15/7   031-bgld 18/23   012-zafk 16/20
     031-bgdf 171/33   Gest No. 405   Toronto No. 456.

Author - (撰) Wang Shou-jên 王 守 仁.

Edition - no notation; dated "i-wei" 1895.   Blocks; "mao-pien"
     paper.

Index - a detailed table of contents for 38 chüan.

Bound in 4 t'ao 24 ts'ê (6 each).

Remarks - an ordinary good edition; the item is complete and in
     very good condition.

569

Accession No. 492   Index No. - 118-hz

Title   " Kuan-tzŭ "
                                   管　子

Classification - C-43 法家
Subject - (Gest No. 3614) - "a treatise on political philosophy,
     legislation, and related subjects."

References - Wylie's Notes page 92   160-1j   163-ggcz 7/9   031-bgld 10/1
     037-ahhg (hsü) 16/3   167-mhfm 14/1   030-iaff 16/1   106-gdkn
     42/10   012-zafk 10/17   031-bgdf 101/1   Gest No. 3614   (#)
Author - attributed to Kuan Chung 管 仲 , also known as Kuan I-wu
     管 夷 吾 , but doubtful.   See 160-1j   Giles B. D. 1006.
     (訂 閱) Ko Ting 葛 鼎 and Ting Tz'ŭ-p'ing 丁 此 聘 .
Edition - no notation; no date.   Blocks; "mao-pien" paper.

Index - a general table of contents for 86 sections in 24 chüan.

Bound in 1 t'ao 10 ts'ê.

Remarks - an ordinary good edition; the item is complete and with
     but a few slight defects. (repaired)

   (#)   Toronto Nos. 469 and 470.

570

The University of Toronto Chinese Library

Accession No. 493　　　　　Index No. - 024-bgzi

Title　　　　　" Wu-t'ing wên pien "
　　　　　　　　午 亭 文 編

Classification - D-33 別集 - 詩文

Subject - an individual miscellaneous collection of prose and poetry.

References - 163-ggcz 15/11　　031-bgld 18/38　　012-zafk 17/10
　　031-bgdf 173/20.

Author - (著) Ch'ên T'ing-ching 陳 廷 敬 ; (輯 錄) Lin Chi
　　林 佶 .

Edition - no notation; (postscriptum) dated Ch'ien-Lung 43/1778.
　　Blocks; "fên" paper.

Index - a detailed table of contents for 50 chüan.

Bound in 2 t'ao 16 ts'ê (8-8).

Remarks - an ordinary edition; complete and without defects.

571

Accession No.   494   Index No. - 072-dzeh

Title   " Ming wên ch'i shang "
               明　文　奇　賞

Classification - D-73 總集一文

Subject - a general collection of prose of scholars of the Ming

 Dynasty.

References - 012-zafk 19/14   031-bgdf 193/37.

Author - (評選) Ch'ên Jên-hsi 陳 仁 錫 .

Edition - a Ming edition; (preface) dated T'ien-Ch'i 3/1623.

 Blocks; bamboo paper,

Index - a general table of contents for 40 chüan; a detailed list

 for the same.

Bound in 3 t'ao 20 ts'ê (8-6-6).

Remarks - a fairly good edition; the item is complete and in

 generally good condition with the exception of some repaired

 worm-holes,

———•—•———

Accession No. 495 (a)   Index No. - 118-eezd

Title   " Ssŭ-ho wên chi "
                         笥 河 又 集

Classification - D-43 別集 一 文
Subject - an individual collection of prose.

References - 012-zafk 17/34.

Author - (撰) Chu Yün 朱筠 .   124-1781

Edition - no notation; (preface) dated Chia-Ch'ing 9/1804.
    Blocks; "mao-pien" paper.

Index - a detailed table of contents for 14 chüan.

Bound in 1 t'ao 6 ts'ê.

Remarks - an ordinary edition; the item is complete and in good
    condition.   012-zafk gives the number of chüan as 2.

————•————

Accession No. 495 (b)   Index No. - 118-eefd

Title   " Ssŭ-ho shih chi "
                        筍   河   詩   集

Classification - D-38 別集 - 詩
Subject - an individual collection of poetry.

References - 012-zafk 17/34.

Author - (撰) Chu Yün 朱 筠 .

Edition - uniform with (a).

Index - a detailed table of contents for 20 chüan.

Bound in 1 t'ao 8 ts'ê.

Remarks - as under (a); but the number of chüan agrees with 012-zafk.

Accession No. 496   Index No. - 030-dfdo

Title   " <u>Wu shih chi lan</u> "
　　　　　　　　　　　吳　詩　集　覽

<u>Classification</u> - D-38 別集一詩

<u>Subject</u> - an individual collection of poetry; with notes and
　　commentaries.

<u>References</u> - none.

<u>Author</u> - (著) <u>Wu Wei-yeh</u> 吳 偉 業 ; (集 覽) <u>Chin Jung-fan</u>
　　靳 榮 藩 .

<u>Edition</u> - the "<u>Liang-yün-t'ing</u>" 凌 雲 亭 ; dated Ch'ien-Lung
　　40/1775.　　Blocks; bamboo paper.

<u>Index</u> - a detailed table of contents for 20 chüan; 談 藪 1 chüan.

<u>Bound in</u> 2 t'ao 16 ts'ê (8-8).

<u>Remarks</u> - a fairly good edition; the item is complete and in good
　　condition.

1126
1773
1329

Accession No. 497   Index No. - 077-lcbh   077-jcbh

Title   " Li-tai shih lun "
                    歷 代 史 論

Classification - B-367 史 評

Subject - critical commentaries on some of the dynastic histories,
    as follows:- (a) Chou 周 Han 漢 Chin 晉 Liu-ch'ao 六朝
    Sui 隋 T'ang 唐 Wu-tai 五代 Sung 宋 Yüan 元 ; (b) Ming
    明 ; (c) Tso-chuan 左傳 .

References - 012-zafk 9/29-30   031-bgdf 90/16   Gest No. 3655.

Author - (論正) (a) Chang P'u 張溥 ; (b) Ku Ying-t'ai 谷應泰;
    (c) Kao Shih-ch'i 高士奇 .

Edition - the "Ts'ang-sung-shan-fang" 蒼松山房; dated Kuang-Hsü
    "kuei-wei" 9/1883.   Blocks; "fên" paper.

Index - (a) a table of contents for 12 chüan covering the period
    down to Wu-tai; a table of contents for 3 chüan at the beginning
    of the Sung Dynasty; same for 1 chüan at the beginning   (#)
Bound in 2 t'ao 12 ts'ê (6-6).

Remarks - an ordinary edition; the item is complete and in good
    condition.

(#) of the Yüan Dynasty; (b) a table of contents for 4 chüan;
(c) a table of contents for 2 chüan.

576

The University of Toronto Chinese Library

Accession No. 498   Index No. - 030-edg

Title   " Shên yin yü "
                     呻 吟 語

Classification - C-13 儒家
Subject - a treatise on mental philosophy and conduct.

References - 160-1j 012-zafk 10/7   031-bgdf 96/26   Toronto No. 38.

Author - Lü K'un 呂 坤 .

Edition - a Ming edition; (preface) dated Wan-Li "kuei-ssŭ" 21/1593.
    Blocks; "mao-pien" paper.

Index - a table of contents for 6 chüan divided into 2 p'ien (內 外).

Bound in 1 t'ao 8 ts'ê.

Remarks - an ordinary Ming edition; the item appears to be complete
    and is in fairly good condition,- a few worm-holes.

Accession No. 499   Index No. - 115-ekzz

Title   " Ch'in-Han jên wên hsüan yü "
              秦 漢 人 文 選 玉

Classification - D-73 總集-文

Subject - an anthology of prose of the Ch'in and Han dynasties.

References - none.

Author - (選) Wang Hêng 王 衡 ; (校) Chang I-ch'êng 張 以 誠.

Edition - officially published; not dated, but of the Ming period.

    Blocks; bamboo paper.

Index - a table of contents for 6 chüan.

Bound in 1 t'ao 6 ts'ê.

Remarks - the item is apparently complete but with a few repaired

    defects.

Accession No. 500   Index No. - 067-zfbi

Title   " Wên chang kuei fan "
                     文 章 軌 範

Classification - D-73 總集 - 文

Subject - (Toronto No. 391) - "a general collection of 69 prose
    compositions by some of the most famous ancient scholars
    of the Han, Chin, T'ang and Sung periods;with punctuations
    and marginal notes ----."

References - 160-1j 163-ggcz 16/5   031-bgld 19/16   030-iaff 38/22
    106-gdkn 114/16   012-zafk 19/4   031-bgdf 187/34 Toronto No.391.

Author - (編) Hsieh Fang-tê 謝 枋 得.

Edition - no notation; no date.   Blocks; "fên" paper.

Index - a detailed table of contents for 7 chüan.

Bound in 1 t'ao 2 ts'ê.

Remarks - a fair edition; the item is apparently complete but 2
    pages are with repaired defects as follows:- chüan 2 page 13;
    chüan 3 page 1.

Accession No. 501   Index No. - 037-zhzh   024-zhgc

Title   " Ta-Ch'ing shih ch'ao shêng hsün "
               大　清　十　朝　聖　訓

Classification - B-67 詔令奏議 一 詔令

Subject - (Gest No. 331) - "Imperial Edicts and Proclamations to
     Governors of Provinces, High State Officials, etc., by the
     Ten Emperors of the Manchu Dynasty, from Emperor T'ien-Ming
     (1616-1627) to Emperor T'ung-Chih (1862-1875), inclusive."
     (Separate notes follow)

References - see under the several works; to the collective work
     Gest Nos. 331 and 1388.

Author - compiled on order of various emperors.

Edition - see under the several works.

Index - none.

Bound in 132 t'ao 856 ts'ê.

Remarks - a very fine edition on the whole. The item was printed
     at different times and contains some replacements. For
     detailed imformation see separate notes.

Accession No. 501 (a)   Index No. - 037-zhae

Title " Ta-Ch'ing T'ai Tsu Kao Huang-ti shêng hsün "
大 清 太 祖 高 皇 帝 聖 訓

Classification - B-67 詔令奏議-詔令
Subject - Imperial Edicts etc., of Emperor T'ien-Ming.

References - 012-zafk 4/27   031-bgld 6/1   031-bgdf 55/1.

Author - compiled on order of Emperor K'ang-Hsi 康 熙 .

Edition - a palace edition; (preface) dated Ch'ien-Lung 4/1739.
    Blocks; "k'ai-hua" paper.

Index - a general table of contents for 4 chüan.

Bound in 1 ts'ê in 1 t'ao with (b) and (c).

Remarks - the item is complete and in perfect condition except for
    some slight stains.

Accession No. 501 (b)   Index No. - 037-zhae

Title   " Ta-Ch'ing T'ai Tsung Wên Huang-ti shêng hsün "
大 清 太 宗 文 皇 帝 聖 訓

Classification - B-67 詔令奏議 - 詔令
Subject - Imperial Edicts etc. of Emperor T'ien-Ts'ung.

References - 012-zafk 4/27   031-bgld 6/1   031-bgdf 55/3.

Author - compiled on order of Emperor Shun-Chih 順 治 .

Edition - uniform with (a).

Index - a general table of contents for 6 chüan.

Bound in 2 ts'ê in 1 t'ao with (a) and (c).

Remarks - the item is complete and without defects.

Accession No. 501 (c)   Index No. - 037-zhde

Title " Ta-Ch'ing Shih Tsu Chang Huang-ti shêng hsün "
大　清　世　祖　章　皇　帝　聖　訓

Classification - B-67 詔令奏議 一 詔令

Subject - Imperial Edicts etc. of Emperor Shun-Chih.

References - 012-zafk 4/27   031-bgld 6/1   031-bgdf 55/4.

Author - compiled on order of Emperor K'ang-Hsi 康　熙 .

Edition - uniform with (a).

Index - a general table of contents for 6 chüan.

Bound in 2 ts's in 1 t'ao with (a) and (b).

Remarks - the item is complete and in very good condition.

Accession No. 501 (d)   Index No. - 037-zhge

Title   " Ta-Ch'ing Shêng Tsu Jên Huang-ti shêng hsün "
          大 清 聖 祖 仁 皇 帝 聖 訓

Classification - B-67 詔令奏議 - 詔令
Subject - Imperial Edicts etc. of Emperor K'ang-Hsi.

References - 012-zafk 4/27   031-bgld 6/1   031-bgdf 55/6.

Author - compiled on order of Emperor Yung-Chêng 雍 正 .

Edition - uniform with (a); but dated Ch'ien-Lung 6/1741.

Index - a general table of contents for 60 chüan.

Bound in 5 t'ao 23 ts'ê (5-5-5-4-4).

Remarks - the item is complete and in good condition,- some stains.

584

Accession No. 501 (e)   Index No. - 037-zhde

Title   " Ta-Ch'ing Shih Tsung Hsien Huang-ti shêng hsün "
大 清 世 宗 憲 皇 帝 聖 訓

Classification - B-67 詔令奏議-詔令
Subject - Imperial Edicts etc. of Emperor Yung-Chêng.

References - 012-zafk 4/24   031-bgld 6/1   031-bgdf 55/7.

Author - compiled on order of Emperor Ch'ien-Lung 乾 隆 .

Edition - uniform with (a); but dated Ch'ien-Lung 5/1740.

Index - a general table of contents for 36 chüan.

Bound in 4 t'ao 16 ts'ê (4 each).

Remarks - the item is complete and in good condition,- 2 or 3
    slight worm-holes.   A number of pages in this item seem
    to have been printed on "fên" paper instead of "k'ai-hua"
    paper.

Accession No. 501 (f)   Index No. - 037-zhze

Title   " Ta-Ch'ing Kao Tsung Shun Huang-ti shêng hsün "
            大 清 高 宗 純 皇 帝 聖 訓

Classification - B-67 詔令奏議-詔令
Subject - Imperial Edicts etc. of Emperor Ch'ien-Lung.

References - 012-zafk 4/28   031-bgld 6/1.

Author - compiled on order of Emperor Chia-Ch'ing 嘉 慶 .

Edition - uniform with (a); but dated Chia-Ch'ing 12/1807.   Blocks;
         "fên" paper.

Index - a general table of contents for 300 chüan.

Bound in 30 t'ao 300 ts'ê (10 each); doubly interleaved.

Remarks - the item is complete, but with many worm-holes the more
         serious ones of which have been repaired.   Parts of the work
         are stained, especially the portions from chüan 157 to 168 and
         from chüan 191 to 192, which are with 2 pages partly missing
         (#)

(#) as a result of the stains.   Chüan 201 to 210 and 221 to
     230 are replacements from another copy.   Chüan 220 is
     duplicated owing to the replacements, and therefore this
     item contains 301 ts'ê and not 300 when actually counted.

Accession No. 501 (g)   Index No. - 037-zhbe

Title   "Ta-Ch'ing Jên Tsung Jui Huang-ti shêng hsün"
大 清 仁 宗 睿 皇 帝 聖 訓

Classification — B-67 詔令奏議 - 詔令
Subject - Imperial Edicts etc. of Emperor Chia-Ch'ing.

References - 012-zafk 4/28   031-bgld 6/1.

Author - compiled on order of Emperor Tao-Kuang 道 光.

Edition - uniform with (a); but dated Tao-Kuang 4/1824.   Blocks;
    "fên" paper.

Index - a general table of contents for 110 chüan.

Bound in 10 t'ao 110 ts'ê (11 each).

Remarks - the item is complete but has been very badly worm-eaten.
    Necessary repairing has been done, however.   A portion of
    this work - t'ao 6, 8, 9, 10 - is in very good condition and
    is apparently a replacement from another copy.

Accession No. 501 (h)   Index No. - 037-zhfe

Title   " **Ta-Ch'ing Hsüan Tsung Ch'êng Huang-ti shêng hsün** "
大 清 宣 宗 成 皇 帝 聖 訓

Classification - B-67 詔令奏議－詔令

Subject - Imperial Edicts etc. of Emperor Tao-Kuang.

References - 012-zafk 4/28.

Author - compiled on order of Emperor Hsien-Fêng 咸 豐 .

Edition - uniform with (a); but dated Hsien-Fêng 6/1856.
    Blocks; "fên" paper.

Index - a general table of contents for 130 chüan.

Bound in 26 t'ao 130 ts'ê (5 each).

Remarks - the item is complete and as new.

Accession No. 501 (1)   Index No. - 037-zhze

Title   " Ta-Ch'ing Wên Tsung Hsien Huang-ti shêng hsün "
          大 清 文 宗 顯 皇 帝 聖 訓

Classification - B-67 詔令奏議 - 詔令
Subject - Imperial Edicts etc. of Emperor Hsien-Fêng.

References - 012-zafk 4/28.

Author - compiled on order of Emperor T'ung-Chih 同 治 .

Edition - uniform with (a); but dated T'ung-Chih (year ?).
    Blocks; "fên" paper.

Index - a general table of contents for 110 chüan.

Bound in 22 t'ao 110 ts'ê (5 each).

Remarks - the item is complete and in perfect condition.

The University of Toronto Chinese Library

Accession No. 501 (j) Index No. - 037-zhke

Title " Ta-Ch'ing Mu Tsung I Huang-ti shêng hsün "
大 清 穆 宗 毅 皇 帝 聖 訓

Classification - B-67 詔令奏議 - 詔令

Subject - Imperial Edicts etc. of Emperor T'ung-Chih.

References - 012-zafk 4/28.

Author - compiled on order of Emperor Kuang-Hsü 光 緒 .

Edition - uniform with (a); but dated Kuang-Hsü 5/1879.   Blocks;
   "fên" paper.

Index - a general table of contents for 160 chüan.

Bound in 32 t'ao 160 ts'ê (5 each).

Remarks - the item is complete and as new.

Accession No. 502   Index No. - 030-ezn

Title   " <u>Chou wên kuei</u> "

周　文　歸

Classification - D-73 總集 - 文

Subject - a collection of <u>Chou Dynasty</u> prose; being selections

from well-known works of that period; with critical

commentaries.

References - 012-zafk 19/11   031-bgdf 193/23.

Author - (選) <u>Chung Hsing</u> 鍾 惺 .

Edition - a Ming edition; (preface) dated Ch'ung-Chêng "kêng-ch'ên"

13/1640.   Blocks; bamboo paper.

Index - a detailed table of contents for 20 chüan; detailed lists

for each of 20 chüan.

Bound in 1 t'ao 12 ts'ê.

Remarks - a fairly good edition; the item is complete and in good

condition with the exception of a few repaired worm-holes.

———•—•———

Accession No. 503   Index No. - 067-zi

Title   " Wên pien "
                         文   編

Classification - D-73 總集 - 文

Subject - (Gest No. 2406) - "an extensive general literary collection,-
    prose; covering the period from the Chou Dynasty 周 to the
    Sung Dynasty 宋 ."

References - 163-ggoz 16/8   031-bgld 19/26   030-iaff 39/12
    012-zafk 19/8   031-bgdf 189/17   Gest Nos. 322 and 2406.

Author - (選) T'ang Shun-chih 唐 順 之 .

Edition - a Ming edition; (preface) dated Chia-Ching "ping-ch'ên"
    35/1556.   Blocks; bamboo paper.

Index - detailed tables of contents at the beginning of each of 62
    chüan with the exception of chüan 37 and 42.

Bound in 4 t'ao 30 ts'ê (7-8-7-8).

Remarks - a fairly good edition.   The item is in generally good
    condition,- defects not being numerous; and shows evidences
    of having been printed from old blocks.   The catalogues give
    the number of chüan as 64, but this item contains 62 chüan only.

Accession No. 504   Index No. - 074-zchi

Title   " Yüeh ling sui pien "
月 令 粹 編

Classification - B-157 時令

Subject - (Wylie) - "----- is a compilation of historical memoranda
for every day in the year -----"

References - Wylie's Notes page 43   Gest No. 153.

Author - by Ch'in Chia-mo 秦 嘉 謨 .

Edition - published by the author; dated Chia-Ch'ing 17/1812.
Blocks; "mao-pien" paper.

Index - a general table of contents for 卷首 and 24 chüan.

Bound in 1 t'ao 6 ts's.

Remarks - an ordinary edition; complete and without defects.

Accession No. 505　　　　Index No. - 181-1cpf

Title　　　　　　" Yen Li ts'ung shu "
　　　　　　　　　顏　李　叢　書

Classification - C-338 雜家 - 叢書

Subject - a collection of reprints of 33 works on the "Four Books",
　the "Classics", literary collections and other subjects.

References - none.

Author - by Yen Yüan 顏 元 and Li Kung (?) 李 塨 of the
　"Shu-ku-nien p'u" - Fêng Ch'ên 馮 辰 .

Edition - the "Ssŭ-ts'un-hsüeh-hui" 四 存 學 會 ; (preface) dated
　Min-Kuo 12/1923.　　Type; "fên" paper.

Index - a general table of the 33 works; separate tables for some
　of the works.

Bound in 4 t'ao 32 ts'ê (8 each).

Remarks - a modern edition.　The item is new.　Of the "Ssŭ-shu
　chêng wu", whole of chüan 5 is missing.　There is no evidence
　to show whether it is missing or unpublished.

Accession No. 506   Index No. - 007-zdhz

Title   " Ếrh-hsi-t'ang wến chi "
二 希 堂 文 集

Classification - D-43 别集-文

Subject - an individual collection of prose.

References - 163-ggcz 15/12   012-zafk 17/18   031-bgld 18/41
031-bgdf 173/26.

Author - (撰) Ts'ai Shih-yūan 蔡 世 遠 .

Edition - no notation; (preface) dated Ch'ien-Lung "ping-tzǔ"
21/1756.   Blocks; "fến" paper.

Index - a detailed table of contents for 12 chūan including 卷首 .

Bound in 1 t'ao 6 ts'ê.

Remarks - a fairly good edition; the item is complete and in
good condition.   Page 37 of chūan 2 is handwritten.

Accession No. 507   Index No. - 009-zkji

Title   " J**ên** **ching** **lei** **pien** "
                   入　鏡　類　編

Classification - C-328 雜家 - 雜纂

Subject - a collection of extracts taken from various standard
    works in explanation of a large variety of subjects in
    connection with various phases of man's life and activities.

References - none.

Author - (輯) Ch'**êng** Chih-ch**ên** 程　之　楨．

Edition - privately published by the Ch'**êng** family; dated T'ung-Chih
    "kuei-yu" 12/1873.   Blocks; "mao-t'ai" paper.

Index - a detailed table of subject headings for 46 chüan.

Bound in 2 t'ao 16 ts'ê (8-8).

Remarks - a very ordinary edition; the item is complete and in good
    condition.

Accession No. 508   Index No. - 019-rif

Title   " Ch'üan shan shu "

勸　善　書

Classification - C-328 雜家－雜纂

Subject - a work of a hortatory character; including examples
taken from the lives of ancient worthies.

References - 012-zafk 13/4   031-bgdf 131/10.

Author - （撰）Empress Jên-Hsiao 仁孝皇后 .

Edition - apparently original; (preface) Yung-Lo 永 樂 5/1408.
Blocks; bamboo paper.

Index - none; 20 chüan.

Bound in 2 t'ao 16 ts'ê (6-10); doubly interleaved.

Remarks - this is indeed a very good edition.　The item appears
to be complete; and although it is not in very good condition
throughout, defects are no more than might be expected in view
of its age.

Accession No. 509   Index No. - 106-ddzb   024-zbcg

Title   " <u>Huang Ming shih-liu chia hsiao p'in</u> "
皇 明 十 六 家 小 品

" <u>Shih-liu ming chia hsiao p'in</u> "
十 六 名 家 小 品

Classification - D-63 總集-詩文

Subject - a general collection of prose compositions with some
poetic writings of 16 authors of the <u>Ming Dynasty</u>; each
author being treated separately as an individual work.

References - 012-zafk 19/14   031-bgdf 193/49.

Author - (編) <u>Lu Yün-lung</u> 陸 雲 龍 .

Edition - a Ming edition; (preface) dated "kuei-yu" 1633.
Blocks; bamboo paper.

Index - a general list of the 16 works, each work in 2 chüan;
separate detailed lists at the beginning of each work.

Bound in 2 t'ao 16 ts'ê; singly interleaved.

Remarks - a fairly good edition; the item appears to be complete
and in very good condition. The table of contents at the
beginning of the work is handwritten.

599

Accession No.   510   Index No. - 030-bbgf

Title   " Ku chin wên t'ung "
                          古　今　文　統

Classification - D-73 總集一文

Subject - a general collection of prose covering the period from
   the Chou 周 to the Ming 明 dynasty; with commentaries and
   criticisms.

References - 085-hchm 1/3.

Author - (論定) Chang I-chung 張 以 忠 .

Edition - a Ming edition; (preface) dated Ch'ung-Chêng 2/1629.
   Blocks; bamboo paper.

Index - a general table of contents for 16 chüan or "chi"; detailed
   list for each chüan.

Bound in 4 t'ao 32 ts'ê; doubly interleaved (8-9-7-8).

Remarks - a good edition; the item is complete and in good condition.
   As it is on the prohibited list of the Ch'ing Dynasty, this work
   is undoubtedly very rare.

Accession No. 511   Index No. - 085-jicp

Title   " P'ang-hsi-chai ts'ung shu "
               滂 喜 齋 叢 書

Classification - C-338 雜家 - 叢書

Subject - a collection of reprints of 54 works on various subjects.

References - 058-jffz 7/36   012-zafk 13/18.

Author - (編) P'an Tsu-yin 潘 祖 蔭.

Edition - the "P'an's Pa-hsi-chai" 潘氏八喜齋 ; undated; blocks
   cut at different times between T'ung-Chih and Kuang-Hsü.
   Blocks; "fên" paper.

Index - separate list of works for each of 4 "han" 函 .

Bound in 4 t'ao 32 ts'ê (10-8-7-7).

Remarks - a good modern edition; the item is complete and as new.

Accession No. 512   Index No. - 173-pjfp

Title   " Ling-chien-ko ts'ung shu "
               靈 鶼 閣 叢 書

Classification - C-338 雜家 - 叢書
Subject - a collection of reprints of 56 miscellaneous works.

References - 012-zafk 13/19   029-pffz 584   058-jffz (hsü) chi/36
    Gest No. 22.

Author - (編) Chiang Piao 江 標 .

Edition - published by the author; (preface) dated Kuang-Hsü
    "ting-yu" 23/1897.   Blocks; "mao-t'ai" paper.

Index - a list of the 56 works in 6 "chi".

Bound in 6 t'ao 48 ts'ê (8 each).

Remarks - an ordinary edition; the item is complete and without
    defects.

The University of Toronto Chinese Library

Accession No. 513   Index No. - 030-be(zb)f

Title   " Ku chien k'ao lüeh "
                        古   雋   考   略

Classification - C-348 類書

Subject - (Gest No. 735) "an encyclopaedia of terms and phrases
    arranged under different categories -----"

References - 012-zafk 13/24   031-bgdf 138/7   Gest No. 735.

Author - (輯) Ku Ch'ung 顧 充 .

Edition - a Ming edition; undated, but apparently of the Wan-Li
    period.   Blocks; "mien" paper.

Index - a general table of "classifications" for 6 "chi".

Bound in 1 t'ao 6 ts'ê.

Remarks - a very good edition; the item is complete and in perfect
    condition.

Accession No. 514   Index No. - 030-gzh

Title   " T'ang wên sui "
唐 文 粹

Classification - D-63 總集－詩文

Subject - a comprehensive general miscellaneous collection of prose
and poetry.

References - 160-1j 163-ggcz 16/2 031-bgld 19/9 037-ahhg 3/38
167-mhfm 23/10 030-iaff 38/11 106-gdkn 112/17 012-zafk 19/3
031-bgdf 186/34 Toronto No. 19 Gest Nos. 367, 856, & 1576.

Author - (纂) Yao Hsüan 姚 鉉 .

Edition - the "Hsü's Yü-yüan" 許 氏 榆 圜 ; dated Kuang-Hsü
"kêng-yin" 16/1890.   Blocks; "fên" paper.

Index - a table of contents for 100 chüan, with separate lists at
beginning of each chüan.

Bound in 2 t'ao 20 ts'ê (10-10).

Remarks - a very good modern edition; the item is as new.   The
following is a supplement to this work:-

    " T'ang wên sui pu i "
    唐 文 粹 補 遺   (030-gzhg)

                                26 chüan

        by Kuo Lin 郭 麐 .

Accession No. 515   Index No. - 096-zg

Title   " Yü hai "
玉 海

Classification - C-348 類書

Subject - (Gest No. 1636) "an encyclopaedia of broad scope, including extracts and references from works covering almost the whole field of Chinese literature."

References - Wylie's Notes page 184   160-lj   163-ggcz 10/14
    031-bgld 14/11   167-mhfm 17/9   030-iaff 20/10   106-gdkn 61/1 (#)

Author - Wang Ying-lin 王 應 麟 .

Edition - a reprint by "Wang-shih" of Ch'êng-tu 成 都 王 氏 ; dated Kuang-Hsü 10/1884.   Blocks; "mao-t'ai" paper.

Index - a general table of contents for 200 & 4 chüan, followed by a general table of contents of the 13 supplementary works.

Bound in 10 t'ao 120 ts'ê (12 each).

Remarks - an ordinary edition; complete and in good condition.

(#)   012-zafk 13/22   031-bgdf 135/48   Gest Nos. 690 and 1636
    Toronto No. 179(a).

Accession No. 516   Index No. - 156-gkcd   098-kcdd

Title   " Chao Ou-pei ch'üan shu "
                      趙 甌 北 全 書
                   " Ou-pei ch'üan chi "
                      甌 北 全 集

Classification - C-338 雜家一叢書

Subject - a collection of reprints of 7 works on history and
    literature by an individual author; with a biographical
    record of the author.

References - 012-zafk 13/15   029-pffz 555   Gest No. 464.

Author - (撰) Chao I 趙 翼 .

Edition - a reprint by "T'ang-shih" of Tien-nan 滇南唐氏 ;
    dated Kuang-Hsü 3/1876.   Blocks; "mao-pien" paper.

Index - a list of the 7 works on the title-page.

Bound in 6 t'ao 60 ts's (10 each).

Remarks - a good edition; the item is complete and in good condition.

Accession No. 517   Index No. - 085-1jjf   085-1jej

Title   " Ch'ien ch'io lei shu "
                   潛 碻 類 書
               " Ch'ien ch'io chü lei shu "
               潛 碻 居 類 書

Classification - C-348 類書

Subject - an encyclopaedia containing upwards of 1400 articles
    classified under 13 sections; with extracts from various
    standard works introduced in explanation of the items
    under discussion.

References - Wylie's Notes page 187   012-zafk 13/25.

Author - (撰) Ch'ên Jên-hsi 陳 仁 錫.

Edition - a Ming edition; undated, but about the close of that
    dynasty.   Blocks; bamboo paper.

Index - a general table of contents for 120 chüan; detailed lists
    at the beginning of each chüan.

Bound in 8 t'ao 80 ts'ê (10 each).

Remarks - a fair edition; the item is complete and in good condition
    with the exception of a few repaired defects.

———•———

Accession No. 518   Index No. – 161-fddf

Title   " Nung chêng ch'üan shu "
                農   政   全   書

Classification – C-53 農家

Subject – (Gest No. 1764) "a thesaurus of agriculture; covering,-
    division of land; husbandry; hydraulics and irrigation;
    implements; planting; silkworms and sericulture; stock-
    breeding; food products; granaries and storage; etc etc."

References – Wylie's Notes page 94 160-lj 163-ggcz 7/10 031-bgld
    10/5 012-zafk 10/19 031-bgdf 102/8 Gest Nos. 518 and 1764.

Author – (纂 輯) Hsü Kuang-ch'i 徐 光 啓 .

Edition – the "Shu-hai-lou" 曙 海 樓 ; dated Tao-Kuang "kuei-mao"
    23/1843.   Blocks; "fên" paper.

Index – a general table of contents for 60 chüan.

Bound in 2 t'ao 16 ts'ê (8-8).

Remarks – an important standard work; the item is complete and in
    practically perfect condition.

The University of Toronto Chinese Library

Accession No.   519   Index No. - 117-fzlf

Title   " Chang shih i shu "
                  章 氏 遺 書

Classification - D-33 別集 - 詩文 C-338 雜家 - 叢書

Subject - an individual miscellaneous collection of prose, with
    some writings of poetical nature; being a collection of
    reprints of works by one author.

References - 029-pffz 366   Gest No. 410.

Author - (著) Chang Hsüeh-ch'êng 章 學 誠 ; （ 編 次 ）
    Wang Tsung-yen 王 宗 炎 .

Edition - the "Chia-yeh-t'ang" 嘉 業 堂 ; dated "jên-hsü" 1922.
    Blocks; "mao-pien" paper.

Index - (main work) - a general table of contents for 30 chüan;
    外 集 18 chüan; 補 遺 1 chüan; 附 錄 1 chüan; 校 記 1 chüan.

Bound in 4 t'ao 32 ts'ê (8 each).

Remarks - a good modern edition; the item is new.

Accession No. 520   Index No. - 085-fhh   145-gefh

Title   " Hsi yüan lu "
                          洗   冤   錄
              " Pu chu Hsi yüan lu chi chêng "
                補 註 洗 冤 錄 集 證

Classification - C-43 法家

Subject - the "Cononer's Hand-book and Guide",- a work on medical
    jurisprudence.

References - Wylie's Notes page 93 160-1j 163-ggcz 7/10 031-bgld
    10/3 030-iaff 16/4 012-zafk 10/18 031-bgdf 101/16 Gest No.
    1453.

Author - of the original work - Sung Tz'ŭ 宋慈 ; additions and
    comments by Wang Yu-huai 王又槐 ; Li Kuan-lan 李觀瀾 ;
    Sun Kuang-lieh 孫光烈 ; Yüan Ch'i-hsin 阮其新 ; and others.

Edition - a reprint of the Tao-Kuang 1844 edition.   Blocks; foreign
    paper.

Index - a general table of contents for 5 chüan; 增 and 附 ,-
    a detailed table of contents at the beginning of each chüan.

Bound in 1 t'ao 5 ts'ê.

Remarks - a good modern edition with "5 - colour" marginal notations.
    In addition to the 增 and 附 sections there are :-
    (#)

610

(#)   " Hsi yüan lu pieh chêng "
洗 冤 錄 辨 正

by Ch'ü Chung-jung 瞿中溶

" Chien yen ho ts'an "
檢 驗 合 參

by Lang Chin-ch'i 郎錦麒

" Hsi yüan lu chieh "
洗 冤 錄 解

by Yao Te-yü 姚德豫

611

Accession No. 521   Index No. - 170-hzdf

Title   " Lu tzŭ ch'üan shu "
                         陸　子　全　書

Classification - C-338 雜家－叢書

Subject - a collection of reprints of 5 works by an individual author;
    with two supplements and a Nien-p'u 年譜 ; being a part of the
    complete collection of 18 works.

References - 029-pffz 354   058-jffz (hsü) ping/15.

Author - by Lu Lung-ch'i 陸　隴　其.

Edition - the "Wu-lin-wei-shu" 武　林　微　署; dated T'ung-Chih
    "mou-ch'ên" 7/1868.   Blocks; "fên" paper.

Index - none.

Bound in 2 t'ao 12 ts'ê (6-6).

Remarks - the work is in fairly good condition.

Accession No. 522   Index No. - 061-dfbz

Title   " K'uai shu wu-shih chung "
                         快 書 五 十 種

Classification - C-338 雜家 - 叢書

Subject - a collection of reprints of 50 works mainly consisting
     of miscellaneous records, sayings etc.

References - 029-pffz 238   058-jffz (hsü) ping/45.

Author - (輯 刊) Min Ching-hsien 閔 景 賢.

Edition - published by the author; (preface) dated T'ien-Ch'i
     "ping-yin" 6/1626.   Blocks; bamboo paper.

Index - a general table of contents for 50 chüan.

Bound in 4 t'ao 24 ts'ê; doubly interleaved.

Remarks - a very good edition; the item is complete and in practically
     perfect condition.

Accession No. 523   Index No. - 067-zzd   040-dagg

Title   " Wên-shan chi "

文 山 集

" Sung shao-pao Hsin-kuo Wên kung Wên-shan hsien-shêng ch'üan chi "

宋 少 保 信 國 文 公 文 山 先 生 全 集

Classification - D-33 別集 - 詩文

Subject - an individual collection of prose and poetry.

References - 012-zafk 15/31.

Author - (撰) Wên T'ien-hsiang 文 天 祥 .

Edition - no notation; (postscriptum) dated Tao-Kuang "ping-wu" 26/1846.   Blocks; "fên" paper.

Index - none; 16 chüan.

Bound in 1 t'ao 9 ts'ê.

Remarks - a very fine and clear-cut edition; the item is complete and in very good condition.

—————•—————

Accession No. 524   Index No. - 040-fejb   024-jbkh

Title   " Hsüan-ho Po ku t'u lu "
               宣 和 博 古 圖 錄

Classification - C-260 譜錄 - 器物

Subject - (Gest No. 1389) "a description,- with numerous illustrations,-
    of utensils, implements, etc. of the period from the Chou to the
    Han dynasties, stored in the Sung dynasty Imperial palace
    (Hsüan-ho-tien) 宣 和 殿 ."

References - Wylie's Notes page 143 160-1j   163-ggcz 9/9
    031-bgld 12/13   037-ahhg 5/50   167-mhfm 16/1   030-iaff 18/1 (#)

Author - Wang Fu 王 黼 .

Edition - the "Po-ju-chai" 泊 如 齋 ; (preface) dated Wan-Li
    "mou-tzǔ" 16/1588.   Blocks; "fên" paper.

Index - a table of contents at the beginning of each of 30 chüan.

Bound in 2 t'ao 16 ts'ê (8-8).

Remarks - an interesting and valuable work; the item is complete
    and in generally good condition.

    (#) 106-gdkn 53/7   012-zafk 12/1   031-bgdf 115/7
         Gest Nos. 626 and 1389.

Accession No. 525   Index No. - 028-clcd

Title   " Ch'ü-wei-chai chi "
                  去 偽 齋 集

Classification - D-33 别集一詩文

Subject - an individual collection of prose and poetry.

References - 012-zafk 16/31   031-bgdf 179/21.

Author - (著) Lü K'un 呂 坤 .

Edition - the "K'ai-fêng-fu-shu" 開 封 府 署 ; dated Tao-Kuang
    "ting-hai" 7/1827.   Blocks; "fên" paper.

Index - a general table of contents for 10 chüan; detailed list for
    the same.

Bound in 1 t'ao 10 ts'ê.

Remarks - a fairly good edition; the item is complete and in generally
    good conditon.

616

Accession No.   526   Index No. - 001-bzpg

Title   " San-ts'ai tsao i "
                         三 才 藻 異

Classification - C-348 類書

Subject - (Gest No. 1134) "a list of things, animate and inanimate,
   for which a name has been selected from some other division in
   nature or chosen in a somewhat similar manner; and other lists
   of nomenclative categories, metamorphoses, etc etc., with
   explanatory and illustrative clauses; together with lists (#)

References - 012-zafk 13/26   031-bgdf 139/5   Gest No. 1134.

Author - T'u Sui-chung 屠 粹 忠 ·

Edition - the "Hsü Yüan" 栩 園 ; (preface) dated K'ang-Hsi "chi-ssŭ"
   28/1689.   Blocks; "hsüan" paper.

Index - a general table of contents for 33 chüan; a detailed list
   for the same.

Bound in 4 t'ao 16 ts'ê (4 each).

Remarks - a good edition; the item is complete and in good condition
   except the last ts'ê, which is stained on the top corner and has
   some repaired defects.

(#)   of pseudonyms or "fancy" names often used in composition,
       literature, poetry, etc."

618

Accession No. 527   Index No. - 030-gdzz

Title   " T'ang Sung pa ta chia wên hsüan "
           唐 宋 八 大 家 文 選

Classification - D-73 總集一文

Subject - a general collection of literary compositions,- prose,
    written by 8 famous scholars of the T'ang and Sung dynasties;
    with commentatorial notes.

References - none.

Author - (評 選) Chung Hsing 鍾 惺 .

Edition - the "I-ching-t'ang" 貽 經 堂; (preface) dated "jên-shên"
    1632 (?).   Blocks; bamboo paper.

Index - a detailed classified table of contents for 24 chüan.

Bound in 2 t'ao 12 ts'ê (6-6).

Remarks - a fairly good edition; the item is complete and in good
    condition with the exception of some stains.

Accession No. 528   Index No. - 040-dbcf

Title   " Sung Yüan i lai hua jên hsing shih lu "
               宋 元 以 來 畫 人 姓 氏 錄

Classification - B-117 傳記一總錄

Subject - a collection of short biographical notes of noted artists
    of the Sung, Yüan, Ming and Ch'ing dynasties, arranged according
    to rhymes.

References - none.

Author - (編 輯) Lu Chün 魯 駿 .

Edition - no notation; (preface) dated Tao-Kuang 10/1830.   Blocks;
    "fên" paper.

Index - a general table of contents for 卷首 and 36 chüan; a
    detailed list for the same.

Bound in 2 t'ao 20 ts'ê (10-10).

Remarks - the item is complete and in very good condition.

620

Accession No. 529   **Index No.** - 001-bhkg   118-ezzz

Title

" <u>San kuo yen i</u> "

三 國 演 義

" <u>Ti i ts'ai tzŭ shu</u> "

第 一 才 子 書

Classification - C-368 小 說 家

Subject - (Toronto No. 141) " an historical novel relating to the
period of the three kingdoms,- <u>Wei</u> 魏 ; <u>Shu</u> 蜀 ; and <u>Wu</u> 吳 ;
in 120 chapters; with illustrations and portraits at the
beginning of the first chüan."   This item is with illustrations
for each chüan.

References - Wylie's Notes page 202   160-1j   Toronto No. 141.

Author - <u>Lo Kuan-chung</u> 羅 貫 中 ; (評) <u>Mao Tsung-kang</u> 毛 宗 崗

Edition - no notation; (preface) dated Kuang-Hsü 14/1888.
Lithographed on "fên" paper.

Index - a table of contents for 60 chüan in 120 hui 回 .

Bound in 2 t'ao 12 ts'ê; singly interleaved.

Remarks - a very fine edition; the item is complete and in good
condition.   A few minor defects, and some stains.

Accession No. 530   Index No. - 030-gfba

Title   " T'ang shih san pai shou chu su "
            唐 詩 三 百 首 註 疏

Classification - D-68 總集一詩

Subject - (Toronto No. 172) "a general collection of some 300 poems
    written by famous poets of the T'ang 唐 dynasty; with notes
    and explanations."

References - Toronto No. 172.

Author - (手 編) Hēng T'ang T'ui Shih 衡 塘 退 士;
    (註) Chang Hsieh 章 燮.

Edition - the "Sung's Chüan-yü-lou" 宋 氏 卷 雨 樓; dated "chia-tzǔ"
    1924.   Blocks; Japanese paper.

Index - a general table of contents for 6 chüan.

Bound in 1 t'ao 6 ts'ê.

Remarks - a good modern edition; the item is new.   This work is a
    duplicate of No. 172, but without supplement.

The University of Toronto Chinese Library

Title

         " Hsi   hsiang   chi "

          西   廂   記

       " Ti   liu   ts'ai   tzǔ   shu "

       第   六   才   子   書

Classification - D-143 戲本

Subject - (Giles' Chinese Literature) "Of all the plays of the
Mongol dynasty, the one which will best repay reading is
undoubtedly the Hsi Hsiang Chi, or Story of the Western
Pavilion, in sixteen scenes.   It is by Wang Shih-fu, of
whom nothing seems to be known except that he flourished (#)

References - 160-1j   012-zafk 20/33   Toronto No. 195.

Author - Wang Shih-fu 王 寶 甫.

Edition - the "Wěn-shêng-t'ang" 文 盛 堂 ; no date.   Blocks;
"mao-pien" paper.

Index - a general table of contents for 8 chüan.

Bound in 2 t'ao 12 ts'ê; doubly interleaved.with margins.

Remarks - a fairly good edition; the item appears to be complete
but with a few repaired defects mainly in the last ts'ê.
The following is a supplement to this work:-

     " Ts'ai   tzǔ   hsi   hsiang   tsui   hsin   p'ien "

     才   子   西   廂   醉   心   篇   (064-zzzi)

     by Ch'ên Wei-sung 陳 維 崧   1 chüan

(#)   in the thirteenth century, and wrote thirteen plays,
all of which are included in the collection mentioned above.
"The dialogue of this play," says a Chinese critic, "deals
largely with wind, flowers, snow, and moonlight," which is
simply a euphemismtic way of stating that the story is one
of passion and intrigue.   It is popular with the educational
classes, by whom it is regarded more as a novel than a play."

Accession No. 532   Index No. - 030-dzlf

Title   " <u>Lu-tzǔ i shu</u> "
                呂 子 遺 書

Classification - C-338 雜家一叢書

Subject - a collection of reprints of 4 standard works; the 2d work
    being made up of 4 small works.

References - none.

Author - (著) <u>Lü Tê-shêng</u> 呂 得 勝 and <u>Lü K'un</u> 呂 坤 .

Edition - no notation; (preface) dated Tao-Kuang 7/1827.
    Blocks; "mao-pien" paper.

Index - separate tables of contents for each of the four works.

Bound in 4 t'ao 24 ts'ê (6 each).

Remarks - a good edition; the item is complete and without defects.

Accession No. 533   Index No. - 075-czhb

Title   " Li Wên-ch'ing kung jih chi "
李 文 清 公 日 記

Classification - B-107 傳記 - 獨錄

Subject - a collection of diaries of Li T'ang-chieh from the 4th
year of Tao-Kuang (1824) to the 4th year of T'ung-Chih
(1865).

References - none.

Author - Li T'ang-chieh 李 棠 階.

Edition - no notation; (preface) dated "i-mao" 1915.   Lithographed
on "fên" paper.

Index - a general table of contents for 16 ts'ê.

Bound in 2 t'ao 16 ts'ê.

Remarks - an ordinary edition; complete and without defects.

Accession No. 534   Index No. - 012-bake

Title   " Liu-jên t'u hsiang "
                  六　壬　圖　象

Classification - C-178 術數 - 占卜

Subject - a work on divination based upon the 64 diagrams; with
    numerous coloured illustrations.

References - none.

Author - not stated.

Edition - an undated manuscript written on "mien" paper.

Index - none; 24 chüan.

Bound in 4 t'ao 24 ts'ê.

Remarks - a very fine manuscript, especially the illustrations.
    The paper has been backed. A small space has been cut off
    every illustration page above the designations. As there is
    no index, it is difficult to tell whether the text is complete
    or not.
        This work seems never to have been published and
    is possibly of the Ming period.